THE ROOTS, RITUALS, AND
RHETORICS *of* CHANGE

THE ROOTS, RITUALS, AND RHETORICS *of* CHANGE

North American Business Schools

After the Second World War

Mie Augier and James G. March

STANFORD BUSINESS BOOKS
An Imprint of Stanford University Press
Stanford, California

Stanford University Press
Stanford, California

Printed in the United States of America on acid-free, archival-quality paper

Library of Congress Cataloging-in-Publication Data
Augier, Mie, 1972– author.
    The roots, rituals, and rhetorics of change : North American business schools after the Second World War / Mie Augier and James G. March.
        pages cm
    Includes bibliographical references and index.
    ISBN 978-0-8047-7616-5 (cloth : alk. paper)
    1. Business schools—North America—History—20th century.   2. Business education—North America—History—20th century.   3. Educational change—North America—History—20th century.   I. March, James G. (James Gardner), 1928– author.   II. Title.
    HF1130.A94 2011
    650.071'173—dc22

                                                                    2010050160

Typeset by Thompson Type in 10.5/15 Minion Pro

Contents

Preface

This is a study of North American business schools during a period, 1945–1970, that is rapidly fading from recollection. It is a period worth remembering, though the number of people capable of doing so is dwindling fast. One of us was not born until after 1970; the other of us lived through the period as a young man, part of it as a faculty member in a business school, but finds that most of the others who did so are either dead or remarkably elderly now.

We have relied heavily on the traces left in writings, archives, and memories of those who were there and of those who have tried subsequently to understand the period, conscious that the records are incomplete, that they are filled with willful and unconscious biases, and that our interpretation of them is only one of many possible interpretations.

We are indebted to numerous colleagues and friends who have contributed to this project. In particular, we owe major debts to the Cynthia and John Reed Foundation, the Sloan Foundation, and the Copenhagen Business School for generous financial support that has made it all possible. We give our thanks to the institutions and also to the individuals involved in approving the grants, particularly John Reed, Finn Junge-Jensen, and Gail Pesyna.

The Stanford University School of Education and the Stanford Graduate School of Business have also provided invaluable support. The Graduate School of Business has provided a small, but flexible, research fund and access to the school's archives. The School of Education has kindly housed us during the time of the project, and we are grateful for the hospitality and many effective efforts to make our lives easier. We appreciate particularly the thoughtfulness of Ona Andre, Deborah Belanger, and Deborah Stipek.

A substantial debt is also owed to the archives and archivists of the University of Chicago, the Ford Foundation, George Washington University,

Harvard University, the Massachusetts Institute of Technology, the RAND Corporation, the University of Rochester, the Stanford Graduate School of Business, Stanford University, and the Wharton School of the University of Pennsylvania. In particular, we are grateful to Vivian Artebery, Ann Horn, Malcolm Palmatier, and Gustave Shubert, for invaluable help during the research at the RAND archives; to Idelle Nissela at the Ford Foundation Archives; to Paul Reist and Kathy Long at Stanford Jackson Libraries; and to Gabrielle Michelek at Carnegie Mellon University Library.

We have talked at some length with a number of people who played important roles in the history. These include Kenneth Arrow, G. Leland Bach, Charles Bonini, Joseph Bower, William W. Cooper, Richard M. Cyert, Robert A. Dahl, William R. Dill, Edward Feigenbaum, Julian Feldman, Charles Holt, James E. Howell, Yuji Ijiri, George Kozmetsky, Gardner Lindzey, Michael Lovell, Andrew W. Marshall, Alan Meltzer, Arjay Miller, Henry Mintzberg, Franco Modigliani, John Muth, William Pounds, Roy Radner, Henry S. Rowan, George Schultz, Bruce Scott, Herbert A. Simon, James R. Schlesinger, Philip Selznick, Richard Snyder, Martin Shubik, Fred M. Tonge, Oliver Williamson, Peter Winters, and Sidney G. Winter. Their memories have been invaluable.

We have also drawn on the willingness of colleagues to talk with us about ideas along the way. In particular, these include Ilker Baybars, Nils Brunsson, Michael Cohen, Giovanni Dosi, Kenneth Dunn, Lars Engwall, Robert Gibbons, Michael Hay, Kristian Kreiner, David Labaree, Daniel Levinthal, Anne Miner, Daniel Newark, Johan P. Olsen, Christos Pitelis, W. Richard Scott, David Tyack, Eric Wanner, Barry Watts, Randall Weingarten, and an anonymous reader for the publisher.

Finally, we are grateful for the effective aid provided by Margo Beth Crouppen, our editor at the Stanford University Press, and her associates, particularly Jessica Walsh. We thank Margaret Pinette for noble copyediting done with grace and care while sitting in Milo, Maine.

As usual with all of this generous help, it would be ungracious to blame any of them for our errors, so we happily absolve them of responsibility.

Mie Augier and James G. March
Stanford, California, U.S.A.
June 2011

THE ROOTS, RITUALS, AND RHETORICS *of* CHANGE

Chapter One

AN INTRODUCTION

Some rather remarkable changes took place in North American business schools in the twenty-five years between 1945 and 1970. The changes altered the character of business schools, the possibilities for their future, and the terms of discourse about them. They transformed the position of business schools in the academic community. They changed the balance between experiential knowledge and academic knowledge in management education. They clarified and articulated several concerns about university education for business and the rhetoric surrounding it. In many respects, the changes constituted a minor "revolution."

The changes in business schools were anticipated by issues that had agitated management educators before the Second World War; and the revolution was, for the most part, a gentle one. There was little sustained conflict. The old guard and old ways were supplanted with only minor whimpers. The traditional lubricants of peaceful change—money, growth, and evolving social consciousness—worked their magic. The resulting developments helped to shape the subsequent history of business schools, in particular a counterreformation that took place in the 1980s and 1990s.

James E. Howell described the transformation in an unpublished memorandum to the Ford Foundation in 1962 that became the basis for a subsequent report of the foundation:

> Ten years ago collegiate schools of business, with a few notable exceptions,
> were regarded as the slums of the educational community. . . . Many business
> schools are today intellectually exciting places in which to teach and to study.[1,2]

The significance of the changes was also acknowledged by business leaders.
Looking back, John Reed, the former CEO of Citicorp and Citigroup, said:

> There was virtually a revolution in the study of business and of decision
> making in organizations. That started I believe at Carnegie Tech at the time
> in the late 50s and the early 60s. . . . This changed business practice just as I
> think it has changed military and policy practice in this country.[3]

The story of this "golden age" became part of the folklore of North American business schools.

1.1 THE UNFOLDING OF CHANGE

During the 1950s and 1960s, coalitions of deans, faculties, foundations, and
business executives sought to change business schools (Bach, 1958; Cyert
and Dill, 1964; Simon, 1967). The effort was both reported and heralded
by a well-known report written for the Ford Foundation by Aaron Gordon
and James Howell (Gordon and Howell, 1959). Their report concluded:

> The general tenor of our recommendations was that the business schools
> (and departments of business) need to move in the direction of a broader
> and more rigorous educational program, with higher standards of admis-
> sion and student performance, with better informed and more scholarly
> faculties that are capable of carrying on more significant research, and with
> a greater appreciation of the contributions to be made to the development
> of business competence by both the underlying . . . disciplines and the judi-
> cious use of . . . materials and methods. (p. 425)

A Program of Reform

The reformers advocated programs of research that might lead to improvements in practice, not so much through diffusion of "best practice" as

through changes in fundamental knowledge. They emphasized closer links with academic disciplines; more rigor, including the greater use of mathematical models and the research findings of psychology and economics; and the substitution of formal analyses for rules of thumb. They proclaimed the importance of problem framing more than problem solving, of a thoroughgoing augmentation of the commitment of business schools to fundamental research. They believed that there was a larger purpose of business education in contributing to society. They had a sense of empowerment and a vision.

The champions of changes in management research and education portrayed the goal of management education as being twofold: First, at all levels in the education of managers—undergraduate, graduate, and executive programs alike—the training of practitioners of management should be based on the foundational disciplines of economics and of behavioral science as well as the quantitative disciplines. The analogy was to the way in which the schools and practice of medicine were based on biology, physiology, and chemistry. Two well-known activists declared:

> The student of management . . . is expected to learn enough about mathematics, statistics, and the computer to be able to understand and use decision models from the management sciences and operations research. He is expected to understand the theoretical and research underpinnings on which economists base their advice to corporations and governments. He is expected to know the main findings and hypotheses about human behavior from psychology, sociology, and political science. (Cyert and Dill, 1964, p. 223)

Second, business schools should be seen, in particular at the graduate level, to be responsible for the education of future teachers and researchers of management and for research that is both relevant to management and respected in the underlying disciplines. The vision was that by doing problem-driven research (research driven by real-world problems but aiming more at understanding than at solving those problems in a specific context), business schools and researchers in management education would both help define and frame practical problems and help advance the disciplines from which they drew.

A Success

The efforts of the reformers were successful to a considerable extent. In the space of two decades, the cultures and practices of many, probably most, North American business schools were changed substantially. Curricula became more analytical and demanding. The quality of students relative to the quality in other programs was improved. New methodologies (such as statistical models), tools (such as computers), and innovations (such as business games) were introduced into business schools. New faculty, particularly those drawn from the disciplines and from research-oriented business schools, became more important and more demanding of a significant research presence in the schools.

Graduate programs became more important relative to undergraduate. Graduate students were drawn increasingly from undergraduate disciplinary programs at major universities. The commitment to faculty research became ritualized in the form of tenure reviews and publicity releases. In the process, many North American business schools sought to become and, in fact, did become academically respectable (Porter, 1963).

The changes were facilitated by the fact that business schools were undergoing dramatic growth in students, faculty, and resources. Many new faculty members were recruited from disciplinary training. The changes were made "on the margin," but the margin was increasing rapidly enough that it quickly swamped the rest of the institutions. The "old guard" was to some extent converted, but mostly it was simply overrun by new immigrants.

Some schools changed more dramatically or more rapidly than others who made fewer changes or moved more slowly. Overall, however, the changes came relatively rapidly and relatively painlessly. The changes were in a certain sense titanic, but the processes were not. They occurred without heroic battles, extraordinary heroes, or prolonged political battles. They were noteworthy, but straightforward, extensions of the times.

In subsequent years, North American business schools found confirmation of the desirability of the changes in their successes. They were successful in establishing their basic MBA programs as primary routes to business success. They were successful financially, developing major support from alumni, foundations, and businesses that freed them from exclusive dependence on tuition income or public subsidies. They were successful in building academic standing by recruiting highly talented students and highly valued research faculty.

They were also successful in building a record of fundamental research with applications to practice. Academic operations research (for example, linear and dynamic programming, queuing theory) transformed business practice in the management of operations. Academic financial economics transformed business practice in financial management. To a lesser extent, academic accounting and academic organizations studies transformed practice in accounting, personnel and human resource management, and strategic management. As academic enthusiasms shifted over time, the ambition to draw from and contribute to fundamental knowledge led to inquiries into the seemingly esoteric wonders of game theory, chaos theory, evolutionary theory, theories of cognition, artificial intelligence, literary theory, neural imaging, and the nuances of cultural differences, some of which seemed similarly to contribute useful ideas to management practice.

Variations on the Theme

The history varied from one institution to another. History and institutional inertia make a difference, and adaptation at the Harvard Business School was different from adaptation at the Wharton School, which was different from adaptation at the Kansas State College of Business Administration. Those differences are reflected in the way the different schools addressed the questions, the answers they reached, the kind of leaders and visions they stimulated or endorsed, and the changes they experienced. Before the changes took place, the University of Chicago Graduate School of Business was different from the Wharton School of the University of Pennsylvania; the two continued to be different after the changes evolved.

Moreover, it is possible to question both the breadth and depth of changes that took place in management education generally. Most of what we know about management education comes from studies or observations of the prestige schools—such as the University of California, Berkeley; Chicago; Columbia; Harvard; Michigan; Northwestern; Stanford; Texas; and the

Wharton School of the University of Pennsylvania. Those schools are important, but they are only a small, nonrepresentative fraction of the faculty and students in business schools in North America. Even the more enthusiastic proclamations (or lamentations) of change would have to concede that business school education in some universities was only superficially altered by the postwar changes that affected the higher-ranking schools.

There appears, however, to be little serious challenge to the proposition that not only the leading schools but many other business schools changed in a fairly consistent direction. It was a direction that increased the emphasis on academic knowledge relative to experiential knowledge and that increased the presence and importance of faculty trained in, and attentive to, disciplinary knowledge. As a result (or at least at the same time), the academic standing of business schools improved. Programs in business at the undergraduate level and the students in them continued to be viewed with various degrees of scorn by disciplinary-based departments; but graduate programs gained a certain amount of academic respectability, as did the research record of business faculties. Those business schools in which the changes came relatively early and were relatively substantial gained (at least temporarily) in academic standing compared with business schools in which the changes came relatively late or were relatively modest.

A Complement to Other Histories

The present book seeks to provide a modest complement to many important recent histories of North American schools of business. Studies of management education range in focus from specific histories of particular business school (such as Sedlak and Williamson, 1983) to broader looks at the institutional history of the community of business schools (Khurana, 2007). Some focus heavily on specific parts of management education such as the MBA (for example, Wanker and DeFillippi, 2006; Daniel, 1998), others on business education in Europe (Djelic, 1998; Durand and Dameron, 2008; Engwall, 1992); and others on the ideas and content of management education through time (Wren, 1994).

Some of the volumes are reports commissioned by major institutional players. For example, the study by Porter and McKibbin (1988) was commissioned by the American Association of Collegiate Schools of Business (AACSB) to focus on the future of management education. It covers issues such as the rise of executive education, the changing market for management education, the role of accreditation bodies, and changes in student motivations and in faculty.

Many of these studies offer observations on the recent history and possible future of business schools and management education. For example, Daniel (1998) provides a history of the development of the MBA program from before 1910 to the future and offers a discussion of the problems of early resistance to business schools in academe. Starkey and Tiratsoo (2007) develop a critique of what they see as a tendency toward "more business and less school" as competition among schools has increased. They also discuss the biases they associate with the use of business cases in teaching management (Chapter Four). Some general aspects of the history can be found in Kast (1965), Edelfelt (1988), and Engwall (1992). And some small parts of the story and its relevance for the development of organizations scholarship are outlined in Augier, March, and Sullivan (2005) and in March (2007).

Many of the books combine analysis with prescription. For example, Khurana (2007) argues that business schools have moved from higher aims to "hired hands," a transformation that he views with little enthusiasm:

> The logic of professionalism that underlay the university-based business schools in its formative phase was replaced first by a managerialist logic that emphasized professional knowledge rather than professional ideals, and ultimately by a market logic that, taken to its conclusion, subverts the logic of professionalism altogether. (p. 7)

Mintzberg (2004) finds that business schools teach the wrong students in the wrong ways. He also decries the lack of diversity among the schools, describing Harvard and Stanford as being differentiated mostly "by geography" (p. 65).

The present chapters should be seen as a set of footnotes to such contributions. They are more modest in aspirations and less sweeping in conclusions. Within the population of North American business schools, variations across time and among graduate and undergraduate schools, private and public schools, large and small schools, rich and poor schools, and all their combinations are daunting to any attempt to generalize. Although we try to be conscious of that variety and to attend to phenomena that extend throughout the North American business school world, we focus our attention, for the most part, on the prestige business schools of North America and consider in detail only a sample of them. As nearly as we can tell, the impact of the period on other important business schools, particularly those in major public universities, was similar; but we have not attempted to confirm that fact directly. Our consideration of the vast majority of less-well-known schools is even more limited. The limitations are real, but so also, we believe, is the general picture we draw.

1.2   A MENU

In the chapters that follow, we examine the context of the 1950s and 1960s, some origins of the efforts at change that typified the postwar period, some features of the ways in which those origins found expression in the rituals and practices of business schools, and some of the key issues and rhetoric that surrounded those efforts. We explore the ways in which the changes after the Second World War were orchestrated in business schools, the stories and heroes they spawned, the arguments they fomented, the truths they enhanced or diminished, the differences they created or reduced, the strains they exposed or concealed. Along the way, we try to find some clues to the underlying processes of change in a set of institutions.

The story we tell has four major components.

The Contexts of Change

In Chapter Two, we consider some major elements of the context in which the changes in business schools took place. Like the rest of North American higher education in the decades after the Second World War, business schools were ripe for change. The United States had emerged from the war with military and economic power rivaled only by the Soviet Union. As the countries of Western and Central Europe and of Asia struggled to recover from the ravages and disruptions of war, North American economies rather quickly established themselves as dominant. Higher education enjoyed a boom. Students flocked to universities in rapidly increasing numbers. The turnover in faculties was substantial, fueled not only by growth but by the replacement of an aging faculty with younger, more recently trained teachers and scholars.

Not particularly by intention but more by happenstance, the conditions and instruments of change were in place waiting for a direction. A number of possible directions might have developed; the course that business school history took after the war was not completely determined by the preconditions. However, by 1960, fifteen years after the end of the war, it was clear that those conditions for change were being exploited for a particular course. Business schools had begun to institute changes that would make them decidedly more academic, more research oriented, and more dedicated to identifying and developing new ideas, concepts, techniques, and procedures for management. They were moving from a vision of being depositories of good practice as established in business to a vision that pictured them as primary creators of good practice.

The Roots of Change

In retrospect, it is possible to identify some aspects of the genealogy of such a direction. In particular, three elementary ancestral threads are important. The first thread is one that traces its history from the Flexner Report. The Flexner Report was prepared by Abraham Flexner in 1910 as a critique of medical schools in the United States. It became the widely acknowledged "bible" of changes that introduced greater rigor into medical education and a greater involvement of medical schools in fundamental research. By 1945 the story that had been crafted around the history of medical schools was a story that lionized Flexner and his report, and that story had become a template for reformers of other professional schools. Flexner and his report are discussed in Chapter Three.

The second thread is one that is critical to the history of North American universities—the development of the University of Chicago creed under Robert Maynard Hutchins. Hutchins championed a university dedicated to intellect, to the idea that the best instrument for a practical life was a mind shaped by fundamental knowledge. The Hutchins conception of a university permeated both the disciplinary departments at the University of Chicago and the famous "committees" of interdisciplinary discourse. It is not an accident that some of the principal purveyors of change in business schools after the Second World War had links less to traditional business schools than to the glorification of the intellect represented by the University of Chicago of Robert Hutchins. The history of the Hutchins creed is examined in Chapter Four.

The third thread is one that emphasizes the contribution of science to society and the solving of practical problems. The thread emerged from experience in the Second World War and was given an added boost by Soviet successes in space and by the Cold War. It found expression in a major expansion of public funding for science after the war, in the founding in 1950 of the National Science Foundation and in 1958 of the Advanced Research Projects Agency, and in the postwar expansion of the National Institutes of Health. Nowhere was this orientation more clearly exhibited than in the RAND Corporation, a nonprofit corporation created in 1948 after evolving from earlier experience working with the U.S. military. Key figures in the development of RAND subsequently became key figures in the reform of business schools. The role of the RAND Corporation in shaping the directions and leaders of the reform of business schools in detailed in Chapter Five.

The Rituals of Change

These three threads were woven together to become the fabric of business school change during the 1950s and 1960s. The existing business schools in North American universities were ripe for change. Each brought its own history to the changes, shaping the elaboration of the adaptation. Each institution struggled to reconcile the pressures of the postwar era with the structures and personnel developed in an earlier period and with a specific institutional history encapsulated in the rituals, routines, practices, and beliefs of that specific school.

In addition, the story implicates two remarkable postwar institutions. The first institution was the Ford Foundation. After the deaths of Edsel

Ford in 1943 and Henry Ford in 1947, the Ford Foundation changed from being a relatively small player in philanthropy to being a very large player. Beginning in 1948 and through the 1950s, the foundation struggled to define its new role. In the course of that struggle, it involved itself for roughly two decades in management education, seeking to change business schools. It commissioned a major report, provided grants to business schools, supported graduate fellowships, established prizes for business school dissertation research, and supported conferences and training sessions in new methods for old faculty. The management education initiative was a relatively minor program in a foundation that primarily pursued other, grander visions of virtue, but for this brief time it was vital to change in business schools. We explore the place of the Ford Foundation in the reforms in Chapter Six.

The second institution was the Graduate School of Industrial Administration of the Carnegie Institute of Technology (GSIA). GSIA was founded in 1949 and became a "poster child" for the Ford Foundation's efforts and more broadly for the reform of business schools. GSIA emphasized fundamental research and a scientific, interdisciplinary approach to management research and education, pioneering in applications of mathematics and computers to solving business problems and to reconstructing economics and other social sciences. Despite its youth and small size, GSIA became a model for those who sought to make business schools more academic, more analytical, more interdisciplinary, and more effectively research based. It was by no means the only model, and the changes would undoubtedly have occurred without it, but, for a relatively brief period, it was a nova of management education and research. The role of GSIA in the postwar period is elaborated in Chapter Seven.

The changes spread through the business school world and deeply affected their character, but the orchestrations of change and its forms were all embedded in the rituals and practices of individual institutions and their histories. In Chapter Eight we detail the different developments in four different leading business schools: the Harvard Business School, the Wharton School of the University of Pennsylvania, the University of Chicago Graduate School of Business, and the Stanford Graduate School of Business. They all responded to the pressures for reform, and they all moved in broadly similar directions, but each found a way to fit the "new look" into an old template. We also consider briefly the evidence for diffusion of the changes through the whole population of business schools and the relevance of the changes in North America for the development of business schools in other parts of the world.

The Rhetorics of Change

The history of change in business schools is preeminently a history of words. The history was unquestionably political. Power was involved. Money was involved. Interests were involved. However, power, money, and interests were all elaborately entangled in argument and ideas. As nearly as we can determine, the principal actors in the history often believed in the justifications they provided and believed that the arguments had persuasive force that was to some degree independent of the power, money, and interests associated with them.

Although it occasionally wanders into other issues, this book, to a larger extent than is typical of histories, is an examination of the rhetorics and arguments associated with change. It seeks to trace and assess the words that were used to justify change or resist it. Such a history of words is necessarily a limited history. We confess the limitations without shame. Academics deal in words and arguments as instruments of conflict, conquest, and resistance. They are the manifest arms and armor of academic discord, thus both one of the tools of academic history and one of its primary artifacts.

The rhetorics of the history decorate three major questions that have organized arguments over the changes and justifications for them. In the later chapters of the book, we consider these questions. None of them is resolvable, although many, perhaps most, of the actors involved believed fervently in resolutions of one sort or another.

The first question is how managerial education connects its teaching to some version of virtual reality, some exposure to the realities of management within the confines of a university campus–based education. The analogue is to the clinical training of physicians, and the instinct is to find a way to make as close an approximation as possible to reality. How does management education provide training in the application of academic ideas to the reality of managerial life? The discussion of this question turns heavily on the role of business cases in business school instruction, but it extends to consideration of other possibilities, for example the prospects for simulating business reality through computer-based business games. This aspect of the rhetoric is detailed in Chapter Nine.

The second question is whether business schools should concern themselves primarily with experiential knowledge of known and immediate relevance to business problems or with academic knowledge with its unclear, uncertain, and distant relevance. Should they gather and disseminate information about the best practices of management as those practices have evolved in business? Or should they be responsible for creating best practice on the basis of academic research? What is the relevance of relevance? We explore such questions in Chapter Ten.

The third question is what kind of vision of managers and management should be reflected by business schools. In particular, should they conceive managers as professionals analogous to physicians, engineers, teachers, or lawyers and themselves as professional schools? In many ways, the issue is whether management education should be driven by a logic of appropriateness or by a logic of consequences (Hirschman, 1977; March and Olsen, 2006). The latter ties business education to a quest for favorable outcomes, to instruction in how to maximize expected individual and social utility. The former ties business education to ideas about managerial behavior that are linked to fulfilling a managerial identity, one that defines rules of proper managerial behavior, including the social responsibilities of professionals. These issues are treated in Chapter Eleven.

In Chapter Twelve, we try to provide some general conclusions that might be drawn from our examination of the 1945 to 1970 period: what the period meant for North American business education and what our explorations suggest for students of institutional change. We also consider briefly the post-1970 history of business schools and its lessons. The forces that shape business schools did not disappear in 1970, but the world changed in important ways.

Chapter Two

THE CONTEXTS OF CHANGE

Under almost any imaginable scenario, North American business schools and management education would have changed in the period after the Second World War. The fundamental engines of change—the extraordinary growth of American higher education, the preeminence of the American postwar economic and political position, the enhanced position of science and operations analysis derived from the lessons of the war, Cold War competition, and exploration of space—all invited change. Business schools were parts of systems of higher education that, in turn, were parts of the social, political, and economic structures of postwar North American society. They existed in networks of relationships and in the cultures and climates that imbued them with the spirits of time and place. As a result, stories told of changes in management education after the war that describe events in specific business schools as though they occurred in autonomous enclaves unconnected to the times or the environment of other schools almost certainly exaggerate the importance of local initiatives and local heroes.

2.1 ELEMENTS OF CONTEXT

The various interests, sentiments, and people internal to business schools that came to be associated with the changes probably would not have come to prominence in another time and place, or if they did they would have been unnoticed and ineffective. Although a number of different possible developments would have been consistent with the conditions the schools faced, the course the reforms took was clearly shaped by the context.

The Context of the Times

The period after the Second World War was an exceptional time in North America. The aftermath of war changed not only the ways in which business was conducted but also the economic, political, and social structures in which it operated. The immediate postwar period witnessed the flowering of the American Empire to unprecedented levels of power and prosperity, a huge expansion of college education in the United States associated with the GI Bill and sustained subsequently by the enhanced educational expectations of the population, the glorification of science and scientists, and the endorsement of science-based systematic analyses as foundations for public policy and as instruments of social and economic progress. North American business schools of the period were surrounded by those transformations and were thoroughly infiltrated by their advocates, patrons, and beneficiaries.

Some indication of the magnitude of the changes is suggested by Figure 2.1, which shows the strong linear increases in U.S. population and the simultaneous much more rapid growth, in constant dollars, of the U.S. gross national product.

It was also a time when there was widespread agreement among leaders on some basic beliefs that profoundly shaped business school reform. The like-mindedness cannot be described precisely, but it included a number of convictions that were widely shared:

- *Optimism.* There was widespread optimism about the possibilities for science, systematic thinking, and intelligent social action. It was taken as a given that individual and social problems could be ameliorated by organized collective action informed by the application of science (including social science) and quantitative analysis.

- *Fundamental knowledge.* There was confidence that the key to the solution of problems was the creation and diffusion of fundamental

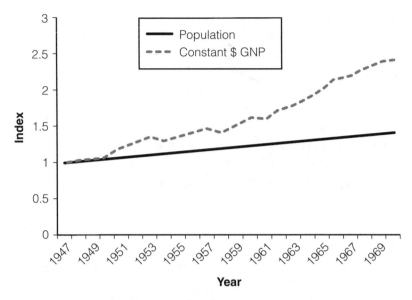

Figure 2.1.   U.S. growth, 1947–1970, indexed to 1947.

Source: The data are taken from the Statistical Abstract of the United States published by the U.S. Bureau of the Census, an agency of the U.S. Department of Commerce.

knowledge based on research. Applications were derivative of fundamental knowledge, and the proper training of professionals emphasized fundamental knowledge based on scientific research. The core foundation was in science and mathematics.

- *Interdisciplinarity.* Knowledge was seen to be appropriately organized into disciplines exhibiting the relative autonomy of individual fields, but there was a parallel belief that the problems of society and business firms typically involved knowledge drawn from multiple disciplines. Their solutions required considerable interdisciplinary exploration and integration.

- *Mindful social intelligence.* It was understood that the processes and institutions of governance, both in firms and in society, depended on structures that facilitated the effective use of intelligently expert analysis based on evidence, knowledge, and analysis. There were shared collective purposes that were served by informed, intelligent choices and plans.

These elements of belief were shared widely among a postwar cadre of activists. They permeated the ideas of the leaders of business firms, government agencies, foundations, and universities who became involved in the reform of business schools.

The Institutional Context

Unlike business schools in most of Europe immediately after the Second World War, North American institutions for the education of managers and business functionaries were positioned as units of larger, more general universities. This location tied North American business schools to the histories and contemporary politics of the larger institutions of which they were a part. Each individual business school was connected to a specific university in an enduring marriage marked by elements of mutual support, discord, mutual disinterest, and interdependence.

Most histories of North American higher education identify three major periods of change in that history before the Second World War. The first was the eighteenth-century creation of institutions for the education of the male gentry, particularly education for careers as clergymen. Colleges such as Harvard, Yale, and Princeton offered variations on a classical education with emphasis on Greek and Latin, philosophy, and religion. The second period was dominated by the mid-nineteenth-century creation of land grant institutions with their emphasis on mass education tied especially to farming, mining, and other practical concerns of an agricultural society but extending to a full range of academic offerings. The third period witnessed the late-nineteenth- and early-twentieth-century augmentation of higher education into an instrument for research and training for research through the introduction of advanced education, research laboratories, research faculty, and the PhD degree, all modeled on German institutions of the time.

As a result of this history, universities in North America had come by the 1940s to be viewed simultaneously as "finishing schools" for the proper gentrification of elites, as schools for the practical preparation of youths for gainful employment, as ways of organizing contact among young adults so as to assure socially appropriate marital ties, as instruments for the democratic substitution of an aristocracy of talent for an aristocracy of inheritance, and as research institutes for the development of both fundamental knowledge and immediately useful practices and products. Over time, they also had become important purveyors of the arts and entertainment, particularly competitive sports. By the start of the Second World War, without any particular grand scheme or intention, this heterogeneous, general purpose social welfare institution had become a significant political, social, and economic entity.

The fact that North American business schools after the Second World War were attached to universities and their histories made a difference. The general purpose university provided business schools with a patina of academic respectability and access to the public and private resources and the social approbation available to a university. Moreover, the university attracted a pool of students for whom the business school could compete.

These advantages came at a cost, however. Business school undergraduate programs had to fit into general undergraduate educational programs that normally involved academic contact with students and faculty from other departments and social contact with students with other foci. Business courses and programs were seen as being in parallel with courses and programs in other fields and as options that could be chosen or rejected by individual students. Business school procedures and budgets were embedded in the procedures and budgets of the university. Insofar as the business school was a part of a university, it became subject to the attention and direction of the university system of governance and to the prevailing prejudices of academics. Business schools sought, and to varying degrees achieved, independence from such controls, but a tension between the desire for autonomy and pressures for conformity were pervasive features of business school relations with their universities.

The Postwar Context of Higher Education

In the decade after the Second World War, North American higher education underwent notable changes, changes that were for the most part simultaneous with related changes in business schools: The demand for higher education and the resources available for it multiplied many fold. Immediately after the war, the GI Bill provided easy access to higher education for

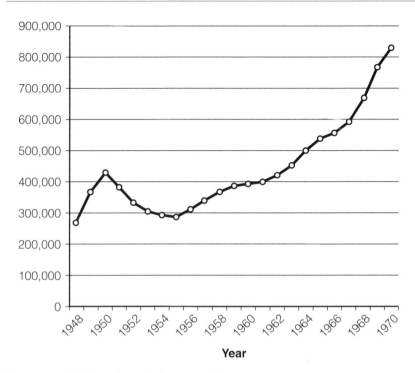

Figure 2.2.   U.S. baccalaureate degrees, 1948–1970.
Source: The data are taken from the Statistical Abstract of the United States published by the U.S. Bureau of the Census, an agency of the U.S. Department of Commerce.

large numbers of returning members of the demobilized armed forces. Subsequently, college attendance came to be viewed as a normal progression in the education of a large fraction of each cohort in the population. There was no need to attract students; they pounded on the door demanding admittance. There was no need to persuade society to support higher education; although university administrators pleaded for more, resources poured into academic institutions at a faster rate than could easily be absorbed.

Figure 2.2 shows the increase in the number of BA degrees awarded by U.S. colleges and universities in the postwar era. By 1970, the number had doubled from its immediate postwar (1950) peak. In 1946, the total enrollment in higher education in the United States was approximately 1.5 million, or 1.1 percent of the total population. By 1970, the total enrollment was approximately 7.1 million, or 3.5 percent of the population.

The link between higher education and the labor market was strengthened considerably. Education came to be acknowledged as the primary route to employment success, and securing appropriate college credentials came to be a necessary ambition for many. Justifications for education came to be articulated primarily in terms of presumed contributions made by education to a graduate's future employability, income, and wealth. College degrees became valuable enough on the labor market to invite fabrication by ambitious liars.

National economic development and social progress were seen as tied to the possession of scientific knowledge more than they had ever been before. Successful programs of research in service of the war effort had created a presumption of a national interest in furthering the development and use of knowledge. As the primary creators and purveyors of scientific knowledge, universities were characterized as vital to economic and social well-being. The model of scholarship was scientific research, and the glories of science were attached to universities, as were the expectations.

These changes were also associated with changes in the prestige of individual universities and in the distribution of resources and power within them. Growth in enrollment brought large public universities to new recognition and made enrollment a major factor in the power of universities and in the distribution of power within them. More importantly, however, earlier trends that shifted the basis for external prestige and internal power from domains of classical scholarship (for example, the humanities) to domains of the new explosions of science and engineering and their applications and to fields linked to employment were accelerated rather decisively.

Business Schools in Context

All of the broad changes in higher education in the years after the Second World War were exhibited in and affected business schools. The number of baccalaureate degrees granted in business doubled during the 1960s alone; the number of doctoral degrees granted increased 88.4 percent in the seventeen years after 1958 (Daniel, 1998, pp. 165, 167). Some indication of the magnitude of the changes is suggested by Figure 2.3. The figure shows that the number of accredited business schools doubled in the two decades after 1949; the number of MBAs granted increased more than fivefold.

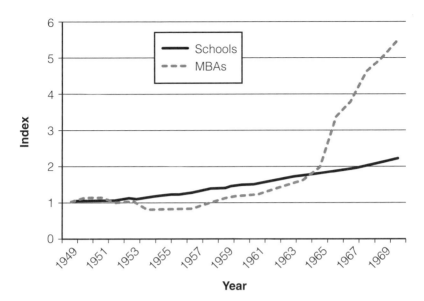

Figure 2.3.   U.S. accredited business schools and MBAs granted, 1949–1970, indexed to 1949.

Source: The data are taken from the Statistical Abstract of the United States, published by the U.S. Bureau of the Census, an agency of the U.S. Department of Commerce.

These elements of growth produced increases in the demand for faculty, straining traditional sources for faculty training, particularly because they were accompanied by pressure to improve the qualifications of faculty. The percentage of faculty in business schools who held doctorates went from 56 percent to 71 percent in the decade after 1954.[1]

Some conception of the magnitude of change for an individual school can be gleaned from a 1963 internal report on "The Financial History and Projected Growth of the Stanford Graduate School of Business."[2] That report shows that, in the eleven years from 1952 to 1962, applications for admission at the business school at Stanford had increased 260 percent; enrollment had increased 119 percent; the number of faculty had more than tripled; annual operating expenditures had increased more than 600 percent. Expenditures were expected to double again by 1970. Stanford was not unique. Similar stories of growth were typical for North American business schools during this period.

The massive expansion of demand for higher education considerably augmented the influence of faculties, including faculties of business schools, relative to the influence of students and outside groups. The increased focus on labor markets made business education, with its manifest vocational relevance, more attractive to students and made business schools more attractive to university administrations and trustees. The glorification of scientific research shifted the balance of power within business school faculties, noticeably strengthening the position of faculty with disciplinary and research involvements and claims to scientific knowledge relative to the position of faculty with practical experience and claims to vocational knowledge.

It was also a period of change in business. North American industry thrived. North American consumer demand rose to unprecedented levels. The numbers and sizes of American firms increased, and the demand for managers increased with it. Management became intellectually more demanding as the techniques of management became more esoteric. Innovation in both products and processes flourished. Public funds were used to provide substantial infusions of money for research and development, an infusion that was conspicuously less both before the war and after 1980 (Mowery, 2009).

2.2   A HISTORY OF TENSIONS

Most leading business schools were well established before the Second World War. Their histories were not long (fifty years or less in most cases), but they were long enough to have created some elements of institutional stability. Their histories can be written to a large extent in terms of the tensions and inconsistencies generated by simultaneous struggles to gain academic respectability and to gain approval in the business community. The tensions were obvious in the early days of business schools; they are obvious today.

Business Schools before the War

As in other professional schools—medical schools and law schools in particular—the roots of business education are found in various apprenticeship arrangements, focused on learning the craft of particular functions in businesses. After the Industrial Revolution, private business colleges began to emerge as places for training workers in the business (for example, bookkeeping, clerical, marketing) sides of industrial operations (Daniel, 1998, p. 20).

Before the rise of the field of political economy (Adam Smith and onwards), however, there was no topical or disciplinary home for business (or commerce, as it was often called) within a university. Business schools lagged behind other professional schools in finding a secure home in academia. Not until the end of the nineteenth century was there appreciable agitation for a university-based education of professionals for business. By that time, however, a president of Boston Board of Trade pointed out:

> You put a man into the pulpit or at the bar or in the school room without any training, and let him undertake to preach or practice or teach, and he will prove a miserable failure. . . . Into business life, however, men rush with no certificate and nothing in the way of qualification for the calling on which a certificate could be based. Without any business talent or training or foresight they buy and sell, but get no gain. Only failure can be looked for in such cases. (quoted in Fitz, 1884 [2009], p. 7)

Proposals for business education in the early twentieth century did not, in general, elicit great enthusiasm from academics. Resistance was grounded to some extent in the low moral reputation that business had among academics, both for its focus on money and for its lack of social consciousness. In addition, universities tended to resist being drawn into the teaching of commercial topics on grounds that they were vocational without intellectual content or basis (Daniel, 1998, pp. 27–28). For example, Charles Eliot, who was president of Harvard University from 1869 to 1909, did not support the idea of education for business at first, considering a traditional academic curriculum to be the best way to develop businessmen. He wrote:

> A young man who is going into business had better take an academic course. That is an indisputable proposition and there is no use discussing it. (quoted in Cruickshank, 1987, p. 25)

The advocates for business education were persistent, however, and advocacy and practical political pressures gradually made it prudent for universities to allow business education into the halls of academe. Much of the pressure for business programs came from employers and potential employees who sought practical training in the routines of business, but that vocational argument was made more palatable to academic sentiments by an argument that business had a function in society and that education for business provided a service to society, improving national competitiveness among other things. Thus, Leon Marshall, an early dean at the University of Chicago business school, wrote:

> However important it may be to turn out business men who can make money, social workers who can command good salaries, civic workers who can rise to positions of influence and affluence, the most important task of all is to aid in promoting the progress and welfare of society. (Marshall, 1913, p. 101)

The number of business schools in North America increased relatively rapidly, from three programs in collegiate business education in 1900 to twenty in 1911 to forty in 1915 and to sixty-five in 1918 (Daniel, 1998, p. 49). However, the reputation of the schools remained relatively low in academe. Some thought a business school was (in the words of a dean at Northwestern) a "very ill defined institution" (Hotchkiss, 1920, p. 92). Alfred North Whitehead, who was in most respects a supporter of collegiate business education, thought that, although business as a vocation had made some progress by 1929, there was still work to do on the works and curriculum of the schools (Whitehead, 1929, 1938).

The establishment of business schools was part of a larger package of proposals for furthering managerial interests and capabilities. Management groups sought to form professional societies. Some were specialized societies like the American Marketing Association, established in 1915, and the American Accounting Association in 1916; there were even narrower ones, such as the Mortgage Banker Association, established in 1914, and the National Association of Bank Women, set up in 1921. There were, however, two that had more general ambitions: The first was the American Management Association (AMA). The AMA was established 1923 as a new version of earlier entity, the National Association of Corporation Schools, which had been established in 1903 and had merged with the Industrial Relations Association, which had been established in 1920. The second was the American Association of Collegiate Schools of Business (AACSB), established in 1916.

The AMA was more oriented toward practicing managers than was the AACSB. Its primary educational objective was to broaden the study of management beyond production issues to include sales and finance and other managerial functions (Wren, 1994, p. 210). The AACSB was focused on academe. Although only twelve schools were represented at its first meeting, AACSB quickly became the primary professional association for business school deans. It held annual meetings where members could debate central issues of business education, such as admissions, students, curricula, faculty, research, and administration.

Both the AMA and the AASCB produced surveys and programs of various kinds during the decades. These included training programs for managers. For example, the Pierson Report (see Chapter Five) noted:

> Undoubtedly, the organization with the most comprehensive and widely used program in this field is the American Management Association, which, in addition to its conferences, courses, and seminars in the major functions of business, offers several courses and seminars specifically in the management development field. (Pierson, 1959, p. 564)

However, unlike the American Medical Association, neither the AMA nor the AACSB undertook to sponsor a major outside, objective, critical look at business schools. AACSB meetings tended to deal with near-term concerns and not the long-term shaping of business schools as institutions (Daniel, 1998, p. 190).

Prior to the Second World War, business schools were well established at many North American universities; but in most respects, they were appendages of higher education, not vital parts. The universities were more centrally concerned with other educational programs and might well have perceived business schools as something akin to intercollegiate athletics—useful to round out a full menu of activities and to attract the support of outsiders but not an essential part of the mainstream academic culture.

Business schools worked to be useful to the business community. They focused on practical instruction in current business practice, particularly in bookkeeping, finance, marketing, and accounting, and often differentiated themselves from other parts of collegiate institutions by their involvement in the part-time education of individuals already in the workforce. They reflected a conception of education as providing practical instruction in useful skills. As an early study of business education put it, "The primary aim of the university school of commerce is to prepare its students for successful and socially useful careers in business" (Bossard and Dewhurst, 1931, p. 55). They hired experienced accountants and executives as professors and tried to replicate experience through the teaching of cases, the involvement of faculty in consulting, and the linking of course work with temporary employment of students in business firms. They sought to become the carriers of "best practice."

This orientation to vocational education left North American business schools with only modest legitimacy in academe. For example, at Wharton, a faculty member noted that the heavy practical emphasis had led by the 1950s to consulting becoming "part of the Wharton way of life" and damaged academic research (Sass, 1982, p. 237). The scholarship component of academe was, for the most part, not a conspicuous part of business schools. Some business schools had doctoral programs, but those programs did relatively little to train research scholars. As a result, business schools tended to have little standing among core academics.

Even the Harvard Business School, probably the best-known North American business school prior to the Second World War, was not always enthusiastically embraced by other departments of Harvard University (Copeland, 1958, p. 17).

Observers differ on the extent to which the inconsequential standing of business schools in the halls of academe reflected accurate academic assessments or stemmed from envy of business school access to business and disdain for business morality; but there was little question that business schools suffered from reputations for mediocre academic capabilities (Gordon and Howell, 1959; Pierson, 1959; Simon, 1991).

A General Indictment

The postwar idea that business schools needed to change was not novel. Throughout the 1930s, there had been calls for reform. For example, the dean of Harvard Business School, Wallace Donham, was concerned with the lack of a broad education, too much specialization, and too little attention to the societal consequences of managerial actions:

> The nation suffers badly from overspecialization of its business leadership. Universities with less excuse have the same fault. Nowhere do we train men to study general social relationships with the broad vision and the philosophic view needed. (Donham, 1933, p. 435)

Critics of management education in the late 1940s and 1950s were more comprehensive in their criticisms. They found fault with the faculty, students, curricula, and research at business schools. The *faculty* was less competent than it should be. Although there were outstanding scholars on business school faculties, faculty in business schools were generally viewed as less distinguished academically than other faculty (Gordon and Howell, 1959; Pierson, 1959).

Although the data did not always consistently support the stereotype, *students* enrolled in business curricula were generally viewed as weaker than students enrolled in most other curricula. The students were too numerous and too callow, and they had less talent than they should have (Gordon and Howell, 1959; Pierson, 1959).

The *curricula* were organized into too-narrow specializations that were neither demanding enough nor linked adequately to research knowledge. The schools failed to provide either instruction or research on fundamental ideas. Thus, the Pierson Report intoned:

> There is considerable evidence that the business curriculum has expanded beyond justifiable limits at most undergraduate business schools. There is need for a general tightening of standards in terms of the scope of the core studies, the variety of majors, the number of courses that can be taken in a major, and the kind of electives students can choose. (Pierson, 1959, p. 196)

And the Gordon and Howell Report chimed in:

> One sign of the low state of collegiate business education is the fact that
> most business schools, particularly at the undergraduate but also at the
> graduate level, are both offering and requiring too many business courses.
> Many of these courses are not only too narrow and specialized, but more
> important, they contain little real substance and provide little or no intel-
> lectual challenge to the student. (Gordon and Howell, 1959, p. 139)

The *research* was too removed from fundamental inquiry and too focused on particulars. As the Pierson Report complained:

> Much of the research at these institutions [that is, business schools] is heav-
> ily weighted on the side of description; much of it centers on particular
> companies or local trade groups; much of it is undertaken because of its
> practical usefulness; very rarely is emphasis placed on developing analytical
> findings which can be fitted into a general system of principles and tested
> in a scientific manner. This misplaced emphasis is almost as serious as the
> dearth of research itself. (Pierson, 1959, p. 313)

Indeed, Robert D. Calkins, the dean of the Columbia University Business School from 1941–1948 and later affiliated with the Ford Foundation,
questioned whether the schools even knew what knowledge was useful.
"What are [the] fundamentals?" he asked:

> What qualifications make for competence in the careers for which we train?
> Frankly, I do not know, and I can think of no one who does. (Calkins,
> quoted in Daniel, 1998, p. 142)

In general, business schools were seen by many academics as using
poorly educated faculty to provide intellectually undemanding vocational
training for students of limited talent. Herbert Simon, whose training and
career were primarily in academic disciplines but who spent ten to fifteen
years of his career (approximately 1949–1963) in a business school, wrote in
his autobiography:

> Accurately or not, we perceived American business education at that time
> [that is, immediately after the Second World War] as a wasteland of voca-
> tionalism that needed to be transformed into science-based professional-

ism, as medicine and engineering had been transformed a generation or two earlier. (Simon, 1991, p. 138)

Looking back later, James Howell also described the inferior quality of faculty, students, and curricula as a major problem:

> The major—and, in some sense, all-encompassing—[problem] was that too often business education was irrelevant to most students, to employers , and to society . . . because of the low quality of its student and faculty and because of the narrowness of the training it provided. (Howell, 1984, p. 3)

The stereotype was sometimes strikingly inconsistent with the facts, as in the case of the superior academic preparation, talent (test scores), and performance of students in accounting at many schools; but the stereotype contained sufficient elements of truth to be troublesome. Business schools struggled with academic legitimacy while offering elements of protection for higher education from the concerns of political and economic leaders about academic snobbery and irrelevance. Their critics argued that business schools needed comprehensive change in order to serve their students, society, and business better.

Connections

Postwar North American business schools were vulnerable to change, and they were linked to a postwar context that invited change in many diffuse ways. Universities were growing rapidly in size and influence, a growth that would ultimately dictate their tighter integration into the social, economic, and political structure of the society but in the shorter run gave them increased autonomy. Wartime experience in the application of statistics, mathematics, science, and analytical tools to the solution of problems in production and logistics encouraged confidence in the possibilities for similar successes in postwar business. The history of reforms in North American medical schools suggested the possibility of similar reforms in business schools.

These preconditions were not simply abstractions but were woven into institutions and personal commitments through a set of institutional connections and life histories. Prior to the war, Robert Maynard Hutchins, president of the University of Chicago, proclaimed an orientation to higher education that emphasized the foundations of fundamental ideas and inter-disciplinary collaboration as essential to the development of practical applications. It was a proclamation that stimulated opposition at Chicago and elsewhere, but it became the basis for a mind-set about higher education that was widely shared among academics as well as significant numbers of educated professionals, including those who would become active in the reform of management education.

During the Second World War, well-trained minds had experimented with applying scientific techniques and methodologies to problems of military strategy and management. With the end of the war, numerous individuals with experience on such problems sought ways to apply their experience and ideas to new domains. Some turned to peacetime strategies in the Cold War and became the backbone of the peacetime elaboration of institutions such as the RAND Corporation. Others saw opportunities in business management for the use of tools developed through wartime (often classified) research. RAND became not only a symbol of the possibilities but a frequent meeting place for individuals committed to them.

Some business executives and management consultants, the natural allies of vocational business schools, had become intrigued by the need for more fundamental research, as reflected particularly in the possibilities for progress and collaboration in the areas of management science and operations research. They spoke of such things as the need for operations researchers (Rader, 1965) and the possibilities for integrating the fundamental knowledge of science and the practice of management (Hertz, 1965).

For the postwar vision of a new era in management to become real, however, business schools had to change. A common rallying cry was "The Flexner Report." In the early part of the twentieth century, Abraham Flexner had written a critique of medical education that came to be known as the Flexner Report and that had spurred widespread changes in schools of medicine. A central tenet of that report was the need to connect the education of physicians to fundamental research and to a sense of professionalism. By the 1930s, the Flexner Report was widely viewed as an unconditional success in improving medical education and had become in the minds of many advocates a model for the reform of business education. After the war, awareness of the Flexner experience pervaded the reform of management education.

The postwar consensus among academic, business, foundation, and government leaders, the legend of Flexner, the spirit of Hutchins's Chicago, and the development of a new version of defense-related research at RAND all shaped postwar developments in business schools. The connections were profound and dense without being organized into any kind of formal command structure. There was a largely shared worldview, a largely shared vision of the future, and a largely shared set of prejudices.

Chapter Three

A Legend of Change:
Abraham Flexner

Beginning in the 1930s and increasingly after the war, a model for business school reform was found in the reform of medical education in the early years of the twentieth century and its most conspicuous artifact—the Flexner Report. Business school reformers of the 1950s and 1960s, consciously or unconsciously and often explicitly, traveled the road of medical school reform in the first decades of the twentieth century. Many of them unequivocally venerated the Flexner Report as a model for change.

3.1 A Model for Change

The publication of the Flexner Report—also know as *Bulletin Number Four* from the Carnegie Foundation, is a key event in the history of modern medical education (Starr, 1984). Within the medical community and the broader community concerned with the state of medical practice, that report came to be regarded as the preeminent instrument and symbol of improvement in medical schools and medical education. The Bulletin of the World Health Organization notes:

> Abraham Flexner's report, commissioned by the Carnegie Foundation, was
> a remarkable attempt to improve the quality of medical education in North

America. It was based on sound principles, which may appear trivial today; medical schools should be university based and their educational programs should have a solid scientific basis. Almost a century later, its influence on medical schools is still felt worldwide. (Boelen, 2002, p. 592)

By the middle of the century, Flexner and his report had been erected as icons of modern educational history. The report and its effects were seen as exemplars of the links among ideas, foundations and education, and some of the political mechanisms involved in the construction of professional education. As Starr notes in one of the most comprehensive discussions of the social history and influence of the changes in medical education:

> Whatever its influence on public opinion, the Flexner report crystallized a view that proved immensely important in guiding the major foundations' investment in medical care over the next two crucial decades. In a sense, the report was the manifesto of a program that by 1936 guided $91 million from Rockefeller's General Education Board (plus millions more from other foundations) to a select group of medical schools. . . . Though the board represented itself as a purely neutral force responding to the dictates of science and the wishes of the medical schools, its staff actively sought to impose a model of medical education more closely wedded to research than to medical practice. These policies determined not so much which institutions would survive as which would dominate, how they would be run, and what ideals would prevail. (Starr, 1984, p. 121)

It is possible to argue that Flexner was less an innovator and instrument of change and more a symbol and focal point for changes and developments that were bound to take place and were already happening, but most subsequent observers are inclined to give substantial credit to Flexner's tenacity and effectiveness. Indeed, conventional stories of the reform of medical education sanctify Flexner and his report. There is no question that the reform was viewed as successful and came to be strongly attached to the Flexner legend. In 1959 the *New York Times* (September 22, 1959) proclaimed that "no other American of his generation" had ever done more for "the welfare of his country and [for] humanity in general."

It was natural for business school reformers to see the Flexner story as an inspiration for their own efforts, but there are features of medical schools, their histories, and their problems that are distinctively different from business schools. Flexner saw the practice of management as radically different from the practice of medicine, and business schools as distinct from, and in most respects inferior to, medical schools. Over the years, he returned to a theme of differentiating business from medicine. From Flexner's point of view, management was not a profession in the sense that medicine was, and medical education was not a particularly good model for business education. He wrote:

> The student who gets his degree in law or medicine is a lawyer or a doctor. The student who passes through the graduate school of business is not a businessman. (Flexner, 1909, p. 367)
>
> Is business a profession? In a loose way, the term "profession" is used merely as the antithesis to "amateur"; . . . we shall not maintain that a changed social and economic order, a changed system of ethical values, a deeper knowledge of economics may not some day convert business into a profession. But is business a profession today in any other than the amateur sense above described? Is the Harvard business school helping or hampering a genuinely professional evolution? (Flexner, 1930, p. 163)

Despite Flexner's reservations, the analogy between medical schools in 1900 and business schools in 1950 became more or less conventional and was used to proclaim the need for a Flexner Report in business education (Porter, 1963). Jeuck noted that:

> In 1957 two major foundations commissioned extensive studies of the field-surveying curriculum, faculty, students and clientele. Not since Abraham Flexner's 1910 report prompted a major reform of U.S. medical education had so much attention been focused on a field of professional education. (Jeuck, 1986, pp. 5–6)

The Gordon and Howell Report of 1959 (see Chapter Six) came to be characterized as a business school "delayed response" (however incomplete and different) to the Flexner Report (for example, Jeuck, 1986; Porter, 1963); commentators noted the similarities (and dissimilarities) of the two reports in terms of their contents and recommendations (for example, Porter, 1963; Simon, 1967, 1991).

3.2   The Prelude in Medical Schools

Studies of the history of North American medical schools are both thorough enough to preclude redoing them (MacDermot, 1952; Rothstein, 1987; Starr, 1984) and controversial enough to be cautious about accepting any broad interpretive summary (Hodges, 2005). However, they paint a basic picture of events that is fairly straightforward and noncontroversial.

Medical education was imported into North America from Great Britain. John Morgan established the first medical school in the original thirteen colonies in 1765 at the College of Philadelphia, an institution that later became the University of Pennsylvania. The faculty had been trained at the University of Edinburgh. Similarly, in Canada the first medical school opened in 1823 (classes began in 1824) as the Montreal Medical Institute, with essentially the same character as European institutions (MacDermot, 1952). Other schools followed, but for the first 100 years or more, medical training was primarily apprenticeship with a small amount of formal instruction. Medical schools generally took students with little or no prior academic preparation and provided relatively brief exposure to lectures before turning students over to practicing physicians as apprentices.

In the early nineteenth century, entry into the medical profession was subject to various licensure procedures instituted by medical societies, medical schools, and governing boards of universities. However, around 1830 licensure laws began to be repealed, and by 1850 legislative control of medical licensure was practically nonexistent in the United States (Fitz, 1884 [2009], pp. 306–307). Attempts to put licensing in the hands of state boards failed repeatedly until about 1875, when the resulting chaos led states to write new laws controlling licensure and practice.

The rising demand for physicians in the nineteenth century stimulated the creation of schools to train them. By 1900, there were 150 medical schools in Canada and the United States with more than 25,000 students and an attrition rate that approached 50 percent. Many of these medical schools were run for profit by the physicians who owned them. Only about 10 percent of the schools in North America required two or more years of college work before admission. It was also possible to practice medicine after an apprenticeship or by graduating from medical schools in Europe.

The practice of medicine had advanced somewhat from the days of barber-surgeons, but even well-trained doctors had few diagnostic capabilities, and their treatments often had little effect on the diseases they treated (Rothstein, 1987). A Harvard biochemist was quoted as saying that

> ... somewhere between 1910 and 1912 a random patient with a random disease, consulting a doctor chosen at random, had, for the first time in the history of mankind, a better than fifty-fifty chance of profiting from the encounter. (Ayers, 1996, p. 12)

As science developed in the nineteenth century, there were persistent efforts to augment the scientific base of medical training, but by the end of the nineteenth century there was widespread agreement that the instruments and procedures involved in preparation for a career in medicine in North America were inadequately tied to scientific knowledge.

Recognition that North American medical training was inadequate in the decades after the Civil War (Shryock, 1930, p. 327) led to proposals for change that gradually bore fruit. As a result of the Morrill Act establishing land grant colleges and universities, premedical education came to be improved. The power and prestige of the Association of American Medical Colleges (AAMC) grew, and the increased status improved the persuasiveness of the association's demands for higher standards from its member colleges. Increasing cooperation between the AAMC and the American Medical Association (AMA) helped to increase the willingness of state legislatures to consider revising the statutory regulation of medical practice; in 1905 the Confederation of State Medical Examining and Licensing Boards adopted the AAMC's standard curriculum as a basis for the granting of medical licenses.

At the same time, the market for physicians changed. Supply exceeded demand. Students were less inclined to clamor for medical training, and schools found themselves in fierce competition to secure students. The competition had a short-run effect of lowering standards but a longer-run effect of eliminating schools. As Flexner noted wryly:

Nothing has perhaps done more to complete the discredit of commercialism than the fact that it had ceased to pay. It is but a short step from an annual deficit to the conclusion that the whole thing is wrong anyway. (Flexner, 1910, p. 11)

3.3 THE AGENTS OF MEDICAL SCHOOL CHANGE

Throughout the nineteenth century but with rising voice toward the end of the century and early in the twentieth century, reformers within the medical profession and medical schools sought to change medical education. Subsequent historians ennobled Flexner, with some justice, but the process began before him. The issues were largely identified and framed before he undertook the preparation of his report. The major organizations that were involved were the AMA and the AAMC. A much later article in the *Journal of the American Medical Association* carefully identified the pre-Flexner AMA efforts, pointing out that for years before Flexner, the AMA had involved itself in efforts to eliminate medical schools that had not adopted a rigorous curriculum based on science (Beck, 2004, p. 2139).

The AMA had been formally established in 1847, and one of its purposes was to seek uniform and elevated standards for the MD degree (Flexner, 1910, p. 14). In particular, the official purposes of the association were (and continue to be) to advance the science of medicine, to improve the standards for medical education, to develop a program of medical ethics, and to improve the health of the public.[1] The AMA Council of Medical Education began to inspect medical schools in 1907 to create a system of classifications and rankings.

Forces within the AMA had battled for reform since the beginning, but their efforts had little effect for many years, primarily because of the structure of the organization itself. One commentator noted:

The best that can be said for the AMA before 1900 is that its monotonous editorial lamentations did keep the matter somewhere in the far reaches of the profession's conscience. (Leavitt and Numbers, 1972, p. 204)

The organizational dilemma the AMA faced was that if physician-owners of proprietary schools were to be induced to join a national organization that strongly favored educational reform, they would have to be offered greater voter representation than their numbers would dictate. On the other hand, giving the medical schools too large a voice would block any chance of reform. The dilemma was resolved by the withdrawal of the medical schools from membership in the AMA. At the AMA convention in 1846, only one-third of the eligible medical schools were present. After 1846, representation of medical schools in the AMA fell, whereas total membership increased.

Eventually the rift resulted both in an attempt to eliminate medical college delegates (see Davis, 1856, p. 37) at AMA meetings and in academic medical professors largely ignoring the AMA. In 1877 the academics formed the American Medical College Association. The new association struggled with unresolved internal conflict among the colleges. In 1880 the organization tried to modify standards to require three years of medical training with at least six months of each year in a "proper medical college." Within two years, ten schools withdrew from the organization, including some of the better colleges. A reorganization took place in 1890. The reorganization, plus a gradual realization of a crisis in medical education, strengthened the hand of those seeking to reform medical schools by establishing higher self-imposed standards. By 1896 the renamed Association of American Medical Colleges (AAMC) could report that 55 percent of the nation's 155 colleges were "cooperating," which meant at least nominal adherence to the curricular standards of the AAMC.

The American Medical Association joined the effort after 1900. In 1901 it began to collect data on medical education in a systematic way. In 1903 Frank Billings, president elect of the AMA, told the association at its annual meeting that the profession was becoming grossly overcrowded and that, to correct this, a medical degree had to become more difficult to achieve and proprietary schools had to be eliminated. At this point it was obvious that, although problems of the quality and scientific basis of medical education were high on the agenda of reformers, some of their primary support in the profession came not so much from a concern with quality as from the perception that an oversupply of physicians was reducing the fees that could be charged for services.

In 1904 the AMA formed a permanent Council on Medical Education. The council began periodically inspecting and grading medical schools, evaluations that probably contributed to the closure or merger of twenty-nine schools between 1906 and 1910. The council completed an unpublished report in 1907 that resulted in many schools agreeing to incorporate more science into their medical education. In 1908 the council helped enlist the Carnegie Foundation for the Advancement of Teaching in support of Abraham Flexner's study and made available to him data accumulated from the council's previous investigations. The secretary of the council, N. P. Colwell, accompanied Flexner on several inspection trips. The council and the institutions it mobilized were the primary institutional forces behind the changes in medical education in North America that took place in the first three decades of the twentieth century. The collaboration between the council and Flexner was not always smooth, but it was effective; the council was both gracious and politic enough to allow Flexner to bear the blame and reap the praise for the reform.

3.4   THE FLEXNER REPORT

Abraham Flexner was not a physician. He was born in Louisville, Kentucky, in 1866, one of eight siblings. After attending Johns Hopkins University (with money saved by his brother, Jacob Flexner), he returned to Louisville in 1886, teaching Latin and Greek at a local high school for four years before starting his own college preparatory school. Although he spent only two years at Johns Hopkins (because of a lack of finances in the family), Hopkins was very influential for Flexner's later life and career. He greatly admired the first president of the university, Daniel Gilman. As he noted in looking back:

> Those who know something of my work long after Gilman's day [that is, Flexner's work at the Carnegie Foundation, the General Education Board, and the Institute for Advanced Study at Princeton] will recognize Gilman's influence in all I have done or tried to do. (Flexner, 1940, p. 29)
>
> I think it is a modest claim to say that the founding of the Johns Hopkins University by President Gilman, was the starting point of higher education, in the modern sense of the term, in the United States. (Flexner, 1940, p. 45)

Flexner may also have been influenced by Gilman's vision of universities being more than (and different from) colleges:

> To Mr. Gilman's mind, a university was primarily a graduate school, and a graduate school was the congenial home of the ablest scholars and students that could be assembled. . . . [The Johns Hopkins University] was founded upon the idea of a university as distinct from a college. (Flexner, 1932, p. 441)

During his study of medical schools, Flexner continued his enthusiasm for Johns Hopkins, finding the medical school at that university to be an exemplar of an ideal school embodying the best of European medical education but adapted to American conditions.

In 1905, in preparation for a trip to Europe to study, he spent time at Harvard studying psychology and philosophy. In 1906, he traveled to the University of Berlin to study psychology with Georg Simmel, Carl Stumpf, and Friederich Paulson. Impressed by Germany, Flexner noted with admiration how "its universities led the world" (Flexner, 1930, p. 66). He admired the German universities, but he also noticed a few things that he considered to be defects: There were great professors but too few of them, and they often led unhappy lives; he found lecturing to be "overdone" (Ibid., p. 70).

Based on his studies in Europe, Flexner published a book on *The American College*, a critique of colleges in the United States as he recalled them at Harvard in the years 1905 and 1906. The book did not receive particularly favorable reviews, a consequence that Flexner attributed to the audience, rather than the book. As he wrote, the book "fell quite flat, for no one was prepared to act on the sweeping criticism which I made" (Ibid.).

The book did, however, give Flexner some kind of presence in discussions of the evolution of higher education in the United States. One of the early readers of the book was the president of the Carnegie Foundation, Henry S. Pritchett. Pritchett had graduated from college in Missouri in 1875 and had been an astronomer and professor of astronomy at various places, director of the U.S. Coast and Geodetic Survey, and president of MIT before suggesting to Andrew Carnegie that he set up a foundation.

When Carnegie did so, Pritchett became president of the foundation and remained in that position from 1906 until 1930.

Flexner thought he might find the Carnegie Foundation an interesting place in which to work, so he asked the president of Johns Hopkins University for an introduction to Pritchett (Bonner, 1998; Flexner, 1940, p. 71). At their second meeting, Pritchett asked whether Flexner would be interested in a study of medical schools. At first, Flexner thought that Pritchett might be confusing him with his brother, Simon Flexner, who was at the Rockefeller Institute, because he, Abraham Flexner, was not a physician and had in fact "never had my foot inside a medical school" (Flexner, 1940, p. 71).

As Flexner recalled it, Pritchett responded: "That [that is, someone outside medicine] is precisely what I want . . . This is a layman's job, not a job for a medical man" (Flexner, 1960, p. 71). Although Flexner at first had some doubts, those quickly dissipated in the face of his self-confidence. He later reported that, unlike writers of insider reports that had to be written diplomatically, he, as a layman, was in a position to be frank and (hence) more objectively truthful (Flexner, 1960, p. 74).

Both the Carnegie Foundation and the AMA were aware of the potential benefits of having an outsider evaluate medical education. In addition to the advantages of frankness, the AMA Council on Medical Education found such a thing tactically congenial from the point of view of its relations with the membership of the AMA. At a meeting held in 1908, the principals agreed to obscure the role of the council in the Flexner effort to increase credibility by sustaining an appearance of independent objectivity. The minutes stated:

> At one o'clock an informal conference was held with President Pritchett and Mr. Abraham Flexner of the Carnegie Foundation. Mr. Pritchett had already expressed, by correspondence, the willingness of the Foundation to cooperate with the Council in investigating the medical schools. . . . He agreed with the opinion previously expressed by the members of the Council that while the Foundation would be guided very largely by the Council's investigation, to avoid the usual claims of partiality no more mention should be made in the report of the Council than any other source of information. The report would therefore be, and have the weight of an independent report of a

disinterested body, which would then be published far and wide. It would do much to develop public opinion. (Shepard, 1960, p. 10)

Flexner observed that the job came with a "modest compensation" but "an unlimited expense account"; so, beginning around December of 1908, he began his work. He worked on the report from 1908 to 1910. Early in the project, Flexner and Pritchett briefly debated the idea of having an advisory committee of physicians. Flexner suggested postponing that decision, and they both forgot about it (Flexner, 1960, p. 74). Flexner read extensively in the literature relating to medical education, discussed the situation in medical education with people such as the then secretary of the American Medical Association (George H. Simmons), consulted the reports that had been prepared for the Council on Medical Education, and invited the secretary of the council to join him on some of his investigative visits to schools.

In the period from January of 1909 to December of 1910, Flexner evaluated 155 schools, based on visiting 167 institutions (some of them had several campuses in different places, so the number of visits was greater than the number of schools) across the country. According to Flexner himself, he visited ninety-six of the schools in the first five months, then took a four-month break, followed by the remaining visits (Flexner, 1940). He used neither questionnaires nor fixed procedures but focused on five questions about medical education:

> First, what were the entry requirements and were they enforced?
> Second, what was the training and size of the faculty?
> Third, what was the money available from endowments and fees and how was it spent?
> Fourth, what was the quality and adequacy of laboratories for instructions and the qualifications of the teachers there?
> And fifth, what were the relations between the medical school and hospitals including rules of appointments for physicians/clinical teachers? (Flexner, 1960, p. 79)

The large number of schools visited in such a short time raised questions of thoroughness for subsequent critics (Hiatt and Stockton, 2003), but Flexner never doubted the solidity of the empirical basis of his assessments.

He quickly became convinced that he could obtain information on these five dimensions by precise, diagnostic questions in his fieldwork that would allow him in a few hours to make "reliable estimates" of the school's capabilities for teaching modern medicine. He reported subjects to be candid and responsive, partly presumably in hopes of possible future support from Carnegie. At some places, he took photographs to document the conditions of particular schools for the edification of Pritchett and others at the Foundation.

Only a year and a half after he had begun his work, Flexner made his report. His findings were transmitted to the Carnegie Foundation for the Advancement of Teaching in a report published in the spring of 1910 and published as *Medical Education in the United States and Canada*—or *Bulletin Number Four*.[2] In June 1910, Carnegie issued 15,000 copies of the report, published with an appendix describing each school by name and a map with the locations of the schools that Flexner suggested closing.

By Flexner's recollection, the report produced "an immediate and profound sensation, making, as we say nowadays, 'the front page'" (Flexner, 1960, p. 87). Part of that sensation, to Flexner's delight, was outrage. Not everyone was happy:

> The medical profession and the faculties of the medical schools, as well as the state boards of examiners, were absolutely flabbergasted by the pitiless exposure. We were threatened with lawsuits, and in one instance actually sued for libel. . . . I received anonymous letters warning me that I should be shot if I showed myself in Chicago, whereupon I went there to make a speech before a meeting called by the Council on Medical Education and returned unharmed. (Flexner, 1960, p. 87)

The report contained (in its second part) survey data from the visits to 155 medical schools in the United States and Canada, but the major findings and arguments of the report were found in the first part. The part began with a relatively long set of comments, but it then moved to the major point that the medical profession was poorly trained. The report urged that state governments accept their obligation to assure competence of physicians by establishing rigorous licensure laws to be administered by professionally competent and incorruptible boards of registration in medicine. An earlier critique of medical schools was quoted:

> The ranks of the profession . . . are . . . filled up with recruits, deficient either in abilities or acquirements . . . (boys too often) indolent and averse to bodily exertion . . . too stupid for the Bar . . . too immoral for the Pulpit. (Drake, 1832, p. 6)

The report proposed that the number of schools be reduced from 155 to thirty-one and that the survivors all be integral parts of universities or colleges. The number of graduates should be reduced from 4,442 to 2,000 annually.

The report found that university medical education should be based on science; so a medical practitioner must be a scientist, even with imperfect knowledge:

> The scientist alone [as opposed to the learner from experience] draws the line accurately between the known, the partly known, and the unknown. (Flexner, 1910, pp. 55–56)

Thus, the report argued that proper training in medicine depended on the underlying disciplines—and on knowledge of chemistry, biology, and physics—knowledge that could not be learned in high schools and required at least two years of college training in the sciences. Flexner was convinced that medical education must be built on science, and he designed a scientific biomedical curriculum for medical schools—one with the six basic biomedical sciences taught in both laboratory and lecture room in the first two years and clinical subjects focusing on internal medicine during the last two.

The report asserted that "the progress of science, and the scientific or intelligent practice of medicine [should] employ . . . exactly the same technique." Thus, he believed that practical knowledge that had no basis in science did not belong in a university medical school (Flexner, 1910, p. 55). Nor should such a school have any room for

> . . . the scientifically dead practitioner whose knowledge has long since come to a standstill and whose lectures, composed when he first took his chair, like pebbles rolling in a brook, get smoother and smoother as the stream of time rolls over them. (Ibid., p. 57)

Flexner became an authority on reform of medical education in the United States and abroad. He subsequently was invited by John D. Rockefeller Jr. to join the General Education Board, where he worked from 1913 to 1928 and expanded his attention to include a general look at higher education. This work culminated in his book, *Universities: American, English, German* (1930). Other board members at the General Education Board included Charles Eliot and Rockefeller, but Flexner was the primary decision maker with respect to funds for medical education. His authority on the board and in the field was such that the other board members refused to make decisions when Flexner was out of town (Bonner, 1998, p. 162).

3.5   THE MEDICAL SCHOOL TRANSFORMATION

It is universally agreed that North American medical schools underwent a transformation in the early part of the twentieth century. There is disagreement about the extent to which the reforms would have occurred without Flexner, but there is no doubt that his report had a role.

The Short Run

The immediate response to the report was mixed. The *New York Times* (June 12, 1910) editorialized that, despite all the defects Flexner pointed out, the nation had a good body of physicians and that the report at times was "contentious and unnecessarily irritating." However, the editorial concluded that reform was needed and the report pointed the way. The *Chicago Daily Tribune* (June 6–7, 1910) made the wry observation that the schools that Flexner had evaluated favorably tended to praise his report while those who were criticized in his report were opposed to it.

The *New York State Journal of Medicine* (1910) thought that the Carnegie Foundation was meddling in the internal affairs of universities. It objected to Flexner's "wholesale and intemperate criticisms" of medical schools in the United States. *American Medicine* (1910) noted that the report exhibited an "animus against smaller institutions" and ignored the progress of the preceding ten years; but the journal also found the report to be "epoch-making" and "fearless" and agreed with the plea to raise requirements in medical education. The *Journal of the American Medical Association* said little about the report itself, perhaps because they felt that the Carnegie Foundation had stolen credit that should have gone to the Council of Medical Education (part of the AMA) or because they didn't want to reveal the extent of their collaboration with Flexner and Carnegie.

In fact, a case can be made that the Flexner Report simply summarized previously advocated changes, accelerating changes that were already under way rather than starting new changes. The Illinois State Board of Health had begun to publish lists of schools whose diplomas should not be recognized, thus undermining the ability of such schools to attract students. The AMA had already announced a goal to eliminate for-profit medical schools and reduce the number of physicians and had already in 1907 begun efforts to make poor schools either improve or close. The AMA was, however, a flawed instrument of change. As Flexner suspected (1960, p. 74) the AMA, with physicians as members, had difficulty articulating sharp criticism for fear of the negative effects on its internal cohesion. The Council of Medical Education of the AMA was engaged in fairly explicit efforts to influence the report and its reception and simultaneously to avoid the appearance of doing so.

The Middle Run

Two years after the report appeared, Flexner joined the staff of the General Education Board, which had been established with Rockefeller money in 1901 and immediately brought medical education into focus there. In 1919 he persuaded Rockefeller to set aside $50 million for the specific purpose of implementing the report's recommendations. He used the board's resources and his own knowledge to raise funds from local philanthropists to work on the transformation of many schools between 1919 and 1928. He sought to establish full-time faculties and to improve clinical teaching facilities. In his overseeing of funds, he was insistent on his principles for medical education; for example, he insisted on full-time clinical faculty in all the medical schools that asked for major funding (Bonner, 1998, p. 163).

Flexner noted in his autobiography that the board had spent $50 million on medical education and that, by leverage, the amount was ten times that. He also praised his tenacity: "We had no authority . . . but we never lost sight of our goals" (Flexner, 1940, p. 308). Flexner retired from the board in 1928, but by that time major reforms of medical education had taken place. The number of schools had been reduced from the 160 of twenty-five years earlier to seventy-six, and most of them had enhanced academic standards and were attached to universities. In subsequent years, schools continued to be closed, although Flexner's ideal number of thirty-one was never attained (Hiatt and Stockton, 2003). Perhaps because of the success in cutting down the number of schools, one historian of medicine characterized Flexner as the man "who did to death more bad schools in less time than any other man in the history of the world" (Fleming, 1954, p. 174), a claim that Flexner enthusiastically and without pretense of modesty supported:

> Such a rattling of dead bones has never been heard in this country before or since. Schools collapsed to the right and left, usually without a murmur. A number of them pooled their resources. . . . The fifteen schools in Chicago, which I had called "the plague spot of the country in respect to medical education," were shortly consolidated into three. (Flexner, 1960, p. 87)

The report probably accelerated the decline in number of schools, but medical schools had been declining in numbers in the United States since 1906 (Flexner himself reported a decline of 20 percent in the number of students from 1904 to 1909). Banta (1971, p. 657) reports that seventeen schools closed in 1908 and 1909 and another eleven by the publication time of the report in 1910; many of the schools covered in the Flexner report were in bad financial health and so may have been on the road to closing regardless of Flexner's evaluation.

The report's recommendations with regard to entrance requirements for medical schools were implemented relatively quickly, partly as a result of revisions in state licensure requirements. By the early 1930s it was impossible for a student to enter an American medical school unless he or she had successfully completed at least two years of college work, including the standard premedical science requirements. By the end of the Second World War, most schools required a baccalaureate degree for admission. The "Flexner medical curriculum," calling for two years of basic science and two years of clinical training, had been installed at Johns Hopkins in 1893, long before the Flexner Report. A few other schools had followed before

1910, but less than ten years after the publication of the Flexner Report, almost all U.S. schools had done so.

Perhaps the most important result of Flexner's efforts in the report and later was the acceptance of the concept of medical schools as "scientific" with emphasis on strong semiautonomous basic science departments, a research orientation, full-time faculty, and effective integration into the university. As Chapman observed:

> After Flexner, every physician was to be a scientist and a scholar, thoroughly conversant with the basic medical sciences and fully capable of applying them to the clinical situation. The purely empirical, rule-of-thumb practitioner was to be phased out. (Chapman, 1974, p. 111)

Although the same study concluded that "the Flexner Report was far more catalytic than innovative" (Ibid.), the report became known as a vital turning point in medical education and a guide to revisions of schools. The transformation and change that became visible in the first quarter of the twentieth century were largely associated with Flexner and his report: "The document ultimately acquired something like Talmudic status; to cite it was de rigeur to criticize it unthinkable" (Ibid.).

The Longer Run

Medical schools in North America continued to grow in size and importance through the remainder of the twentieth century. Many of the changes were part of the same postwar climate that fueled change in business schools. The rapid expansion of the National Institutes of Health stimulated research and rationalized the importance of research in medical schools.

However, some of the key changes instigated by the report came to be viewed as obsolete in medical schools. By 2006 an article in *New England Journal of Medicine* reported that "medical education seems to be in a perpetual state of unrest" (Cooke et al., 2006, p. 1339). In particular, population growth and increased demand for health care created strong pressures counter to the Flexner advocacy of reduced numbers of medical school graduates and lengthened training.

The "Bane Report" (Bane, 1959) and the "Coggeshall Report" (Coggeshall, 1965) both quoted Flexner but urged dramatic increases in the number of MD degrees; a new Carnegie Commission report stated that, based on 1966 figures, facilities for 75 percent more medical students would be required by 1976. In 1970 another Carnegie Commission report recommended a shortening of the time required to attain the MD. By the 1970s, the Flexner Report's demand for limiting the number of medical graduates was reversed, and the mostly scientific curriculum that that report envisaged was being deemphasized.

At the same time, there were developments in the underlying medical sciences (in directions probably not predicted by anyone). They had profound effects on medical education, effects that essentially confirmed the result for which Flexner aspired. The practice of medicine had become embedded in science. Lippard noted that, after the Second World War:

> In the basic sciences, scientific advances rather than changes in methods of instruction determined the emphasis given to courses and topics. Introduction of the electron microscope made possible the study of the morphology of subcellular elements and broadened the scope of courses in microscopic anatomy. Instruction in biochemistry became more concerned with enzyme systems and biochemical genetics. Physiologists became more interested in the study of fundamental processes, such as membrane permeability and nerve conduction, than in organ function. Pharmacologists became more biochemically oriented and, until the introduction of a new breed of clinical pharmacologists who combined interest in basic pharmacology and clinical medicine, more divorced from therapeutics. Bacteriology departments were appropriately redesigned as departments of microbiology. They ceased to be concerned with identification of bacteria, and dealt more extensively with viruses and other microorganisms as well as microbial genetics. (Lippard, 1974, pp. 4–5)

The Historical Run

Most historical accounts have pointed to Flexner's revolutionary role in reforming medical education (for example, Fleming, 1954; Starr, 1984). For example, a historian of the Johns Hopkins University of Medicine wrote that "Mr. Flexner's epoch-making investigation" led to "a sharp reduction in the number of medical schools in the United States within an incredibly short period of time" (Chesney, 1963, p. 143). And Corner wrote that Flexner's report had "shaken American medical education to its very roots" (Corner, 1965, p. 211).

Some criticism of Flexner's report and viewpoint emerged in the 1970s and 1980s, reflecting perhaps some general changing trends in society in the 1970s and 1980s more than anything else. For instance, one described Flexner as a "prize academic snob" because he insisted on higher standards (Perkin, 1984, p. 38); others claimed marks of racism and sexism in his attitude toward women and people of color (Brown, 1979, p. 154). Even a former editor of the *Journal of the American Medical Association* described the report as "the most grossly overrated document in American medical history" (King, 1984, p. 1079).

Some also criticized Flexner because medical education became too standardized in the United States. It was a criticism that curiously echoed Flexner's own sentiments. A little more than a decade after his study, he wrote that medical students:

> . . . move through medical school in tight lock step, and have little time to stop, read, work or think . . . anything more alien to the spirit of scientific or modern medicine or to university life can hardly be contrived. (Flexner, 1925, p. 149)

Regardless of these criticisms, Flexner's legacy remains, and newer articles have again begun talking favorably about his study and even pointing to the need for a (new) Flexner Report (see, for example, Gilbert, 2008). For instance, an article titled "Abe Flexner, Where Are You? We Need You!" published in 2007 (Arky, 2007) argued that, whereas the report at first changed medical education, medical education had not been changed subsequently to reflect underlying changes in the medical sciences and clinical practice. Once again, it was argued, there was a need for a

> . . . modern day Abe Flexner—someone to pull the disparate parts together, to shape up the lethargy and complacency, to streamline medical education into the 21st century. (Ibid. p. 89)

In discussions in medicine, as elsewhere, the Flexner Report had become an icon of an age and a symbol of change, attributes loosely connected to the history but tightly connected to the growing sanctification of the Report. Flexner became a saint. Flexner himself, describing the celebration of his ninetieth birthday, wrote with his characteristic resistance to modesty five decades after the publication of the report that

> Deans from every medical school in America came to the Waldorf-Astoria Hotel in New York, together with the nation's top cabinet officials, to hail him as the man who made "the greatest single contribution" in the history of the teaching of medical school. (quoted in Bonner, 1998, p. 161)

3.6   THE WORDS AND THE ISSUES

The reform of medical schools emphasized concrete objectives of reducing the number of schools, particularly those not associated with universities, reducing the number of graduates, improving the quality of medical school students, and improving the rigor of medical school training. To justify and accomplish those objectives, the Flexner Report, and the discussions it reflected and initiated, developed a rhetoric that found echoes fifty years later in the efforts to reform business schools. Flexner used words as weapons, both in the Flexner Report and in his activities before and after the report. Those words were organized by a few central themes.

Fundamental Knowledge as a Basis for Medical Education

Flexner believed that the practice of medicine should be based on fundamental knowledge about the human body and its functions. Medical diagnosis and treatment should be derived from scientific principles and research; thus, medical education should be education in fundamental scientific knowledge and its applications, and the teachers of medicine should be scientists. Flexner was scornful of a "century of reckless overproduction of cheap doctors" by schools whose budgets accommodated "advertising costs more than laboratories" (Flexner, 1910, p. 19).

In a discussion of "the proper basis for medical education" (Ibid., p. 38), Flexner noted how the past "empirical training of varying excellence" and procedures such as apprenticeship did not allow for the generation of general knowledge in the students; the fundamental sciences are "the essential basis of medical education" (p. 26). As the proper use of scientific method was the foundation both for medical education and for research and practice, Flexner emphasized that the medical sciences should be taught regardless of their applicability to immediate medical practice or to student's career goals; research should be "untrammeled by near reference to practical ends" (Ibid., p. 59).

To Flexner, the link to science was (or should be) pervasive in medical education. Admission requirements for medical students should emphasize basic scientific training. The curriculum for medical schools should include two years of exposure to the relevant sciences and courses in practice that are science based. Medical schools should be sites for fundamental research, and medical faculty should be researchers. Medical schools should be linked with the traditions of fundamental scholarship associated with major universities; only in the universities can the sciences relevant to medicine be cultivated.

Medical education should build on prior university education that is characterized by its breadth and depth, rather than its focus on medicine per se:

> The college will, within its limits, train broadly when, free from any immediate technical responsibility such as exists in the professional school itself, it presents every subject philosophically as well as technically. The student of biology, physics and chemistry is thus on the technical side preparing for the study of medicine; meanwhile the bearing of modern scientific methods and discoveries on the whole trend of social speculation and activity may be simultaneously made clear to him. (Ibid., p. 366)

Professions and Professionalism

The role of fundamental knowledge was linked to a conception of the practice of medicine as a profession. Flexner saw professionalism as an essential feature of good medical practice. For him, medical education was professional because it built on several sciences in a cross-disciplinary and problem-oriented way. Flexner's understanding of professionalism did not, however, end with that idea. The professionalism that he embraced involved four vital elements. First, it was based on scientific knowledge. Second, it was oriented to a patient's health, not a doctor's wealth. Third, it was conscious of, and dedicated to, the general social good, not narrow self-interests. Fourth, it was self-organizing, enforcing standards on itself (Flexner, 1915).

In the name of professionalism, Flexner opposed the involvement of medical school faculty in "lucrative private practices," a point elaborated in a private report to the General Education Board in 1911 arguing that they support full-time clinical faculty at Johns Hopkins University Medical School:

> The clinicians have with very few exceptions proved too easy victims of the encroachments of profitable practice. Not only has productive work been sacrificed to private professional engagements—routine teaching and hospital work go by the board when a large fee is in prospect. Classes are turned over to subordinates in order that the chief may leave town to see patients, not because they were scientifically interesting, but because they are pecuniarily worth while. (in Chesney, 1963, p. 300)

The rhetoric of professionalism, particularly with its emphases on scientific knowledge and on altruistic commitments to values beyond the self-interests of doctors, permeates the Flexner approach. Medical education should involve training in practice based on the best fundamental knowledge available. It should also involve socialization into an altruistic code of medical virtue. For Flexner, professions should aspire to be "objective, intellectual and altruistic" and "devoted [more] to the promotion of larger and nobler ends than the satisfaction of individual ambitions" (Flexner, 1915, p. 56).

The Usefulness of Useless Knowledge

The link to science was later extended by Flexner to a more general point involving the pursuit of useless knowledge. In a speech given at Bryn Mawr College in June of 1937, subsequently repeated at the opening of the Squibb Institute for Medical Research and published as part of the proceedings for the latter (Flexner, 1938), he argued for the "usefulness of useless knowledge." His argument combined a paean to the aesthetics of irrationality with a utilitarian defense of arbitrary curiosity:

> Throughout the whole history of science most of the really great discoveries which had ultimately proven to be beneficial to mankind had been made by men and women who were driven, not by the desire to be useful, but merely by the desire to satisfy their curiosity. (Flexner, 1938, p. 2)

His argument was even more extreme: Criteria of relevance and usefulness are not only irrelevant; they are deleterious:

> It is almost certain that efforts aiming at the immediately practical will fail unless they are based upon a long succession of experiments and endeavors that have no such practical use in mind. (Ibid., p. 6)

Flexner recognized that the uncontrolled generation of ideas would result in a lot of craziness, but he thought the costs were clearly less than the benefits:

> To be sure, we will thus free some harmless cranks. To be sure, we will thus waste some precious dollars, but what is infinitely more important is the fact that we will be striking the shackles off the human mind in setting it free for the adventures which in our own day have taken Hale and Rutherford and Einstein and their peers millions upon millions of miles into the uttermost realms of space and loosed the boundless energy imprisoned in the atom. (Flexner, 1938, p. 5)

3.7 The Legend and the Analogy to Management Education

The early-twentieth-century history of medical schools in North America and the role of the Flexner Report in them became a mythic legend in subsequent years. Although there were challenges to various parts of the story on the part of subsequent historians, by the time of the Second World War the essential elements of the legend had become insulated from challenge in all but the most skeptical quarters. Few people any longer studied the history or read the report, but almost everyone knew and repeated the story.

The successes of medical school reform were embraced as triumphs of modernity and models for other fields. The role of the Flexner Report in producing those changes became a matter of sacred belief. The legend captured and extended the spirit of the times. The essential elements of the story included a skeleton of the events and a theory of their causal basis. The skeleton of events had three parts:

- First, by the end of the nineteenth century North American medical education was woefully deficient. There were too many medical schools of too little distinction educating physicians of too little competence.

- Second, the Flexner Report and its author Abraham Flexner symbolized and mobilized a movement to correct the faults of medical schools, providing a diagnosis of the problems and a course of treatment for them.

- Third, by 1920 North American medical schools had been changed by the movement. The number of schools had been radically reduced; the quality of students, faculty, and instruction had been radically improved; and the practice of medicine had been thoroughly embedded in fundamental knowledge.

The events confirmed an analysis reflected in Flexner's diagnosis and treatment. He argued that the deficiencies in North American medical education were created by a failure to enforce standards of excellence on students, faculties, and programs and that this failure stemmed from the isolation of medical education from its basis in fundamental knowledge. The schools were too separate from institutions that conducted fundamental research, and medical education was too removed from the scientific knowledge on which medical practice should rely. In Flexner's view, medical education would be drastically improved by significantly tightening standards and by bringing students, faculty, and curricula closer to fundamental research.

The Flexner rhetoric framed the events. That rhetoric emphasized the symbols of fundamental knowledge, professionalism, and dangers of enforcing standards of immediate relevance. It propagated a vision of medicine that glorified science and the pursuit of useless knowledge and that advocated a medical calling more akin to a priestly dedication than to a self-interested ambitious career.

The Flexner Legend became grounds for reform in areas far removed from medicine. For example, the Committee on Legal Education and Admissions to the Bar of the American Bar Association wrote to the then-president of the Carnegie Foundation (Henry Pritchett) that it was "greatly impressed" by the Flexner report and "most anxious to have a similar investigation made by the Carnegie Foundation into the conditions under which the work of legal education is carried on in this country" (Schudson, 1974, p. 359). A Carnegie staff member was asked to take up this work, which resulted in a similarly spirited report, the "Reed Report" (Reed, 1921).

It was this legend and this rhetoric that were carried by the ghost of Abraham Flexner into discussions of management education. Flexner and the Flexner Report were parts of the mind-set for business school reformers starting as early as the 1930s. For instance, an article in the *Journal of Business* in 1931 was entitled "Dr. Flexner on University Training for Business" (Le Rossingol, 1931). Although noting Flexner's skepticism about the parallel with medical education, the article commended his insights for thinking about business education.

After the Second World War, the Flexner legend became a dominant theme in discussions of business school reform. The analogy to medical schools was, of course, not perfect. Indeed, Flexner himself implicitly pointed to the inadequacy of the analogy by criticizing business for not being a profession (1915, 1940). Proprietary schools of business existed, but they played a much less significant role in management education than medical schools had in medical education fifty years earlier. There was nothing equivalent to the licensing of physicians involved in the legitimacy of managers. There were important differences between the professionalization of medicine and the professionalization of management.

On the other hand, there were similarities. Students in business schools seemed poorly qualified; business school faculty seemed less academically qualified than other faculties; management science had flourished in the 1940s in a way reminiscent of the flowering of biomedical research in the final decades of the nineteenth century. Management education in 1945 suffered in a way similar to medical education in 1900 by its isolation from fundamental research.

Whatever the merit in the analogy, there was no question about its status as a cliché. Flexner was cited repeatedly as a model in discussions of business education. The parallel was noted in an article in 1973:

> Investigators commissioned by two major foundations embarked on extensive surveys of the field [management education] in 1957—curriculum, faculty, students, and clientele. Not since Flexner's 1910 evaluation of medical schools had so much attention been focused on a field of professional education. Both reports were published in 1959: Frank Pierson's *The Education of American Businessmen* (supported by the Carnegie Corporation) and Gordon and Howell's Ford-financed *Higher Education for Business*. (Jeuck, 1973, pp. 284–285)

Or, as the Carnegie Corporation Review committee stated in their written preface to the Pierson report,

> The Carnegie name has long been associated with scholarly studies in professional education and in educational policy generally. One of the notable landmarks in medical education, in many minds the most important, was the report published in 1910, "Medical Education in the United States and Canada," authored by Abraham Flexner and sponsored by the Carnegie Foundation for the Advancement of Teaching. (Pierson, 1959, p. vii)

Robert Trueblood, a noted accountant and collaborator with Richard M. Cyert in advancing the uses of statistics in accounting, described the Pierson Report and Gordon and Howell Report as delayed responses to Flexner (Trueblood, 1963, pp. 86–94):

> More recently, the Carnegie and Ford Foundation each have sponsored studies on business education, patterned somewhat after Flexner's famous study on medical education fifty years ago. (p. 87)

The report by Rowan Gaither to the Ford Foundation (see Chapter Five), first formulated in 1949 and published in 1951, also reflected an awareness of the Flexner legend:

> Often remarked, but worth repeating, is the fact that some of the greatest achievements by foundations in quite specialized fields were the work of laymen. Abraham Flexner, a layman, did enough for medical education on a Carnegie grant . . . (Gaither, 1951, p. 131)

This awareness was not isolated within the community of management education reformers but extended very broadly through postwar activist groups in the social sciences who knew about Flexner and recognized him for his contribution to education in general as well as his role in reforming medical education (Berelson, 1961; Calkins, 1961: Wallis, 1964). For example, a 1952 meeting of a planning group for the Ford Foundation Center for Advanced Study in the Behavioral Sciences (an institution that would have some significant connections with important early scholars in business schools) mentions Flexner several times and quotes from his writings.[3]

In the minds of the reformers of management education in the 1950s and 1960s, Flexner was an inspiration. Robert Calkins, president of the Brookings institution (and involved in the Ford Foundation's initiatives (see Chapter Five), noted that "what is needed is a comprehensive appraisal of business education comparable to the Flexner report on medical education of 1910" (Calkins, 1961, p. 1). Flexner was credited with changing medical schools, in particular by increasing their links to fundamental research, by embedding education in its scientific foundations, and by improving the quality of students, faculty, and curricula. The Flexner legend suited the enthusiasms for science, the criticisms of management, and the opportunities for growth that the postwar period provided for business schools. The analogy was far from perfect and explicitly rejected by Flexner himself, but it provided both optimism about what could be done and support for the major theme of the reformation of business schools—the need to link professional education to scientific research and academic values.

Chapter Four

A Spirit of Change:
Hutchins's University of Chicago

The Flexner Report and the reform of medical schools provided rather direct (if not entirely precise) analogues to business schools and management education. The advocates for change in business schools in the 1950s and 1960s were conscious of and envious of the Flexner example. It was part of their worldview and a conspicuous part of the discourse about change. Repeatedly, enthusiasts for business school reform evoked the ghost of Abraham Flexner as a model of what they hoped to achieve.

A second source of their worldview was more diffuse and less explicit but nonetheless quite pervasive. It was the spirit of Robert Maynard Hutchins's University of Chicago, a spirit that was shaped originally by Hutchins's efforts to reform the university but became a broader set of intellectual commitments marking and motivating not only a generation of Chicago faculty and students but also many others. It was a spirit of educational reform that was conspicuously arrogant in its intellectual pretensions and uncommonly naïve in its academic ambitions, but it was embraced widely among the intellectual elites of university communities.

Flexner and Hutchins shared a number of prejudices, including a lack of enthusiasm for humility. A story is told that during the 1920s when Flexner was working to implement his medical education changes, he offered some Rockefeller Foundation money to Hutchins, then at Yale University, to allow him to read and extend his knowledge and deepen his wisdom. Hutchins declined the offer; and, when he ran into Flexner some years later, Hutchins is supposed to have said, "If I'd taken your ten thousand, I wouldn't be president of the university." The story records Flexner's response as "Maybe not . . . but you would have been prepared to be" (McDonald, 1956, p. 78).

Hutchins was a prophet of the intellectual university. One symbol of that orientation at Chicago was the elimination of intercollegiate football at the university, a declaration of the primacy of the mind. The intellectual climate that Hutchins fomented and symbolized created an academic culture in which the precocious development and ostentatious display of intellectual prowess were essential. The resulting mood at Chicago was often internally contentious, and it ultimately disavowed some of the specific innovations that were important to Hutchins, but it sustained a set of attitudes that the debates at the University of Chicago stimulated, attitudes that extended well beyond the boundaries of that university and influenced the reform of business education as it was later implemented in individual business schools.

4.1 Building the Chicago Spirit

Robert Maynard Hutchins became president of the University of Chicago in 1929 at the age of thirty. He left the university in 1951. Hutchins was combative, articulate, and controversial. He had only partial success in implementing the structural changes that he sought at Chicago. His fascination with metaphysics led to well-publicized conflicts with other leading intellectuals, most notably with John Dewey. His efforts to mute the importance of disciplines while at the same time glorifying fundamental knowledge proved ultimately to be self-defeating. After he left Chicago in 1951, he himself became a relatively minor voice in discussions of the ideological, social, and political bases of democracy; and although it never completely lost the Hutchins stamp, the University of Chicago drifted back toward the mainstream of American universities.

For more than two decades, however, Hutchins maintained a voice for a strongly intellectual view of higher education. During the time he was at Chicago, he, his allies, his opponents, and the debates they initiated created a climate that shaped the thinking of many who were there as well as many others who resonated with the prejudices Hutchins espoused. As those individuals moved into positions of importance in the 1950s and 1960s, they carried with them the thrusts of the Hutchins themes. Those themes would become prominent in the thinking and rhetoric of the leaders of business school reform, especially those who had connections to the University of Chicago during the Hutchins era.

Hutchins's themes were built on two fundamental axioms. First, higher education should be grounded in fundamental scholarly knowledge, not in the accumulation of facts or vocational preparation (or intercollegiate football). Out of this came, among other things, the emphasis on "great books" as a foundation of undergraduate instruction and on research-based graduate education. Second, discipline-based education created barriers to the exciting intellectual opportunities found in interdisciplinary work. Out of this came efforts to create multidisciplinary "committees," such as the Committee on International Relations, the Committee on Child Development, and the Committee on Social Thought, with authority to hire professors and grant degrees in parallel with disciplinary departments.

Leading business school reformers in the 1950s saw an opportunity to reconstruct management education to make it consistent with a view that echoed Hutchins's perspective. In doing so, they built on the Hutchins's aura and sought to overcome the deficiencies in business education that were alien to that aura. They were committed to fundamental knowledge and interdisciplinarity as essential elements in a reformed business school. Their intellectual arrogance echoed that of Hutchins.

Hutchins and Business Education

Like Flexner, with whom he occasionally exchanged views, Hutchins himself was little disposed to support business education as it existed, viewing it as involving the kind of rampant vocationalism that he fought. In a discussion of the role of professional schools in universities, he argued that

. . . the tricks of the trade [vocations] cannot be learned in a university, and . . . if they can they should not be. They cannot be learned in a university because they get out of date and new tricks take their place, because the teachers get out of date and cannot keep up with current tricks, and because tricks can be learned only in the actual situation in which they can be employed. (Hutchins, 1968, p. 47)

He argued that the case method and the study of current events usually resulted in keeping up with past events instead and that one should focus not on learning the particulars of time and place and practice that change every day but instead on underlying principles and general knowledge.

His exchanges with Alfred North Whitehead were instructive (see Woodhouse, 2000). Hutchins and Whitehead shared many prejudices. They both decried thinking of universities as businesses. Whitehead wrote that "the learned and imaginative life is a way of living, and is not an article of commerce" (Whitehead, 1929, p. 97). However, Whitehead published an essay on "Harvard: The Future" that argued that the university and the world of business and markets may go hand in hand. He wrote that "celibacy does not suit a university, it must mate itself with action" (Whitehead, 1936, p. 267).

In response, Hutchins criticized how the pursuit of "immediate utility" was emphasized at Harvard "to the exclusion of [the] intellectual tradition" of seeking to undermine knowledge (Hutchins, 1936, p. 585). Hutchins's response to Whitehead's metaphor was to state that

. . . the danger of the American universities is not celibacy, but polygamy. They are mated to so many different kinds of action that nothing but a few divorces can save them from the consequences of their ardour. (Hutchins, 1936, p. 583)

Defending the emphasis on thought (not action), Hutchins argued against the "pressure of the practical" and the "fragmentary and scattered" courses that he saw in (especially) the Harvard Business School. "The classics and the Liberal arts have almost disappeared . . . [into] fragmentary and isolated remains" (Hutchins, 1936, p. 585). Thus, as a university president he argued that students in the professional schools should take courses in the underlying disciplines and that faculty, for instance in the medical school, should keep links with the sciences that enabled them to be "more definitely part of the University" (Hutchins, 1949, p. 29) rather than be isolated:

> I suggest that vocationalism is not merely bad for the universities; it is bad also for the professions. I beg to lay down this fundamental proposition, that every profession requires for its continuous development the existence of centers of creative thought. To the extent to which universities and professional schools abandon creative thought and degenerate into trade schools the profession must degenerate into a trade. (Hutchins, 1968, p. 44)

Hutchins also believed that the professions, if they were to contribute to the university, should be based on "mutual interchange" with the disciplinary departments (Hutchins, 1968, p. 43). He argued that where the medical schools were strong, it was where they were not "slaves" of any professional group but had "intimate relationships" with "strong disciplinary departments" (p. 45).

In addition, professions that relied on a market logic rather than a logic of pursuing the common good did not really belong in educational institutions. In this respect, he questioned the status of business as a profession (Hutchins, 1968). A profession was to him a group of "men trained in a subject matter which had intellectual content in its own right. The aim of the group was the common good" (Hutchins, 1936, p. 586).

While Hutchins was critical of the pursuit of profit and immediate knowledge, he was not opposed to the pursuit of fundamental knowledge relevant to business. For example, in 1936, he endorsed the idea of an "Institute of Accounting" at the University of Chicago. Referencing models such as the Institute for Advanced Studies at Princeton and the Brookings and Mellon Institutes, he advocated "research into practical problems only in so far as these illustrate or serve to develop general or theoretical principles of the science of accounting."[1]

The Hutchins History

Robert Hutchins came to the University of Chicago from a position as dean of the Yale Law School, where he had encouraged the integration of social science theory and law and was highly critical of what he considered to be inferior legal education, a dark world to which he consigned most existing law schools. He also voiced criticism of the dominant method of case studies that permeated the law schools' curricula, arguing that the case method represented significant progress from earlier methods of instruction but was insufficient. While cases provided knowledge of particulars or facts, they lack general and fundamental knowledge (Hutchins, 1928).

At Yale, Hutchins was instrumental in securing funding for the Institute of Human Relations, which was intended as an organization for the "cooperative study of man" (Hutchins, 1929). Connecting the biological sciences and medicine with social science and law (through psychology), the institute focused on research and seminars "overlapping the boundary lines of the traditional boundaries" (Hutchins, 1929, p. 187). It was a theme to which he would return at Chicago.

Although Hutchins saw himself as designing an educational framework for a democracy, the visions were Platonic and elitist: He never lost the moral fervor of his Presbyterian childhood, reinforced by his experiences at Oberlin College, where he earned his baccalaureate degree. He was convinced that there was a right way, that he knew what the right way was, and that his responsibility was to help others to find the way (Dzuback, 1991, Chapter 1). In his view, educational leaders had intellectual and moral responsibilities for the community; educational institutions were responsible not only for making coming generations of society's leaders and citizens more capable but also for educating them in their responsibilities. The character of society was determined to a large extent by the character of education, and knowledge was the key to enabling students to become good citizens and leaders (Hutchins, 1937).

To implement his vision, Hutchins turned particularly to philosophy and the "great books" ideas imported by Mortimer Adler from Columbia University. He regularly taught "great books" classes during his tenure at Chicago and was attracted to the vision of finding a solid (and philosophical) intellectual foundation for the sciences as well as other scholarship. He thought that making this the central core of the University of Chicago would assure its primacy (Hutchins, 1941).

The Hutchins Creed

Hutchins wrote many words, debated many issues, and proposed many changes, but there was one overriding consistent element in his pronouncements. He embraced unconditionally the glories of the intellect. He sought to raise the intellectual level of the university and the society. He saw intellectual capabilities as the fundamental capabilities of a good life and a good society. He saw intellectual discourse as the foundation of society and intellectual display as the true manifestation of modern machismo.

He urged a "return to vicious intellectualism," as represented by Descartes. He described the purpose of higher education as "to unsettle the minds of young men, to widen their horizons, to inflame their intellects" (Hutchins, 1936, p. 48). And he wrote that

> A university education must chiefly be directed to inculcating the intellectual virtues, and these are the product of rigorous intellectual effort. Such effort is the indispensable constituent of a university course of study. (Hutchins, 1934a, p. 182)

It was only a short step from an enthusiasm for the intellect to a position that placed research scholarship at the center of the university. He wrote:

> The University is not an instrument of popular education; the university is an organization for the promotion of scholarship. (Hutchins, 1933, p. 484)
>
> The object of faculty and students in the university should be the highest kind of scholarly and professional work in a scholarly and professional atmosphere. (Ibid., p. 485)
>
> A university may be a university without doing any teaching; it cannot be one without doing any research. (Hutchins, 1934b, p. 349)

Hutchins's commitment to the intellect included a persistent inclination to support explorations of novel ideas. His proclivity for supporting innovations led him to become one of the primary contributors to two of the more conspicuous post-Hutchins developments at the university, developments that certainly were contrary to Hutchins's own political preferences. The first innovation was the free-market radicalization of the Department of Economics and the Graduate School of Business. Over the objections of senior members of the department, Hutchins invited Friedrich Hayek to visit the university and give a seminar (Dzuback, 1991). It was a critical step in the development of "Chicago economics." The second innovation was the so-called law and economics movement at Chicago associated with scholars such as Richard Posner, Gary Becker, Harold Demsetz, Ronald Coase, and Henry Manne (Kitch, 1983). This movement also became an arm in the free-market branch of economics, both in scholarship and in antitrust law and policy (Posner, 1986). Hutchins saw both initiatives as the kind of intellectually based deviant directions that should be encouraged at a university.

The Hutchins Legacy

The primary legacy of the Hutchins period at Chicago was not institutional. Most of the institutional changes he championed were either not introduced or were gradually transmuted to forms rather different from his vision. For example, Hutchins tried systematically to reduce the power of disciplinary departments. He removed them from responsibility for undergraduate education. He encouraged the creation of interdisciplinary committees able to hire faculty and grant advanced degrees. He welcomed outside institutes such as the Cowles Commission that provided alternative centers of intellectual effort. He saw interdisciplinarity as an integral part of a commitment to the intellect. He wrote:

> Whitehead may have been right when he said not long ago that "the increasing departmentalization of universities has trivialized the intellect of professors." (Hutchins, 1934a, p. 180)

The Hutchins years produced enthusiasm for the possibilities for cross-disciplinary engagement. For example, students of economics thrived on contact with the mathematical statisticians and mathematicians who gathered around the Cowles Commission. Social scientists thrived on contact with the systems ideas of Nicholas Rashevsky and his colleagues at the Committee on Mathematical Biology.

Hutchins's enthusiasm for intellectual deviance was shared by a few but resisted by many. Allen Wallis, who later became the dean of the University of Chicago Graduate School of Business and a staunch supporter of the Hayek-based directions in economics, observed, not entirely with enthusiasm:

> There were always things being started. There were innovations all the time, and nobody ever resisted them. (Wallis in Kitch, 1983, p. 189)

In the end, what survived at Chicago was a set of attitudes that defined education as the pursuit of knowledge and knowledge as stemming from fundamental research; that set of attitudes ultimately became the basis for increased authority for the disciplines. In the institutional struggles at Chicago, the parallel part of the Hutchins gospel that emphasized interdisciplinary scholarship succumbed to the disciplinary implications of the emphasis on fundamental research. The free-market radicalization of Chicago economics, which generated a political realignment of economics that differentiated it politically from Hutchins and earlier giants in economics at Chicago, tended to obscure the part played by the Hutchins era and Hutchins himself in creating a climate that facilitated that development.

The primary legacy of the Hutchins years was a culture of attitudes that evolved in two decades of argument. It was a culture that drew its spirit from disdain for the low level of intellectuality in American universities. Hutchins wrote:

> Everybody knows that the American student is less mature intellectually by at least two years than his British or European contemporary. (Hutchins, 1943, pp. 294–295)

The legacy culture reflected the academic arrogance and intellectual elitism that Hutchins fostered, as well as many of the beliefs on which they were based, without a commitment to the specific institutional forms that Hutchins associated with those attitudes or to the fascination with metaphysics as a fundamental basis for thought that filled many of Hutchins's pronouncements.

4.2 The Tentacles of Chicago

Many of the specific curricular and organizational initiatives that Hutchins championed either were not adopted or were later abandoned, but he built on an earlier University of Chicago excellence in graduate education to confirm a culture in which intellectual discourse was central. "Great books" and metaphysics became metaphors for a concern with fundamental scholarship, a concern that in the spirit of the times became particularly focused less on philosophy than on mathematics, science, and the creation of new interdisciplinary domains. As students and faculty moved from Chicago to other parts of the academic world, they frequently carried recollections of an intellectually exciting place and exhibited a desire to replicate its intellectuality elsewhere.

The Cowles Commission

The Cowles Commission illustrates both a general point about the stimulation of fundamental research and intellectuality and a more specific point about the ways in which the University of Chicago spirit permeated the reform of business schools. The Cowles Commission was created in 1932 by the businessman Alfred Cowles. In a move in which Hutchins was actively involved, the commission moved to Chicago from Colorado in 1939.

Alfred Cowles was an investment analyst who became suspicious of traditional stock market analysts after the crash of 1929. Instead he wanted people with statistical knowledge to do economic analysis. He was introduced to the Econometric Society (created in 1930), which at the time was in need of money. When Cowles offered an annual budget of $12,000 for a journal and a research institute, the Cowles Commission was founded (see Christ, 1952, pp. 5–6).

Ultimately, in 1956, the Cowles Commission was driven from Chicago to Yale by the radicalization of the Chicago Department of Economics under the leadership of Milton Friedman and George Stigler, but the commission illustrates both the influence of Hutchins and the way in which the Hutchins spirit was transformed into a dedication to fundamental research on deep questions of economic analysis. The commission championed the use of mathematics, statistics, and economic theory, both to develop new ideas for economics and to solve complex problems of planning and management.

Scholars at Cowles saw themselves as using high-level theoretical and statistical tools to clarify issues of management. Kenneth Arrow (Arrow, 1964) focused on issues of coordination, control, and hierarchy; Jacob Marschak discussed adaptive programming (Marschak, 1963); and John Harsanyi (1962) analyzed bargaining in cooperative and non cooperative games—all in the context of management decision making. Abraham Charnes and William Cooper (1962) discussed the works of Tjalling Koopmans and others in the context of linear programming and the structure of decision problems; and Martin Shubik (1962), who was at Cowles after the move to Yale, discussed game theory and experimental gaming as two perspectives for representing and understanding decision making and the use of game theory in the study of industrial administration (Shubik, 1960).

Both intellectually and institutionally, the interests and themes that flourished at Cowles were natural allies for the movement to reform business schools. Cowles found common cause with reform-minded scholars at the Graduate School of Industrial Administration of the Carnegie Institute of Technology (see Chapter Seven). Jacob Marschak (working closely with Tjalling Koopmans), recognized that GSIA was a place for kindred spirits and initiated a series of connections between the two groups that involved substantial intellectual cooperation and exchange.

Cowles became an important bridge between economists and operations researchers at the RAND Corporation (see Chapter Five) and the academic world of business schools. It also became a gathering place for several of the key actors in the subsequent reform of business education and a source for a conception of economic research that was highlighted in that reform. In many respects, the Cowles Commission was an almost pure illustration of the linkage between the Hutchins vision of a university dedicated to fundamental, interdisciplinary scholarship and the reform of business schools. Its eviction from the University of Chicago at the same time that the Chicago Graduate School of Business was seeking Ford Foundation support for reform of that school is one of the anomalies of the era, an anomaly attributable primarily to the deep personal and political antagonisms of the individuals involved but also to the complications of combining enthusiasms for fundamental knowledge and interdisciplinarity.

The Ford Foundation

The Ford Foundation, which played a critical role in pushing the reform of business schools, drew many of its ideas and personnel from the Chicago, Cowles, and RAND community. It is a curiosity of that reform, however, that although Hutchins himself was a Ford Foundation officer during the critical years in which the foundation's support for business school reform was formulated, he had almost nothing to do with it.

When Paul Hoffman became president of the Ford Foundation in 1951, Hutchins left the university to become his associate. Hutchins did not thrive at Ford. His stay there was short and acrimonious. A substantial part of his problem was widespread hostility, both within the foundation and among its enemies, toward Hutchins. When the trustees became unhappy with Hoffman and pressured him to resign, Hutchins stayed on for a short time, but he left in 1954 to become president of the Fund for the Republic. Few at the foundation are recorded as lamenting his departure.

One of Hutchins's principal rivals for position and influence at Ford was H. Rowan Gaither, who would become, as we will detail in Chapter Six, one of the principal architects of the reform of business schools. He was an organizational rival of Hutchins but far from antagonistic to the Chicago spirit. Several of his key associates had strong ties to Hutchins's University of Chicago, most notably the sociologist Bernard Berelson, the educator Ralph Tyler, and the statistician and economist Allen Wallis. He also had close connections to the RAND Corporation and the Cowles Commission. In these groups, the Hutchins dream of an intellectual elite based on a grounding in metaphysics and Thomastic rationality morphed rather easily to confidence in the intellectual primacy of science, mathematics, and theory. It was this version of the Chicago spirit that thoroughly infused the Ford Foundation's contribution to the reform of management education.

Carnegie Institute of Technology

The aura of Hutchins's Chicago envelops much of the 1950s reform of management education, but it is particularly visible in two of the leading schools in that effort, the University of Chicago Graduate School of Business and the Graduate School of Industrial Administration at the Carnegie Institute of Technology. The Chicago Graduate School of Business was neglected under Hutchins. He considered business schools as inferior academic institutions and made little effort to stimulate the development of the Chicago version. However, as we detail somewhat in Chapter Eight, the ideas about fundamental knowledge and interdisciplinary integration that he championed ultimately became established as the "Chicago approach" to business education. Under Allen Wallis, James Lorie, George Stigler, and George Schultz, the school took firm steps toward a research orientation in both its faculty and its curriculum.

However, as we consider at greater length in Chapter Seven, the business school that came most to typify the new approach to management education was the Graduate School of Industrial Administration (GSIA) at the Carnegie Institute of Technology. It was a tiny new school at an engineering school in Pittsburgh. It assembled a faculty that was, in retrospect, an exceptional collection of distinguished scholars. It codified an ideology for business education and exhibited an exemplar of its implementation. It also provided the stimuli and key personnel that led to the transformation of Carnegie Tech into Carnegie Mellon University.

The key actors in the creation and early development of GSIA were G. Leland Bach, the dean; Herbert A. Simon, the associate dean and unquestioned intellectual leader; W. W. Cooper, the leader of the developments in operations research; and Franco Modigliani, the leader of developments in financial economics. Others were important to the evolution of GSIA subsequently, but in the early years Bach, Simon, Cooper, and Modigliani formed the core group. They set the tone, constructed the culture, and built the school.

It is striking that each of them had close personal and professional ties to Hutchins's University of Chicago and shared in the key aspects of the Chicago spirit. Bach and Simon both received their doctorates from Chicago, Simon after earlier doing his undergraduate work there. Cooper studied and taught there. Modigliani was closely associated with the Cowles

Commission and Jacob Marschak. Moreover, several of the other leading faculty members in the early years of GSIA (including Charles C. Holt and Harold Guetzkow) were products of Hutchins's Chicago. The threads of Hutchins's intellectual understanding and arrogance are woven into the GSIA mantle.

4.3   THE HUTCHINS BUSINESS SCHOOL HERITAGE

After the Second World War, there were numerous North American universities with claims to distinction, most notably schools such as UC Berkeley, Chicago, Columbia, Harvard, MIT, Michigan, Northwestern, Princeton, Stanford, Texas, Wisconsin, UCLA, and Yale. In the period from 1950 to 1970, these schools and many others grew substantially in numbers of students and faculty, in resources, in productivity, and in international research reputations.

Business schools grew with the rest of the institutions. They grew and changed in a way that was distinctive. They became more intellectual. It was a change that was not entirely dictated by postwar conditions; growth, yes, but why intellectuality? The answer lies in many features of the context, but part of the answer lies in the prejudices and enthusiasms that came from the Hutchins era at Chicago. That era left its mark upon the University of Chicago, including its business school, but its larger mark was on the rest of the business school community.

The rhetoric of change was much more sedate than the proclamations of Robert Hutchins. It was more disposed to see intellectual challenge in practical problems. But it was unquestionably Hutchins in spirit and in genealogy. The voices of reform were echoes of the voices of Robert Hutchins and the academic intellectuality and passion for research that he fostered. Much of the leadership and predispositions of the reform movement came not from business schools but from the core of academe as that core was shaped and represented by a particular era in the history of the University of Chicago, the era of Robert Hutchins.

Hutchins's Chicago symbolized, proclaimed, and exhibited an American version of intellectual snobbery, one that assigned priority in ideas and imagination to academe, that denigrated academic participation in the practical details of vocational preparation, and that exalted the intellect and intellectual combat. In the mélange of ideas and people that produced the changes in business education, the intellectual spirit that was associated with the Hutchins era at Chicago played an important role. Many of the people at the heart of the reform movement had been weaned on Hutchins,

Chapter Five

An Incubator of Change: The RAND Corporation

Among the many new institutions spawned by the experiences of the war and the postwar era, there was one improbable organization that distinguished itself by exhibiting the possibilities for harnessing fundamental knowledge as an aid to practical problem solving. That institution was the RAND Corporation. The name, RAND, was an acronym for Research ANd Development, although some referred to RAND as "Research And No Development" because the organization never produced any real hard outputs (such as weapons) (Kaplan, 1983, p. 9). John Williams, who was a major figure at RAND for eighteen years, noted in a 1961 paper that RAND "manufactures nothing. Its product is intellectual" (Williams, 1962, pp. 1–2).

RAND championed a creed that celebrated multidisciplinary work, problem framing, mathematical social science and operations analysis, and the application of refined intelligence and educated technique to imagining new ways of resolving old social problems, beginning with problems of national security and extending ultimately to a wide range of public concerns. In particular, the focus was on the use of decision theory, mathematics, statistics, and microeconomic analysis to improve the choices made by leaders of social collectivities (such as armies, firms, nations).

The changes that business schools experienced in the 1950s and 1960s were infused with that creed. The sentiments were not unique to RAND, and their incorporation into the litany of business schools certainly cannot be attributed entirely, or even primarily, to the influence of RAND. However, as we shall see, the linkages between RAND and the reform of business education were extensive. Although business schools were not consciously on the RAND agenda, and RAND played little or no direct role in the changes, RAND was a place where ideas about the future course of research and policy making were exercised and elaborated by a community of scholars that included some of academia's best-known and most-influential social scientists.

In addition, RAND served as a home for several of the key people behind the idea of reforming business school education. These included H. Rowan Gaither, an early board member at RAND, who later at the Ford Foundation wrote the Gaither Report that led to, among other things, the Ford Foundation's decision to support changes in management education (see Chapter Six). They included Bernard Berelson, who was recruited to RAND in 1947 to do social science and later became one of the key people at Ford supporting the behavioral social science movement and associated funding. They included Hans Speier, who was chief of the Social Science Division at RAND and who later was a primary consultant to Gaither at the Ford Foundation. They also included many of the scholars whose work would form the 1950s through 1960s core of many of the fundamental contributions in key areas of business school research, such as operations research and organization theory. Among others, the list includes such luminaries as Kenneth Arrow, Tjalling Koopmans, Duncan Luce, Jacob Marschak, Richard Nelson, Roy Radner, Howard Raiffa, Philip Selznick, Herbert Simon, Vernon Smith, Oliver Williamson, and Sidney Winter.

5.1 Creating a Think Tank

Postwar interest in the systematic application of science to practical problems had been stimulated by the scientific work that was done for the military during and after the Second World War. That war witnessed a large-scale mobilization of scientists to work on concrete national policies and problems. They were enlisted to work on military issues at all levels, including the atomic bomb project at Los Alamos, the MIT Radiation Laboratory, the Office of Scientific Research and Development (headed by Vannevar Bush), the Statistical Research Group (SRG) at Columbia University, and the Secretary of War's panel of expert consultants from science and industry. Although the story of those efforts included numerous mistakes and quarrels, the immediate postwar evaluation of them was decidedly positive.

After the war was over, it seemed obvious to many leaders in the postwar academic and policy-making communities that collaboration of scientific and military minds was important to stay ahead in the global military competition and to expand knowledge related to future developments in peace, war, and national security. It would be interdisciplinary from the beginning. As one former RAND staff member put it, there was a need

> . . . for a mobilization of all the disciplines—physical sciences, engineering, mathematics, whatever you have—to study and give advice to the military on the problems . . . of national defense that were going to come up in the future. (Bornet, 1961, p. 2)

The Allied victory in the war had validated the success of such wartime cooperation among scientists, the military, and industry; not just to win any future wars and conflicts but also to create and maintain peace. That validation, in turn, encouraged postwar discussion of ways to allow peacetime scientists, now mostly returning to universities, to continue to work on national security problems. Dwight Eisenhower was among the enthusiasts. "The armed forces," he noted in a memorandum from April 30, 1946, on "Scientific and Technological Resources as Military Assets,"

> . . . could not have won the war alone. Scientists and business men contributed techniques and weapons which enabled us to outwit and overwhelm the enemy. (quoted in Bornet, 1961, p. 5)

A peacetime institution was needed to sustain the partnership that had emerged during the war, and the RAND Corporation was one result of those sentiments. Rather than simply negotiate separate contracts with individual university faculty members, the Scientific Advisory Board to the Army Air Force's chief of staff adopted a "think tank" model for recruiting expertise and doing research.

Initially it was assumed that, to have stability and attract top-flight scientists, the effort should be housed in an industrial research facility; so, in 1946, the Douglas Aircraft Company was persuaded to sign a contract with the Air Force to provide the facilities. RAND was created as a separate division of the Douglas Aircraft Company to produce long-term scientific and technical planning for the Air Force. A special office in the Pentagon, headed by General Curtis LeMay, was established to handle the contract.

LeMay saw RAND as an experiment to explore ways of organizing the nation's scientific capabilities in the service of military and civilian policy making. As he wrote to Arthur Raymond in February of 1947:

> The Army Air Forces consider RAND one of its most important projects. We are interested not only in the end-results we hope it will achieve, but in the philosophy behind this type of contract. We believe it to be a distinct forward step in correlating the thinking and planning of the Army Air Forces and its scientific civilian partners. We cannot help but feel that if RAND should fail for any reason whatsoever, it would be a severe set-back to the Army Air Forces and to the nation. (quoted in Bornet, 1961, p. 8)

The idea that RAND might be a prototype of future relations between university experts and military policy making was received with enough enthusiasm to lead the Navy to ask for permission to study the contract.

Almost immediately, the initial arrangement with the Douglas Aircraft Company came to be seen as less than perfect. In particular, there was concern about protecting the independence of the research effort in a commercial establishment beholden to the Air Force. The founders of RAND wanted researchers to have freedom to contribute to basic science and civilian sector research, without too much direction from the military. John Williams noted that

> . . . it is an unpleasant fact that on a number of occasions in recent years the Air Force, the Department of Defense, or the Executive Office of the President has shown a tendency to gag us. (Williams, 1962, p. 17)

Rather quickly, widespread agreement arose that it would be advantageous to have RAND be an independent nonprofit research corporation to help create a better research environment as well as better relations with the outside world and academic scholars (Goldstein, 1961; Smith, 1966). RAND was constituted as a nonprofit corporation under California law.

A central actor in accomplishing the transformation was H. Rowan Gather, who would later become a key player in the Ford Foundation's program in management education. Gaither, who was born in 1910, was the son of a San Francisco banker. After graduating with a law degree from the University of California, Berkeley, in 1933, Gaither worked with the Farm Credit Administration in Washington, and with the law firm of Cooley, Crowley, and Supple, where he became a partner specializing in trusts and the law of nonprofit corporations. During the war, Gaither was assistant director of the Radiation Laboratory at MIT, and he quickly was identified as an effective organizer with an interest in both pure research and the application of ideas to practice. While at MIT, he also gained a reputation as a skillful mediator between scientists and the military. He became a close associate of Karl Compton, the president (from 1930 to 1948) of MIT and a leading figure in the wartime science policy establishment.

RAND president Frank Collbohm had first met Gaither in 1943 when Gaither was at the MIT Radiation Laboratory. Their contacts led naturally to Gaither being made a legal counsel to RAND on December 1, 1947. His principal assignment was to advise whether the organizational form for RAND should be a nonprofit corporation and (if so) to help in the organization and funding of the new project.

After being unsuccessful in an attempt to secure money from the Sloan Foundation, Collbohm and Gaither turned to the Ford Foundation in 1948 and were successful in securing a loan of $1,000,000 from the foundation to RAND. Subsequently, the loan was converted to a grant at the suggestion of Henry Ford II, the son of the founder of the Ford Motor Company who had become president of the company in 1945.[1] On November 1, 1948, RAND became a nonprofit corporation, and Gaither was chosen to be the chairman of the board of trustees. Although he later moved to the Ford

Foundation, he remained keenly interested in RAND affairs until he died in 1961 (Bornet, 1961, p. 15).

5.2   AN EVOLVED VISION

To say that anyone present at the birth of the RAND Corporation had more than a dim idea of what the organization would do or become would be to attribute unusual perspicacity. The overall mission of RAND was framed as a program of

> . . . study and research on the broad subject of Aerospace Power with the object of recommending to the United States Air Force preferred methods, techniques, and instrumentalities for the development and employment of Aerospace Power." (Goldstein, 1961, p. 3)

In that spirit, the first two major projects undertaken by RAND were a study requested by General LeMay of the feasibility, design, and military utility of an Earth-circulating satellite and a comparison of ramjets and rockets, including ballistic missiles, as strategic offensive weapons systems.

From the beginning, however, RAND was given unusual independence. Although the Air Force expected RAND to contribute to Air Force intelligence and to solve some of its pressing problems, it tolerated, even encouraged, a RAND that was significantly autonomous. In particular, RAND was not required to accept suggestions from the Air Force for topics of research and could develop elements of its own agenda. As one commentator noted looking back:

> By a policy that ensured that the organization and its people would be largely free of routine requests from units of its enormous military establishment, the Air Force made it possible for the scientists to devote their full efforts to independent and original research. The RAND that developed through the years, therefore, is the direct result of the wise planning of national leaders in and out of the RAND family in the formative years, as well as of the many individuals who zealously guarded the important freedoms and prerogatives of the new research body. (Bornet, 1961, p. 13)

The result was an organization that sometimes seemed unreal or chaotic to those who worked there. John Williams cites a colleague's comments on the unique intellectual freedom at RAND:

> At the time of my arrival . . . I was impressed by the anarchy of both policy and administration which I found in Santa Monica. Since such an atmosphere exists only rarely . . . I was shocked and disturbed . . . [But] I soon was carried into a stream of interests in which questions of orderliness in corporate policy and administration no longer seemed important. Subsequently, I have come to regard this anarchy as the strength if not the substance of RAND . . . obviously, what I am calling anarchy is not really anarchy but rather a degree of intellectual freedom which is so unique that it seems like anarchy in terms of my earlier experience [in government and academe]. (Williams, 1962, p. 19)

The combination of broad military obligations and considerable independence served both to make RAND unusually innovative and to make the organization vulnerable to criticism from different directions. Bellman noted that "RAND had to be careful. It had powerful enemies in the Air Force, the Congress and in the Universities" (Bellman, 1984, p. 157). The Air Force worried about relevance; Congress worried about fuzzy-headed academics; and the universities worried about involvement in military research. The original intent had been to keep RAND relatively small, but it grew from seven employees in March 1946 to 247 in 1948 and to 1,090 in 1961.

The autonomy of RAND encouraged the visionary sentiments of the founders. They had the enthusiasms and ambitions of their age, and they believed they had found a way to stimulate more effective problem-oriented research that engaged scholars of different disciplinary persuasions, using broad ways of thinking rather than narrow immediately practical instruments. More importantly, however, they created an institution with the flexibility to become something considerably different from what might reasonably have been anticipated.

The RAND vision, insofar as it can be said to have existed, was the product of time, opportunities, and the unpredictabilities of fortune, but it evolved into a clear set of prejudices. RAND became interdisciplinary and quantitative (though also interested in what nonquantitative disciplines such as anthropology and psychiatry could offer), focused on choices and strategies, more academic than the academy, and entirely persuaded of the potential gains to be secured from analysis and intelligence in the service of collective goals.

Interdisciplinary Problem-Solving

A working premise in the imaginations of RAND was that military problems rarely fit a particular academic category very neatly. Indeed, the idea that problem-focused work required interdisciplinary teams became part of the sacred dogma of the institution. The RAND building was designed to facilitate interdisciplinary communication, with patios connecting the offices and departments across disciplines. Because of the nature of the problems addressed, departmental lines were frequently treated as arbitrary. Once projects started, research projects would often migrate through several departments, involving individuals of different skills.

Several departments (numerical analysis, logistics, mathematics, economics) were established at RAND to accommodate the growing diversity of scientific expertise required. A social science department was set up in 1948, in part because it was realized that an emphasis on systems analysis and quantitative research could not fully capture the essence of warfare. As John Williams explained in a RAND discussion paper from 1962, the span of RAND was much broader than the interests of most people. As a result,

> . . . while individuals often feel they perceive clearly what it is, or what gives it its character, or what made it viable in the first place, when you combine the images, the picture gets fuzzy.[2]

The interdisciplinary ideology at RAND affected several projects and activities devoted to topics that would later be important in the reform of business schools, as well as in the development of postwar social science.

RAND's pursuit of an interdisciplinary, long-term approach to problems led to an interest in social science. The interest was institutionally but not intellectually deviant. It reflected a sentiment among many leading scientists that contemporary problems of strategy required knowledge about human behavior and that the social science disciplines might be able to provide such knowledge. At a 1947 conference in New York devoted to re-cruitment for the RAND Corporation, Warren Weaver, head of the applied mathematics panel of the National Defense Research Committee (NDRC) during the war and a board member at RAND but perhaps best known for his work on the mathematics of communication (Shannon and Weaver, 1949), articulated the contemporary creed:

> ... since the last war there has been a change in the character of war, a change in the character of the inevitable amalgamation of all the intellectual and ma-terial resources of the country which are necessary to maintain our position in peace and to enable us to defend ourselves ... There have also emerged some patterns of working together, particularly among the biological, physi-cal and social sciences, which seem to me to have great promise ... the whole fields of the social sciences and of the physical sciences must be brought more closely together.[3]

The conference involved several well-known names in the subsequent development of RAND and the Ford Foundation, as well as the disciplines associated with economics and the behavioral social sciences. They included people such as Armen Alchian, Bernard Berelson, Bernard Brodie, Frank Collbohm, Herbert Goldhamer, Olaf Helmer, Charles Hitch, Abraham Ka-plan, Harold Lasswell, Frederick Mosteller, Donald Marquis, Edward Shaw, Hans Speier, Jacob Viner, Allen Wallis, Warren Weaver, and John Williams.

This embrace of interdisciplinary research fed on the prejudices of the day. The necessity of multidisciplinary collaboration was a cliché of the principal architects of postwar science. These prejudices significantly influ-enced the Ford Foundation's vision for the behavioral sciences; they were later shared with most of the business schools favored by the foundation.

The Glories of Mathematics and Statistics

If the RAND Corporation had one overarching enthusiasm, it was for mathematics and statistics, for the use of quantitative analysis and quanti-tative data in furthering an intelligent approach to practical problems. The enthusiasm led to an emphasis on domains such as operations research.

The emphasis on quantitative analysis arose, in part, because of Frank Collbohm, who was an active partner of Warren Weaver in staffing the organization originally. Collbohm had worked for Weaver doing operations research for the Air Force during the war. One of Weaver's earliest steps was to hire John Williams, who had spent the war years as a statistical consultant to the U.S. Army Air Force, as a scientist with the Statistical Research Group (SRG) at Columbia University, and with the Applied Mathematics Panel of the NDRC. Collbohm told Williams that he would like to have RAND "permeated by the kind of analyses that the Applied Mathematics Panel had done during the war."[4]

The NDRC had been created within the Council of National Defense by order issued from President Roosevelt in 1940. Superseded by the Office of Scientific Research in 1941, it was originally headed by Vannevar Bush and directed to conduct and oversee research on the problems underlying development and mechanisms of warfare. Some of the better-known projects on which it worked were the Manhattan Project and the creation of MIT's Radiation Laboratory (Bush, 1970).

Williams was the first of a number of people who came to RAND from Columbia and Princeton, including Edward Paxon (head of systems analysis), Olaf Helmer, and Abraham Girshick. RAND built its strengths and unique character less by open recruitment than by exploiting networks of friends and colleagues. The techniques anticipated the recruitment of nerd friends that typified the later development of innovative computer-related start-ups.

The emphasis on mathematics and statistics meshed particularly well with trends in the development of economics. As economic theory became more decisively mathematical and the analysis of economic data more decisively based on mathematical statistics, the work at RAND became more relevant to economic research, and economic research became more relevant to RAND. Leading economists found the RAND organization congenial, particularly as more and more of them participated in conferences and projects sponsored by the organization. The list of economists associated with RAND in one way or another in the 1950s and 1960s includes most of the early North American Nobel laureates in economics.

The RAND Corporation became closely related in orientation, personnel, and spirit to the Cowles Commission at the University of Chicago (see

Chapter Four). The Cowles Commission was a center of postwar efforts to develop better ways of linking economic theory to economic data and economic policy. The commission recruited an extraordinary roster of scholars who would play critical roles in the fundamental development of mathematical economics and econometrics. Among the key actors were such names as Kenneth Arrow, Gary Becker, Carl Christ, Gerard Debreu, Leonid Hurwicz, Tjalling Koopmans, Jacob Marschak, Franco Modigliani, Roy Radner, and Herbert Simon (Christ, 1952; Hildredt, 1986).

The mission of the Cowles Commission was the "conduct and encouragement of research in economics, finance, commerce, industry and technology, including problems of the organization of these activities, and of society in general" (Christ, 1952, preface). Its original motto was "science is measurement," which was later changed to "theory and measurement" (Ibid., pp. 61–62). The Cowles scholars worked primarily on problems associated with matching theory to data. Under Marschak's leadership they studied, in particular, systems of simultaneous equations and the problems of using aggregate and time-series data.

A Focus on Choice

The evolution of RAND from an organization devoted to doing technical and scientific research for the Air Force to a hotbed of ideas about the uses of mathematics and the behavioral and social sciences in thinking about the making and implementing of decisions occurred in the first decade after the end of the war. The decision theorists, statisticians, and mathematical economists at RAND (and the Cowles Commission) were closely connected to the burgeoning academic developments in those fields. A focus on developing the tools of linear programming, game theory, decision theory, and other instruments of intelligent choice became embedded in an emphasis on rational choice. As Kenneth Arrow, who was closely associated with both RAND and Cowles, noted,

> My ideal in those days was the development of economic planning, a task which I saw as synthesizing economic equilibrium theory, statistical methods, and criteria for social decision making. (Arrow, 1983, p. vii)

The focus on choice permeated many of the activities at RAND. The contract with the Air Force directed RAND to recommend "preferred instrumentalities and techniques" to the military. The word *preferred* evoked the need for a theory of choice, a domain that included elements of the social sciences. Thus, a project, headed by the mathematician John Williams, was established for "analyzing military worth." Williams had a taste for trying to augment intelligence through rational analysis:

> While we would doubtless be revolted by a perfectly rational world, our bias is that the present one would be better if the rational element were a little stronger. So we try to enhance it, through such analysis, insights, and techniques as we can devise.[5]

Subsequently, this focus was extended substantially, and the group was expanded to include several economists and political scientists, but it retained an emphasis on using mathematics, statistics, and technology to clarify decision contexts and options and to improve choice.

One major organizing idea for the analysis of choice was game theory. Williams was influenced by the mathematician John von Neumann, whom he had met at Princeton, and particularly by von Neumann's work with Oskar Morgenstern on *The Theory of Games and Economic Behavior* (Von Neumann and Morgenstern, 1944). Olaf Helmer and Williams started a game theory research project at RAND, and they courted von Neumann to entice him to a relation with the group. As Williams wrote to von Neumann, "Paxon, Helmer and the rest are going to be especially nice to me if I succeed in getting you on the team."[6]

Apparently, von Neumann had become disenchanted with the lukewarm reactions to game theory by economists in the 1940s and decided that the prospects for acceptance were more promising within the fledgling community of strategy and operations analysts. Both von Neumann and Morgenstern came to be affiliated with RAND; over the next two decades, a virtual Who's Who of early game theorists traveled the road to Santa Monica (Poundstone, 1992).

For the people at RAND, game theory was a method to improve rational behavior for people or nations in competitive situations, such as the Cold

War. For instance, in 1949, Olaf Helmer initiated a conference on "applications of game theory to tactics." Conference participants included Kenneth
Arrow, Leonard Savage, Lloyd Shapley, Abraham Girshick, and others. The
conference was held according to Helmer because of

> . . . the feeling that the recent progress in the theory of games and its ap-
> plications had reached a stage where it might be profitable for the various
> agencies concerned with one or another aspect of this work to get together,
> to exchange ideas and information, and to decide on the principal directions
> in which further research in this field ought to proceed.[7]

The discussions at RAND highlighted some limitations of the original
game theoretic formulations. There was concern about the "zero-sum" character of the game and the avoidance of complications involved in forming
coalitions. The psychologist, Merrill Flood, who worked closely with RAND,
developed a program of experiments that were interpreted as raising serious
doubts about the rationality assumptions underlying game theory (Flood,
1958; Poundstone, 1992).[8] Flood objected particularly to the von Neumann
and Morgenstern concept of "solution" and the prospects for its application
(Flood, 1958, p. 5). In other RAND quarters, the analysis of game theory was
criticized for overlooking human aspects of competition and choice.

An early rationale for the work at RAND on decision making was the
absence of a good framework for considering the long-term strategic competition with the Soviet Union. A RAND document written in 1954 and
called "The Next Ten Years" asked a set of questions regarding Soviet nuclear
systems, U.S. strategic positioning, and other related issues.[9] The report discussed changes in the strategic balance and factors, including geographical
and technical factors, affecting the strengths of the United States and the
Soviet Union.

RAND scholars pioneered research across a broad range of topics relevant to choice, particularly strategic choice, importing techniques from
systems analysis, game theory, and linear programming. In many cases,
scholars working at or in conjunction with RAND established the intellectual bases that continue to underpin the state of knowledge in those fields

today. Scholars at RAND were principal contributors to the development of Cold War strategy in the United States and its allies and thereby in the Soviet Union. Much of the history of debate about game theory, its elaboration, and its extension occurred within RAND.

RAND was also a site for the development of ideas about what came to be called "organization theory," particularly that part of studies of organizations that emphasized decision making. Olaf Helmer asserted that "organization theory can be viewed as a very natural extension of game theory,"[10] and Oskar Morgenstern was involved in a study designed to develop a mathematical theory of organization, drawing considerably on game theory. A long paper written by Morgenstern at this time was never published, but it indicates the interest in organizations within the RAND community at the time.[11]

The RAND effort extended, however, well beyond game theoretic approaches to contribute to the elaboration of a choice-oriented theory of organizations. In August 1951, RAND hosted a conference on organizations, in which Kenneth Arrow, Merrill Flood, Oskar Morgenstern, and Allen Newell (among others) participated.[12] RAND attempts to develop a mathematical theory of organization were built partly on Herbert Simon's early work, which was unconnected to game theoretic ideas but focused on the limits to rationality in choice. Simon was a frequent visitor and consultant to RAND in the 1950s and 1960s. James March, Simon's coauthor in writing *Organizations* (March and Simon, 1958) and Richard Cyert, March's coauthor in writing *A Behavioral Theory of the Firm* (Cyert and March, 1963), although less involved with RAND, were visitors there often enough to be seen as part of the group.

The RAND work on organizational adaptation extended into several domains, particularly microeconomics, evolutionary economics, and decision theory, with early participants including Richard Nelson, Thomas Schelling, and Sidney Winter. The later publication of *An Evolutionary Theory of Economic Change* by Nelson and Winter (1982) was presaged by several RAND working papers and in particular by Winter's paper on a "NeoSchumpeterian Theory of the Firm,"[13] which initiated their collaboration.

The work on organizations also became the basis for work at RAND on understanding the organizational basis of Soviet behavior.[14] Joseph Loftus joined RAND in 1954 after service as a civilian analyst for the Air Force, where he had worked on intelligence relating to the Soviet nuclear program. Loftus joined discussions on "The Next Ten Years," strategic warning issues, and Soviet developments. He and Andrew Marshall started talking with one another about experiences with the Soviet nuclear program. Another set of meetings and seminars around organizations resulted in the well-known book by Graham Allison on the Cuban Missile Crisis (Allison was the rapporteur of the meetings), using different kinds of conceptions of decision making to understand the decision process during the crisis (Allison, 1971).

Ultimately, Marshall was to become a leading guru of American intelligence and director of net intelligence in the Department of Defense, a position he held for more than thirty-eight years through numerous changes in the presidency and the secretary of defense. In 2010 he was eighty-nine years old and continued in office. Marshall was trained as a statistician originally at the University of Chicago (where he had studied with Rudolf Carnap, Milton Friedman, and W. Allen Wallis, among others).

At RAND, Marshall and Loftus wrote several papers together that explored organizational aspects of Cold War competition. Several of these are still classified, and there is not yet a complete list.[15] A memo by Richard Nelson and James Schlesinger[16] advocated the application of ideas drawn from organization studies. Ultimately, these discussions led to a proposal drafted by Marshall and Sidney Winter (in collaboration with James Schlesinger and Richard Nelson).[17] The intent was to begin a long-term project, carefully researching all the existing contributions to organizational behavior, and to extend and adapt the ones suitable to understanding military organizations. The project was never undertaken within RAND, but several of the key people associated with RAND subsequently became pivotal in the development of organizational studies in business schools, and organizational behavior became an important intellectual foundation for the concept and practice of net assessment within the Department of Defense. As late as 2010, Marshall continued to propose and support studies of organizations and organizational change to an often reluctant community of intelligence and defense strategists.[18]

More Academic Than Academics

In developing the ideas that typified its contribution, RAND successfully involved an elite group of academic physical, biological, and social scientists (primarily but not exclusively economists). Its success in this endeavor came initially perhaps because of the prestige of, but ultimately more in spite of, working with the military establishment on issues of national security. A list of RAND employees and consultants in the 1950s and 1960s would include a large number of leading social scientists of the time, including Armen Alchian, Robert Aumann, Kenneth Arrow, Gary Becker, Richard Bellman, James Buchanan, Ronald Coase, Richard Cyert, Gerald Debreu, Merrill Flood, Leonid Hurwicz, Tjalling Koopmans, Harold Lasswell, Nathan Leites, Charles Lindblom, J. C. C. McKinsey, James March, Harry Markowitz, Jacob Marschak, Oskar Morgenstern, John Nash, Richard Nelson, Allen Newell, Edmund Phelps, Howard Raiffa, Paul Samuelson, Thomas Schelling, Theodore Schultz, Lloyd Shapley, William Sharpe, Martin Shubik, Herbert Simon, Vernon Smith, Robert Solow, Hans Speier, James Tobin, Albert Tucker, William Vickrey, Oliver Williamson, Sidney Winter, Albert Wohlstetter, and many others. Several of these RAND-connected figures were to become well-known as scholars within business schools.

RAND produced this concentration of talent in large part by offering a combination of academic freedom and colleagues of intellectual power that was hard to find in academe. The level of discourse was uncommonly high. John Williams contrasted the RAND culture with that of the Statistical Research Group:

> [Life at the SRG] was something like life in RAND but gone to hell: too much time in bad airplanes, in bad hotels, producing bad studies too quickly.[19]

Allen Newell, one of the early cofounders of the field of Artificial Intelligence, recalled,

> RAND was a fairly free place at that time, bubbling with ideas and people could sort of go off and . . . do everything, and they saw themselves as sort

of experimenting with a whole way of life in terms of research, not in the university setting, with people who sort of consciously and rationally sort of decided what they were going to do and ideas could come up from the bottom of the organization and so forth. It was an exploration of the scientific way of life.[20]

When Newell first arrived at RAND, he worked on logistics problems.[21] Newell's immediate boss in the mathematics department was John Williams, but he worked closely also with Merrill Flood. Like many others, Newell found the place to be highly stimulating and enjoyed the flow of people and ideas, particularly during the summer seminars. He became interested in organizations and in experimental research, in part as a result of a visit to the Pentagon where he worked on a study of the Munitions Board (the logistics organization within the Department of Defense). After looking at their problems of supply and logistics and spending weeks talking to officers, Newell authored a paper on "The Science of Supply."[22]

Foreshadowing his later views, the paper argued that existing mathematical approaches were too abstract and that conventional models were inadequate: "Organizational factors and so forth made large amounts of differences and that sort of got me interested in organizations" (Ibid., pp. 14–15). This led to an effort to develop a laboratory for studying organizational behavior and to contact with the Harvard sociologist Robert Freed Bales, who was a consultant to RAND at the time.

The broad range of interests at RAND was further stimulated (or made possible) by the high degree of intellectual freedom at the place. The talent of the people attracted to RAND, either as employees or as consultants, made RAND not only a locale for the development of many kinds of technical analyses relevant to military policy but also a focus for conversations over the future nature and role of knowledge, particularly in the social sciences and the fields that draw on them. There were many other actors who were unconnected to RAND, but RAND wrote the textbook and expressed the vision about interdisciplinary, quantitative, and problem-driven research that was reflected in the development of postwar social science and the postwar changes in business schools.

5.3   A LEGACY

Just as Flexner and the Flexner Report and Hutchins and the Chicago spirit permeated the ethos of business school reformers in the 1950s and 1960s, so also did the RAND Corporation and the biases it reflected. RAND had no direct role in the changes in management education, but many of the key players in the transformation of business schools and several key elements of the intellectual spirit they reflected were nurtured by the RAND experience and the larger community of elite social science from which it drew.

This RAND perspective considerably influenced the thinking about training, research, strategic thinking, and management in and around the military forces of the United States, most spectacularly in the introduction of the attitudes and techniques of Robert MacNamara and his "whiz kids" in the Kennedy and Johnson administrations and more enduringly in efforts such as those of the Advanced Research Projects Agency (ARPA) and the Office of Net Assessment in the Department of Defense.

The effects were, moreover, not limited to the military or to thinking about national security. The lessons drawn from the war by students of national security problems led to a widely held view that the problems facing the United States and the world called for interdisciplinary collaboration and quantitative analysis. The new thrust in social and behavioral sciences seemed congenial to such directions. During the 1950s and 1960s, many academic institutions considered the establishment of "policy research" institutes that would mobilize multidisciplinary social science and engineering knowledge along with systematic quantitative analysis to address broad sets of national problems, particularly those that were rather distant from issues of national security—problems of poverty, discrimination, education, health, environmental degradation, economic growth. The RAND history of applying intelligence and fundamental knowledge to framing problems relevant to the Air Force shaped the ideas, but similar formulations were also current in discussions of health policies, educational policies, social welfare policies, and other elements of the public domain.

These directions were entangled with discussions of the future of the behavioral and social sciences. The term *behavioral and social sciences* developed from being a relatively clumsy collective noun of ambiguous reference to becoming a standard expression within science policy circles such as the National Science Foundation (NSF), National Institutes of Health (NIH), ARPA, and the Committee on Science, Engineering, and Public Policy (COSEPUP) to symbolize the "new" social science (Berelson, 1963). The conversations surrounding these efforts, like the conversations at RAND, proclaimed the need for an invigorated, multidisciplinary, and more scientific social science. Similar conversations involving many of the same people were common within the National Research Council, the National Science Board, the National Science Foundation, and the Social Science Research Council. They helped the behavioral and social sciences gain a footing within the science establishment (Berelson, 1963, p. 10). For example, behavioral and social sciences became defined as part of the mission of the National Academy of Sciences and the National Science Foundation (National Academy of Science, 1986). A panel was also set up in the President's Science Advisory Committee, which published a report on the strengthening of the behavioral sciences in the journal *Science* (1962).

It was only a short leap to the problems of management and management education. The emergence of the modern model of business education was embedded in this climate of policy research and of the rise of the idea of interdisciplinary collaboration among the behavioral and social sciences and between them and the natural sciences and engineering. The postwar culture of business schools was a culture in which traditional historical, institutional, and qualitative academicians were challenged by younger scholars with new research tools developed or highlighted during the Second World War and with enthusiasm for quantitative analysis of data and theory; for perspectives drawn from economic theory, decision theory, systems theory, and game theory; for developing more mathematical, analytical, and rigorous behavioral and social sciences; and for the enlistment of those sciences in the interdisciplinary solution of social and economic problems.

Many of the modern tensions of academic institutions stem from the complications of engaging problems that cut across disciplines within an organization that is organized by disciplines, but such an interdisciplinary vision was a part of the postwar rhetoric of business schools and management education. To many business educators, problems in business organizations, like problems in military and national security organizations, seemed to fit any one discipline poorly and required insights from many disciplines to be genuinely understood.

Without deliberately intending to do so, RAND developed the skills, commitments, and ideologies of a cadre of individuals who would take the lead in extending the thrust of postwar sensibilities into business schools. At the same time, RAND sowed the seeds that were later to be harvested in the form of disillusion with the instruments it forged and exported to business schools. Enthusiasm led inexorably to disappointment. Cleverness led inexorably to excess. The quantitative techniques, rational perspectives, and enthusiasms for intelligence that animated RAND and the reformers of the 1950s and 1960s were implicated in the misfortunes of Vietnam and the financial collapses of the first decade of the twenty-first century. Moreover, to a substantial extent, the enthusiasms of economics shifted from a vision of collective problem solving and decision making coordinated through intelligence to a vision of decision making by self-interested individuals coordinated through competitive markets.

Chapter Six

AN ENGINE OF CHANGE:
THE FORD FOUNDATION

As we have described in earlier chapters, many of the ideas and prejudices that were to change North American business schools in the two decades after 1950 trace their origins to the legends of Flexner and of Hutchins's Chicago and were incubated in the RAND Corporation. The incubation did not occur because of any explicit interest at RAND in business education. Rather, it was because RAND provided a home for some of the key ideas that animated the postwar social science community and for people committed to the use of quantitative analysis and the natural and social sciences in solving social problems.

The incubation was important, but it might have been a much smaller factor in the history of business schools were it not for the links forged between those postwar communities and business schools by another institution—the Ford Foundation. The foundation and its officers were key players in directing the capabilities represented in the postwar consensus toward business school reform. They did this by articulating the intentions of the reform of business education, by organizing a coalition of supporters, and by nudging business schools along.

The Ford Foundation and RAND were tied together by the role of the foundation in the early funding of RAND, by the involvement of H. Rowan

Gaither in the management of each, by the interest of the foundation board in solving social problems, and by numerous overlaps in personnel. The linkages were extensive and, from the point of view of the reformers, fortunate. The foundation nurtured the reform of business schools by providing institutional leadership and financial inducements for a relatively brief period when business schools were ripe for change.

In this chapter, we focus on three elements of the changes:

(1)   The building of a *coalition*. For change to occur, supporters had to be activated and organized, and resources had to be brought to bear on business school reform. The members of a potential coalition were identified and recruited through conversations among postwar groups dealing with various postwar issues of science and education. It was a conversation-rich and resource-rich time, both in higher education and in foundations, and this richness was exploited in a particular way.

(2)   The articulation of a *manifesto*. The postwar bouillabaisse of ideas, justifications, beliefs, and proposals for reform that bubbled to the surface created the conditions for change. However, they needed some definitive articulation that could be used to proclaim a revolution. This articulation came through two reports commissioned by two different foundations and providing a clear compilation and integration of the sentiments of the coalition.

(3)   The creation of a *model*. In a world in which legitimacy depends on conformity, institutional change requires institutional models that exhibit possibilities for change. Such institutions have to be foolish enough or corrupt enough to become models of the revolution. These institutional deviants become exemplars of possibilities, the sources of new infectious institutional changes, and the poster children of reform.

None of these elements was simple. The members of the coalition and their resources came from multiple sources with multiple interests. Some features of the coalition building in this case are sketched in Section 6.1. The articulation of a manifesto had to make choices among the various elements of the consciousness. Some features of the manifesto in this case are reviewed in Section 6.2. The recruitment of model institutions required balancing the advantages and disadvantages of legitimacy and deviance. A "poster child" in this case is examined in Chapter Seven.

6.1   Building a Coalition

The Ford Foundation played a major role in creating and supporting a coalition for reform in business schools. To speak of "the foundation" as a coherent body, however, may be misleading. It was a time of turmoil in the foundation's history. Many things were happening. The board was changing; the management was changing; the ethos was changing. Programs were begun but quickly ended. Grand plans were announced without clear implications. In the midst of all this, a handful of individuals committed the foundation opportunistically, briefly, and (from the point of view of the foundation's total resources) in a minor way to a reform of business schools.

Elements in the foundation built links to the social and behavioral science community; they developed the implications of sentiments within that community for management education; they identified and embraced particular schools of business as moving in the right directions; they provided financial resources for schools and programs that supported the litany of change. Foundation involvement covered a relatively brief period, but it came at a critical time and was sharply focused. The foundation rode a wave of enthusiasm among the elite of the social and policy science communities into the somewhat backward and momentarily vulnerable academic neighborhood represented by North American business schools.

The Postwar Community of Social and Policy Science Activists

As was described in Chapter Five, the community of social and policy science activists that developed in the United States after the Second World War infiltrated the RAND Corporation extensively, as well as such institutions as the Cowles Commission, the National Research Council of the National Academy of Sciences, the National Science Foundation, and the Social Science Research Council. They came to be recognized as the embodiment of postwar social science with a strong commitment to behavioral and mathematical social science. Gradually after the war, this community established significant presence in all of the social science disciplines in the United States.

The ideas that were reflected in the halls and conferences of academic and semiacademic institutions of the time and incubated at RAND provided a consciousness on which to build changes in management education. This consciousness was shaped by a fairly loose network of individuals who shared the worldviews of the time, including the idea that society and democracy could be strengthened through the intelligent application of rational analysis to social problems. Those worldviews were reflected in words and phrases such as *interdisciplinary, behavioral and social science, problem-focused, mathematical/analytical/scientific,* and *policy science.* The individuals involved included many leaders of the economics establishment as that establishment became transformed after the war as well as many other social scientists who were recognized as disciplinary leaders.

Extension to business schools was a natural step but one that was hampered by the modest links between existing business school faculties and the postwar enthusiasms for mathematical and behavioral social science that permeated elite social scientists. Proponents of the new operations research and decision theory as bases for an analytical conception of management and newly recruited professors in business schools with disciplinary training and ambitions for contributions to fundamental research constituted an internal base for change, but they were relatively weak within the schools and were far from organized.

To a substantial extent, the mobilization and organization of the coalition relied on a small handful of foundation officers and individuals in business schools who advised them. They could not have achieved what they did without the existence of a widely shared consensus among critical leaders in academe, government, and business; some features of vulnerability in schools of business; and the abundance of resources available to them; but they took the spirit and content of the discussions that permeated the 1940s and 1950s social science consciousness and molded them into a vision of a modern business school and concrete programs for achieving that vision.

Although both the Sloan Foundation and the Carnegie Corporation also played parts in the story, the key institutional actor was unquestionably the

Ford Foundation. People at Ford assumed the leadership of the coalition of interests and attitudes that evolved into a program for reform of management education. The efforts also helped give direction to the foundation, which was struggling to find its place as an instrument of social change, groping for a way to harness the ideas of academe to serve the social attitudes of progressive business leaders.

The Gaither Report

Some of the key actors involved in the Ford Foundation's participation in the development of RAND were also important figures in the foundation's contribution to business school reform. They were committed to building a bridge between social policies based on systematic analysis and the new social science. They enlisted in that endeavor both many of the same people and much of the same rhetoric that had energized RAND. Their vision covered huge domains of social policy that came, by a series of somewhat contentious steps, to include management education.

The most important single individual was H. Rowan Gaither. He led the group that defined the Ford Foundation's program after the Second World War, and he ultimately became president of the foundation. Gaither's thinking was shaped by his wartime experience and by his connections with RAND, the social and behavioral science community, and the higher education community. Those linkages helped to mold a particular response of the foundation to the opportunities and pressures of the postwar scene.

Gaither met Henry Ford II during the meetings concerning Ford Foundation support for RAND (described in Chapter Five). When negotiations over the support to RAND were concluded, Ford asked Gaither to develop a policy statement for the Ford Foundation. After completing his commitments to RAND in November 1948, but while still serving on the RAND Board, Gaither started to advise the Ford Foundation Board of Trustees on the foundation's future program, policies, and organization.

The board was receptive to Gaither's formulations. Henry Ford II wished to change the foundation from an institution closely controlled by the Ford family into an institution with wide national as well as international concerns. He set into motion a set of actions that would ultimately eliminate the Ford family from significant influence in the foundation. His first step was to make the board of trustees stronger and more independent by electing new people to the board, people such as Karl Compton from MIT and Donald David from the Harvard Business School, as well as several prominent people from business.

Ford saw Gaither as a man who could help him in outlining a mission statement that would expand the foundation's purview. One of the first steps Gaither took once he had arrived at the foundation was to gather a committee of academics with different backgrounds to write a report that could be used to help the board set policy. This report became known as the Gaither Report. It was approved by the trustees in 1950.[1]

Although not a social scientist himself, Gaither was a persistent supporter of the social and behavioral sciences in the face of significant opposition among key people at Ford. He produced a report that was unequivocal in proclaiming both the importance of the social and behavioral sciences to the Ford mission and the need for fundamental research that would strengthen those sciences. The introduction to the report noted:

> In the committee's opinion, the evidence points to the fact that today's most critical problems are those which are social rather than physical in character—those which arise in man's relation to man rather than in his relation to nature.[2]

The report was not bashful in proclaiming both a need and a possibility to improve American society (and competitiveness) and to build a better world. Toward that end, it was important to be ahead not only in the physical and biological sciences but also in the social and behavioral sciences. The report proposed that the Ford Foundation contribute to policy analysis and fundamental research in five program areas, breathtaking in their scope. Although each of these involved policy domains with long traditions of policy development, each also could be imagined to involve the application of social science knowledge and perspectives to social problems.

Area I, "the establishment of peace," was intended to support initiatives that could potentially influence national or U.N. policies or procedures, through giving assistance to the formulation or execution of policy matters, research, and analysis, and through helping create the public awareness and understanding necessary for better execution of policy.[3]

Area II, "the strengthening of democracy," was intended to support activities directed toward things such as elimination of restrictions on freedom of thought; maintaining democratic control over large concentrations of power (while preserving freedom for scientific and technological matters); strengthening political processes for policies; and improving the organization and procedures involved in adjudication of private rights and interpretation and enforcement of law.[4]

Area III, "the strengthening of the economy," involved the support of "activities designed to advance the economic well-being of people everywhere and to improve economic institutions for the better realization of democratic goals."[5]

Area IV, "education in a democratic society," focused on supporting activities "to strengthen, expand, and improve educational facilities and methods to enable individuals more fully to realize their intellectual, civic, and spiritual potentialities; to promote greater equality of educational opportunity; and to conserve and increase knowledge and enrich our culture,"[6] including activities directed toward the clarification of educational goals and improving conditions and facilities for scholarly research and the quality of teachers throughout all levels of education.[7]

Finally, program Area V, first named "individual behavior and human relations," was intended to support "scientific activities designed to increase knowledge of factors which influence or determine human conduct, and to extend such knowledge for the maximum benefit of individuals and of society."[8] This program was quite different from the others in that its domain was defined not by a set of social problems but by a variety of knowledge. Where the other programs areas drew on existing knowledge in pursuit of policies, program Area V was concerned primarily with generating useful knowledge.

The Gaither Report was an immediate success among the foundation trustees and became the basis of the public report on the program, published in 1950. Gaither became the part-time director of the foundation's Area V—the better understanding of man, an area that became known as the behavioral science area. In 1951, the trustees began authorizing the behavioral science program to make grants to universities and to other institutions, such as the Social Science Research Council.

The foundation also set up several panels and commissions to discuss issues currently deemed important to the development of social science, such as the role of mathematics in behavioral social science and the relations between the different traditional social science disciplines (particularly economics) and the emerging area of behavioral social science. Many of the individuals involved in these efforts were later associated with business schools (for instance, G. Leland Bach, Thomas Carroll, Herbert A. Simon).

The Gaither Report endorsed the litany associated with the postwar social and behavioral sciences establishment as illustrated by the efforts at RAND. The objective of Area V was to:

> . . . support scientific activities designed to increase knowledge of factors which influence or determine human conduct, and to extend such knowledge for the maximum benefit of individuals and society.[9]

Research had to be scientific. Thus, the Ford Foundation's understanding of the behavioral science concept endorsed an "emphasis upon the scientific approach to problem solution."[10] Scientific interdisciplinary research was particularly valued. Thus:

> The program is interdisciplinary and inter-field. Its goal is to acquire and apply knowledge of human behavior, and segments of all fields and disciplines will make contributions in varying degrees.[11]

Research also had to be useful. The foundation was interested in "knowledge which promises at some point to serve human needs."[12] The language identified "usefulness" as an inevitable product of research knowledge, and an emphasis on the usefulness of fundamental behavioral science research in understanding and solving broad social problems became a part of the foundation mantra. Thus, the emphasis was consciously double edged. On the one hand, it favored basic research over applied research and basic research rather than "immediate solution of practical problems";[13] at the same time, it justified basic research by its contribution to solving practical problems, and thus claimed practicality for it.

Creating a Team and a Mission

In early 1951 Gaither, acting in his role as director of Area V, appointed Donald Marquis (a social psychologist from the University of Michigan) and Hans Speier (chief of the Social Science Division at RAND) as his consultants in building up the behavioral science research area. In the summer of that year, Bernard Berelson was named a senior staff member of the program. He would later head it. Berelson was born in 1912 and received his PhD in library science from the University of Chicago in 1941. Before coming to the Ford Foundation in 1951, he had been a professor of library science and dean of the Graduate School of Library Science at Chicago during Robert Hutchins's tenure as president of the university and a project leader under Paul Lazarsfeld, the noted mathematical sociologist at the Bureau of Applied Social Research at Columbia University.

Prior to Berelson's arrival, the foundation leadership was under attack from elements of the board. There was dissatisfaction with the slow development of the program areas specified in the 1949 report and the limited collaboration among them. In 1951, having secured a board commitment to pursue the ideas of the Gaither Report, Gaither succeeded Paul Hoffman as president of the foundation. His first move was to name as associate directors Dyke Brown (a partner in Gaither's law firm), William McPeak, Donald Price, and Thomas Carroll—all of whom had assisted Gaither in working on the study committee report.

Although Gaither did not initiate any formal changes in the structure of five programs, the trustees began a review of existing routines and programs, resulting in long reports on each of the research areas. Donald Price became vice president in charge of international development (Area I), Dyke Brown for public affairs (Area II), Thomas Carroll for economic development (Area III), and William McPeak for education and behavioral sciences (Areas IV and V). The changes in leadership, the jockeying for position, and the inherent ambiguity of the programs produced an abundance of conflict, uncertainty, and imaginative invention but less in the way of clear direction or accomplishments.

The struggles within the foundation can be illustrated by the history of two bellwether tenets of the postwar consciousness, the importance of behavioral science and the idea that social and economic policy required interdisciplinary attention. At Ford, much of this effort was organized by Berelson, who became the director of the Behavioral Science Division. He was influential in establishing the legitimacy of the term *behavioral science* (Berelson, 1963) and played a leading role in the creation of the Center for Advanced Studies in the Behavioral Sciences.

However, Berelson's time at Ford would be relatively difficult. Neither Berelson himself nor the program in behavioral sciences secured much enthusiasm within the foundation. Although Berelson was a product of Hutchins's university, Hutchins asked the record to show he had nothing to do with his appointment at Ford. He explained that he did not want to be accused of favoring people from Chicago,[14] an explanation that may have been less than totally satisfactory given Hutchins's efforts to secure support for Mortimer Adler. Other observers noted the elements of personal antagonism between Berelson and Hutchins. Berelson also met opposition both from Donald David, a key member of the board, and from other members of the board who were not impressed by the possibilities in social science.[15] Moreover, social science sounded too much like socialism to some members of Congress;[16] and the program raised hopes in the behavioral science part of academe that proved impossible to satisfy.

Gaither (with the advice of Hans Speier) was Berelson's primary supporter, and Gaither's support was of considerable value. As Berelson observed in his final report in 1957:

> . . . the top administrative officers of the Foundation were not fully convinced of the value of the Program and it was only through the direct support and personal responsibility assumed by Rowan Gaither that implementation began as early as mid 1951.[17]

The Behavioral Science Division supported the field with grants of $38 million between 1951 and 1957 and contributed to establishing the legitimacy of the term *behavioral science*, but the division was eliminated in 1957.

Although rhetorical enthusiasm for behavioral science and interdisciplinary work flourished for a time in the foundation, the programs explicitly associated with them did not. For example, the foundation created several advisory groups focused on interdisciplinary efforts, one of which was an "Advisory Group on Economics and the Behavioral Sciences," which was initiated to consider the question whether and how the Ford Foundation should attempt to establish more fruitful relations between economics and the behavioral sciences. After an initial meeting in New York, smaller one-day conferences were held in San Francisco, Chicago, and New York, and participants included such distinguished economists as Armen Alchian, Kenneth Arrow, Kenneth Boulding, George Katona, Jacob Marschak, Charles Lindblom, Franco Modigliani, and Oskar Morgenstern. Herbert Simon also participated, but the imbalance between the representation from economics and the representation from other social sciences was manifest.[18]

From the outset, there was "unanimous agreement" that cooperation between economics and the behavioral sciences was "highly desirable." The economists on the Advisory Group were as unstinting in their ambitions for the behavioral sciences as they were naïve in their understanding of them. The report from the meeting observed that the potential benefits of such cooperation were mutual:

> Such cooperation would be valuable both in the development of new theories about economic behavior and in "mopping up" operations designed to document and refine earlier theories. On the other side, it would be valuable in providing new data and new techniques for the behavioral science.[19]

The heroic sentiments influenced foundation aspirations, but the aspirations with respect to behavioral science were mostly not achieved. The discipline of economics veered decisively away from conceptions of economics as a "behavioral" science, leaving behavioral economists as a small, deviant cluster. Efforts of the foundation to infuse business education with behavioral science were largely unsuccessful.[20]

Moving into Management Education

After Gaither became president of the foundation and Thomas Carroll became head of the program on Economic Development and Administration, the EDA program moved in the direction of concerns about business and business education. Carroll was born in 1914 in San Francisco and studied at USC and the Harvard Business School, where he received MBA (1936) and DCS (1939) degrees. He served on the faculty at HBS from 1939 to 1942 (including a year as assistant dean when he was just twenty-six). After wartime service, he was dean at Syracuse University Business School (at age thirty-two), then dean at the University of North Carolina Business School before moving in 1954 to a full-time position on the Ford Foundation staff. He had been involved with Ford already in 1946 as a program area advisor and became vice president in 1954. In 1961, he left Ford to become president of George Washington University. He died in 1964.

There were numerous reasons for the movement toward business. One was a political context produced by the attacks on social science and foundations by Senator Joseph McCarthy and his allies. In 1952, a House of Representatives Select Committee (the Reece Committee) undertook hearings in response to House Resolution 561. The resolution instructed the committee

> . . . to conduct a full and complete investigation and study of educational and philanthropic foundations and other comparable organizations which are exempt from Federal income taxation to determine which such foundations and organizations are using their resources for purposes other than the purposes for which they were established, and especially to determine which such foundations and organizations are using their resources for un-American and subversive activities or for purposes not in the interest or tradition of the United States.[21]

In pursuit of this charge, the committee took testimony about the Ford Foundation from Henry Ford, Rowan Gaither, Paul Hoffman, and Robert Hutchins. The questioning highlighted the skepticism of some members of congress about programs involving academics and foreigners, particularly programs in social science.

From the foundation's point of view, business education was a "safe haven," or as James Howell was to call it later, "a philanthropoid's dream."[22] The foundation had been profoundly buffeted by Congress, a buffeting that Robert McNamara later attributed largely to the presence of Hutchins.[23]

The attacks contributed to the departure of Paul Hoffman from the foundation and shaped foundation sentiments for some time to come.

At the same time, there were struggles in the foundation between leaders of the economics profession and leaders of business schools over possible directions for foundation programs in economic development. Carroll was viewed in some quarters as an ally of business school deans in their conflicts with economists over resources from Ford. There was a basis for the view. About half of those chosen to serve on the advisory committee for the program were affiliated with business schools or business firms. And, under Carroll's direction, the title of Research Area III changed to "Economic Development and Administration" to signal the potential for a focus on business administration.

Institutional support to places such as the Harvard Business School and the Graduate School of Industrial Administration at the Carnegie Institute of Technology began in 1954, when the distinct program in EDA, outlined in the Gaither Report, came into operation; a significant part of the EDA vision became the idea of reforming management education. With Carroll in charge, the foundation involvement in management education was relatively intense and relatively brief. It was also, by most standards and appearances, relatively effective. This direction was heralded by a report submitted by an advisory group to the Program on Economic Development and Administration. The group consisted of scholars from a variety of universities and think tanks, as well as one business man, and included G. Leland Bach (from Carnegie Tech), Kenneth E. Boulding (Michigan), Robert D. Calkins (Brookings Institution and chairman of the group), John Maurice Clark (Columbia), Robert Aaron Gordon (Berkeley), Walter E. Hoadley (Amstrong Cork Company), John Lintner (Harvard), Howard B. Myers (Committee for Economic Development), Lloyd G. Reynolds (Yale), Edward S. Shaw (Stanford), Gordon Siefkin (Emory), and R. Miller Upton (Washington University). The group recommended:

> That support be given to the improvement of graduate study and research training in economics and administration especially through pioneering centers of graduate study and research training with a problem orientation.[24]

More particularly, the group recommended

... that, to encourage pioneering work of a higher order in both research and teaching, the Foundation provide substantial support for a limited number of university centers of graduate training in economics and administration.[25]

The perceived low academic standards of business schools were an early priority. As early as 1947, a Ford Foundation report on possible future activities mentioned professional schools (including business) as ripe for support.[26] Later, an EDA internal memo linked the initiative in business schools to the lack of academic quality (a major theme in the later Gordon and Howell report) and the decline in the quality of students:

> If the purposes of Area III are to be achieved, both economics and business administration badly need more men of outstanding ability entering on graduate study. During the depression of the 1930s, economics, and the social sciences generally, held a strong attraction for outstanding minds. More recently, the physical sciences appear to have drawn a more than proportional share of the nation's outstanding young minds, while economics and business administration have drawn considerably less than their share. This problem seems to us especially acute in business administration because of the small number of first-class men who go on to the doctoral field and hence to university teaching or basic research in this field.[27]

The diagnosis reflected the tension between seeing business schools as contributors to the relatively immediate well-being of business firms, on the one hand, and a conception of business schools as contributors to knowledge relevant to the long-run health of business firms and economic systems, on the other. The programs sponsored by the Ford Foundation were built on a conviction that the American business schools of the time were too much oriented to the former and too little oriented to the latter.

For example, Thomas Carroll reported on a meeting advising the foundation's EDA area on their initiatives in business school research in the 1950s. A top executive of "one of America's largest corporations" explicitly pointed to the need for general knowledge:

> ... the training for business given ... tends to spoil the kids for business ... students, he said, need to get broader, more liberal education background; the business firm, he added, is a better place to learn the "how-to-do-it" techniques. There were no dissents among those present. (Carroll, 1958, p. 3–4)

Professors and administrative officials of schools of business are, of course, accustomed to slighting remarks by "unworldly souls" in academic life who may regard business as not quite "respectable." But these were hard-headed, successful business executives who are active also in educational affairs and who devote a surprising amount of time in reflection on optimum education as preparation for business. (Ibid., p. 4)

The mantra became one that was well known to the Flexner, Hutchins, and RAND traditions: Management education should be focused on the use of fundamental knowledge to frame classes of problems. Learning how to solve specific problems would be better done outside of the business school environment and when graduates were well underway in their careers.

Within the foundation and outside, the thrust into management education involved a somewhat unlikely and somewhat fragile coalition between the advocates of business schools, identified particularly with the Harvard Business School and personified by Donald David, and the advocates of a new managerial and social science, represented particularly by Rowan Gaither and G. Leland Bach. Thomas Carroll proved to be an effective leader of the coalition. To David and HBS, he offered support for business schools; to Gaither and Bach, he offered reform of them.

In many respects, it was an unlikely coalition because many of the reforms that were being proposed involved obvious criticisms not only of established business schools in general but particularly of the Harvard Business School. Carroll held them together by a combination of shared resources and somewhat two-faced rhetoric. With respect to the resources, Carroll proposed as early as 1953 that the foundation should support case study programs in business school administration.[28] At the same time, he worked closely with G. Leland Bach to support the work at Carnegie Institute of Technology to develop managerial and organizational science.

With respect to the rhetoric, for example, the 1957 Annual Report of the Ford Foundation noted:

The "clinical" approach pioneered by the Harvard Business School long ago demonstrated a usefulness that has guaranteed it a firm place in business school research and teaching. Recently, however, two newcomers to the business school, both components of engineering institutions, have embarked on imaginative research and teaching programs.[29]

In that spirit and with clear echoes of Flexner, Carroll (1958) drew parallels between medical schools and business schools and noted that medical schools focused their clinical training on a solid foundation in the sciences such as anatomy, biochemistry, pathology, and physiology. He then acknowledged, without explicitly endorsing, the feelings of "certain influential business educators" who

> . . . regard social psychology, cultural anthropology, sociology, mathematics, and statistics, as well as economics, the business analogues of the medical students' anatomy, biochemistry, pathology, and physiology. Rather than devote most of the professional curriculum either to a description of business practice or to tackling business problems via the case method, these educators would concentrate on training in the so-called behavioral sciences and on mathematics and statistics. (Ibid., p. 6)

The emphasis continued to be on economics, and the first grants in the area were in that field, but the rhetoric frequently reiterated that management education should rest on a solid foundation of mathematics and behavioral and social science. The Ford Foundation Report of 1954 had emphasized the connection between the two programs of economic development and administration and of behavioral social science:

> We believe that joint support of projects by two or more of the five programs of the Foundation to be desirable. . . . Collaboration is conspicuously appropriate, for example, . . . where joint research under programs III and V appears almost essential to obtain a thorough understanding of the behavior and decision making processes of economic organizations[30]

In 1958 a grant was suggested (but not made) for $1,250,000 to a "multiphase program designed to improve business education through increased application of the social sciences, mathematics and statistics to business problems." The proposed program included summer seminars, visiting professorships, and other tools to engage faculty and students in social science research. An Institute of Basic Mathematics for Application to Business was launched at Harvard and MIT in 1959.

This blurring of "social sciences, mathematics, and statistics" into a common initiative followed the lead of the RAND Corporation and its advisors and helped to focus business school social science on issues of decision making (organizational or otherwise) (Bach, 1958). However, it tended to conceal the lack of integration of the main ideas and the extent to which the major thrust (beyond economics) would become a thrust toward mathematics and statistics, rather than behavioral science.

In a memorandum to the Ford Foundation in 1960, G. Leland Bach summarized the proposals that had come to fill Foundation reports. In substance, he characterized the reports as centered on five major changes:[31]

- More integrated use of the foundation disciplines in teaching and research in business administration—the behavioral sciences, economics, modern quantitative methods, and mathematics, in application to managerial problems.

- More fundamental teaching with an analytical approach— combining case- or problem orientation with the use of organized theory and analytical concepts, in contrast to routine description, pure case method, or unapplied theory.

- Less emphasis on narrow specialization.

- Higher intellectual standards for faculty and students.

- Beginnings of fundamental research and increase in applied research—to supplement and replace traditional descriptive research, which has been focused merely on reporting prevailing practices; and faster introduction of these research results into teaching and teaching materials.

These ideas were by no means immediately acceptable to the majority of faculty and administrators in a majority of business schools. They may have defined a "revolution," but it was not a revolution of the masses. The main advocates of reform were connected to leading business schools. They had been successful in securing access to the considerable financial resources of the Ford Foundation, partly because their cause fit the postwar consensus, but also probably because it was politically more acceptable in the McCarthy era than other possible foundation programs.

From modest beginnings, a full program in business emerged. In total, the foundation spent over $35 million in its programs to improve business schools and management education (including about $4 million to support international programs). The major categories of grants included $12 million that went to general institutional support, $8 million to research support, $6 million to doctoral and faculty fellowships, and $4 million to workshops and seminars designed to improve the teaching and research in specific areas.

In 1956, predoctoral fellowships, faculty fellowships, and a program for faculty research support were initiated; and a study by Gordon and Howell (see Section 6.2, following) was commissioned. A program of flexible grants to institutions also was designed to support problem-oriented research at four selected schools—the Harvard Business School, the Columbia Business School, the University of Chicago Graduate School of Business, and the Graduate School of Industrial Administration at the Carnegie Institute of Technology. The Stanford Graduate School of Business was later added to the group.

As James Howell noted later:

> The strategy evolved by vice-president Carroll and consultant Bach [G. Leland Bach; see Chapter Seven] was simple: pour large sums of money into a few reasonably good or promising schools of business which would then be the instruments of change for the rest of the field. These demonstration centers came, inevitably, to be called centers or peaks of excellence.[32]

As a result, the money spent by the foundation was concentrated in leading schools. The sum of $11 million (31 percent) went to just two schools (Stanford and Harvard), $22.5 million (64 percent) went to eight schools (Stanford, Harvard, Chicago, Carnegie Tech, Columbia, UCLA, UC Berkeley, MIT), and all of the major grants went to these schools (excluding Columbia). The amount of $26 million (75 percent of the total) went to twenty-two schools. Of the fellowships that were awarded by the foundation, 90 percent went to students and faculty at those schools, and all of the research grants went to seven of the eight.

In addition, the Ford Foundation supported competitions for research excellence in doctoral dissertations. As might be expected, the awards went disproportionately to students at elite schools. In a "Foreword" to the published version of one of the selected dissertation, that of Victor Vroom, Thomas Carroll reiterated the foundation's emphases:

> The competition is intended to generalize standards of excellence in research on business by graduate students. It should give widespread professional recognition to persons recently awarded doctorates in business whose dissertation research is especially distinguished by its analytical content and strong roots in underlying disciplines. It is also intended to give recognition to a select number of persons outside business schools who in their doctoral dissertation pursued with distinction interests relevant to business. (cited in Miner, 2006, p. 131)

A final conspicuous part of the Ford Foundation program was the sponsorship of "outreach" from the elite schools in the form of fifty-nine workshops intended to disseminate the latest research and curricular developments to faculty members in business schools. Altogether, 1,500 faculty members from nearly 300 different institutions participated. Thirty-eight (64 percent) of the workshops were organized by one of the top eight schools using faculty drawn primarily from those schools.

There were some general differences in the configurations of the grants. Among the leading schools, the foundation tended to give money in the domains of a school's excellence, rather than try to strengthen its weaknesses. For example, half of the money given to Stanford and Carnegie was earmarked for research, whereas the maximum among the others was 28 percent. Of the grants given to Harvard, 50 percent of money was for doctoral teaching, whereas the maximum among the other four institutions was 13 percent. Harvard received support for summer programs in the development and use of cases; Carnegie Tech and Chicago received money for workshops, seminars, and conferences on new developments in analysis and research. Over time, research grants became more widespread relative to doctoral grants and endowments. Overall, direct grants for research amounted to about $8 million with all but about $1 million going to eight leading schools.

6.2 Articulating a Manifesto: Two reports

The development of a consciousness in the community of scholars around a vision of mathematical, scientific, interdisciplinary, and analytical approaches both to policy problems and to the social and behavioral sciences involved several years of conversations among key leaders in and around business schools. Those conversations yielded a certain amount of closure on the core fundamentals of needed change in the schools, but they did not provide a clear manifesto, a document that could be a guide and a lightning rod.

To generate candidate documents, the Carnegie Corporation and the Ford Foundation commissioned separate reports. The issuance of these two reports came to be key events in the records of business school history. The reports were, however, more legacies of the Ford Foundation programs than progenitors of them. Many of the participants in both reports were people who had previously been involved in discussions with groups in and around the foundations. The general themes of the reports were implicit in the choices made of authors and in the conversations around them that involved many of the same people who had come to be associated with Rowan Gaither, Thomas Carroll, and their advisors.

The reports clarified the arguments, developed supporting data, and articulated the prejudices that had come to be shared widely in the foundation and among its major grantees in business schools. Their primary audience was not the foundation, which was relatively soon to remove itself from the scene, but the many business schools in North America who were just beginning to feel the pressures to change. The reports articulated a manifesto that would justify the revolution and possibly carry it forward.

The charges in the two cases were quite similar. Each report was to provide some answers to the directions in which business schools should go. Although they were prepared during the same period, the two reports were done independently. The authors had one joint meeting and shared some data, but the analyses and conclusions were generated separately. The similarities in their analyses and conclusions stemmed less from their explicit coordination than from the extent to which they drew on a community that had developed a substantially shared view.

The approaches used in preparing the two reports were different. The Carnegie Corporation report, thereafter called the Pierson Report after its principal architect, involved a collection of essays written by different people, including some suggesting specific curriculum changes in functional areas and paying attention to undergraduate education for business. The Ford Foundation report, thereafter called the Gordon and Howell Report after its two authors, was written by the two authors themselves after considerable consultation with a wide group of individuals and devoted itself primarily to questions of graduate education and research.

The two reports suggested numerous things, but the central theme of their recommendations was a desire to make business schools more academic. It was a desire that resonated not only with the academic establishment but also with important leaders in business. In developing that theme, the contents of the two reports overlapped considerably, as did their recommendations. In particular, both reports argued that business schools had inferior students, inadequate bases of fundamental knowledge and intellectual skills, and too-specialized curricula. As Thomas Carroll noted:

> The reports reach essentially similar conclusions. There is agreement that much of present-day business education is excessively specialized and vocational and that there is a need for the substitution of a broad-based core curriculum. Wherever practicable they prefer that professional education for business be pursued at the graduate level. They recognize the continuing need for education at the undergraduate level, however, and urge greater breadth, improved analytical tools, and stronger requirements in the underlying disciplines, especially in economics, the behavioral sciences, mathematics, and statistics. (1959, p. 159)

Considerable credit—and blame—has been awarded to the reports for the revolution in management education and the simultaneous changes in business schools. For example, an article looking back at management education in the *Academy of Management Review* noted:

> The landmark studies of business education by Pierson (1959) and Gordon and Howell (1959) have had great influence. The often unsubstantiated descriptive content of earlier business school curricula and research has been replaced by quantitative description based on rigorous data collection, computer-assisted mathematical modeling, and the foundational concepts of science—testable hypotheses (or, at least testable networks of hypotheses), correlated observations, and causal explanation. (Mulligan, 1987, p. 593)

However, not everyone granted to either report the same iconic status granted to the Flexner Report in medical education. For example, Porter commented that the reports, despite the way in which they are usually interpreted, were inadequately committed to a scientific foundation for management:

> Neither the Pierson nor the Gordon and Howell reports, in my opinion, went to the heart of the problem; namely, the need to shift from the study of current practices toward scientific research. (Porter, 1963, p. 140)

The Pierson Report

The Pierson Report was issued in 1959 (Pierson, 1959). It was commissioned by the Carnegie Corporation, an institution founded by Andrew Carnegie, as was the Carnegie Foundation for the Advancement of Teaching, which had earlier in the century sponsored the Flexner Report that helped reform medical education in the United States. The connection was noted explicitly in the preface and probably shaped the thinking of the authors. The report emphasized the problems of raising standards in business education and moving toward an educational experience that was better grounded in fundamental knowledge.

Frank Pierson was an economics professor at the University of Swarthmore, where he taught for a total of thirty-nine years, many of them as chair of the Economics Department. He received his PhD in economics from Yale in 1948. A labor economist, he also served as an arbitrator in several labor disputes in the United States. In his introduction, he observed that universities and colleges are

> . . . the product of two distinct and sometimes conflicting traditions. According to the first . . . knowledge is pursued for its own sake. . . . Most proponents of this view . . . would regard direct preparation for particular careers as basically alien to the purpose of academic work. . . . The other great tradition . . . would leave ample room for those students desiring to prepare for particular careers. According to this tradition, the search for truth is not impugned because it proves useful nor is education necessarily unworthy because it is pursued for its career value. (Ibid., pp. 16–17)

Against the background of that general dichotomy, the chapters in the first half of the report (almost all the chapters in the first two parts of the book) were written by Frank Pierson. Part 1 discussed the principles underlying higher education for business. Part 2 applied those principles to existing programs of undergraduate and graduate schools. The second half of the report (parts 3 and 4) consisted of contributions from thirteen others, including Kenneth Andrews (dean of the Harvard Business School), George Leland Bach (dean of the Graduate School of Industrial Administration at the Carnegie Institute of Technology), and George Shultz (who would later [1962–1964] be dean of the University of Chicago Graduate School of Business). Part 3 examined some selected areas of the business school curriculum, and part 4 discussed the programs of other institutions such as engineering schools and liberal arts colleges.

In keeping with its assessment that "the central problem confronting this branch of higher education is that academic standards need to be materially increased" (Ibid., p. ix), the Pierson report criticized the large number of specialized courses in fields such as marketing or production with relatively simple techniques and little analytical content or educational value:

> The besetting weakness in this branch of education, as perhaps in many others, is the tendency to build up areas and sub-areas far beyond their true academic worth. (Ibid., p. xi)

The report argued that the most promising development in management education was the increasing emphasis on managerial decision making (and the correspondingly lesser emphasis on specific skills). In endorsing a more fundamental, less vocational approach, it noted that:

> . . . no more subject specialization should be encouraged, particularly at the undergraduate level, than is necessary to secure a start in industry. Primary emphasis could then rest where it belongs—on analysis and application of underlying disciplines and widely usable tool subjects. (Ibid., p. xiii)

The report discussed issues such as the difficulties of raising standards because the field of business was relatively new; because the practice of business was increasingly complex; because of heavy enrollment pressure;

and so on. It found that the problems apply to both undergraduate and graduate levels, so one of the more important steps required was to limit enrollment to students who were interested in "serious academic work." Such work, they found, should be largely general rather than specific and mostly centered around decision making.

The report supported the importance of developing skills at applying abstract knowledge in concrete real world situations, but it returned time and again to a theme declaring the necessity of a significant foundational part that drew on the scientific disciplines:

> Implicit in the conception of business education set forth in this study is the prime role which should be accorded research. The need is not for just any kind of research, as that rather elastic term is often defined, but for research which meets high scientific standards and is aimed at problems of general significance. (Ibid., p. xv)

> Primary emphasis could then rest where it belongs—on analysis and application of underlying disciplines and widely usable tool subjects. (Ibid., p. 30)

> . . . in this area, as in any other field, the first obligation of a college or university is to put its work on a challenging intellectual basis. This is the purpose of such institutions, and where it is not fulfilled, their reason for being disappears. (Ibid., p. 33)

The theme was emphasized by a quotation attributed to Allen Wallis, who was dean (1956–1962) of the University of Chicago Business School:

> Social science training in school is the optimum way of hastening, stimulating, and making more profound that education which is acquired on the job. It raises pertinent questions, increases sensitivity to relevant phenomena, and provides a coherent frame of reference into which the individual can assimilate his complex and occasionally untidy vocational experience. (cited in Carroll, 1958, p. 246)

The Gordon and Howell Report

In 1956, the Ford Foundation commissioned a three-year study of management education by two University of California, Berkeley, economists, Aaron Gordon and James Howell. Both were "outsiders" in the sense that neither was then associated closely with a business school, though by no means as much "outsiders" as Flexner had been to the medical education community. As economists, both were familiar with business education in a general way, but neither had been heavily involved.

Aaron Gordon was a senior respected economist at Berkeley, known for his role in making the Berkeley economics department a well-known one and for speaking his mind (Pechmann, 1978). Born in Washington, DC, Gordon had gone to Johns Hopkins University and received his PhD in economics from Harvard in 1934. He was a contributor to the Keynesian revolution in the United States and a student of business fluctuations. In his work, he was interested in the role of firms and corporations in society and sometimes critical of the ways in which corporations (and especially corporate management) could (mis)use their powers (Gordon, 1945). James Howell was a young economist who had received his doctorate in 1955 from Yale University. He was recruited to the Ford Foundation to work on this project and later came to Stanford. In fact, as will be discussed in Chapter Eight, his hiring in 1958 was a part of the Stanford Graduate School of Business's effort to revamp its image to fit what the Ford Foundation wanted.

Working with an advisory committee consisting of university administrators, foundation leaders, and business practitioners, and on the basis of conversations with businessmen, educators, and administrators in business schools, the two authors produced a report, issued in 1959, that became a manifesto for a major change in business school education and research in North America.

Partly perhaps because of its link to the Ford Foundation programs that had already anticipated many of its recommendations and partly because of its greater coherence, the Gordon and Howell Report (Gordon and Howell, 1959) secured greater attention (as reflected in citations) than did the Pierson Report. To a considerable degree, the report anticipated, reflected, or shaped current controversies. Among other things, it considered education for undergraduates and "the graduate core," the role of specialization versus general knowledge, composition and quality of business school faculty, the role of research and teaching in management education, the need for a scientific basis for management education, and how to develop curriculum to best reflect this. It discussed topics such as: "To what extent is management a profession?" "What are the aims of business schools?" "What are the basic elements in the practice of business that management education should address?" "What is the market for business school graduates?" and "What is the role of education in the development of business competence?"

The primary conclusions of the study were that academic standards in American management education were too low; that the methods used in teaching were insufficient for the development of analytical and managerial capabilities in future managers; that the management curriculum had too many specialized vocational courses with little value for the building of managerial competencies; that business schools failed to attract students of high ability; that research in business schools was inadequate in quantity and quality to advance knowledge underlying either the theory or practice of management; and that the academic quality of teachers in business schools was inadequate.

The report documented symptoms of weakness in the quality of students recruited into management education. Noting that "business schools and departments enroll a disproportionate share of very weak freshmen" (Ibid., p. 325), the authors also found that, according to most studies, a large fraction of business students were below the average, at least in part because "business attracts a smaller proportion of really good students" (Ibid.).

Similarly, the report was harsh in its judgment about business school faculties, noting that "a school is no better than the abilities and interests of its faculty" (Ibid., p. 140). It decried the number of narrowly vocational specialists on the faculty:

> The "vocationalists" tend to attract the poorer students wanting a "practical" training. By the nature of the case, they are not interested in research. They do little thinking about the field of business administration as a whole, and, perhaps even more than the other specialists, they defend the inviolability of their own specialties. (Ibid., p. 349)

The report called for higher levels of competence and ability in both students and faculty, in particular for retraining and upgrading many faculty members so that they, too, would become more oriented toward the disciplinary foundations for management education:

A number of things can be done to improve the quantity and quality of research in the business schools . . . [A] general improvement in the scholarly climate in the business schools is the first need—for its effect on teaching as well as its possible long-run effects on the quality of research . . . It is important to increase the level of technical competence and scholarly activity . . . there is urgent need for arrangements that will help existing faculty members to bring themselves up to date with recent developments in their fields and in the related underlying disciplines. (Ibid., pp. 390–391)

In addition, the report noted the need for social scientists in the business schools; and, as social scientists, "we include the applied mathematicians and statisticians, as well as the economists, psychologists, and other social scientists who, while primarily concerned with some discipline, are also interested in applying the analytical tools of their field to business problems" (Ibid., p. 347). In an echo of the standard dogma of the time, the report observed that the significance of behavioral science, mathematics, and statistics needed to be recognized and integrated with the business school's focus on economics:

This implies seeking to interest more behavioral scientists, mathematicians, and statisticians in business problems (whether they move into a business school or not), more interdisciplinary research and more training in these related areas for doctoral candidates in business and for present faculty members seeking to keep up with the latest developments. (Ibid., p. 392)

The Gordon and Howell Report was a remarkable report. It captured the spirit of the times and helped to mobilize a coalition of forces to overcome potential problems in inducing dramatic changes in management education, including problems of institutional and organizational inertia and path dependency and the problems with multiple constituencies and interest groups in business schools (March and Sutton, 1997).

6.3 Moving On

With almost as much alacrity as the Ford Foundation had shown in creating programs to reform management education, it withdrew from the effort. In 1961, five years after the foundation programs in business education had begun, they were evaluated by an advisory group in a special report on the EDA program in business administration. The report was generally positive:

> The Foundation's [then—in 1961] $20 million investment in business education appears to have made a real difference in the level of education acquired by large numbers of present and future students.[33]

At the same time, however, the evaluation noted that the majority of business schools still were not what the foundation might hope:

> Necessarily, certain phases of the program have been weaker than others. Grants to support activities at the less prominent schools, for example, despite the attractiveness of such action from a democratic point of view, have not always worked out well. It appears that these schools can be more effectively aided by inviting their faculty to participate in seminars under the direction of leaders in the field, and by providing them with fresh blood in the form of young faculty trained at the leading institutions.[34]

The evaluation signaled a waning of foundation interest. As might be expected, the recipients of foundation largess were reluctant to see it end. A memo from G. Leland Bach proclaimed the importance of continuing support:

> The Foundation has been instrumental in bringing about a major revolution in the field of business education over the past five to seven years . . . This revolution . . . is in full swing at a number of the leading business schools, and is getting under way in others to varying degrees. But the revolution is still in its early stages; the forces of mediocrity and stand-patism are on the run but still hold substantial power in most universities, including most of the leading ones. Thus, the next few years are crucial ones for capitalizing on the remarkable progress made to date and for developing momentum. . . . continued strong external support for the central elements of improvement and change is crucial while new curricula are being developed.[35]

The Bach plea fell on institutionally deaf ears. The foundation creed called for efforts to spur the initial developments, diffuse the model, diffuse the major reform, and then gradually pull out. The years of initial funding (1954–1955), years of major grants (1956–1957) and subsequent dissemination activities were followed by about four years of fewer and smaller grants. By 1960–1964 the initiative turned to the planning and implementation of "terminal" grants to end foundation support in business education.

The process of termination was probably accelerated by Gaither's death in 1961, by Carroll's 1961 departure from the foundation (and death in 1964), and by the departure of several other foundation officers with similar orientations to join the new administration of the U.S. government after the election of John F. Kennedy as president in 1960. Foundation enthusiasm veered away from most of the spirit of the Gaither and Carroll initiatives, indeed from much of any concern whatsoever with business schools, fundamental research, or behavioral science, presumably assessing its programs in those areas as providing fewer potential gains to the human estate than other grander activities.

Chapter Seven

A Poster Child of Change: GSIA

Ford Foundation officers guiding the business school reform movement of the 1950s and 1960s saw themselves as working primarily with major existing business schools, but they also found a renegade school that could be made a poster child of the desired changes. The school was the newly established Graduate School of Industrial Administration (GSIA) at the Carnegie Institute of Technology—a small, unranked, and unaccredited school at a second-tier engineering institute. As Henry Mintzberg noted in 2004:

> The Irish monastery of the business school Dark Age was a remarkable place in Pittsburgh, Pennsylvania, called the Graduate School of Industrial Administration. (Mintzerg, 2004, p. 25)

7.1 The Right Time and the Right Place

In the early 1950s, GSIA was substantially unknown among leading business schools, but it was known at the Ford Foundation. G. Leland Bach, the dean of GSIA, was an advisor to the foundation and had been involved in one of the study committees leading to the Gaither Report. Before the Ford Program in Economic Development and Administration (EDA) began its support program in management education, the foundation's behavioral science division had been supporting research at Carnegie, beginning with a grant in 1950 "to finance an inventory of knowledge in the field of human behavior in business and other organizations."[1]

GSIA was built on the kind of vision that the Gaither Report to the Ford Foundation advocated. The context was the Cold War. Economic growth, educational advances, and other aspects of national strength in the competition with international communism and the Soviet Union were central concerns of public policy. There was widespread agreement that the national interest required the mobilization of science and new techniques of decision making in the service of efficiency and competitiveness. There was widespread optimism about the possibilities for progress through informed intelligence.

GSIA fit these prejudices. The school was small, but researchers at GSIA appeared to be doing the kind of research that was heralded in the new vision of socially relevant quantitative science. They were eager to promote mathematical models for decision making; they were interested in interdisciplinary studies of organizational and social behavior; they were involved in using advanced quantitative and statistical techniques to solve scheduling and allocation problems; and they were committed to the use of such research in framing problems of business management and in contributing to what they anticipated as a new era of social science.

As James Howell noted with respect to GSIA's role in "the construction of a science of administration":

> Under the guidance of Bach and Simon, [Carnegie] was going to mobilize the methodologies, attitudes and recent advances of the social sciences to investigate the phenomenon of organizational administration. The ultimate goal was the construction of a science of administration using economics and the behavioral and quantitative sciences as the starting points. If even partially successful, the Carnegie group would provide the intellectual basis for the hoped-for revolution in business education. Here was the advanced projects laboratory, the R&D group that EDA had to find or create; fortunately, it already existed.[2]

The Ford Foundation found a poster child in GSIA, and GSIA found a sugar daddy.

7.2 The Beginnings

GSIA was established by a gift from William Larimer Mellon, a somewhat renegade member of the Mellon family who had founded the Gulf Oil Company. He gave Carnegie Tech $6 million to build a new school of industrial administration. Mellon's explicit motivations were simple. He objected to the idea that the Pittsburgh area produced engineers at Carnegie Tech and then saw them leave Pittsburgh to go to Harvard Business School to learn management. He wanted a program in which engineers learned to use managerial tools to go with their engineering skills.

Although Mellon's interest in a school at Carnegie Tech was relatively parochial, the location in Pittsburgh was favorable. In 1952, at a time when commercial airplane travel was still in its infancy, Pittsburgh was only an overnight train trip from Washington, New York, Boston, Detroit, or Chicago. It was close enough to firms interested in new directions that the school's research could become entwined with practical business concerns.

The school's dean, George Leland Bach, worked with E. Dunlap Smith, the provost at Carnegie Tech, to design the new school's character and mission. Smith was committed to expanding engineering education to encompass a broader set of intellectual concerns. Bach was the son of a small-town Iowa banker and had a PhD in economics from the University of Chicago. During the war he had served as a special assistant at the Federal Reserve Bank and at the U.S. Department of Commerce. He dressed in the style of an old-school banker and, in many ways, thought like one. He was conservative in politics, economics, and administration. He combined this deep conservatism with outstanding skills at analysis and a brutally unemotional capacity for good judgment. Bach was recommended to Smith by Theodore Schultz, who had been his dissertation advisor. He came to Carnegie as chair of the Department of Economics, which had been temporarily eliminated during the war, and became dean of GSIA when it was established.

Bach came to be pivotal in the development of the Ford Foundation program and more generally in the reforms of management education. As the history unfolded, he was actively involved in advising the foundation with respect to its Program in Economic Development and Administration

(EDA). He also contributed a chapter to the Pierson Report (see Chapter Six) (Pierson, 1959) and became a leading advocate of reform.

Bach was a respected macroeconomist and author of a leading introductory college textbook in economics, but the primary basis for his exemplary reputation was less in his scholarship than in his organizational leadership. His genius lay in administrative judgment. He was legendary for the austerity of his manner, the purity of his demands for excellence, and the brilliance of his personnel choices. Herbert A. Simon, who was one of Bach's early personnel choices, recalled

> The spectacular growth of GSIA owed much to the leadership style of Lee Bach, who served as dean from 1949 until 1961, and whose strength of conviction and character kept the enterprise on course. (Simon, 1991, p. 148)

Bach's attitudes about management and management education were not unique to him but reflected a substantial body of contemporary enthusiasm for building both on a foundation of quantitative skills and scientific knowledge. For example, it was also (independently) expressed by A. P. Sloan in correspondence in anticipation of the Sloan Foundation Grant that led to the 1952 Establishment of the Sloan School of Management at MIT:

> While the exercise of sound business judgment will always be the keystone of a successful industrial executive and a progressive enterprise, yet to reach the highest level of effectiveness, executive decisions must be supported by a scientific appraisal of all related facts and circumstances. Industrial management has passed through a long process of development as our industrial age has evolved. Today it has become in every sense of the word, a matter of science.[3]

GSIA found a congenial home at Carnegie Tech. In 1936 Robert E. Doherty, an engineering professor from Yale University, had been appointed president of the institute, which had by that time become a well-respected engineering school. Doherty established what came to be called the "Carnegie Plan." He emphasized that the program should cultivate a student's ability to think through problem situations independently—give a student a clear grasp of the fundamental scientific knowledge relevant to the situations; lay the basis for subsequent learning from experience; and develop an interest in responsibilities as a citizen and a person. These were the values that he saw as requirements for the new kind of engineering education he had in mind. As he stated,

> The program must place less emphasis upon routine "know-how" and miscellaneous technical information, and much more upon intellectual skills and upon the fundamental knowledge and understanding essential to the constructive use of such skills in coping with practical situations—situations, that is, which the student may meet later as a professional man, a citizen, and as an individual. (Doherty, 1950, p. 7)

Among other things, the Carnegie Plan had an "interdisciplinary social relations program," with courses in the tools (logic and method) for the application of engineering techniques to behavioral and social problems; and later a program also in the "Historical Development of Western Civilization," which had courses in "Economic Analysis of Contemporary Problems" and "Problems of Population."[4]

The onset of the Second World War delayed implementation of the full Doherty vision, but after the war ended he reiterated his interest in expanding the role of humanities and social sciences at Carnegie Tech. After exploring several alternatives, he concluded that economics and psychology were the most promising for research contracts and graduate study (Cleeton, 1965, p. 86). In addition, he was encouraged by William Larimer Mellon's interest in creating and endowing a Graduate School of Industrial Administration "for developing the kind of interdisciplinary instruction which he felt was not being adequately covered in work offered at other institutions" (Cleeton, 1965, p. 87).

When the gift became available in 1949, GSIA was created, and G. Leland Bach was named its first dean. In 1986, Bach recalled the task of starting the program, noting that his conception

> . . . called for a teaching program that would stress analysis and flexible problem solving while simultaneously emphasizing the importance of organizational behavior, economic analysis, and modern quantitative methods in understanding how decisions are made and implemented, and could

be made and implemented better, in the complex, uncertain world. (Bach, 1986, p. 39)

Bach worked closely with Doherty (as well as Provost Smith) as long as Doherty was president. Not surprisingly, Bach's attitudes in many respects echoed those of Doherty, the man who hired him. However, they did not agree on everything. For example, Doherty did not want the word *graduate* in the school's name at first, but Bach did. With Mellon's death and Doherty's retirement in 1950, the rebels at GSIA found themselves with more freedom. The new president of Carnegie Tech, John Warner, was a chemist who had worked on the Manhattan Project. He was inclined to delegate responsibility for GSIA to Bach while working to improve the quality of the institution as whole (Fenton, 2000, p. 5).

In 1949, GSIA had seventeen faculty members, many of them carryovers from the earlier departments of Industrial Management and Economics. In the following years the faculty grew in numbers at a rapid, but not extraordinary, rate. By 1965, GSIA had fifty-five faculty members. Of the faculty who had been present at the "birth," only four remained.

The core curriculum at GSIA was created by Bach and a handful of faculty. It reflected the sacred script of the postwar reforms, partly because key people at GSIA were involved in writing the script. As Franco Modigliani, one of the major figures in the early years, recalled:

> The whole group eagerly took part in devising the curriculum for a new business school that, unlike the practice prevailing at that time, was to be based not on common sense and imitation of the "best existing practice" but would have a strong analytical component. It was to be underpinned by disciplines like economics, administrative science, mathematics, statistics, accounting, and the use of computers that was targeted on "problem solving." (Modigliani, 2001, pp. 85–86)

The economics that was taught was not "business economics" but the advanced micro- and macro-theory courses of an economics department. Accounting was combined with statistics into a course on quantitative control. Management and organizational behavior were transformed into an interdisciplinary course on "organization theory." Marketing emphasized analytical models for assessing demand and developing marketing strategy. Production management morphed into operations research, much of it using linear and dynamic programming methods. Almost as soon as computers were available, a computer management game was developed and used. Courses in which students were exposed to things such as the history of Greece and the Peloponnesian Wars, philosophy of science, or theories of revolutions were introduced.

The school's small size made its early survival financially possible. The building that it occupied was paid for by the Mellon endowment, which also yielded a modest annual return. A major source of the resources required to sustain the research effort came from the Ford Foundation. As James Howell later noted,

> [Harvard] didn't receive the first big grant [from the Ford Foundation]. That honor went to Carnegie . . . To all but a few insiders, the inclusion of Carnegie in the list of primary centers was a surprise; it failed completely to meet two of the five "official" criteria: a small school, it was not only new (1950) but also part of a minor technical institute rather than of a major university . . . [But] Carnegie by 1954 "knew where it was going." (Howell, 1966, p. 9)

Ford Foundation support was critical, but it was not the only source of early support for research at GSIA. In the years of research enthusiasm after the Second World War, early Carnegie scholars were able to secure useful research contracts. For example, the U.S. Air Force sponsored a study in 1950 on "Intra-Firm Planning and Behavior," which focused on "the application of new analytical methods and techniques to the production planning and control of intra-firm behavior." Another early contract was from the Controllership Foundation on "Centralization and Decentralization of Accounting and Control Functions in Business" (Simon et al., 1954). Other studies were funded by or in collaboration with the Cowles Commission, the Office of Naval Research (ONR), and Westinghouse Corporation. Among the papers written with ONR support were Simon and Holt, "The Control of Inventory and Production Rates" (Simon and Holt, 1954), and Modigliani and Simon, "On the Relation Between a Heuristic and an Exact Production Decision Rule."[5]

7.3 CREATING A CULTURE

Many of the things that were said about the RAND culture in its heyday were also said about the GSIA culture in its. It was a culture of intense commitment. In standard terms, most faculty members were workaholics. The norms required working at night and on weekends, talking primarily about research at social gatherings, and being prepared at any time to defend even the most apparently innocuous assertion. It was immensely internally supportive, with a strong sense of being an embattled core of the virtuous facing a hostile, misguided, and mostly incompetent world.

At the same time, it was immensely internally competitive; faculty seminars were fought with the intensity of mortal combat. The standards were the highest standards of the disciplines, but there was no respect for disciplinary lines. Trespassing across lines was dangerous because it required demonstrating competence in a foreign field, but it was common. The faculty was diverse, ambitious, and brash; the individuals were engaged with each other; no quarter was given to age, seniority, or scholarly status.

Franco Modigliani recalled:

> It was during the eight years spent at the Carnegie Institute of Technology that I matured as an economist. . . . The atmosphere at the Carnegie Institute was one of tremendous ferment and novelty. (Modligliani, 2001, pp. 85–86)

In a letter to Herbert Simon, he also noted the culture of collaboration (and of disputation):

> GSIA was an exciting place, we felt at the center of the universe and . . . maybe we were. And, what's most important, we had a lot of fun working hard together, and arguing even harder."[6]

In many respects, GSIA was a first generation product of the University of Chicago of Robert Maynard Hutchins. The four scholars who are usually credited with primary roles in creating GSIA's character were G. Leland Bach, William W. Cooper, Franco Modigliani, and Herbert A. Simon. Bach received his PhD in economics from Chicago. Cooper was educated there and taught there from 1942–1946. Simon also was educated there and received his PhD in political science from Chicago. Modigliani (who was educated largely in Italy) spent much of his early years in the United States with the University of Chicago's Cowles Commission and had as his primary American mentor Jacob Marschak, who was on the faculty there. These four scholars were steeped in the Hutchins ethos and catechism.

The Chicago connection is important. As we have noted in Chapter Four, Hutchins was president of the university from 1929 to 1951. While he was president, the university created a culture that was enormously committed to the intellect, to pursuing knowledge fundamentals as a basis for making the world better. That commitment was a major matter of faith for many who were connected to the university during the 1930s and 1940s. It was carried into the Chicago Graduate School of Business by Allen Wallis and his associates. It was carried into GSIA by Bach, Cooper, Modigliani, and Simon.

Cooper was the first person Bach brought to GSIA. He had briefly been a professional boxer before going to the University of Chicago to study economics. Simon later described Cooper as "a 'revolutionary' whose indifference to convention was a critical ingredient in the successful GSIA effort" (Simon, 1991, p. 141). As Simon recalled,

> Of the three members of the triumvirate—Lee, Bill, and I—that assumed the leadership of GSIA, Bill was the radical, the least constrained by the established conventions of business education or by the realities of organizations. (At the same time, of the three, he had had the most extensive organizational experience). His influence prevented Lee and me from conceding too much to the pressures of the outside business and academic worlds. (Simon, 1991, p. 143)

After finishing at Chicago, Cooper went to the Tennessee Valley Authority (TVA) on a government project, followed by a fellowship at Columbia University and more government work in Washington during the war. When Bach approached him in 1946 with an offer of a job teaching economics at Carnegie Tech, Cooper was working in Washington for the Division of Statistical Standards in the Bureau of the Budget, coordinating programs across various government agencies ranging from the Securities Exchange Commission to the Office of Price Administration and many military programs. Despite his relative youth, he was chairman of an interagency committee on accounting and financial statistics that was charged with planning significant aspects of the postwar statistical activities of the government. At the same time, Lee Bach had been hired by the Carnegie Institute of Technology and was a chairman of a similar postwar planning committee for the Federal Reserve Bank.

Cooper was attracted to the job at Carnegie; but he asked his friend, Herbert A. Simon, what he thought.[7] The link between Cooper and Simon was important to the development of GSIA. Among other things, Cooper had served as Simon's teacher in boxing at the University of Chicago and in a later conversation recalled how the grade he gave Simon may have helped Simon chose a career outside of boxing:

> The only B [Simon] got the whole time he was in college was a B that I gave him. That was in boxing! I kept telling him, "the reason I gave you a B was that I could see you weren't going to be a world champion in boxing so I suggested you look at another career—and I was right, you had a very good career." He was a terrible boxer![8]

Cooper's inquiry to Simon in 1946 was an echo of an earlier exchange in 1942. When Cooper had tried to recruit Simon to Washington, Simon had declined and had added,

> I hope that your own sojourn in Washington is planned as a temporary one. Important as the work of the bureaucracy may be, there still remain certain very important tasks of theory construction which persons with creative talents like your own need to help with before they dissipate all their energies helping the day-to-day operation of the machine.[9]

In 1946, Simon responded that the offer from GSIA to Cooper seemed "very attractive" and that "engineers are not a bad bunch to teach, and you should be able to recruit some first rate mathematical economists from among them."[10]

Shortly after Cooper's arrival at Carnegie, he wrote to Simon about the development of the courses there, and in 1948 he arranged for Simon to come to Carnegie for a short visit during which he gave a seminar on some economic aspects of technological change.[11] In due course, Bach wrote Simon a long enthusiastic letter discussing "the possibility of [Simon's] coming to Carnegie."[12] "We all want you to come and play a leading role," he wrote.

"We had to persuade him," Cooper said.[13] The persuasion was ultimately successful. "Bill Cooper can be very persuasive," Simon recalled (Simon, 1991, p. 140). Much later, Bach would describe inducing Simon to join GSIA as "the most useful thing I ever did as dean at Carnegie."[14]

Simon's fit with the postwar spirit of increased use of mathematics in the social and behavioral sciences was clear and expressed in his correspondence with Bernard Berelson:

> It is an article of my scientific credo that the behavioral sciences are going to follow economics in becoming more and more mathematical. . . . Virtually every important advance in theory since the last quarter of the nineteenth century has been made by men with considerable knowledge of mathematics.[15]

In the very early years, the school's culture was built by the team of Bach, Cooper, and Simon and shaped by their ideas, many of which could be traced to their experiences at the University of Chicago. As Cooper recalled, discussing his and Simon's common roots at Chicago:

> Herb and I shared the background provided by the survey courses which were required of all students during the intellectually exciting days when Robert Maynard Hutchins was president of the University of Chicago. These courses, which occupied the first two years of college, were designed to cover, broadly, the entire field of human knowledge in our four separate packages consisting of the humanities, the social sciences, the physical sciences, and the biological sciences. . . . these survey courses made it possible to communicate easily with each other since they continued to provide a broad basis for understanding what we were each doing (and learning) both in the university and thereafter. (Cooper, 2004, p. 68)

In 1953 the initial trio was augmented by the appointment of Franco Modigliani, who was at the University of Illinois when he was recruited to GSIA in 1952. Modigliani knew Simon and Cooper through their interactions in the Cowles Commission (Cooper, 2004; Modigliani, 2001, p. 58; 2004).

He had organized a seminar with Simon at Cowles to discuss the research of their groups. Simon also had extensive discussions with Jacob

Marshack, Modigliani's mentor, and had been influenced by his early work on expectations and uncertainty. Simon wrote to Marschak in 1952, sending one of his own manuscripts that

> you will see it [the paper] was stimulated by a restudy of the Modgliani—Hohn paper, and by Franco's presence on the campus here.[16]

Simon worked with Marshack on a study of the economic aspects of atomic energy for the Atomic Energy Commission (Schurr and Marschak, 1950) and saw Modigliani as an essential part of the "Cowles people."[17]

The team of Bach, Cooper, Modigliani, and Simon formed the core of GSIA from 1953 to 1960. They set the tone, defined the program, and recruited the faculty. They organized and molded a culture of intense intellectual commitment and self-confidence. They were, in many ways, a Robert Maynard Hutchins mafia dedicated to the cultivation of the intellect through the elaboration of fundamental knowledge and molded by postwar sensibilities into a commitment to science, mathematics, analysis, and problem solving through intelligence informed by formal models. As the other faculty members they recruited became established, the original four gradually withdrew, but their imprint remained for at least two decades.

7.4 An Academic Nova

GSIA turned out to be a nova in the history of academic institutions. The school assembled a small, extraordinary group of faculty members (or made its faculty members extraordinary). It recruited an exceptional group of students (or made its students exceptional). It created a program for graduate business education that became a model for other schools. It established a culture for collegial interaction and intellectual discourse that has few equals in the recent history of academic institutions. And it developed a research program that transformed important areas of research. It was a tiny school that played a key part in changing management education and business schools in North America and ultimately in the world and contributed ideas that came to be critically important to the development of several scholarly fields.

The Students

One of the features of GSIA that made it attractive as a place to showcase the possibilities for a new, analytical management education was its student niche. At the start, the program offered an MS degree in business, rather than an MBA, and it admitted to the MS program only students with baccalaureate degrees in engineering. In many respects, the program could have been more properly seen as a competitor to the Sloan School at the Massachusetts Institute of Technology or to programs in industrial or engineering management offered by engineering schools, rather than as a competitor to university-based business schools.

The student niche assured a group of students who would be prepared for mathematically based courses and would have an engineering approach to the use of fundamental knowledge drawn from economics, psychology, and sociology. The MS students were in considerable demand in the expanding economy. In some management quarters, the GSIA product became the model. Arjay Miller, later an influential dean of the Stanford Graduate School of Business who had been CEO of the Ford Motor Company, recalled believing at the time that GSIA had the brightest, best-trained students among American business schools.[18]

A striking feature of the student body was the productivity of the doctoral students. The doctoral program was very small. It was selective but probably not as selective as leading economics programs of the time. Nevertheless, GSIA yielded an exceptional crop of scholars, including Albert Ando, Dwight Crane, Justin Davidson, William Dill, Edward Feigenbaum, Julian Feldman, Yuji Ijiri, David Klahr, Kenneth Kotovsky, Arie Lewin, Michael Lovell, Dale Mortensen, John Muth, Allen Newell, Louis Pondy, William Pounds, Edward Prescott, William Starbuck, Fred Tonge, and Oliver Williamson, all of whom graduated from the program in the early years and built outstanding careers in academia.

The Faculty

Although the GSIA faculty in the 1950s and 1960s was considerably smaller than many economics departments in North American universities, it included such luminaries as William W. Cooper, Richard M. Cyert, Harold Guetzkow, Charles Holt, Yuji Ijiri, Harold J. Leavitt, Robert Lucas, Edwin Mansfield, James G. March, Allan Meltzer, Merton Miller, Franco Modigliani, John Muth, Richard Nelson, Allen Newell, Herbert A. Simon, Victor Vroom, and Harrison White. Except for Ijiri, Muth and Newell, who gained their PhDs from GSIA, and Cooper, who aborted his PhD training at Columbia University over a disagreement with his principal advisor, all of these faculty members received their doctorates from social science disciplinary departments, not from business schools. Most were economists, but there were also political scientists, psychologists, and sociologists among them.

In later years, almost all of these scholars left GSIA. Bach moved to Stanford on the explicit invitation of the dean (Arjay Miller) to help make the Stanford Graduate School of Business more like GSIA. Cooper moved first to a public policy school at Carnegie Mellon and then to the University of Texas. Cyert stayed for a while as dean of GSIA after Bach left, but later became president of Carnegie Mellon University. Guetzkow moved to Northwestern University. Holt moved to the University of Texas. Leavitt moved to Stanford University. Lucas moved to the University of Chicago. Mansfield moved to the University of Pennsylvania. March moved first to the University of California, Irvine, and then to Stanford University. Miller moved to the University of Chicago. Modigliani moved to MIT. Nelson moved to Columbia University. Newell moved to the Department of Computer Science at Carnegie Mellon. Simon moved to the Department of Psychology at Carnegie Mellon. Vroom moved to Yale University. White moved first to the University of Arizona and then to Columbia University. Almost all of the key figures left, but, for a brief period of perhaps fifteen years, they created an exceptional intellectual milieu.

After the departures, GSIA continued to be firmly established as a leading business school, but its aura of uniqueness faded. Neither the faculty nor the students glowed as brightly as in the 1950s and 1960s. Partly this was because other schools became more scholarly, thus making distinctiveness more difficult. Partly it was because neither the intensity of the GSIA pursuit of excellence nor its commitment to fundamental interdisciplinary knowledge could be sustained. The school had established itself as one among several leading business schools, but the glitter of distinctiveness glowed less brightly.

7.5 Fundamental Research in a Business School

The GSIA creed was a creed dedicated to fundamental research. Bach thought that basic research was essential for schools of business, and he recognized that it had to have both a long-time perspective and a propensity to challenge established practices. He wrote:

> . . . I want to stress as strongly as I can my own belief that fundamental research is a major part of every leading business school, especially those which offer graduate work . . . The function of the university is to be ahead of best practice, not to be trailing a few steps behind the operating business world. (Bach, 1958, pp. 363–364)

Bach was committed, but he recognized the costs:

> As in the development of the physical sciences and engineering, educational institutions probably must take the lead in original basic research in the area of management, especially since much of this research will inevitably appear slow and impractical—even "long haired." Moreover, many findings may well be disruptive for long-established patterns of business operations . . . American management will be highly skeptical of basic research in this field for many years, just as it was skeptical of the usefulness of early research in the physical sciences. (Bach, 1951, p. 7)

Perhaps understandably, Bach and his colleagues were defensive about accusations that they pursued knowledge "only for knowledge's sake." They saw fundamental research in business schools as a basis for solving practical business problems and involvement in research focused on business problems as contributing to better fundamental research. A key notion was that research could be both problem focused and fundamental. This was particularly conspicuous in operations research. The mathematical tools in OR included game theory, probability theory, linear and dynamic programming, and queuing theory—tools that were used in many disciplines and were (often) tools used by many at RAND and Cowles (Mirowski, 2004).

Operations research also became an important focal point for the use of the computer and its ability to solve analytical and managerial problems (Augier and Prietula, 2007).

A conspicuous example of problem-focused research at GSIA was the work by Holt, Muth, Modigliani, and Simon on a set of problems in inventory management. The inventory control project sought to develop theory and contribute to science, but it was fundamentally problem driven. "We didn't want to work on 'just academic problems,'" Holt recalled, "we wanted to work on *real* problems."[19] The work was centered around the Pittsburgh Plate Glass Company. The purpose was to develop analytically based tools that would improve the performance of the factory. In the course of solving the practical problems involved, the book made important technical contributions to the theory and practice of dynamic programming.

The Holt-Simon-Modigliani-Muth collaboration resulted in the development of several significant models, as evidenced in the resulting book, *Planning Production, Inventories and Work Force* (Holt et al., 1960) as well as several papers (for example, Holt and Modigliani, 1961; Muth, 1961). The group developed a model involving quadratic payoff functions with linear constraints, building on a mathematical model from control theory. This was ultimately extended to produce a general model of how to run a paint factory (as a model for other factories), with production—employment scheduling and the like. After some considerable problems in securing acceptance of the scheme within the company, the group ultimately was able to exhibit large improvements in the practice of the PPG factory.

The work in operations research joined easily at GSIA with work on decision making and organizations, exhibiting an unusual combination of rational and behavioral approaches to choice. For example, Modigliani, who was in most respects a committed "rational economic actor" theorist, had earlier noted in an *American Economic Review* discussion paper his unhappiness with traditional economic theory's inability to explain behavior under uncertainty:

> Even in those cases where the theory of rational behavior exists, we frequently suspect that actual behavior follows from a different pattern, and that this pattern is not an erratic one. This pattern may be simply irrational. . . . or

it may be rational, or close to it, though in a sense not fitting our postulate of rationality. For instance, the cost of making the best decision, both psychological and material, is hardly taken into account in our theorizing, though it may in fact be a very important factor in explaining rule of thumb and non-optimal decisions. (Modigliani, 1949, p. 203)

Decision theory had flourished in the context of operations research, particularly in the context of research at RAND. Much of the activity at RAND had decision making at its core (Simon, 1991, p. 131). This research stimulated interest not only in optimization problems but also in understanding the ways in which actual decisions were made in actual organizations and how organizations learn from their experience. These lines of research made it natural for GSIA to establish close working connections not only with RAND but also with the Cowles Commission of the University of Chicago (see Chapter Four), where Jacob Marschak and Roy Radner were beginning the work that would lead to their theory of teams (Marshack and Radner, 1972).

In the 1950s, Cowles and GSIA initiated a series of formal cooperative agreements. These agreements made Cowles discussion papers and seminars available to GSIA scholars, made GSIA research notes on organization theory available to Cowles scholars, made Herbert Simon formally a consultant to Cowles, and provided for the establishment of a series of special Cowles Commission–Carnegie Institute Conferences. These included a conference on organizations held in 1952 at Carnegie with an emphasis on how organizations influence economic behavior. It was attended by people from Cowles (including Jacob Marschak, Tjalling Koopmans, and Leonid Hurwicz) and from Carnegie (including Cooper, David Rosenblat, and Simon). A follow-up conference was arranged at the University of Chicago and also included a future Carnegie faculty member, Franco Modigliani.[20]

Along the way, GSIA became a major source of theoretical ideas about how organizations make decisions and learn (Cyert and March, 1963; March and Simon, 1958). The research included field studies of organizations, laboratory studies of decision making and learning, and mathematical and computer-simulation models of organizations. A whole host of ideas that subsequently considerably influenced theories of organizations, decision making, and adaptation can be seen as initiated by this work.

A symbol of this culture of research was Herbert A. Simon. He was the first social scientist (other than anthropologists) elected to the National Academy of Sciences, one of the very few who received the National Medal of Science, and the winner of the Prize in Honor of Alfred Nobel in economics. Simon's interests and style affected the GSIA culture simply by virtue of his intellectual power and the intensity of his commitment to intellectual discourse. Simon's interdisciplinary interests and research program fit the Ford Foundation vision quite well. He was interested in economics and made important contributions to it but also explored its limitations, as evidenced, for instance, in his famous paper, "A Behavioral Model of Rational Choice" (Simon, 1955), which introduced the idea of bounded rationality.

Simon was an indispensable part of the GSIA culture and typified the main themes of the postwar transformation in business schools, but he was also to some extent a symbol of the difficulty of sustaining fundamental behavioral science research in a business school. By 1960, Simon, working particularly with Allen Newell, had turned his creative attention almost entirely to artificial intelligence and cognitive psychology and away from economics and business. After the mid-1960s, he stayed at Carnegie Mellon University but moved out of GSIA. Most of his leading doctoral students (for example, Feigenbaum, Feldman, Kotovsky) ultimately had distinguished academic careers, but they found homes not in business schools but in departments of computer science or psychology, as Simon and Newell did.

Similarly, many of the distinguished faculty who left GSIA and Carnegie went not to business schools but to disciplinary departments. Harold Guetzkow, James G. March, and Harrison White all went to social science departments (though March later moved partly to a business school). Robert Lucas, Edwin Mansfield, Merton Miller, Franco Modigliani, John Muth, and Richard Nelson went to economics departments (though in some cases with links to business schools).

Overall, GSIA faculty research created or profoundly influenced several fields of study, most notably organization studies, strategic management, information processing perspectives on management, linear and dynamic programming, accounting theory, decision theory, transaction cost economics, uses of statistics in accounting, analysis of financial risk, rational expectations theory, and game theoretic, statistical, and other mathematical approaches to accounting. The success of GSIA in such projects, along with the parallel successes of other schools favored by Ford Foundation grants (notably Chicago, Berkeley, MIT, Stanford), was a critical part of the postwar changes in North American business schools.

7.6   ANOTHER LEGEND

GSIA became a poster child of the reforms and, ultimately, a legend of the period. It pioneered a new version of management education and a new version of a business school. Kermit Gordon, who served as a member of the Council of Economic Advisors and director of the budget under Lyndon Johnson and later was president of the Brookings Institutions, said in a oral interview in 1972:

> Today it is widely recognized that one of the most important, and certainly the most influential, graduate school of business administration in America is the Carnegie Tech Graduate School of Industrial Administration. It has done more, I think, to influence the strategy and structure and general level of intellectual respectability of graduate business education than any school; more so than Harvard and I think the people of Harvard would concede on this.[21]

In particular, in retrospect, it is clear that for about fifteen to twenty years GSIA was an extraordinary place for research. Testimony on that point can be had from any number of the people involved (for example, Ijiri, 2004, p. 110; Leavitt, 1996, pp. 288–300; Modigliani, 2001, pp. 85–86; Starbuck, 1993; Williamson, 1996); and although personal testimony can be notoriously self-serving, the independent evidence is strong. A small faculty and small student body generated a large output of influential research.

Among the faculty, Abraham Charnes and William Cooper produced a series of articles that considerably shaped the development of operations research. Robert Lucas built on the ideas of John Muth to formulate the basic ideas of what came to be called "rational expectations theory." Edwin Mansfield began his work on technological change and innovation. Harrison White started his work on vacancy chains. Richard Nelson (in conjunction with Sidney Winter) initiated new directions in evolutionary economics. Franco Modigliani and Merton Miller published their ideas on the cost of capital and theories of investment. Richard Cyert, James March, and Herbert Simon produced a series of studies and two books that became foundations for the field of organization studies. Harold Leavitt contributed a series of studies and a much-admired textbook on managerial psychology. Simon and Allen Newell began a research program that would influence considerably the field of cognitive psychology and artificial intelligence. Victor Vroom published his much-cited book on the motivational bases of work.

Among the students, Davidson, Pounds, and Dill became deans of major business schools. Feigenbaum, Feldman, and Newell became leaders of the new field of artificial intelligence. Williamson pioneered transaction cost economics and ultimately received the Nobel Prize in Economics. Prescott began his work on business cycles, and Mortensen began his work in labor economics, for which each later received the Nobel Prize. Muth published the first paper with the fundamental result underlying rational expectations theory, and Lucas began the elaborations that ultimately earned him a Nobel Prize. Starbuck became an early editor of the premier organizations research journal and Lewin the first editor of its major modern competitor. Pondy, before his untimely death, was recognized as a major contributor to organization studies. Ando, Crane, and Ijiiri became distinguished figures in business school research.

Ultimately, Lucas, March, Modigliani, Newell, Simon, White, and Williamson were all elected to the National Academy of Sciences; Feigenbaum was elected to the National Academy of Engineering. March, Simon, Starbuck, Vroom, and Williamson all received the Scholarly Contributions to Management Award from the Academy of Management. Lucas, Miller, Modigliani, Mortensen, Prescott, Simon, and Williamson all received Nobel Prizes in Economics.

What made GSIA so special? Although lists of factors generated by observers tend to sound suspiciously consistent with their prior prejudices and suffer from the problem of distinguishing causality from covariation, a few may be worth noting.

One factor frequently cited is the interdisciplinary spirit of the school. For example, Simon recalled,

> In almost all projects faculty from diverse backgrounds worked hand in hand. Everyone was encouraged to approach whatever problems they tackled in the most fundamental way, using whatever tools—mathematics, computer simulation, systematic empirical work in the field, plain English words—seemed to be useful for the task. The constant mingling of disciplines caused many ideas to stray across disciplinary boundaries—from economics to psychology and back—so that economics illuminated organization theory and vice versa.[22]

As dean, Lee Bach decreed that GSIA would not have any departments. Bach wanted all faculty to interact without respect to discipline. In practice, they did so. Participants in faculty seminars routinely challenged or elaborated presentations across disciplines.

A second factor that is cited is the extent to which collegial interaction occurred without distinctions of labels or status. In particular, the status distinctions among faculty or between faculty and students were largely ignored. Younger faculty members routinely challenged their elders. There was very close interaction between faculty members and students. "Graduate students were really treated like jewels," Feldman recalled.[23]

A third factor was the GSIA attitude toward "relevance." Fundamental research was honored without regard to current discernable relevance. It was assumed that any good idea would ultimately find its own usefulness, but it was not viewed as helpful to insist on justification in terms of relevance. This suited Simon particularly well, and he was always cheerful when reminising about the early GSIA spirit: "No one ever asked (or hardly ever), 'what does this have to do with business management?'"[24]

A fourth factor was a collection of features—small size, lack of history or a sense of it, and a Protestant work ethic that encouraged innovation. There was no heritage to be acknowledged, or at least none that was acknowledged. There was no model to be imitated. There were few barriers to interaction. The emphasis on work was unremitting. Most conspicuously of all, there was arrogance. Even before there was any persuasive external basis for such a judgment, the faculty viewed itself as an elite cadre, better than any other, and passionately communicated that confidence to its students and to outsiders.

All of these factors seem reasonable, but they seem better recognized as necessary than as sufficient causes. Other factors have been cited, but the truth is that no one knows, and the search for reasons by looking at the practices of GSIA may be misguided. There clearly are factors other than those associated with the way the organization functioned. Undoubtedly, there was good judgment in personnel. Undoubtedly, there was luck in timing. Undoubtedly, GSIA's reputation was enhanced by its irrelevance in the competition for ranking among major business schools. The reforms needed heroes, and heroes could be more tolerated at an inconspicuous school than at one of the main contenders for rank.

Moreover, it may be well to contemplate the extent to which the distinctive standing of GSIA depended on the distinctive standing of one man, Herbert A. Simon. Simon was a giant of American social science. His works, as well as his person, were well known and widely admired in several disciplines. Although, as we have seen, GSIA's research program also involved a number of other distinguished scholars, the stellar research reputation of the school in the early years was tied to Simon's reputation to a considerable extent. It declined when he became less prominent in the school. To be sure, the decline can be attributed to the simultaneous departure from the school of other major figures, but it seems probable that none of the "factors" commonly cited as leading to GSIA's position would have produced the results without Simon's presence.

All of the necessary qualifications about the difficulty of understanding the phenomenon notwithstanding, the indisputable fact remains that GSIA was a place where almost all of the changes that were advocated by the postwar reformers were implemented and where their hopes for favorable consequences were realized. As a result, the GSIA story became a story of a glorious time and place that accumulated more luster as the years went on. In time, GSIA was probably remembered more fondly than it was experienced, probably acknowledged more fervently than it was remembered, probably honored more than it warranted; but it became an obvious legend of the revolution.

Chapter Eight

Spreading the Gospel of Change

A vision of enlisting fundamental knowledge, particularly knowledge drawn from mathematics, science, and the behavioral sciences, in the service of economic and social policy attracted many of the leading scholars and political and business leaders of the postwar era. It was a vision that was reflected and refined at RAND, as well as at the National Science Foundation, the National Research Council, and the Social Science Research Council. It was adopted by the Ford Foundation in its efforts to define a role for itself. The vision found expression in many visionary hopes after the war, including hopes for changes in business schools and management education.

The vision spread less by broadcast from any single source (for example, RAND, GSIA, or the Ford Foundation) than by the generation of parallel efforts in numerous institutions and by a mobile and ambitious faculty and administration in business schools. The schools were expanding; they were recruiting newly trained young faculty with the aspirations and methods of postwar science; they saw opportunities to make substantial improvements in the academic standing of business schools in universities. As Pfeffer and Fong (2002, p. 92) observed, "In implicitly or explicitly rejecting the so-called trade-school model, business schools gained respectability and approval on their campuses."

8.1 The Dissemination of a Vision

The times were favorable. There was support from significant business leaders for a new approach to management education, and an emerging demand for a better education of managers. The MBA became not only in high demand but also respectable. In 1969, an article in *Fortune Magazine* noted that business schools had raised academic standards and also were hiring scholarly stars from the disciplines (Zalanznick, 1986). The postwar era of growth had produced a rising wave of discipline-trained faculty in business schools who provided particularly eager allies for the kinds of changes proposed by the Ford Foundation message and program.

Change occurred in many different places and assumed many different forms, and the relations among changes in different institutions at different times involved something more than simple imitation. For instance, at the University of Texas, a book about the university reported that the members of the faculty were "sensitive to the need for broad general education, even before the Gordon and Howell and the Pierson reports were issued" (Smith, 1962, p. 75). When the major studies on business education were received, the reports were reviewed by the faculty in order to determine "how the recommendations advanced would fit the requirements of a school of business in a state university of the Southwest" (Ibid., p. 146). Specialized programs were cut, and more emphasis was put on more rigorous courses and the use of computational methods (Ibid., p. 147).

The revolution produced changes in institutions and in scholarly fields. Merton Miller, who was on the faculty at GSIA before moving to Chicago and who shared the Nobel Prize in Economics in 1990, reflected on how modern finance resulted from the unique "blending" that business schools could provide of foundational or theoretical approaches and empirical research (Miller, 1986). It was a blend familiar to Miller's colleagues who shared in the prize. Harry Markowitz had spent much of his career at the RAND Corporation, and William Sharpe was on the faculty at the Stanford Graduate School of Business.

Despite the generality of the spirit of optimism and the breadth of the effects achieved, the reforms of the 1950s and 1960s, for the most part, did not represent a revolution of the masses. There were supporters, even enthusiasts, in various places; but the bulk of business school faculties throughout North America were probably not particularly attracted to the new agenda. Some faculties were openly hostile, as were some officials in major associations. The faculty and administration at some premier business schools were largely indifferent or inclined to say (and believe) that they were already fulfilling the "new" (or better) expectations. For many of the lesser-known schools, the terms of discourse about contributions to fundamental research were terms from some distant planet. The forces in opposition were largely muted by the times, but they were extensive and did not disappear. Their day would come.

The Ford Foundation assumed leadership of a program to stimulate and support change in management research and education. The reformers did not think in terms of a broad-based pattern of support. Foundation officers were clear in seeing the movement toward change as more of an elite coup d'état than a popular revolutionary response to a groundswell of discontent among ordinary faculty, business people, or alumni. They embraced a "trickle-down" view of change in which changes in elite schools were seen as leading inexorably to changes throughout business schools.

Most of the efforts of the Ford Foundation were focused on a few leading schools in expectation that others would follow. Ford was careful to enlist (and to offer financial incentives to) the major "centers of excellence" among business schools. The strategy led to relatively substantial grants to schools such as the Harvard Business School, the Columbia University Business School, the Wharton School at the University of Pennsylvania, the University of Chicago Graduate School of Business, the University of California, Berkeley, School of Business, the Sloan School of Management at the Massachusetts Institute of Technology, and the Stanford University Graduate School of Business.

Except for the Sloan School, which was new, these were high-ranking business schools. Moreover, they were housed at elite universities in which pressures to make the business school more respectable academically were generated and sustained. The response in some of the schools was lukewarm, but generally the foundation was able to encourage elite transformations.

Doubtless for reasons that extended beyond the resources provided by the foundation but were facilitated by those funds, there were observable changes in leading schools.

The strategy of directing Ford Foundation attention to the leading schools was a defensible one, but it was not certain to work. The "trickle down" of changes at leading schools to less prominent schools was inhibited by the extent to which leading schools were distinctly different from less prominent schools. A rich, private, graduate school of business located in a prestigious academic institution was not automatically a model for a poor, public, undergraduate school located at a university of modest reputation.

The foundation also made the somewhat problematic assumption that leading schools would be susceptible to reform. Precisely by virtue of their status rankings, leading schools might be imagined to be self-satisfied and resistant to external pressures for significant change. The prestigious are rarely revolutionaries. The Graduate School of Industrial Administration at the Carnegie Institute of Technology illustrates the point. GSIA became a model for the "new look" in management education. It was, however, not a leading school. It was a newly established, small school located not at a major university but at a second-tier institute of technology. It had few students, a small faculty, virtually no alumni, and no reputation. Although these attributes made GSIA especially vulnerable to radical reform, they made the school, by the same token, an unlikely model for imitation by business schools wishing to follow highly rated schools.

For the Ford Foundation strategy to work, leading schools had to become more like GSIA, but there was very little chance that they would do so in anything approaching a slavish way. No leading school would easily become an explicit "follower," least of all a follower of a new school. Each school would have to imagine that it invented a new direction. Whatever course was followed would be seen as a distinctive "Harvard Way" at Harvard, "Wharton Way" at Wharton, "Chicago Way" at Chicago, and "Stanford Way" at Stanford. Whatever local histories were written would overlook the extent to which the local orchestration of change involved a variation on themes of Flexner, RAND, Hutchins's Chicago, the Ford Foundation, GSIA, and the overall spirits of the time.

We explore this interaction of the global spirit of reform, the elements of history, and the history and arrogance of uniqueness in a few leading schools of business. Any such exploration is incomplete, both in the small number of schools examined and in the limitations of archival search. We consider particularly how the desires of the present fit into the memories and artifacts of the past. Each leading business school had a distinct history that shaped its adaptation to the revolution. Each institution had its own story, replete with its own heroes and its own picture of its own centrality.

The major North American business schools were mostly founded during a relatively short period around the start of the twentieth century; all struggled to achieve stability within relatively hostile academic environments; and all shared the rigors of survival during the Great Depression of the 1930s. However, their individual histories were remarkably different. Each found a different route to survival, a route that affected the response to pressures to change in the 1950s and 1960s.

In the following brief ministries, we try to capture some of the distinctive ways in which the specific historical evolution of four different business schools—the Harvard Business School, the Wharton School at the University of Pennsylvania, the University of Chicago Graduate School of Business, and the Stanford University Graduate School of Business—affected both the way they participated in the changes following the Second World War and the stories they tell.

Harvard Business School

The Ford Foundation and the movement for change had to deal with the Harvard Business School. HBS was generally conceded to be the premier business school in the world of 1950. The leadership at Ford had strong connections to HBS. Both Thomas Carroll and Donald David had been on the faculty there, and David had been dean. They were perceived at Ford as advocates for business schools, and any such advocacy was viewed as necessarily advocacy for HBS. It was expected by them, and by the leadership at HBS, that any program of support for management education would necessarily involve support for HBS.

Nevertheless, the school was not an easy target for the Ford Foundation. The changes foundation leaders were advocating threatened some of the established bases of the HBS reputation and the ideology of instruction that permeated the institution. HBS had endured a long history of debate about fundamental knowledge, professionalism, rigor, and relevance, as well as a long history of coping with the academic armaments of Harvard University. The school prided itself on its success in resolving the issues in a way that provided it with a rationale for its particular conception of business education and business research.

The earliest suggestion that Harvard might want to explore possibilities for professional education in business came from Harvard's overseers in 1869. The original suggestion morphed very slowly into a proposal for a school of business, but there was no immediate response. Charles Eliot, during his presidency at Harvard, had been involved in the transformation or creation of professional education at the graduate level in several fields (medicine, law, botany), but business was to come last. Indeed, Eliot at first saw little room for undergraduate business education because he felt that "thorough mental training" was essential for business, and that was to be found in liberal arts undergraduate education (Hawkins, 1972, p. 219).

In 1889, however, Eliot suggested that the university consider establishing a school in diplomacy and government, a suggestion that led ultimately (in 1906) to Eliot appointing Frank Taussig as chair of a committee to consider a graduate-level school that would be designed to offer training both in public service and in business. Taussig was an economist who thought that a graduate education for business that was based on economics could improve business practice. His own work had been used among businessmen and politicians who opposed protective tariffs for manufacturers in the United States, and he had served as chairman of the U.S. Tariff Commission.

In 1907, A. Lawrence Lowell (who became president at Harvard in 1910 after Eliot), wrote a letter to Taussig (who had asked for Lowell's advice):

You particularly ask for my opinion on the public service part of it; and I will say frankly that I do not like it. . . . In the business side of the plan I take a great deal more interest. . . . [However] I feel very doubtful whether any such idea would commend itself to the economists any more than a law school of our type would ever commend itself to professors of jurisprudence. (Copeland, 1958, p. x)

Lowell's prediction of resistance from disciplinary economists was consistent with those made by many in the academy. As one early instructor in marketing at the HBS recalled:

By many professors and by numerous Harvard Alumni, it was deemed to be degrading for the University to offer instruction in the venal subject of Business Management. Some of the academic animosity toward the young Business School was outrightly expressed. Some of it was covert, albeit thinly concealed. Later, as an instructor in Marketing in the School, I was made especially aware of the academic animosity toward us, for with the development of the courses in Marketing some of the sharpest barbs of the critics were directed at that subject as being one particularly unworthy of academic recognition. (Copeland, 1958, p. 17)

Beginning in 1900, Taussig and William Morse Cole had taught some business-related courses in the economics department, but the first real cohort of business students began in 1908 with twenty-four regular students and thirty-five other students taking only certain courses. The fledgling status of management education was recognized in a brochure published that year:

Unlike the older professions, with their well-established University instruction and tried methods, Business, as a department of University training, has still, to a large extent, to invent its appropriate means of instruction and to form its own traditions. (Copeland, 1958, p. 27)

The first head of the program, Edwin Gay, believed that business schools should teach students about the societal role of business, and he also had an approach to business education that was broader than instruction in the specialized functions of business. He wrote in 1909 about the science (and teaching) of business:

I am constantly being told by business men that you cannot teach business. . . . I heartily agree with them; we do not try to teach business in the sense in which business men ordinarily understand their routine methods, or in the sense in which you speak of teaching young men to be "money makers" or "to get the better of their competitors." We believe that there is science in business, and it is the task of studying and developing that science in which we are primarily interested. It is our aim to give our young business men the breadth of horizon, as well as the equipment of information and grasp of principles, which will enable them, as you say, to be better citizens and men of culture, as well as broader men of business. (Gay, cited in Cruickshank, 1987, p. 54)

Under Gay's leadership, efforts to produce "broader men of business" included a course in business policy (Copeland, 1958, p. 43) that reflected a commitment to "general management" that would continue to distinguish the rhetoric of HBS.

The program in business remained inconspicuous at Harvard until Edwin Gay resigned in 1919. Gay's departure gave Lowell, who by that time had become president of the university, a new opportunity to shape the school. He chose Wallace Donham as the new dean. Lowell noted retrospectively:

When [Gay] left the position open, my mind turned at once to Donham. . . . I offered him the position and he accepted at once. . . . I found that his ideas were extraordinarily like mine in a general way, in dealing with the problem as to what a professional school should be. He felt that it should have its own atmosphere, its own temperament, its own standards, its own loyalties. (Cruickshank, 1987, p. 95)

Donham had been a student of Lowell and had business experience as a banker. He had given lectures at the school before but had no other experience in education, although he had strong beliefs about the importance of education for business. Whereas Gay and the former president, Eliot, believed in the role of general knowledge as a basis for learning about business, Donham looked for an alternative that would build on the earlier idea of providing "laboratories" in which students could learn about the realities of business.

The idea of "laboratories" elided to the idea of "cases." Donham was a graduate of the Harvard Law School, as were both Lowell and Taussig; so, perhaps not coincidentally, their model became not the disciplines but the law school. The adoption of the case method at HBS was at least in part a result of Donham's desire to reinvent the school in a way closer to the practice of business; and to close the gap between his own lack of knowledge in theoretical aspects of business and (what he found to be) the faculty's lack of interest in practice.

However, the primary motor for the adoption of the case method lay in stories about its early successes. One instance of such stories involved a marketing professor, Melvin Copeland. As the story was recorded, Donham had asked Copeland to reorient his marketing course around case studies, in part because students found Copeland's classes boring. Using cases as a mode of teaching coincided with a reduction in student complaints. Copeland became a popular teacher, produced the first case book at Harvard (Copeland, 1920), and was appointed director of a center to convert statistical data to case collections.

The Harvard Business School invested much of its early financial and political resources in the development and legitimization of cases and the case method of instruction. Donham noted in his report for the 1920–1921 school year:

> When the case system is once installed, the expense of keeping it up to date should be considered a part of the cost of instruction, but this initial cost is in the nature of a capital expense. (Copeland, 1958, p. 104)

It turned out to be a good investment. The school thrived both financially and in terms of reputation. In 1922, the school was authorized to grant a Doctor of Commercial Science degree, and it quickly became the preeminent training ground for professors of business in North America. With only a slight hiccup in 1932, enrollment grew rapidly. So did the endowment. Cases became a major source of revenue as Harvard case studies were sold to business school programs across the country.

As the country moved into the postwar era, HBS had established itself as the best-known and best-endowed business school in the world. The connections between the Ford Foundation and the school were substantial. Thomas Carroll, one of the key Ford Foundation executives in charge of the programs for management education, had previously been an assistant dean at the Harvard Business School, and Donald David, who became a trustee at the Ford Foundation in 1948 and had good personal relations with Henry Ford, had been dean. Indeed, Henry Ford had asked David to become president of the foundation, an invitation that David declined. David was an important force behind the scenes for implementing the Gaither Report at Ford and for getting Gaither on the board, too; he was also actively involved in the reorganization of the foundation that began with Gaither's presidency later.

Given the extent of the linkages and the position of HBS among North American business schools, it was natural for people at Ford to see success in reforming management education as requiring the involvement of HBS. As one Ford Foundation insider reported:

> Harvard met all of the official criteria [for being a center of excellence in the Ford Foundation initiatives in business education], although the non-scholars on the right bank of the Charles far outnumbered the few genuine scholars who had taken up residency there. There were many special reasons, however, why the Harvard Business School had to head any list: by size and history it dominated business education to the extent any school could; it carried high the banner of "administration and general management" . . . and two of the three strategists, Carroll and David, had been intimately associated with it.[1]

Although the financial strength of the HBS made foundation support a less significant factor there than equivalent support to another school would have been, Harvard became one of the principal beneficiaries of foundation grants. However, the spirit of the foundation program as it developed out of its Flexner, Hutchins, RAND, and postwar operations research and mathematical social science roots was quite distant from the traditions and primary capabilities of HBS.

HBS had pioneered an approach that explicitly modeled management education on law school education—with its focus on cases rather than on medical school education with its focus on fundamental scientific knowledge. It valued its close consultative relations with the business community and published a leading journal, the *Harvard Business Review*, that was oriented strongly to providing practical information for managers. Most faculty at the school were better known for their development of business cases and related consulting services than they were for their contributions to major scholarly journals.

The Harvard Business School spoke with more than one voice; but the institution, in general, prided itself on its cases and was, at best, tolerant of the postwar emphasis on mathematics, statistics, theoretical economics, interdisciplinary work, and the other accoutrements of the "new" academic social science. HBS had turned back repeated efforts by other parts of Harvard University, particularly its arts and sciences faculties and its presidents, to make the school more academically respectable through more academic research and a greater commitment to academic definitions of fundamental knowledge. The school was successful in its own market, was well-connected to important Harvard alumni, and it was rich—three properties that made it less susceptible than others to the administrative pressures of university presidents, the persistent scorn of disciplinary faculty, or the monetary blandishments of the Ford Foundation.

A conspicuous thrust of the postwar reforms was to reduce the significance of several of the more treasured aspects of HBS, especially its emphasis on cases and consultation and its deemphasis of academic research. The people both at the foundation and at HBS were aware of the potential mismatch between the main objectives of the program and the main commitments at HBS. Both groups chose, however, to be flexible. On the one hand, there was little inclination among the Ford Foundation staff to eliminate case methods of instruction from business education. Indeed, the foundation provided substantial support for improving the quality of cases and their dissemination.

At the same time, the HBS took steps during the 1950s to reflect the new trends. In 1955, it used money from Ford to support two research professorships, one chosen from the ranks of HBS professors, one from Harvard's Department of Social Relations. In 1956, the faculty considered "the inclusion of statistical and mathematical techniques in our basic curriculum," and a seminar on mathematics was offered to a small group of HBS faculty to enhance their quantitative skills. In 1957, Howard Raiffa, Raymond Bauer, and Renato Taguiri were appointed to the faculty to create faculty research training courses and to serve as "transmission lines with the behavioral sciences." Raiffa, in particular, proved to be an inspired choice who bridged the HBS gap between excellence in mathematical statistics and excellence in the practice of management. In 1958, the faculty approved a major expansion of the doctoral program with Ford Foundation support. And in 1959, HBS established a twelve-month "Institute of Basic Mathematics for Application to Business" to teach faculty in business doctoral programs at thirty-two universities.

In effect, HBS and the Ford Foundation entered into a marriage of convenience for which neither had unbounded enthusiasm, but each found more useful than open hostility. In retrospect, the calculations on both sides may have been correct. The foundation, by involving HBS in the initiative, neutralized a major potential opponent within the community of business schools and avoided a risky confrontation. The Harvard Business School, for its part, probably lost position in the short run as a result of the changes that occurred in management education. It became less important in the training of business school professors and slipped in ratings of business schools made by business school faculty and deans. However, by not being overtly antagonistic, the school retained the possibility of subsequently introducing elements of the changes and of recovering much of its earlier position.

Over time, without compromising its fundamental culture, HBS used its resources to appoint more research-oriented faculty and to forge collaborative doctoral programs with disciplinary departments at Harvard. Indeed, early in the twenty-first century, an untenured faculty member at HBS created a blog on the web in which he accused Harvard presidents Derek Bok and Lawrence Summers of

> ... pushing very hard to increase the academic respectability of HBS, using the club of the President's control of the tenure process. . . . [The result] was that HBS began to hire more "outsiders," respected business scholars from leading research institutions. This set in motion a process of increasing "capture" of HBS by discipline-oriented academics and strengthened the forces taking the school in the direction of academic respectability. This process of capture has continued through the administration of the current Dean, Kim Clark (himself an economist). It has accelerated recently because the school has reached a "tipping point" in terms of the declining influence of the old guard and the rise of the young academics.[2]

The complaint may have had some merit, but the commitment of HBS to consulting was not abandoned. In 2010, the Harvard Business Press (the publishing arm of HBS) published a book by Walter Kiechel III the former editorial director of the press, extolling the role of consulting and consulting firms in the development of what he called the "corporate strategy revolution" (Kiechel, 2010). The book contrasts the intellectual success of ideas emanating from consulting firms, particularly those of HBS product Bruce Henderson at the Boston Consulting Group, with the failure of ideas from more academic research on organizations (Ibid., pp. 161–164).

The Wharton School of the University of Pennsylvania

The Wharton School, alone among the schools considered here, was heavily involved in undergraduate business education as well as graduate. It was also less tightly linked by personal or professional connections to the leaders of the reform efforts. Wharton's response reflected the general tenor of the times as interpreted through special features of that school's program and history. As a result of the school's long-established emphasis on multiple, specific fields of business, changes were less focused on conceptions of business management as involving general skills in problem solving and decision making than were Ford-supported changes elsewhere; and Wharton never became the darling of the reformers. Nevertheless, Wharton received substantial Ford Foundation support, and the school changed in ways that were generally consistent with most of the main thrusts of the reforms.

The idea of a business school at the University of Pennsylvania was proposed to the trustees of the university by Joseph Wharton in 1881. Wharton's parents had wanted to send him to Harvard, but because of illness he stayed in Philadelphia where he became interested and competent in chemistry before being apprenticed by his parents to a counting house to learn business procedures. Ultimately, he established himself in industrial metallurgy and became a successful businessman.

Wharton became convinced that the problems of industrial operations in a firm should be approached through "systematic management, rather than searching for some unusual or extraordinary man" (Taylor, 1923, p. 3).

Toward this end, at one point he hired Frederick Taylor as a consultant to install a system of scientific management at his company. His business experience led him to a conviction that the apprentice system of training in business was obsolete.

Wharton complained that the existing commercial colleges trained men "to become clerks, not business leaders." He wanted business to build on social science because he felt that social science provided the best conceptual background for business problems, and he also wanted to create a liberally educated class of leaders for American society. Consequently, he wanted business training to be embedded in a university. In his March 24, 1881, memorandum to the trustees of the University of Pennsylvania, he wrote:

> I hereby propose to endow the school with the securities below named, amounting to $100,000. . . . To provide for young men special means of training and of correct instruction in the knowledge and in the arts of modern Finance and Economy, both public and private, in order that, being well informed and free from delusions upon these important subjects, they may either serve the community skillfully as well as faithfully in offices of trust, or, remaining in private life, may prudently manage their own affairs and aid in maintaining sound financial morality: in short, to establish means for imparting a liberal education in all matters concerning Finance and Economy.[3]

Wharton urged the trustees to place business education on a level with education for other professional callings—lawyers, doctors, clergymen—by creating a comparable school. His vision was unabashedly elitist, seeing the possibility of creating a new cadre of leaders for society:

> It is reasonable to expect that adequate education in the principles underlying successful business management and civil government would greatly aid in producing a class of men likely to become pillars of the State, whether in private or in public life. An opportunity for good seems here to exist, and fairly comparable with that so largely and profitably availed of by the technical and scientific Schools.[4]

After some jostling between Wharton and the university, the Wharton School opened its doors in 1883. Much of the subsequent history of the school has been written in terms of two tensions: The first is the tension between specialized subfields and more general management, and the second is the tension between practical knowledge and academic knowledge. With respect to the first, general management had a harder time at Wharton than at Harvard. Management was not seen as a separate category or function. There was bank management or transportation management but not "just" management. With some variations over time, the school grew to emphasize the specialized subfields of business, such as banking and finance, marketing, transportation, and accounting.

With respect to academic knowledge and practical knowledge, Joseph Wharton recognized (and endorsed) the tension, but he placed an emphasis on introducing fundamental knowledge:

> Instead of teaching and perpetuating the narrow, various, and empirical routines of certain shops, they base their instruction upon the broad principles deduced from all human knowledge, and ground in science, as well as in art, pupils who are thereby fitted both to practice what they have learned and to become themselves teachers and discoverers. (cited in Sass, 1982, p. 22)

As the school evolved, it followed a course for a while that took it in the direction of becoming a more general school of political and social science before turning its emphasis more narrowly to business, but Joseph Willits, who became dean in 1933, shifted the focus to a greater attention to scholarship:

> . . . just as a medical school, or any other professional school worth the name, is not performing its full function unless it is contributing to thoroughgoing research on the fundamental problems in the field of medicine, so should a . . . school of business aim to contribute its share toward the solution of the fundamental problems of business.[5]

The research tradition would subsequently be involved in postwar efforts at reform, but the advocates for more fundamental scholarship were confronted consistently with their critics. For example, in the 1950s debates among the faculty, one leading faculty member commented:

> . . . the public at large has differences in tastes and the Wharton School offers an excellent education for business for those whose intellect will be stimulated more by a study of business than by a study of the liberal arts.[6]

Despite these reservations, the calls for reform after the Second World War resonated with Wharton history. Substantial involvement in consulting and reduced attention to fundamental research made the school vulnerable to the critiques of business school reformers. At the same time, however, the history of concern about scholarship and science at Wharton provided the school with both an historic basis for joining the reform and with active groups in the school predisposed to the changes.

Any change, however, would have to deal with two distinctive features of the Wharton setting: First, undergraduate education was a major part of the Wharton tradition and involved a major part of the resources and faculty. Second, Wharton business education placed an emphasis on specialization. Finance, marketing, insurance, accounting, production, and other fields had autonomous standing. Because a main thrust of the reforms was to emphasize graduate education and to deemphasize specialization, they encountered considerable opposition among Wharton faculty, alumni, and students.

On the other hand, concerns about improving the quality of students and faculty found greater support. The problems at Wharton were seen as partly related to weakness in the university as a whole; and when, in 1953, a leading physicist, Gaylord P. Harnwell, was named as president of the university, he and his supporters on the board undertook a program of renewal for the university. As part of that program, the university launched a five-year educational survey of the university. The survey included a section on Wharton that involved people from both academia and business. The Ford Foundation program provided grants of $10,000 in 1955 and $50,000 in 1956 in support of these efforts.

In anticipation of the educational survey, the school created a "presurvey" committee, chaired by Reavis Cox. In its report of November 1956,[7] the committee recommended that the educational survey focus on four questions:

- What are the goals and objectives of the Wharton School? Is it a school of administration? Or a school for training in functional business specialties? Or a school of social science? Or a school the goes in whatever direction the talents of faculty take it?

- What is the relation between the Wharton School and the University of Pennsylvania? How are teaching functions allocated between the school and other units of the university? How are university funds allocated?

- How can Wharton best deal with internal problems facing it? Specifically, how should it be organized? How can it arrange the integration of social science with management education? What teaching methods should be used? How are new mathematical and computational theories and techniques to be introduced? How can the faculty be strengthened?

- What resources and funds are essential?

The recommendations of questions to be asked may have been useful in identifying issues, but they provided little guide to the answers. To develop ideas further, the school created a board of consultants, generally called the James Committee after its chair, F. Cyril James, who had previously been on the Wharton faculty but was at the time of his service in this capacity a vice chancellor and principal of McGill University.[8]

In 1958, the James Committee issued a report that concluded the Wharton program had declined from an outstanding program to being at risk of becoming a run-of-the-mill program. The committee made recommendations to increase and "integrate" the exposure of undergraduates to the liberal arts. It devoted less attention to the graduate program, but it urged a faculty development program to upgrade the quality of the faculty and suggested that "attention should be given to a study of outside activities by Wharton faculty."[9]

The response of the school to the James Committee Report was measured. The first draft of the report was described by Joseph Willits as having been "met with a good deal of reserve by the faculty."[10] A committee chaired first by William Loucks and subsequently by John P. Horlacher was appointed to review the James Report and submitted alternative proposals that came to be known as the Horlacher Report.

The Horlacher Committee concluded that:

   . . . it is perhaps too early to tell whether the future path of business education lies in the direction of graduate training emphasis, or whether such emphasis is part of a more or less temporary phenomenon in educational circles. In this sense, our Five-Year Program is proposed as a systematic attempt to explore and support the graduate training movement without being definitely forced to put all our eggs in one basket.[11]

The school was conscious of the outside pressures toward reform. Sass (1982, p. 251) reports that Pierson had spent time at Wharton and that three members of the Wharton faculty had consulted with him when working on the James Report. A November 1957 draft report from the Wharton Survey Advisory Committee observed,

> Following World War II further changes took place in American business education, the most important of which, perhaps, was the emphasis on research and the utilization of empirical research methods.[12]

The report cautioned against "boarding of the fad-and-phase bandwagon." It doubted the efficacy of concentration on things such as courses in decision making, or research courses, or social science, or liberal arts:

> It is self-evident that business school curricula should be periodically overhauled and revised. But it appears equally self-evident that this process should, as far as possible, rest on a solid and demonstrable base rather than a series of temporary foundations.[13]

The Horlacher Report was, however, sharp in its critique of Wharton research efforts:

> If our aim is to raise the Wharton faculty to the number one position among business schools, this elevation can be achieved only through a diligent and continuing search for young men with research-promise, and by the creation of an academic climate favorable to sustained research efforts.[14]

There was a basis for concern about the faculty. Joseph Willits was outspoken in his characterization of the effects of the university's policies toward the financing of Wharton on faculty recruitment and retention:

> The School has long been operated as a "proprietary school" on a very low-cost basis. The figures for 1954–55 may be taken as suggestive of Wharton's history. In that academic year, the School met all of its own expenses out of tuition (and some few grants) plus its small endowment income, provided an overhead of $419,000 plus an excess of income over all expenses of

$525,000 to the University. . . . the average basic salary for Wharton full professors in 1945–55 was $7,485 which was below that of all other schools in the University except Social Work, Education, Nursing and Allied Medical Professions. It was slightly above average salaries in Social Work and Education but less than half the average salaries for full professors in the Law School.[15]

The faculty was underpaid relative to other faculties at major institutions. It was also parochial. In the fall of 1956, the faculty of the Wharton School included 245 individuals. Of the 245, 124 held the PhD degree. Of the 124, eighty-eight had received their doctorate from the Graduate School of Arts and Sciences at the University of Pennsylvania.

Much of the debate at Wharton turned on the role of an emphasis on the specialties of business (finance, accounting, marketing, transportation, and the like). Wharton spokespeople generally came down strongly on the side of specialization. "Traditional business studies"—that is, work in specialized domains of business—were defended against the pressures for Harvard-style case-based emphasis on "general management" and also against the pressures for a broad focus on "decision making" or "problem solving."

In many ways reluctantly and incompletely, and with only modest involvement in the Ford Foundation's efforts, by the end of the 1950s, the school had moved perceptively in the direction of the reforms, particularly as they affected undergraduate curricula.[16] At a meeting of the Educational Council of the University of Pennsylvania on May 14, 1959, the council approved the recommendations of its Policy Committee with respect to the recommendations of the Educational Survey of the Wharton School. The recommendations included:

- Wharton's requirements for the undergraduate degree should be increased to the equivalent of three years of academic work by expanding the requirements for courses in the liberal arts and sciences.

- Courses oriented to professional purposes should be limited to approximately one year of undergraduate academic work.

- The Wharton undergraduate program should increase the emphasis on students with superior abilities and on increasing the demands made on students and the academic opportunities for them.

- The Wharton undergraduate program should place a strong emphasis on the concepts and methods of natural science.

- However, the Educational Council specifically rejected a proposal from Wharton that the first three years of the curriculum consist in courses developed within the school that covered the "behavioral, biological, physical and social sciences, the humanities, and communications," apparently preferring that the first three years be concentrated in courses outside Wharton.

Though they were steeped in the traditions and institutional framework that the school had developed earlier, the changes at Wharton were recognizably part of the transformation of business schools from 1945 through 1970. They came with a rhetoric that embraced management science and the idea of creating a science of management and an art of business based on that science.

In 1960, Wharton received $700,000 from the Ford Foundation in support of its efforts, and the school opened a Management Science Center in 1962. There was a new commitment to academic values and fundamental research. Although Wharton persisted in maintaining a significant undergraduate program, there was an increased emphasis on graduate programs, and successful efforts to hire economics and social science faculty with distinguished research reputations. As might be expected from its history, however, Wharton responded more forcefully to strengthen fundamental research within its specialties than to move to new, interdisciplinary efforts or to broader conceptions of managerial decision making.

University of Chicago Graduate School of Business

As at other comparable schools, business education at the University of Chicago dated from the start of the twentieth century. After two years of research and planning, plans for a business school were prepared and presented to the university senate in 1894. The creation of a College of Commerce and Administration was approved. A group of courses was set up within existing departments, but financial issues delayed the plans so that no separate dean or faculty for the college existed until 1902 when a report on the organization of the College of Commerce and Administration was approved by the trustees (Marshall, 1913, p. 97).

It was an inauspicious beginning. The school was born into neither academic respectability nor innovative approaches to management education. An early dean wrote in 1913 that the school "succeeded in little more than making provision for the grouping of existing courses in economics and closely related subjects; and while its registrations rose to 261 in the academic year 1910–1911, the vitality of the college was low" (Marshall, 1913, p. 98).

A gift of $10 million to the university from John D. Rockefeller helped to fund a study (by the dean) of other North American schools of commerce and a design of an action plan for the school. The study found that the school should build its curriculum on a base of fundamental knowledge:

> The first aim is to secure for the student a broad cultural foundation in the main divisions of human knowledge. Above this foundation is placed a broad survey of social sciences. (Marshall, 1913, p. 100)

Only later in the education would students specialize and then gradually and not too narrowly.

Education in the school was clearly linked to social science, and although it was partly a "training school" it was also "partly an opportunity to extend the bounds of present knowledge." It was important that faculty did research:

> Important will be the investigations by the instructors . . . in this formative period of such education, it is clear that the college must expect to carry, as one of its most important functions, its research divisions." (Marshall, 1913, p. 103)

Over the years, the school struggled to meet the early hopes and to find a distinctive character consistent with the University of Chicago to which it was attached. The university had developed a strong program of graduate education in the disciplines, including anthropology, economics, political science, psychology, and sociology. The departments and the disciplines they defended were challenged in the 1930s by a charismatic and insistent president, Robert Maynard Hutchins, who supported the idea of a university committed to fundamental knowledge but saw the disciplines as too narrowly focused enemies of innovation. He championed interdisciplinary committees dedicated to fundamental research.

The business school had difficulty satisfying either the graduate department culture or that of the new committees. It was too broad for the former, too narrow for the latter, and not fundamental enough for either. The school gradually lost standing at the university, a process that was accentuated by the Hutchins administration. Hutchins decried any symptoms of vocationalism in higher education and had little enthusiasm for business education. Although he supported ideas for the establishment of a basic research institute in accounting and was instrumental in bringing the Cowles Commission to Chicago, his main initiatives and primary enthusiasms emphasized the humanities, fundamental scholarship, and interdisciplinary research. Hutchins also was eager to support intellectual mavericks. The Business School provided very few exemplary efforts in any of those directions.

Ultimately, however, the school's direction was considerably affected by Hutchins's success in bringing Friedrich Hayek to the university over the objections of many of the leading economists at Chicago. Over time, the directions Hayek and his disciples advocated came to dominate the Chicago Business School, though the school played no significant role in early efforts by Hutchins to bring Hayek to Chicago.

In 1951, Hutchins, who found himself increasingly at odds with the faculty (Dzubeck, 1991), left the University of Chicago to take up his position working with Paul Hoffman at the Ford Foundation. In 1956 Allen Wallis was appointed as dean of the Chicago Business School. It was a choice that both symbolized and helped realize a marriage of Chicago traditions, Ford Foundation ambitions, and Hayekian economics. Wallis was born in 1912 and studied at the University of Minnesota and Chicago and Columbia. During his career prior to becoming dean he also had been at Yale, Stanford, and the Ford Foundation. Subsequently, he was a frequent advisor to the Eisenhower and Reagan administrations and was president of the University of Rochester.

Prior to the deanship, Wallis had established a reputation as an effective research administrator by his work with the Statistical Research Group

(SRG) at Columbia University during the Second World War. The SRG was part of the National Defense Research Committee, which was part of the Office of Scientific Research and Development. It had been started by Warren Weaver and was an explicit model for the early thinking about the RAND Corporation. It resembled in many intellectual respects the Cowles Commission. Wallis later referred to SRG as "as big and brilliant a galaxy as has been collected at any one place" (Olkin, 1991, p. 124). It attracted people such as Milton Friedman, Abraham Girshick, Harold Hotelling, Frederick Mosteller, James Savage, George Stigler, Abraham Wald, and Jacob Wolfowitz. Albert Bowker, subsequently chancellor of the University of California at Berkeley, who had worked with the SRG, recalled that:

> Allen Wallis was hired to work in this group. He had been an economist but had come East to work some with Hotelling on statistical questions. It became pretty clear that he was going to have to run the group if anything happened, so he really became the director, and Hotelling was called principal investigator.[17]

There were at least three conspicuous features that Wallis brought to the deanship: (1) He was a highly regarded quantitative economist and statistician. He had no doubts about the relevance of mathematics and statistics and theoretical economics to business education. (2) He had close connections to the Ford Foundation. As a consultant to the foundation he led an overview of grants and projects for survey studies at the foundation and was also on the Ford staff for a full year.[18] He knew and had worked with the major figures involved in the foundation's programs in economics, social science, and business. (3) He knew and was known by major figures in academic economics, particularly such stars as Kenneth Arrow, Milton Friedman, Harold Hotelling, and George Stigler.

Wallis later recalled that, when he became dean at Chicago,

> . . . its period of great distinction was long past. It was nearly defunct and the university administration was considering abolishing it. (Olkin, 1991, p. 136)

Wallis and James Lorie, who worked closely with him, used the Hutchins history at Chicago, the Ford initiative, and the free-market transformations in the Chicago Department of Economics to pursue a set of changes that combined the Chicago spirit with the Ford program in a distinctive way.

Ford (like Hutchins) was committed both to fundamental research and to interdisciplinarity. Wallis's background was steeped in both. He was an economist, but he had majored in psychology as an undergraduate at the University of Minnesota and had taught statistics to students from a variety of disciplines. He was well acquainted with Bernard Berelson, the architect of the Ford Foundation program in behavioral science.

At the outset, Wallis and Lorie did what they could to encourage the Ford Foundation to view their plans for Chicago as being in line with the foundation prejudices. Their grant proposal to the foundation closely resembled G. Leland Bach's proposal for GSIA in putting economics and behavioral social science at the center of the program (van Overtveldt, 2007). When it came time for the foundation to identify "centers of excellence," they included the Chicago Graduate School of Business. Ford awarded $1,375,000 to Chicago (and a total of $2,900,000 over the period from 1954 to 1964).[19] It was a commitment, according to one observer, that reflected a hope Chicago would, with Carnegie, be a "Midwestern counterweight" to the more "clinical" program at Harvard (Schlossman, Sedlak, and Wechsler, 1998, p. 18).

As the Chicago program evolved, however, Wallis's close personal, professional, and political ties to Milton Friedman and George Stigler and a commitment to free-market economics negated any commitment to other disciplines or to interdisciplinarity. It was a direction that was anticipated (and decried) in a 1957 letter to the Ford Foundation from Aaron Gordon, in which he observed,

> Emphasis on the economic ingredient of the curriculum (and probably of a traditional Chicago mold particularly if George Stigler accepts the Walgreen professorship) might override the other social science elements.[20]

The direction was confirmed by the Wheeler Report in 1965 (Wheeler, 1965) which noted that Chicago was not successful in "its announced wedding with the social sciences" that "never came off" (p. 129). The changes reflected intellectual and institutional developments in the university, where the economic and political philosophy of Friedrich Hayek as interpreted and elaborated particularly by Milton Friedman and George Stigler and a coterie of radical free-market faculty members challenged and ultimately replaced the earlier mainline economic prejudices and personnel.

The changes did not come instantly. Initially, a deviant economics based on free-market ideology faced the hostility both of establishment economics and of the rest of social science. To establish a pocket of true believers buffered from establishment control, the Chicago disciples of Hayek set out to accomplish five things: first, to gain clear control over the economics department at Chicago; second, to extend that control to the Chicago Business School; third, to eliminate the threat from high-quality establishment economics represented at Chicago by groups such as the Cowles Commission; fourth, to replace peer-controlled (establishment) sources of funds with politically reliable sources; and fifth, to repudiate the idea that economic questions should be approached in a multidisciplinary way (because other disciplines were not only ideologically and politically hostile but also inferior). The Chicago radicals were largely successful in all of these endeavors and established a base for a different vision of economics, one that was to have considerable influence on North American business schools in the last quarter of the twentieth century.

The resulting Chicago version of management education was as stridently academic and intellectually arrogant in its pretensions as might be expected in the wake of Robert Maynard Hutchins. In that respect, it fit into the postwar reformation easily. The Chicago Graduate School of Business became a conspicuous outpost of a management education linked to fundamental knowledge and committed to a faculty distinguished by its research productivity.

However, the link to theories of free-market economics left little room for the interdisciplinary work or the behavioral sciences that Wallis's initial proposals, or the Ford initiatives generally, envisioned. Nor was there a strong basis for those parts of the postwar enthusiasms that embraced improving the rationality of collective action. The imputation of purpose (or utility functions) to nations, and thus the planned intervention of governments in markets, became mostly unacceptable.

Perhaps less obviously, the imputation of purpose to business firms became equally problematic; the whole superstructure of decision theory applied to management and operations research seemed questionable, though it was given the imaginative but somewhat uncertain foundation of agency theory by which organizational collectivities were transformed into instruments of single actors (Fama, 1980).

The directions taken by the school may have been encouraged in part by the end of Ford Foundation support and the school's increasing financial links with private conservative foundations; but one primary factor was the decision to offer the Walgreen Chair for the Study of American Institutions to George Stigler, which also made Stigler the director of the Walgreen Foundation and hence gave him substantial freedom in setting a research agenda. Just as Lee Bach's decision to bring Herbert Simon to Carnegie Tech had profound consequences for the Graduate School of Industrial Administration, the decision to bring George Stigler back to Chicago had profound consequences for the Chicago Graduate School of Business. Stigler was a smart, forceful, and overwhelmingly committed proponent of "Chicago economics."

The Stigler vision of business education was different from that at Carnegie and also from that of Wallis's early proposals. It shared the idea that the foundation for managers was academic knowledge rather than experiential knowledge and that business education should have an emphasis on quantitative methods and skills. However, there was no behavioral science involved; the neoclassical economics perspective was dominant; there was little interest in trying to understand actual business decision making; and notions of business social responsibility were subordinated to the maximization of stockholder wealth. Indeed, Stigler found the concept of social responsibility a uselessly fuzzy one:

> It is hard for me to make sense out of any concept of social responsibility which does not rely exclusively on profit maximization and conformity with the law.[21]

In the catechism as it developed, there was only one social science, and it was economics. On May 8, 1963, Wallis wrote to Stigler for advice on a report to the Ford Foundation reviewing its support for the behavioral and social sciences in the past, present, or future. Stigler responded on May 21, 1963, without any mention whatsoever of the behavioral sciences.[22] As he noted in a memo on "the Chicago view":

> [The] view of economics as *the* science of the efficient pursuit of objectives, a calculus of human rationality, gradually expanded to where it has become the dominant train of the present Chicago School.[23]

Stigler believed in interdisciplinary work, but his interdisciplinarity was imperialist. He listed several areas (for example, marriage, divorce, fertility, and altruism) as topics previously considered by other disciplines that economists could study with economic tools and economic interests.

Like the Harvard Business School, the University of Chicago Graduate School of Business established an external support group and financial base that gave it considerable independence from the broader academic community at the university and the broader association of North American business schools. The primary cost of that independence lay in the increased intellectual and political dependence on the Chicago Department of Economics, but it was a dependence from which the school undoubtedly gained more than it lost.

Despite the deviation from the Ford Foundation litany (or perhaps because of it), the transformation established the Chicago Graduate School of Business as one of the top North American schools. As an internal Ford Foundation document commented in 1965,

> The qualitative change in the programs is very difficult to evaluate but these programs appear to be regarded generally as among the top ten programs, with Carnegie Tech, Harvard and Chicago probably ranked one, two, three in that order by most people in the field. (Wheeler, 1965, p. 127)

In subsequent years, as the recognized rankings of business schools became the rankings made by various organs of the business press, and as the economics embraced by business schools generally, as well as their business constituents, became increasingly the economics expounded by the Chicago department, the school strengthened its position at or near the top of North American business schools.

Stanford University Graduate School of Business

The Stanford Graduate School of Business is perhaps the clearest example of a school reinventing itself to fit the image of the so-called New Look of business schools. An internal Ford Foundation report commented on their change:

> Stanford is the Cinderella of the business education field in that it rose in just a few years from a poor institution to one of the top five and it gives promise of being a leader for many years to come. Their research program has been slow in starting but promising signs have begun to appear and it could well be second to Carnegie Tech in research in five years. (Wheeler, 1965, p. 129)

By adopting an emphasis on research and behavioral social science, Stanford came to look quite a bit like GSIA at Carnegie (even hiring people from GSIA to reinforce the "look").

The idea of a business school at Stanford had been around from the early years of the university after its founding in 1891, but it didn't take hold until one influential alumnus, Herbert Hoover, took an active interest in the early 1920s. He brought a group of friends together at the Bohemian Club to solicit support for the creation of the school.[24] Hoover felt that the formation of the business school was part of a movement to

> . . . lift business training out of the category of formalism with its previous inclination towards vocational training in the narrower meaning of that term and to elevate it to professional dignity . . . [a movement that] . . . promises a most valuable contribution to the advancement of American education. (Hoover in Pelz, 1926, p. vii)

The president of Stanford at the time, Ray Lyman Wilbur, had clear ideas about what he thought a business school at Stanford should do, probably informed by his previous experience as dean of the medical school where he had helped restructure medical education in the post-Flexner years to build on the underlying sciences of biology and chemistry. He later reflected back on his experience as dean:

> [It] was a time of revolutionary change in the medical schools of the United States. They were discontinuing their old lecture system with staff made up

of part-time clinical professors. Many of the schools were appointing academic professors to the various medical chairs on academic salaries, with the idea that they could engage in teaching and research . . . From the first we considered research as one of the most important functions of the medical schools. (Wilbur, 1960, p. 172)

Wilbur's sentiments on business schools came to be quite similar to his views on medical schools. He wanted the school to emphasize "fundamental knowledge" and found economics and psychology to be particularly relevant underlying disciplines for understanding issues in business (Wilbur in Pelz, 1926, p. 4).

The first dean of the Business School was Willard Hotchkiss, who served from 1925 to 1931 (he was on leave 1930–1931). Hotchkiss had graduated from Cornell and taught industrial management for several years at Northwestern. He had also taught briefly in the political science department at Stanford. He was an active consultant to such enterprises as the National Industrial Federation of Clothing Manufacturers, the Institute of American Meat Packers, and the United States Coal Commission.[25]

Hotchkiss shared some of the Wilbur's sentiments, but he also saw the virtue of a close alliance with business:

However great the necessity of making business the object of systematic professional study, teachers must see to it that they draw wisely on the hidden reservoirs of educational knowledge to be found in business itself. In order that these reservoirs of experience may become accessible, it is important that the men who teach business in the universities work in close cooperation with responsible businessmen. (Hotchkiss in Pelz, 1926, p. 9)

Moreover, he was skeptical about an approach that treated economics as an adequate foundation for instruction in business:

There can be no doubt about the potential disciplinary value of studying economics. But taking the situation as we find it . . . until the objectives and the organization of economic study are somewhat further clarified, we shall probably have to admit, however much we may call economics the science of business, that there is in American universities no science of economics which can be regarded as basic for business in the sense in which doubtless biology and chemistry are basis for medicine. (Hotchkiss in Pelz, 1926, p. 20)

The school gradually added students and faculty, including J. Hugh Jackson, an accountant recruited from the Harvard Business School in 1926. Jackson became dean in 1931. He changed the focus of Stanford to be more specialized and more closely linked to business experience. He hired practitioners to serve on the faculty. Such moves, and Jackson's long tenure as dean, changed the course of the institution quite significantly. The GSB developed a focus that deemphasized research and pursued a much closer alliance with business than with academe, including the appointment of significant numbers of "consulting professors," a title accorded to teachers whose primary credentials were experiential rather than academic.

Jackson's deanship was relatively long and marked toward the end by conflict with Stanford presidents that focused on Jackson's disinterest in strengthening academic research at the school. Donald Tresidder, who served as president from 1943 to 1948 discussed with Herbert Hoover (as well as others, including Donald David from the Harvard Business School) how to improve the school, including how to replace Jackson as dean.[26]

At one point, Jackson resigned; but, due to the Tresidder's death, he was asked to stay on. In 1949, the new president (Wallace Sterling) solicited long-term plans from the various schools. The plan submitted by the GSB, with the low priority it gave to research and its emphasis on what appeared to be a predominately vocational approach to management education, pleased neither Sterling nor his powerful provost Frederick Terman.[27]

Terman had earned a degree in chemistry from Stanford in 1920 before doing his graduate work in electrical engineering at MIT, working with Vannevar Bush. Sterling and Terman had embarked on an ambitious (and ultimately successful) program to move Stanford from the ranks of good regional universities to a position as one of the premier universities in the world, a position it achieved first in its professional schools, particularly the School of Engineering. Terman, in particular, is given much of the credit for the transformation (Gillmore, 2004).

In a 1951 letter to Sterling, Jackson characterizes (accurately) the president's and provost's attitudes about the Stanford Graduate School of Business:

> (i) the School had raised no money; (ii) the School had a faculty of inferior scholarship; (iii) the School had done no worthwhile research; and (iv) the

School's alumni were not taking any important place in the business of the country.[28]

In 1956, Jackson finally retired from the deanship. His farewell remarks at the alumni dinner for his retirement May 26, 1956, were addressed to Sterling. He was aware that his vision of business education differed from the president's. He pointed out that his longevity as dean had been greater than the longevity as president of any of the presidents under whom he had served. "You see that we kill off presidents more rapidly than we do deans," he said (Jackson, 1958, p. 7). He mentioned that his Harvard background was what made him shape Stanford in that image. And he recognized that the school was now going to take a different direction.

In 1958, after two years with an interim dean, Sterling appointed Ernest Arbuckle as dean. Born in 1912, Arbuckle had initially studied at Stanford Law School for one year before changing to the business school where he got his MBA in 1936. He served in the U.S. Navy, as well as in several businesses and banks in the San Francisco area, before becoming dean.

Arbuckle shared Sterling's vision of a more research-based school and began a restructuring of the school that would change the institution significantly. As he noted in his first article in the alumni magazine, he wanted the school to "create new knowledge and advance intellectual frontiers" (Arbuckle, 1959, p. 5), and he wanted to improve the conditions for research, noting that, since the war, the School "has not produced enough in the way of research and publications." His commitment was clear:

> As an educational institution, we should be ahead of business institutions in terms of solutions to and improved methods of handling current and future business problems. This job cannot be done without research. In this context I am not speaking of that research which surveys and reports current practices . . . but of creative research which develops new concepts and new principles. (Arbuckle, 1959, p. 6)

Arbuckle and Sterling wanted to put Stanford on the radar screen of the Ford Foundation because that was one way to secure more funding for the school as well as improve its academic reputation. Rowan Gaither and Allen Wallis assisted Stanford in self-studies of the behavioral sciences. The school began an active courtship of the foundation that involved hiring faculty from GSIA and RAND and upgrading the engagement in research and research conferences.

The president, provost, and dean lobbied actively to become visible to the foundation.[29] The school hired James Howell, the coauthor of the Gordon and Howell Report, as a faculty member. It hired G. Leland Bach, the architect of the GSIA at Carnegie Institute of Technology and prominent Ford Foundation advisor, whom they had approached at least once earlier to become dean of GSB.[30] It hired a trio of recent GSIA PhDs (Charles Bonini, Peter Winters, and Gert von der Linde). It sought to interact with the decision makers at the Ford Foundation, including Gaither, Carroll, and Berelson.[31] It obtained grants from the behavioral science division. It organized conferences featuring Ford Foundation speakers, Rowan Gaither and Thomas Carroll. One conference in particular was held on the "growing dimensions of management." The final speaker at the conference was Rowan Gaither.

The definitive statement of Stanford's commitment to research and the Ford vision came in the school's long-term plan, a core document that appeared shortly after the conference at which Gaither spoke. The long-range plan was produced by a committee appointed by Arbuckle and mirrored the Ford reports and the Gaither vision in most ways: It argued that business schools relied too much on cases and too little on the sciences and analysis.[32]

The document can be read as an integration of Gaither's speech and his 1951 report, as applied to a business school eager to transform itself and secure funding for the transformation. It proclaimed the necessity of a high-level MBA program; continuing education through conferences and programs, a doctoral program of high quality, and a vigorous research program:

> Research is necessary for the expansion of knowledge of the administrative function and of the environment in which it is performed; it is an integral and indispensable part of a doctoral program of quality; and is necessary for imaginative, alert teaching. Thus high priority must be given to research if a faculty is to interpret and to contribute to the changes constantly taking place in management, and in the underlying and supporting disciplines.[33]

This plan became the basis for the first application to Ford directly related to management education (Stanford had received money before, for example, from the behavioral science area). Lee Bach retrospectively noted in taking stock of business education in general (and Stanford in particular) in 1984, that "GSB is pretty much matching . . . the kind of activities and attitudes that the 'shakers and movers,' the Gordon-Howell and the Pierson reports call for."[34]

The campaigns to gain the attention of the Ford Foundation and to change the Stanford Graduate School of Business were successful. Carroll wrote to Sterling on receiving an application from the business school to the foundation that

> I already knew of your dedication to the advancement of the School's program . . . Needless to say, we have been watching each step that Ernie has taken during this past year and we share your belief that the promise of these things to come at the School has been substantially increased as a result of his moves.[35]

Stanford became one of the principal beneficiaries of Ford grants given after 1956. These resources were combined with vigorous efforts to upgrade the faculty. One student paper written later observed that the percentage of faculty holding PhD or DBA degrees moved from 30 percent to over 80 percent.[36] The changes at the school moved the Stanford GSB in about a decade from a relatively low position to a position at or near the top of business schools in North America. The Ford Foundation noted its success in moving to the "new model" of business administration; and the difficulties of doing so for institutions (such as Stanford) with a long history (relative to new ones such as GSIA):

> It is one thing to assist a school which has a clear sense of direction, but quite another to help a school with a distinguished past and a mediocre present to shake off complacency and organizational fetters, set entirely fresh targets, and initiate new undergraduate and graduate programs. This has, however been accomplished with Foundation assistance at . . . Stanford.[37]

Although the 1950s and 1960s leadership of the school explicitly pursued a strategy of emulating many of the features of the Graduate School of Industrial Administration at Carnegie as well as the dogma endorsed by the Ford Foundation, it was careful to present the Stanford approach as distinctively its own and reflective of its history. In 1960, in a special supplement to the Alumni Bulletin, Dean Arbuckle set out to define the Stanford approach in an essay entitled "Training Men to Solve Problems of the Future" (Arbuckle, 1960). He wrote about three different approaches to business education: one based on basic knowledge of behavioral sciences, theory and analysis; one based on economics and mathematical sciences; and one based on training for practice. Stanford, he proclaimed, provides a unique Stanford blend of the approaches:

> Stanford's philosophy and objectives have been more closely related to the third view . . . but in the future we have a unique opportunity to develop a better blend . . . We will be criticized by the intellectuals for not being theoretical enough and by businessmen for not being practical enough. But the very difficulty of the job presents its real challenge—and the stakes in this area are high. (Arbuckle, 1960, p. 3)

The Stanford rhetoric recognized the limitations of the Jackson era without entirely rejecting its premises. It acknowledged the limitations of case instruction while retaining it. It exalted fundamental research without granting it exclusive merit. In the tradition of a school that sought to honor its history while moving on, Stanford positioned its program as a uniquely balanced combination of the old and the new.

History Matters

As numerous studies have documented, most of the stories and routines that are products of history are conservative. In general, they inhibit the introduction of change from outside and mold the changes that are accepted in ways that make them more consistent with established internal attitudes, beliefs, and practices (Czarniawska and Joerges, 1996; Kiesler and Sproull, 1987; Zald and Denton, 1963). It is not hard to see important ways in which the business schools at Harvard, Pennsylvania, Chicago, and Stanford changed in the 1950s and 1960s. By some crude measures, Harvard seems to have changed the least and Chicago and Stanford the most, but each of the four schools became stronger both in the management education market and in the world of academic reputations. By the end of the century, they were clustered at the top in most rankings of business schools. It is also not hard to see that the ways in which the schools changed were affected by their earlier histories so that each remained different from the others in consistent ways even as each changed.

As always, it is hard to distinguish the effects of history from the effects of interests and their power. The postwar reforms of business schools were executed at a time in which there was considerable pressure from other parts of the universities in which they existed for building greater academic respectability in business schools. Greater respectability meant, in most cases, making business schools look more academic. This pressure was expressed through administrative channels, through contact with colleagues in other departments and fields, and through newly appointed business faculty with disciplinary training and allegiances. The strength of each of these pressures and the avenues through which they were exerted varied across schools, and those differences tended to covary with elements of history.

GSIA was the recognized model, but it was replicated precisely in none of the four schools. The schools varied in their acknowledgment of the importance of the GSIA model, but each of them believed that its own variation on the theme was distinctive. In some sense, they were all right. The best combination of practices depends on the capabilities developed over history and the demands of a particular market. It would be unimaginable to superimpose the Chicago Graduate School of Business model on the Harvard Business School, or the Stanford Graduate School of Business model on the Wharton School. Rhetorics of universality are denials of the heterogeneities of market position, contemporary institutional context, and history.

There are, however, some consistencies in these stories of elite schools that should not be overlooked.

First, change was facilitated by a breakdown of the established order in the schools. All of the schools were stressed (HBS the least) by challenges to their normal ways of doing business. Most of them were struggling for academic respectability and conscious that they were losing the struggle. All of them faced a significant problem of finding faculty adequate to meet rapidly expanding demand for management education.

Second, expectations with respect to academic research on the part of faculty were raised substantially in all of the schools. There remained clear differences among the schools, but the academic research expectations increased in all of them. Research publications became an important currency of standing. Case development continued to be respected in most schools, but it was increasingly categorized as a contribution to teaching rather than to research.

Third, the prejudices of the time (mathematics, quantitative analysis, interdisciplinarity, behavioral science) were not equally successful in gaining implementation. In every case, it was possible to increase significantly the role of mathematics and quantitative techniques of analysis both in courses and in research. In addition, microeconomic theory, including game theory and decision theory, and operations analysis, including linear and dynamic programming and queuing theory, became more important. On the other hand, concepts drawn from interdisciplinary fields and the behavioral sciences did not. And the notion that ideas drawn from analytics based on decision theory could become vehicles for planning and collective choice in society sometimes collided with ideas drawn from enthusiasms for markets.

8.2 Beyond the Elite

We know of no systematic, large-scale efforts to assess the Ford Foundation's assumption that other schools would be influenced by changes in elite schools. Anecdotal reports suggest that there were significant enduring changes, but it is hard to measure the magnitude, character, or durability of the changes precisely. The gradual infusion of faculties with individuals having doctorates either from the disciplines or from business schools that themselves had strengthened the disciplinary respectability of their faculties almost certainly increased the scholarly pretensions of many business schools. It led to the creation of several major scholarly journals that became outlets for business school research reports. However, the extent to which significant curricular or research reforms were initiated or persisted is not easy to calibrate.

There were not many contemporaneous attempts to evaluate the Ford Foundation's programs and their effects. However, there was one that has survived in the archives. In its effort to assess the changes produced in business schools by its own efforts and by parallel efforts in similar directions, the foundation in 1965 asked John Wheeler to make a confidential analysis of what had happened in business schools. His report, entitled "Report to the Ford Foundation on Changes in Collegiate Business Education in the United States 1954–64 and the Role of the Ford Foundation in These Changes," was never published but represents a contemporaneous look at changes in North American business schools during the 1950s and 1960s.[38]

John Wheeler was not by any means an outsider, but he was also not a clear insider. Although he had participated in some aspects of the efforts to reeducate business school faculty and was a senior faculty member at the University of California, Berkeley, a school that was relatively active in supporting the reforms, he was less heavily involved with the reforms than were many others. He clearly had sympathy with the changes being pushed by the Ford Foundation, but he was not a zealot.

In general, Wheeler concluded that 1965 was probably too early to determine the effectiveness of the "trickle-down" character of the foundation strategy, but he noted the general dilemma of effectiveness research: The longer you wait, the more any genuine signal can overcome short-run noise; but the longer you wait, the more any effect is distorted by intervening factors. He wrote:

> . . . the "trickle down effect" can best be judged in ten years rather than today although by then other influences will obscure the particular impact which Ford had upon business administration.[39]

Wheeler undertook to collect several different kinds of data:

(1)   A comparison of 1954–1955 catalogues of schools that were members of the American Association of Collegiate Schools of Business (AACSB) with 1964–1965 catalogues.

(2)   A similar comparison of the leading textbooks used in 1954–1955 with those used in 1964–1965.

(3)   Interviews at a sample of thirty business schools in the United States.

(4)   Responses to a questionnaire sent to all AACSB schools.

(5)   A comparison of test scores received by students on nationally administered tests.

(6)   A study of the journals published in business administration.

(7)   Studies of applications and postfellowship questionnaires for Ford Foundation programs in faculty and doctoral fellowships.

Although the report was filled with the results of these efforts, it did not attempt to provide the usual statistical qualifications associated with research reports (that is, response rates, tests of hypotheses, estimates of error). Rather, it was an attempt by an experienced researcher to make sense of the data. Wheeler provided ample warnings about the difficulties of addressing questions as comprehensive as he attempted:

> In a study as comprehensive as this one many impressions are gathered which cannot be documented—and may be wrong: trends are perceived which may be illusory; and findings are obtained which may be spurious.[40]

Nevertheless, he formed some conclusions. The conclusions were organized around the eight specific goals enunciated by the Ford Foundation for the Economic Development and Administration Program:

(1)   *To increase the emphasis on graduate curricula relative to undergraduate.* With respect to this goal, Wheeler concluded that "it is obvious from the data on enrollments that this objective was achieved."[41] The number of graduate degrees awarded annually in business administration more than doubled in the decade after 1954; the number of undergraduate degrees increased by less than 40 percent. He went on to observe that one consequence was that many of the earlier weaknesses of undergraduate programs reappeared in new graduate programs; indeed, they were accentuated. In that respect, he cited the problem that some graduate programs were actually weaker in their mathematical requirements than were undergraduate programs.

(2)   *To decrease the amount of specialization.* Wheeler concluded that the evidence was persuasive about a decline in specialization at the undergraduate level but that the record indicated very little about changes at the graduate level, or indeed about efforts to affect such changes.

(3)   *To increase the role of the disciplines in business programs.* The presumption was that a movement away from the purely descriptive nature of many business courses to courses

that involved more analysis would require a grounding in mathematics, statistics, economics, psychology, and sociology. Wheeler noted the widespread introduction of quantitative courses, but he observed no increase in the low exposure of students to the fundamentals of psychology and sociology and little sign of increase in exposure to economic theory. In the end, he concluded, "In the typical business school course, however, neither quantitative analysis, economic theory, nor the behavioral sciences are utilized effectively. The typical course is still a highly descriptive course with little analytical content."[42]

(4)   *To raise the intellectual level of students in business administration.* This objective was presumably to be accomplished by increasing the intellectual demand of business courses at both the undergraduate and graduate levels and raising the standards for admission to graduate programs. Wheeler observed that the absolute intellectual level of students in business was raised substantially during this period but that the level relative to other fields was raised only slightly. As the elite business schools had raised standards of admission and the intellectual demands of their courses, the intellectual level of their students had been raised; but there was no strong evidence for a general increase across all business schools. As the demand for business school graduates increased, business schools responded by expanding programs and lowering admission requirements.

(5)   *To improve the courses by changing the approaches and methods of teaching.* The program emphasized substituting more analytical material for descriptive material in courses. This effort succeeded to a significant extent at the better schools, but it was not clear that it made much of an impact in general. The program also emphasized improving teaching methods. Wheeler concluded that the major effort in this respect was to increase the use of cases in teaching, an effort that he believed probably improved the average level of teaching. Moreover, he asserted that business school courses appeared to be better taught on average than were courses in the humanities and social sciences. However, he bemoaned the limited effort to improve other aspects of teaching,

particularly the limited use of simulation, audiovisual methods, small group sessions, and the like.

(6)   *To raise the scholarly level of the faculty.* Wheeler felt that the Ford Foundation programs had made some useful contributions to improving the research capabilities of faculty at business schools, particularly through the workshops that were organized in the 1960s. He also felt that the increasing numbers of PhD holders among new appointments to the faculties would contribute to the goal. Overall, his data showed that the proportion of regular faculty in business schools with doctorates increased in the decade beginning in 1954 from 56 percent to 71 percent, with the percentage in the top schools reaching 88 percent. However, he was decidedly pessimistic about business schools as sites for encouraging continuing development and productivity among faculty, citing particularly the relatively large teaching loads, the temptations of consulting and textbook writing, and the lack of a scholarship-oriented association of business school professors.

(7)   *To increase the quantity and improve the quality of basic research in the field.* Wheeler's report was unstinting in its praise of the effectiveness of Ford Foundation support for research at the top eight schools:

> The Top 8 schools in which the majority of funds were centered significantly increased the quality and quantity of their research and incorporated developments from mathematics, statistics, psychology, sociology, and economics. In fact, in a number of cases they made major contributions to developments in the basic disciplines. Such research served to increase the visibility of business schools, raised their status, and made it easier to recruit faculty and students from other disciplines.[43] . . . Individuals or small groups at some of the next 17 schools initiated projects under Ford Foundation support which give great promise of significant breakthroughs in research.[44]

However, Wheeler saw serious impediments to further development lying in the emphasis in business schools on programs (for example, MBA, DBA) without suitable research specialization or focus and in the absence of any long-term institutionalized support for fundamental research in business.

(8) *To expand and improve doctoral programs in business administration.* The Ford Foundation programs had direct effects on just five schools but provided secondary effects (primarily through doctoral fellowships) for a larger number. Wheeler assessed these efforts as having effects within a relatively small number of institutions and speculated that they would have been more effective if spread across a wider number:

> The large sums spent to develop a few centers of excellence achieved their desired result and each of these centers developed a distinctive character which will provide a base for future development. These centers plus a few other schools received research support which led to the development of a body of knowledge upon which many new concepts in business are and will be developed. It is the author's opinion that beyond this point the programs were less effective in achieving their objective because they failed to recognize the regional nature of educational development and the need for concentrated programs of support if major changes are to be accomplished.[45]

In general, Wheeler's report confirmed three important intimations of the look at elite schools. First, there were very substantial changes in the ambitions of business schools. They became more explicitly academic with a greater emphasis on research and graduate education. Second, the changes fit into the histories and contexts of existing schools in ways that maintained considerable heterogeneity among schools, reduced the global impact of the reforms, and seemed likely to leave them vulnerable both to subsequent innovation and to future backsliding. Third, it was not clear that the changes in elite schools heralded a comparable change in others. Wheeler's data were limited but seemed to raise doubts about the Ford "trickle-down" strategy.

8.3 A REVOLUTION EMBRACED AND CONTAINED

There is a consistent thread through these stories. Each of the institutions we have considered endorsed the reform project as its own. Each fit that project into its own conception of a proper business school derived from its own history and from its own integration into outside interest groups. For example, Wharton presented the denigration of vocational work as simply a confirmation of its traditions:

> Vocational oriented work was not emphasized in Joseph Wharton's design for business education, nor is it given much emphasis in the present Wharton curriculum.[46]

As a result, the revolution was both embraced and contained. Each elite school declared its version of the revolution as uniquely its own. The Wheeler Report suggested a similar phenomenon in other business schools. With the possible exception of the Harvard Business School, each school raised a banner declaring it as a preeminent carrier of the new reforms. Among the schools we considered, this was most evident in the cases of Carnegie Tech, which saw itself as a model of the changes; Chicago, which labeled the revolution "The Chicago Approach"; and Stanford, which proclaimed itself as following "The Middle Way." In each case, the reforms were made to fit the particular history in which the individual school existed.

The revolutionary price, of course, was that the reforms, while not entirely losing strains of more general principles, tended to become transformed into a local instrument of local interests and preferences. Mathematics became variations of decision theory at Harvard, variations of financial economics at Wharton, and variations of microeconomic theory at Chicago. Interdisciplinarity became business cases at Harvard, economic imperialism at Chicago, and the economics of politics at Stanford. Fundamental research became business cases at Harvard, theorems in economic theory at Chicago, and applied game theory at Stanford. Behavioral science became business cases at Harvard, economics at Chicago, and organizational sociology at Stanford.

In most respects, the reforms appear to have penetrated deeply into the business school world with extensive changes attributable to them. The teaching and thinking about accounting was transformed (Jeanjean and Ramirez, 2009, p. 115) with consequences that extended to the Financial Accounting Standards Board (Zeff, 1999).[47] The teaching and thinking about finance and financial management was transformed with consequences that considerably altered financial markets and the role of finance in management (Litzenberger, 1991; Merton, 1994).

The teaching and thinking about production management was transformed with consequences that extended into artificial intelligence (Simon, 1961; Simon, 1987). And the teaching and thinking about organizations was transformed with consequences that extended to the creation of a new quasi-discipline of organization studies (Augier, March, and Sullivan, 2005).

The recruitment of faculty from the disciplines provided a strong internal base in support of many of the changes. However, in most other respects, the structure of interests in the business school world was left untouched; and the recruitment of faculty was destined to become more internalized to business schools as business schools developed their own research-oriented doctoral programs. In the long run, business schools faced the same array of interests and structural constraints that earlier had led them to the academic doldrums.

8.4   THE INTERNATIONAL EPIDEMIOLOGY OF CHANGE

Our focus has been exclusively on North American business schools and management education during the 1950s and 1960s. However, the history of business education is obviously not confined to North America. Until about 1970, North American business education was relatively self-contained. After 1970, attempts to emulate or improve the North American model spread through much of Europe and ultimately to Asia. A more comprehensive study would extend the perspective to include European and Asian management education and institutions. Because we have not undertaken such an extension (for some efforts to do so, see Djelic, 1998; Durand and Dameron, 2008, Chapter 1; Engwall, 1992; Koenig and Tapic, 2008; Moslein and Huff, 2008; Thomas, 2008), we will limit ourselves to a few general observations.

The changes in European and Asian management schools came later than the changes in North America. Recovering from the physical, human, and financial devastations of the war was a priority in most of Europe and Asia that delayed attention to possible reforms of management education. The timing and location made a difference. The academic worldviews that animated the changes in North America earlier were different in important ways from the academic worldviews in Europe twenty years later, and these later worldviews led to a somewhat different kind of business school. More-over, developments in Europe came at a time when the European Union was seeking to introduce elements of standardization into European man-agement education.

When educational attention in Europe and Asia turned to business schools by the 1970s and later, many of the reforms were explicit echoes of earlier North American reforms (Djelic, 1998; Durand and Dameron, 2008, p. 5). European and Asian business schools sought to gain legitimacy by adopting frameworks taken from North American schools. One anoma-lous result of the timing of the flowering of European and Asian business schools was that they tended to copy North American business schools and particularly changes in those schools during the 1950s and 1960s, at a time when many of the North American schools were undergoing the changes of a counterreformation and when the social science context in Europe was different from the postwar North American context.

Business schools in Europe and Asia differentiated themselves from North American schools at least in part by contrasting their international and intercultural flavors with the more parochial style of North Ameri-can schools (Durand and Dameron, 2008, Chapter 6). North American schools, in general, found it difficult to meet such a challenge in terms of course material or in terms of the backgrounds of their faculty. At the same time, however, the major elite North American schools probably enrolled a higher fraction of foreign students than did many of their European and Asian competitors.

The postwar convergence of academic publishing into primarily English-language journals gave North American scholars an advantage but resulted in considerable sharing of research results and orientations, more in some fields than others. However, as European- and Asian-based English-language journals became established, there was some tendency for the sharing to de-cline as scholars in each region tended to publish in journals from their own region; and as North American hegemony declined, so also did the inclina-tion to mimic American schools.

Chapter Nine

THE RHETORIC OF REALITY

As was true throughout the period after the Second World War, and perhaps forever, the main artifact of academe was words. Academics used words, and the words they used and how they used them certainly distinguished and possibly affected the history. Words provided rationale for changes; words provided justifications for resistance to change. Words decorated memoranda and reports.

The words associated with changes in business schools were partly local to specific schools. They involved particular institutional histories and specific internal rivalries that affected events. However, they also resonated with some issues and dilemmas that were general and around which substantial parts of the debates circled. The barrage of words focused particularly on three grand issues that framed the discussions:

- *The infusion of reality into management education.* How are business school students exposed to problems and situations that are similar to those they will encounter as managers? To what extent should they be? How can a business school assess the relative merits of business cases as compared with other simulations of reality?
- *The pursuit of relevance in management education.* What should be the temporal and spatial dimensions of business school usefulness?

What is the relation between the pursuit of fundamental knowledge and the education of managers? Between academic knowledge and experiential knowledge?

- *The attribution of professional status to the practice of management.* To what extent is management a profession? What does it mean to be a profession? What is the relation between social obligations and self-interest in professional life? How is professionalism (or the lack of it) manifested in managerial education?

Issues such as these are exercised by the debates of history but are not resolved by them. As they had for many years, they inhabited the rhetoric of conflict and the proclamations of advocates during the quarter-century after the Second World War. In the next three chapters, we explore some elements of the rhetoric of those debates, the issues underlying them, and the "resolutions" that might be achieved. The present chapter considers the infusion of reality into management education. Chapter Ten considers the pursuit of relevance. Chapter Eleven considers professionalism in management.

9.1 Simulating Reality in Management Education

To a substantial extent, the recent history of professional education is a history of shifting from experiential knowledge to academic knowledge. That process is obviously involved in the history of business education after the Second World War. By most measures, business schools became more dependent on the lessons of academic research and less tied to the lessons of practical experience. For example, the practice of financial decision making was largely removed from rules of thumb derived from experience and became embedded in the theorems of financial economics and decision theory.

At the same time, however, almost everyone agreed that professional education should provide opportunities for students to refine their skills at applying and elaborating academic knowledge in "real" situations. Professionals do not merely recite theories; they use them. Engineers and architects use theories of the strength of materials to construct bridges and buildings using specific materials in specific locations. Physicians use theories of physiology and disease to identify and treat specific ailments in specific patients. Teachers use theories of learning to develop teaching plans for instruction of specific students in specific topics. To develop capabilities in the skills relevant to such professional tasks, professional schools provide both theoretical knowledge and various forms of exposure to the virtual reality of simulated problems. Devising and implementing settings to accomplish the latter training is a major responsibility of professional schools, including schools of business.

The problem arises from one of the earliest and most highly praised bases for modern professional education—the separation of education from the direct experience of an apprenticeship. Committed as most business schools have been (and are) to a physical separation of business education from the locales of business, they seek to develop ways of mimicking the realities of managerial experience within an academic setting. Faculty enthusiasm for such efforts varies across the fields of study involved in management education, but even the more rigid advocates of academic knowledge accept the necessity of some version of "clinical" training within business training programs.

In the pursuit of an aura of reality, business schools expose students (and faculty) to emanations from the real world of business organizations. They infuse the teaching of abstract concepts with examples drawn from business experience. They exhibit successful managers as manifestations of practical wisdom. They tell stories drawn from experience to give meaning to speculations. They provide simulated experience. They try to extract real-world implications from speculative constructs. They are committed to making a connection between the neat theorems of academe and the messy confusions of reality.

Reality is, however, a difficult scholarly concept. To Giambattista Vico, reality is captured by myths that survive. To a survivor, reality is encased in his survival. To the dead, no doubt, reality is death. Some years ago, a leading school of acting (Meisner, 1987) advised actors to imagine themselves as creating in themselves the thoughts and emotions of the character they portray. Acting involved the appropriation of reality. At about the same time, a leading sociologist (Goffman, 1959) argued that reality consisted in acting. Life was a script performed by role players. Where is the anchor in that orgy of coevolution?

For some scholars, reality is socially constructed and has no meaning that is independent of human awareness. For them, reality is what we make it. For others, the idea of an extrasubjective reality is easily accepted, but discerning and understanding that reality are difficult, particularly because any particular observation may be specific to the context in which it occurs. The main claim of higher education is not that it is connected to a specific reality with its subscripts of time and place but that it provides general principles about reality that are, to some extent, independent of the vagaries of specific realities. The claim is that the reality portrayed in academic theories is general and fundamental and that when experience seems to conflict with the theories, the error lies with the interpretation of experience, not with the theories.

Reality is a difficult scholarly concept, but it is not difficult in ordinary terms. For a business school, reality is life in business as it is experienced by those who inhabit business organizations. It is comprehended through credible stories about the events of business life and through credible theoretical characterizations of the causal structure underlying them, but it is experienced through exposure to it. A conventional aspiration for business education is that a graduate will recognize subsequent work in business as familiar, something already experienced. The transition from business education to business employment should be smooth.

Students try to imagine reality and to judge whether their education prepares them for it. They lobby for educational experiences that conform to their imaginations of reality. Those imaginations are informed by their previous business experience and by the teachings of peers and parents, but they are unlikely to be accurate. If the objective is to prepare a graduate for positions of significant responsibility, the appropriate "reality" of education is likely to be the reality of several years after graduation rather than immediate or previous employment. There are problems in preparing for yesterday's reality or for the reality of someone else.

Almost all business schools include elements of experiential reality in their extracurricular programs. They encourage students to spend time on jobs (for example, internships) that can be used to supplement their studies and to seek educationally (as well as monetarily) useful employment during summer vacations. They invite experienced managers to talk to their students. They encourage faculty to enrich their awareness of business (as well as their incomes) through consulting for business firms.

Business schools also seek to construct activities within their curricula that simulate elements of experiential reality. These include the telling of "war stories" by teachers, anecdotes of life in business. They include the draping of analytical problems with a superficial mantle of business problems, abstract problems with real-world labels. The more elaborate manifestations of virtual realities in management education are found, however, in the simulations of reality in business cases and in business games. These are primary teaching instruments by which a business school eases the transition from the equations and other fulminations of theories to the experiences of daily life in business.

9.2   BUSINESS CASES

By any measure, the primary pedagogical tool used by North American business schools to simulate reality is the business case. The changes in business education in the 1950s and 1960s, although they were accompanied by critiques of the use of cases, did not lead to a significant diminution of the role of the case method of instruction.

In a study for business school admissions advisers (based on self-reporting from the schools themselves), leading business schools characterized the distribution of instructional effort devoted to such alternative representations of experiential reality as are found in lectures, cases, experiential learning, and simulation games.[1] The results are summarized in Table 9.1. The reported penetration of case studies ranged from 80 percent at the Harvard Business School to 25 percent at the University of Chicago Graduate School of Business. Lectures, the next most popular teaching method, represented more penetration than cases at a minority of schools (including Chicago, Duke, UCLA, Carnegie Mellon, Texas, Yale, Rochester, Vanderbilt, and USC). Simulation was a distant contender, never achieving more than 15 percent.

TABLE 9.1

Reported Distribution of Instructional Effort (as percentages)

Business School	Cases	Lecture	Experiential	Simulation	Other
California, Berkeley (Haas)	50%	30%			20%
California, Los Angeles (Anderson)	30%	50%			20%
Carnegie Mellon	30%	60%			10%
Chicago	25%	50%		5%	10%
Columbia	40%	40%			20%
Cornell (Johnson)	40%	25%			35%
Dartmouth (Tuck)	40%	30%	10%	10%	10%
Duke (Fuqua)	40%	45%		15%	
Harvard	80%	15%			5%
Indiana (Kelley)	40%	30%			30%
Massachusetts Inst of Tech (Sloan)	45%	30%		10%	15%
Michigan	40%	40%	20%		
New York University (Stern)	37%	38%			25%
North Carolina, Chapel Hill	40%	35%		10%	15%
Northwestern (Kellogg)	33%	33%			34%
Pennsylvania (Wharton)	55%	30%	15%		
Purdue (Krannert)	50%	25%	25%		
Rochester (Simon)	30%	50%			20%
Southern California (Marshall)	30%	50%	20%		
Stanford	55%	30%		10%	5%
Texas, Austin (McCombs)	35%	45%		5%	15%
Vanderbilt (Owen)	30%	50%			20%
Virginia (Darden)	70%	15%		5%	10%
Washington, St. Louis (Olin)	45%	25%	10%	10%	10%
Yale	35%	60%	5%		

SOURCE: Retrieved in July 2008 from www.businessschooladmission.com/teaching_methods.php.

The Law School Origins

North American law schools have used a case method of instruction for many years without completely agreeing on the pedagogical logic of doing so. As early as 1870, a Harvard University professor (Christoffer Langdell) concluded that law students could learn more from cases than from textbooks. He proclaimed that law was a science and its principles could best be learned through cases:

> . . . law, considered as a science, consists of certain principles or doctrines. . . . and the shortest and the best, if not the only way of mastering the doctrine effectually is by studying the cases in which it is embodied. (Langdell, 1871, p. 11)

Interestingly, the argument that is sometimes used for promoting the use of cases in business schools—that business is not so much a science as an art—was reversed in Langdell's formulation; it was because law was a science that teaching cases made sense:

> If law be not a science, a university science, it is a species of handcraft, and may best be learned by serving an apprenticeship to one who practices. (Langdell, 1871, p. 125)

The Harvard Law School dean who succeeded Langdell, James Ames, on the other hand, thought the purpose of the case method was not to teach principles because they were too complex and multifaceted but to teach how to solve legal problems—to teach students how to think like lawyers (Williston, 1910).

Subsequently, without fully coalescing on a single justification, professors at the Harvard Law School began to expand the use of cases and casebooks, combining cases with textbooks emphasizing legal principles. In a relatively short time, they made the case method the all-embracing Harvard approach to training lawyers (Keener, 1894). In the early twentieth century, the case method of legal education—the "Harvard method of instruction"—was, thanks to Harvard's intellectual and political influence, seen as the main innovation in legal education, and, despite some complaints (for example, for being "unscientific"; Patterson, 1995, p. 200), cases and casebooks came to dominate legal education in the United States. Indeed, Charles Eliot in his Annual Report of the President managed to credit the case method with making university-based law schools the primary bastion of legal education:

> So long as lectures were the only means of teaching in the law and medical schools of this University, the heterogeneous character of the class did not much affect the efficiency of the institution, except so far as the lecturers

felt obliged to adapt their teaching to the ignorant and untrained portion of their audience. But with the adoption of catechetical methods in both schools, the presence in the recitation room of a considerable proportion of persons whose minds were rude and unformed became at once a serious impediment. (Currie, 1951, p. 370)

Later, criticism of the case method would come and go in legal education and controversies surrounding the role of science too (Patterson, 1995). But adoption of the case method was a significant step in the professionalization of the law schools and legal education; Eliot even spoke of the case method causing "the climax of success in professional education" (Eliot, cited in Stevens, 1983 [2001], p. 59). And it became the turning point for schools going from good to "elite," such as Yale (Stevens, 1983 [2001]).

The Spread of the Case Method to and among Business Schools

In 1919, Wallace Donham, the dean of the Harvard Business School and a graduate of the Harvard Law School, began to promote cases as an instrument for teaching business students (Donham, 1922). At first, the case method was limited at HBS to courses in commercial law but spread eventually to other subjects (Copeland, 1954). Melvin Copeland, a faculty member at the time, recalled how Donham called him into his office and asked him to give up other plans to develop a casebook in the field of marketing (Copeland, 1954, p. 30). This resulted in the first book of cases in marketing (Copeland 1920). Donham next suggested that a collection of cases be collected in industrial management. Although the professor in charge of that topic was not too enthusiastic at first, he found it prudent not to "attempt to dissuade the Dean"; so he went ahead with the project.

According to Copeland, although the initial push for cases came from the dean's insistence on using the method, there also was increasing demand from students:

As more and more courses were converted from lectures to class discussion, the students showed a strong preference for the case method, and their attitude soon became apparent to the instructors. This student attitude was a major factor in accelerating the use of cases in the classroom. Hence, within a period of about four years following 1920, a high proportion of the courses in the School were transformed from lecture courses to discussion courses. (Copeland, 1954, p. 33)

Aided by the organization of the HBS Bureau of Business Research (Swanson, 1914), case work expanded. Recent business school graduates were hired to collect cases. Researchers used assistants to gather cases from field work. According to Copeland, the investment required by HBS to sustain the case initiative was daunting. He reports that Donham had to raise almost $2 million between 1920 and 1940 for that purpose alone, having begun with just $5,000 in hand (Copeland, 1954, p. 33). "His unflagging interest in the objective," Copeland noted in writing about Donham, "supported him in his crusade; and once started, the work never faltered" (Copeland, 1954, p. 33).

And indeed, the effort had considerable success. The case method and HBS as its principal supplier thoroughly penetrated the market for management education. Despite some persistent resistance from academic quarters throughout the decades (including at times from Harvard's own corners), cases became a major instrument of teaching in most business schools (Table 9.1). Although the position of the case method as part of a sacred litany of pedagogy sometimes induces individuals to define almost any method of teaching as reflecting the "case method" (Argyris, 1980, p. 291), the importance of the case method is still obvious even when instances are limited to variations on a classic definition by Kenneth Andrews, by which a case is:

> . . . a carefully written description of an actual situation in business which provokes in the reader the need to decide what is going on, what the situation really is, or what the problems are—and what can and should be done. (Andrews 1951, p. 60)

Moreover, teaching based on cases came to be closely associated with the Harvard Business School and with its thrust toward a "general management" perspective. As a result, discussions of the case method often became framed in terms of support of or competition with HBS. Just as it was sometimes hard to distinguish praise of the case method from praise of HBS, it was hard to distinguish criticism of cases from criticism of the school. Schools happy to be protected by the shadow of HBS tended to become enthusiasts for cases; schools seeking to differentiate themselves from

HBS tended to become critical of cases; and the debate over cases often became a proxy for a debate over the hegemony of the Harvard Business School in the world of North American business schools.

Cases and the Reformers of the 1950s and 1960s

It is perhaps not surprising that several individuals significant to the post–Second World War revolution in management education implicitly and explicitly disagreed with the heavy use of cases in management education. Thus, Gordon and Howell noted,

> Heavy reliance on the case method involves two serious dangers. Systematic knowledge may be neglected, and the student may be left to use relatively crude and weak analytical tools when he might have been trained to use more refined and powerful ones. Equally or more important, preoccupation with the preparation and teaching of cases may lead a faculty to neglect research on significant problems. Teachers who heavily emphasize case teaching tend to distrust generalizations . . . (Gordon and Howell, 1959, pp. 371–372)

G. Leland Bach, one of the recognized architects of the 1950s–1960s reformation of business schools was more restrained, attempting to differentiate teaching in which cases might be useful from teaching in which it would not be:

> Uses of cases, for example, is excellent for many purposes—for integration, for emphasis on orderly problem solving, for experience in the application of analytical concepts. One the other hand, it does not seem to me very useful where the primary emphasis is on development of sharp analytical concepts. (Bach, 1958, p. 358)

Bach in particular recommended the (limited) use of cases after a year of solid foundation program covering organizational behavior, economics, behavioral science and methods, as well as applications. Only on a solid foundation would it make sense to use cases, for example in an elective course on "business policy and its administration":

> While cases would play a vital teaching role, their function would be largely as exercises in the use of analytical tools from earlier courses in reaching reasoned decisions. (Ibid., pp. 356–357)

These concerns about cases led to little or no change in the use of cases. Indeed, the concerns were not universal among the proponents of business school reform. As part of its efforts to support the reformation of management education, the Ford Foundation provided substantial resources to the Harvard Business School to strengthen its case development program.

At a symbolic level, by virtue of the increased glorification of fundamental research and theoretical analysis, the reforms struck a blow against the case method. At a pragmatic level, however, cases thrived. Most business schools seemed to find it relatively easy to proclaim a commitment to fundamental knowledge while investing heavily in case method pedagogy. To some extent, the apparent contradiction was ameliorated by returning to a prior law school justification of cases as showcases for fundamental principles, rather than as opportunities for learning problem solving skills; but the continued penetration of case instruction was probably a symptom that the reforms were not as universal as they appeared.

The Rhetoric of Cases

The Harvard Business School is thoroughly persuaded of the value of its cases. On its website, HBS notes,

> The cornerstone of the School's renowned general management approach, the case method provides students with the transcendent skills, insights, and self-confidence required to meet the interdisciplinary demands of real business situations.

Although the words have the taint of advertising excess, they reflect a deeply felt and widely shared belief in the efficacy of case instruction. Students have accepted cases as providing elements of relevance; business executives have accepted cases as honoring business sensibilities; and business school instructors generally have found cases a congenial and effective form of teaching.

By far the primary theme in the advocacy of cases, is the claim that participation in case discussion develops problem-solving skills in domains in which there is no clear answer. Thus:

> Cases should be used with the clear consciousness that the purpose of business education is not to teach truths—leaving aside for a moment a discussion

of whether there are or are not such things as truths—but to teach men to think in the presence new situations. (Dewing, 1954, p. 4)

The use of cases is seen as a method for conveying knowledge and for learning, but, unlike traditional educational methods, it puts less emphasis on training students to know abstract knowledge than on training them to act in concrete situations (Dewing, 1954). In contrast to the search for legal principles that had motivated the introduction of cases in legal education, cases are usually presented in management education as contributing to understanding how to approach a problem.

To some extent, the rhetoric surrounding the case method revisits the rhetoric of the struggle between proponents of experiential and academic knowledge. Advocates of cases are commonly proponents of experiential knowledge; opponents of cases are commonly proponents of academic knowledge. In fact, Roland Christensen has described the case method as a protest movement directed at academic conceptions of knowledge and traditional academics.

> Its founders thought that applied economics was not a very useful way to prepare people for leadership in business. Nor did they believe that the then-current academic values would ever permit the emergence of a practice-oriented professional school. Therefore, they refused to hire traditional academics. (in Schmotter, 2000, p. 48)

Part of that movement involved redefining "research." For business schools located in research universities, it was important to exhibit evidence for the research productivity of its faculty. This could be done, as it was done to a substantial extent during the 1950s and 1960s, by hiring and supporting faculty interested in and capable of generating academic knowledge. It could also be done by defining the production of cases as a form of research.

Wallace Donham, the original Harvard proponent of cases, saw the collection of business cases as a fundamental form of research. In the lead article in the first issue of the *Harvard Business Review*, he wrote:

> Methods of research in science vary as widely as technique in business, but while the technique of research varies, the conception that scientific studies should be approached through the collection and classification of facts

and through the development from recorded facts of generalizations and theories into which the facts fit, is the basis of all science. This method has been applied with great effectiveness to such fields as the law, which lack the exactness of national sciences. In this respect business resembles the law more than the natural sciences, and therefore the probable course for the development of theory in business is more analogous to the similar development of the law than it is to chemistry or physics. It will require, however, the application of the same scientific method. (Donham, 1922, pp. 5–6)

Schools such as the Harvard Business School with its commitment to cases are inclined to view case development and writing as an important form of research and to reward faculty members for it. Schools such as the University of Chicago Graduate School of Business, with their commitment to disciplinary scholarship, are not inclined to view case development and writing as significant in assessing the research contribution of a faculty member.

The Rhetoric of Opposition

Not everyone has shared the unabashed enthusiasm of the Harvard Business School for the use of cases. Robert Hutchins, for example, saw them as inherently out of date:

The case method in schools of business leads to the study of cases which occurred during a boom, a year or so after a depression has set in. (Hutchins, 1968, p. 48)

A 1921 report from the Carnegie Foundation for the Advancement of Teaching pointed out some limitations to the methods (Reed, 1921), and Walter Donham, although strongly supporting the case method, identified some limits:

There are certain limitations which may affect the application of the case method of teaching to other fields. Primarily, it appears to be applicable only where the principal effort is to develop the student's power of analysis and synthesis. Secondly, the substance of the method depends upon the ability of the instructor to draw upon a wide variety of written cases. The field in which it is to be applied, moreover, must be thoroughly classified. Another serious objection to the case system is that it is not a rapid method of transmitting facts. (Donham, 1922, p. 54)

Some have questioned the analogy to legal or medical education, point-ing out among other things the difference in the underlying knowledge that forms the basis for cases:

> A business case differs from a law case. It also differs from a case history as used in medicine and social work. The difference is largely due to the fact that there exists a so-called body of substantive knowledge in law and medi-cine which does not exist in business. (Roethlisberger, 1977, p. 123)

Business cases have been criticized for their simplification of problems, for their providing too clear a specification for students, and for removing the student too far from the real-world experience of living with the situa-tion. Thus:

> Although the case method has realism, it is by no means identical with re-ality. The case writer has made a selection of the facts for the student, who gains little practice in seeking and recognizing pertinent facts and relation-ships in the continuum of daily detail that makes up the life of people in business. . . . Finally, the student faces a given problem for a relatively short time and without operating responsibility. In the actual situation, of course, operating personnel must live with their problems. (Carson, 1954, p. 86)

Cases have also been criticized for encouraging too great a separation from research knowledge. It is argued that, while cases were not necessarily antiknowledge, they were built on the assumption that "wisdom can't be told" (Cragg, 1954) and that only by examining real and particularized cases and by discussing them can students learn to observe the patterns behind business decision making. Thus, students were given facts, not theories or ideas or hypothesis, but specifics from particular business situations.

An editorial for the journal *Marketing Science* noted, under the title "Save Research—Abandon the Case Method of Teaching," that the case method ig-nores research findings and therefore destroys the link between academic re-search and learning (Shugan, 2006). The author notes that the case method:

> . . . often lacks the spirit of inquiry and the worship of the truth associated with the scientific method. . . . Students lose because they lose the benefit of important research findings while leaving the classroom with a false confi-dence about what they know. (Ibid., p. 114)

A similar set of observations can be found in Flexner's comments on the case method. He argued that cases are "discrete" and that "students rarely possesses sufficient generalizing power to redeem it from scrappiness" (Flexner, 1910, p. 98). Students obtain only specific knowledge from cases from which they cannot easily generalize in a scientific way. Thus, the applicability to new situations of the heuristics that are developed through case discussion is left to the vagaries of metaphorical habits.

Cases and Innocence

Neither the advocacy of cases nor their opposition is entirely innocent. From the start, the primary purveyor of cases for use in North American schools of business has been the Harvard Business School. The market for cases has a dominant firm. A substantial part of the school's investments and revenue have been linked to the production and marketing of cases, creating a financial incentive to develop rhetoric supporting the idea that cases should be central to business education. An annual report for 2008 notes the production of more than 8,000 cases, yielding revenue of more than $29 million (or more than 6 percent of the school's income).[2] A major part of the rhetorical efforts of schools with heavy investments in cases has been involved in promoting the use of business cases. The causal arrow runs from investments to rhetoric as well as from rhetoric to investments.

Moreover, links between individual faculty members who prepare cases and the firms that appear in them are often sources of mutual benefit. As is well known from debates over case studies as data in social science, anthropologists and "natives" are involved in complicated games that encompass sentiments of attachment, mutual dependence, and manipulation (Harris, 2003). Case writers can easily become enthusiasts or apologists for the firms they study; if not, they are likely to find access more difficult. Business executives are likely to see cases as forms of public relations. In some cases, relationships are financial with faculty who write the cases being compensated as consultants by the companies portrayed (Harris, 2003). It would be remarkable if these financial linkages were entirely irrelevant to the case portrayals.

The use of cases has met with persistent criticism that is no more reliably innocent than the enthusiasm of advocates. The rhetoric of opposition to cases comes particularly from business schools seeking to challenge the primacy of the Harvard Business School, usually by promoting some version of more academic knowledge. The University of Chicago Graduate School of Business and the Graduate School of Industrial Administration of the Carnegie Institute of Technology were particularly active in the 1950–1970 period. Critics of the case method are less obviously direct economic beneficiaries of the use of alternatives than are the advocates of cases with their use, but the whole industry of teaching materials is filled with incentives for corruption in procurement and advocacy (Borden, 1998; Harris, 2003; Kopelman, 1994).

9.3 Computer Simulation

In 1950, the pedagogy of virtual reality in business schools was dominated by the use of cases. In pedagogical terms, Harvard was king. In 1970 (and even in 2011), cases were still, by far, the primary way of simulating reality in business classrooms. The reforms of the 1950s and 1960s, however, coincided with and to some extent stimulated a second device of virtual reality—computer-based simulations and management games. The introduction of management games was heralded by the postwar reformers as a major pedagogical development. It became a symbol of a new approach. However, management games penetrated the market only slowly and never became a significant challenge to case teaching. They remained to a large extent an artifact of the massive infusion of information technology and computer-based games into modern life and thereby symbols of modernity in business education.

Educational Exercises

Although the use of business games, or the idea of simulation in business, has been linked to Chinese war and board games going back at least to 3000 BCE, the modern use of business games was very much linked to the development of electronic computers and the postwar years of defense-related projects at places such as the RAND Corporation and the Systems

Research Laboratory (SRL). The use of computers and the introduction of simulations and other techniques into business schools were embedded in (and a reflection of) the postwar environment of innovations in management methods derived from management science and operations research (Cooper, 2002). Places that pioneered those innovations came naturally to an enthusiasm for the use of computers in understanding and improving organizational decision making, particularly in the training of organizations to respond to rapidly changing environments.

SRL, a spin-off of RAND, was instrumental in the integration of computer technology and management by blending computers and the psychology of groups and organizations. Several ideas from organization studies concerned with motivation, leadership, learning, adaptation, and task environment, turned out to be important for the SRL research.[3] Indeed, Allen Newell with coauthor Joseph Kruskal described SRL as doing "organization theory in miniature,"[4] and he and James March were both consultants to SRL.

While RAND in general prided itself on emphasizing individual decision making and resource allocation (see Chapter Five), SRL sought to focus on groups and decision processes in groups, including studies of command, communication, information and the organization of personnel.[5] Social psychologists were brought into contact with operations researchers and computer scientists to help understand the connections between individual and group behavior through the human–machine simulation of organizational behavior in laboratories (Chapman et al., 1958).

Along the way, SRL pioneered the use of simulations as educational devices. The underlying model was that of flight simulators by which pilots were trained to deal with air combat situations, and much of the early work focused on developing simulations of military reality. SRL researchers constructed experiments involving air traffic patterns combined with a series of different and complicated enemy attacks (such as enemy planes mixing with commercial planes). The experience of experimental subjects in coping with the simulated patterns was then used to improve the training effectiveness of the simulations. The possibilities for uses in more general management education were noticed relatively early, and the SRL work stimulated efforts to devise management games.

Management Games

As early as 1955, RAND had developed a simulation exercise called "Monopologs," focused on the U.S. Air Force supply system logistics. In 1956, the American Management Association developed its "Top Management Decision Simulation"; in 1957, McKinsey and Company offered the "Business Management Game."

The first recorded classroom use of a management game was at the University of Washington in 1957 (Faria and Nulsen, 1996), and the use of games as a method of teaching spread among business schools in the late 1950s and early 1960s. By early in the 1960s a handbook of training simulations listed about 200 games. The *Wall Street Journal* noted,

> The soaring popularity of business games stems from their effectiveness in supplementing the pamphlets, lectures, and case studies on which most management training . . . [is] based. (Ibid., pp. 25–26)

One survey reported that sixty-four out of ninety business schools had integrated management games into their curriculum from 1956 to 1966. Of the remaining twenty-six respondents, six were planning to introduce the games shortly and twelve when they had the necessary resources (Raia, 1966, p. 339). Two 1967 surveys of samples of AACSB schools found that over 90 percent of the respondents used simulation games in at least one course on at least one day (Day, 1968; Graham and Gray, 1969), a rate repeated in subsequent surveys (Faria, 2004).

By 1990, Faria (1990) estimated that there were approximately 228 business games available, and that 1,733 four-year schools were using business games in 3,813 courses. The usage was substantially greater in courses in marketing and strategic management than in accounting. At the same time, he noted that over 40,000 instructors in business schools were not currently using business games. The penetration was extensive but not complete, and compared to the penetration of cases it was miniscule.

The Rhetoric of Simulation

The justification of management games tended not to be focused on specifics or particulars:

The game was not intended to teach specific concepts or techniques of management as we try to do, say, in a course in marketing or finance. It was designed as part of the integrative stem of our curriculum to challenge students to deal effectively with the kinds of problems that real executives face. (Dill and Doppelt, 1963, p. 31)

The argument was that the games would enable students not just to see the interrelatedness of the different areas and functions of firms and organizations but also that would help them develop four skills (Ibid., p. 32):

- An ability to seek out and evaluate information from a variety of data and organize it to guide future decisions.

- An ability to plan and take action in situations with hundreds of variables.

- An ability to be both a generalist and a specialist and to handle problems that rested on "imaginative and thorough analysis" as well as those where solutions rested on "fast, intuitive judgment."

- An ability to work in teams with other people outside and inside the firm (Ibid., p. 32).

Such justifications, however, hardly distinguish management games from other forms of virtual realities, in particular from business cases. Abilities at analysis, planning, decision making, and relating to people are much to be valued; but advocacy of management games as instruments for teaching such skills has to link some unique features of simulations to the achievement of such abilities.

The great claim of management games lies in the dependence of the unfolding history on the intermediate actions taken and in the compelling generation of more or less continuous feedback. These, in turn, put considerable pressure on participants to discover ways of developing analyses, strategies, and experiments that increase the long run information obtained without unduly sacrificing short-run achievements. Thus, they encourage confronting the issues of balancing exploration and exploitation that are central to managerial effectiveness (March, 1991).

Insofar as the intention is to teach general abilities to deal with such problems, a wide variety of computer simulation games are candidates: Simulated air combat, road racing, or dragon hunting. The difficulty is identifying a special claim for games that have the appearance of business environments and actions. The greater "reality" that is simulated obviously has some motivational advantage with business students, but does it have additional pedagogical value that extends beyond that advantage?

It was argued that games provided learning at several levels and in several ways. For example, faculty directors overseeing the games were found to believe that by observing changes in the behavior of players they could improve the way in which the game evoked analytical tasks. And the students within the organizations became more aware of the factors involved in having good working relationships in teams (Dill and Doppelt, 1963, p. 34). The comments and feedback included,

> "I learned a great deal about coordination and what it really means and what is needed to get it done"; "One thing we naturally did . . . was to establish routines and to set things up so that they would become easier . . . this allowed us to place greater emphasis on longer range planning in all areas" . . . "I have learned to look for influence patterns and have learned about their importance" (Ibid., pp. 35–36).

The testimony is impressive, but it is not clear what advantage a simulation might have over many other kinds of group tasks.

The Rhetoric of Opposition

Management games based on simulations never became a serious threat to the status of other forms of virtual realities in business schools, particularly business cases. In general, games thrived most where cases did not; but they never achieved the kind of economic success that would be required to solicit the resources required to maintain and develop them. As a result, there was less rhetorical jousting around simulation than there was around cases. For the most part, the champions of cases ignored any potential threat to their hegemony from simulation games.

Nevertheless, there were some obvious problems with simulation games. The most obvious problem was the resources required to develop, maintain, and use a computer-based game. Direct commercial incentives for the development of management games exist within the market for such games, but no business school saw the financial opportunities as warranting the investment required. Costs were relatively substantial, sales were relatively modest, and the opportunities for unauthorized reproduction were relatively large.

Few business schools were organized in such a way as to make the use of games routine. Few had the technical resources available to deal with the inevitable technical problems. Rarely could an individual professor implement a large-scale management game unilaterally with the same ease as he or she could implement a case. Some of the more complicated management games have been developed within academe, but it has proven hard to sustain faculty commitment to the elaboration and improvement of those games in the absence of explicit recognition for the effort.

Even where resources were available and committed, simulation games did not always gain the enthusiasm of professors or students. It was not clear what could be learned from such a complex world because experience in it would sample only a small fraction of the possibilities. Although later enthusiasts have argued that complex games are more effective pedagogically than simple games (Baillie, 1993), there were persistent concerns about the confused lessons drawn from complexity.

In addition, students might very well treat the game as a game, familiar as they are likely to be with a wide variety of computer games that have become an essential part of youthful maturation. With that background, they are likely to ask not what they would do if they encountered this problem in the business world but what can they guess or ascertain about the game designers' view of the world. Can we beat the program? Almost all observers report that students seek to imagine or deduce the model that is embedded in the game, often by the assumption that instructors are deliberately trying to induce certain behaviors. Thus, the students' definition of the problem involved in the game is not to learn how to act in a business situation but how to be victorious in this particular sport. The result is a kind of infinite game between game designers and students, each trying to fool the others, a game that arguably might be educationally useful for some purposes but not particularly for simulating specific features of business reality.

Moreover, management games rather naturally represent reality as more reliable than it is. The game format typically creates a simulated reality through a set of functions that reflect a considerable simplification of the reality they simulate. Game designers are reluctant to introduce too many random anomalies, though the world is filled with them. Or, if they do introduce such features, they (and their students) find it difficult to determine what can be learned from one particular realization in a stochastic world.

When successfully simulated, reality is a mixed benefit. If a game appears "real," experienced managers are likely not to learn anything from it but simply to apply rules they have used in the "real world." Inexperienced students are likely to be swamped by the problems of simply understanding what is going on. Thus, Dill and Doppelt observed:

> Trial runs show that for sophomores with little or no knowledge of business, it is a major task to read the information which they have to work with and to comprehend the basic dimensions of the decision problems that they face. With executives from industry who think that they know how to manage firms, there is likely to be less experimentation with strategies and more consistent effort to maintain strategies which they are convinced are good. (Dill and Doppelt, 1963, p. 43)

Finally, insofar as games are interactive in the sense that the decisions of one group of players affect the outcomes to other players, as is true in most games that seek to simulate competition, the "reality" that is produced is not the reality of "real-world" actors but the reality of interacting student novices disconnected from real-world obligations or rules. It seems unlikely that the result will reliably have the characteristics of the real world that it purports to simulate.

Simulation and Research

From the beginning, simulation games were seen as offering arenas for research (Babb, Leslie, and Van Slyke, 1966; Cohen and Rhenman, 1961). It was not hard to imagine treating a management game as an experimental setting and observing behavior in the game. It was argued that the realism of a management game provided a better basis for studying managerial behavior than did the simple choice situations provided in conventional psychological experiments.

As early enthusiasts clearly recognized, the experimental advantages brought with them some clear disadvantages that have limited studies using complicated games. In particular, the interactive character of management games in which the actions of one player affect the outcomes of another result in loss of experimental control over the experiences in the game. Moreover, the elements of realism introduced by the game result in an unmeasured mix of actions based on structural features of the game itself and actions based on generalization from knowledge about the real world the game simulates. In general, the complexity of the game makes studying behavior within a management game more akin to studies of individual cases in the field than to laboratory experiments.

9.4 VIRTUAL REALITY IN MANAGEMENT EDUCATION

Business schools are arenas for debate over alternative ways of introducing virtual realities into management education. The debates occur in general curriculum discussions and in the individual discussions leading to individual course decisions by individual faculty. The debates and their outcomes have spawned repeated generations of arguments over the place of different virtual realities in management education.

The Pedagogical Argument for Instruments of Virtual Reality

In a world of obeisance to reality, the rhetorical justification of virtual realities takes many different forms, but the arguments are rarely complicated. Overwhelmingly, the pedagogical advantages of instruments of virtual reality are found in one or more of three general claims:

- First, human learners grasp concepts more easily when they are embedded in narratives than when they are presented as abstractions. Virtual realities are forms of storytelling in the service of the transmission of theoretical knowledge. They are effective insofar as they efficiently communicate academic knowledge that has been gleaned from research and analysis.

- Second, virtual realities are exercises in applying general principles to confusing concrete situations. The match between academic knowledge and experience is complicated by the fact that academic knowledge is derived by abstraction and simplification of experience. Using academic knowledge to advantage in a world of experience requires an ability to select among alternative academic concepts to apply in a particular case and an ability to deal with confounding features of the situation. Virtual realities provide training exercises in those abilities.

- Third, virtual realities and the associated discussions of them provide more general training in ways of thinking. The exercise of dealing with a simulated world and articulating the reasons for action develops skills at intelligent action. The argument is similar to an earlier argument for the teaching of Latin—that it develops the mind's capabilities for dealing with new situations.

Thus, uses of virtual reality can be justified either as devices for experiential acclimatization or as devices of intellectual development. As instruments of the former, they are likely to suffer by comparison with genuine experience. The comparative advantage in education seems unlikely to lie in imitations of life except with respect to experiences that are unlikely to occur often in real life.

As instruments of the latter, they are likely to suffer by comparison with games of chess or the study of great books. Education has long sought to teach students how to think. There is considerable testimony to its successes (as well as its failures) in this regard. However, the mechanisms of success are obscure. Even precollegiate education, which depends much more than higher education on pedagogical research as a source of pedagogical innovation, is not particularly distinguished by its solutions to the teaching-to-think problem. Skill at thinking abounds, but the manner of its development is clear only to enthusiasts for particular gimmicks. Great teachers are identified and honored, but their skills are difficult to characterize or to replicate.

Debates over virtual realities focus attention on what is potentially a false issue. There is nothing inherent in business cases or management games that makes either a particularly good or particularly poor instrument of fundamental instruction. Each provides a useful illusion of reality to satisfy a student's quest for relevance, but it *is* an illusion, and the varieties of ways in which such illusions have been used or avoided in management education with (as nearly as can easily be ascertained) approximately the same final result may suggest that neither instrument is particularly important to the education beyond the illusion of reality it provides. It is possible to argue that the capabilities of the virtual realities of cases and management games to provide instruction depend more on the knowledge and capabilities of instructors than on the properties of the virtual realities themselves.

Not by Argument but by Power

Many students of organizations would argue that debates over creating virtual realities in management education are likely to be settled, if at all, not by argument but by power. Insofar as cases and simulation are contenders for favor, they bring forth two important bastions of power: On the one hand, there is the power represented by the Harvard Business School and other business schools heavily committed to case development and teaching. These are substantial educational and economic forces with considerable investment in business cases as the foundation of business education. They can easily produce variations on the arguments outlined here in defense of cases. They are in a position to mobilize considerable political support by virtue of their close connections with management and the business press. And they have substantial economic incentive to do so.

On the other hand, there is the power represented by the information technology industry and its various associates in higher education committed to extending the reach of the technology into education and business. In the early days of computer science, the extent to which the field would develop as a part of mathematics, engineering, or business was not obvious. Over time, however, business schools proved to be relatively hostile environments, and the development of information technology as an instrument of business took place almost entirely outside of business schools. They became relatively tardy consumers of the software of business operations, rather than producers or researchers. This places the information technology industry at a disadvantage in business schools, but its position in the economy and in the world of the intellect makes it a formidable potential participant in management training.

When political, institutional, and economic forces of this scale are involved, anticipating future developments requires anticipating the elaboration and utilization of power in a world in which competing opportunities for using power are numerous. Business schools have their internal systems of power; they are connected to numerous powerful actors for whom business schools are occasional concerns; and they are subject to other, even more powerful, actors who are almost entirely indifferent to management education but whose actions affect the schools. Developments in management education come out of this ecology of attention and inattention. Along the way, of course, the rhetoric of arguments about using virtual reality to teach, about bringing reality to theory, and about learning to think will decorate the process. It may occasionally even contribute marginally to its outcome.

Chapter Ten

The Rhetoric of Relevance

Because professional education is intended to prepare students for employment in a profession, a fundamental pedagogical issue concerns how to mix the basic concepts of the academic knowledge underlying the profession with the rules evolved through experience by practical professionals. Throughout the twentieth century, university-level business schools in North America were forums for argument over that mix. The conflict extended to questions of staffing, organization, curriculum, and research programs. It showed no signs of abating at the start of the twenty-first century (Chia and Holt, 2008; Knights, 2008).

10.1 Two Kinds of Knowledge

At least from the time when Aristotle undertook to teach Alexander the Great, the relation between the knowledge gained from experience by skilled practitioners, on the one hand, and the knowledge gained from scholarship by skilled academics, on the other, has shaped the formal training of practitioners. *Experiential knowledge* is derived from practical experience in the field. It is stored in the routines and wisdom of experienced

This chapter is not identical to but draws heavily from Augier and March (2007) and March (2004).

practitioners and communicated by them. Its hallmarks are plain language and direct relevance to practice. *Academic knowledge* is derived from scholarship. It is stored in the theories of academics and communicated by them. Its hallmarks are predilections for intellectuality and an aesthetic of ideas.

Knowledge derived from practical experience tends to emphasize immediacy and applicability in a specific context. It is ordinarily more focused in time and space than is academic scholarship. Conversely, the academic perspective tends to emphasize the timelessness and generality of its relevance. As a general rule, the shorter the time horizon and the narrower the scope, the greater the comparative advantage of experiential knowledge.

This dichotomy oversimplifies the relationship. Experiential knowledge and academic knowledge are in many ways better seen as intertwined than as in opposition. Experience is interpreted within frames that reflect academic sensibilities, and the research on which academic knowledge is based is deeply affected by observations and understandings of experience (sometimes interpreted as data).

The relation between experiential knowledge and academic knowledge is related to, but different from, the relation between basic research and research applied to practical problems (Labaree, 2004, pp. 66–67). The latter relation is also contentious in a professional school. For example, Herbert Simon argued that an institution such as a business school should:

> . . . include both the pursuit of knowledge for its own sake, and the application of knowledge to practical pursuits. It does not assume that one of these goals is the sole possession of the disciplines, the other, the sole possession of the profession. On the contrary, there is no reason why knowledge about physics should be useless; and no more reason why knowledge about optimal inventory control or organization structure should not be intellectually and aesthetically interesting. (Simon, 1967, pp. 3–4)

Questions of the appropriate mix of experiential and academic knowledge and their relation to each other are not resolved in the modern history of North American management education, but they are displayed by it (March and Sutton, 1997). Two contending assertions dominate the debates in professional schools. The first assertion proclaims that professional education has sacrificed relevance to the esoterics of academic purity. For example, Jerome Frank critiqued law schools for being too academic and too little focused on the lessons of practice:

> The Law student should learn, while in school, the art of legal practice. And to that end, the law schools . . . must repudiate the absurd notion that the heart of a law school is in its library. (Jerome Frank, "What Constitutes Legal Education," speech, quoted in Stevens, 1983 [2001], p. 156)

The second assertion bemoans the subordination of academic knowledge and research to the limited perspectives of experience. Thus, Abraham Flexner, whose fulminations decorated much of the debate around medical schools, argued that, instead of worrying about practice, it was precisely when medicine emphasized scholarship and did not worry about practice that it became more important and capable of engaging in continuous cross-fertilization:

> Chemistry made no progress as long as men were concerned immediately to convert base metal into gold; it advanced when, for the time being, it ignored use and practice. Today chemical theory and chemical practice are continuously fertilizing each other. So, again, medicine stood almost still until the pre-clinical sciences were differentiated and set free—free to develop without regard to use and practice. (Flexner, 1930, p. 14)

He argued that medical schools should pursue knowledge and research that was "untrammeled by near reference to practical ends" (Flexner, 1910, p. 59).

The rhetorical flourishes associated with the debate are often overly dramatic, but they reflect an enduring problem of professional schools that is manifest in the histories of schools of medicine (Rothstein, 1987), engineering (Reynolds, 1991), law (Hurst, 1950), education (Labaree, 2004), and public policy and administration (Haskell, 1977). All of these schools exhibit tensions between "experiential" knowledge and "academic" knowledge.

10.2 BALANCING EXPERIENTIAL AND ACADEMIC KNOWLEDGE

The prototypic response to tensions between the two forms of knowledge is to call for some form of "balance" or "integration." The idea is to determine the appropriate mix of experiential and academic knowledge by

invoking an analysis in which the costs and benefits of alternative investments are assessed from the point of view of some conception of the common or collective good over time, or to find a conception of knowledge
that integrates what is generated through practical experience with what
is generated through academic research. Much of the discourse over business education tacitly accepts some version of such a formulation. There is
widespread obeisance to the mantras of "balance" and "integration" (Adam
and Salipante, 2003; Amabile et al., 2001; Vermulen, 2005).

One common vision is that by doing research driven by real-world problems but aimed more at understanding than at solving those problems in
a specific context, business schools and researchers in management education both help define and frame practical problems *and* help advance the
disciplines from which they draw. The "balance" and "integration" problems are reduced or "solved" by declaring them potentially nonexistent.

In particular, the idea of "balance" as a solution to conflict is an under-
standable predilection of leaders. They long for some kind of institutional
coherence, with conflict resolved through reference to some higher aspirations. One early president of the American Collegiate Schools of Business
proclaimed,

> . . . the future of collegiate education for business lies wholly within our abil-
> ity to integrate successfully the work of a professional school and the basic
> academic disciplines that underlie that work. (Lee, 1960, p. 10)

Such sentiments can be found in the pronouncements of many other leaders
of the effort to transform business schools in the 1950s and 1960s (Bach, 1958;
Carroll, 1958; Cyert and Dill, 1964; Simon, 1967), as well as in essays by writers who are skeptical about that transformation (Behrman and Lewin, 1984).

Similar proclamations are found in debates over medical education.
Contributors to that debate saw a need to "restore" a balance between research and practice (and teaching) (Ginsberg, 1984). An article in the *New
England Journal of Medicine* argued also that although medical professionals have to master knowledge in the academic disciplines, the "final test" of
their efforts will be "not what they know but what they do" (Cooke et al.,
2006, p. 1341). Thus, they argue, the purpose of medical education post-
Flexner is to

... transmit the knowledge, impart the skills, and inculcate the values of the profession in an appropriately balanced and integrated manner. (Ibid.)

These longings for balance and integration have shaped the ways in which the debate has been framed. Talk of balance is an obligatory ritual. It is, however, a ritual that often appears to be a transparent mask for a more extreme position. Although almost everyone may agree that a balance between experiential and academic knowledge is essential, there is little agreement on the current mix, on the optimal mix, or on the criteria by which the optimum might be determined.

Although almost everyone may agree that experiential knowledge and academic knowledge need to be integrated, there is little agreement on strategies for strengthening that integration or even for ways to describe the level of integration desired or achieved. As a result, there is little or no dissent from the desirability of integrating experiential and academic knowledge, but little consensus on what that means in terms of educational practice.

Debates over relevance are engaged without any significant chance of being resolved by data or by derivation from shared assumptions. A few stylized "facts" are presented from time to time, and some crude empirical summaries are put forth, but the support for one side or the other turns less on facts than on perspectives and prior prejudices. Each side enters the debate with an inclination to be intransigent; and neither the supporters of greater use of experiential knowledge nor the supporters of greater use of academic knowledge feel they can afford to be unilaterally reasonable.

The discussion is often characterized more by rhetorical ripostes from contending advocates than by thoughtful engagement about "balance" or "integration." Thus, a critique of business schools as intellectually shallow and academically second rate (Gordon and Howell, 1959; Mintzberg, 2004) is counterposed to a critique of the schools as far removed from managerial reality, thus irrelevant to, or destructive of, good management practice (Bennis and O'Toole, 2005; Chia and Holt, 2008; *Financial Times*, 2005; Ghoshal, 2005; Lavelle, 2005).

Over time, the argument has become standardized into conventional talking points. Advocates for a practical and relevant approach, the supporters of experiential knowledge, habitually identify a few generic advantages of such a curriculum:

- *Content*. Students learn practical business under instruction from faculty members skilled through practical experience. Their mastery of managing and solving business problems can be tested and corrected before they go into business.
- *Motivation*. Business students are more highly motivated by courses taught about the immediate practice of business by faculty members with practical experience than by more abstract courses taught by faculty members with primarily academic skills.
- *Risk avoidance*. Business firms are at risk if untrained business managers go through management education without a focus on solving practical business problems. Without such attention, business ethics and business performance are both endangered.
- *Concreteness*. By focusing on realistic, practical situations and solutions, education is made more effective. The teachings of academic knowledge and disciplines, on the other hand, are abstracted from practical situations so that students fail to see their usefulness; indeed, their usefulness is likely to be illusory.

Their opponents habitually list some disadvantages with an emphasis on experiential knowledge relative to an approach that emphasizes fundamental knowledge:

- *Vulnerability to change*. The practical aspects of business change rapidly, and the education will become obsolete soon after (or even before) students become managers.
- *Narrowness*. By not teaching the general principles and rationales behind managerial techniques, an education focused on experiential knowledge and specific techniques fails to prepare students for the variety of unanticipated problems they will face.
- *Inattention to social roles*. Business professionals need to know more than the techniques of their specialty. They should be educated also to understand the role of their profession in society and the nature and significance of business and firms generally.

As business schools (and other professional schools) and their constituencies struggle with the problems, the conversations tend to swing from one extreme to the other in their conclusions without significant resolution of the argument. A revolt of those who see relevance as defined in terms of long-time and global perspectives and of problem framing mobilizes forces to advance that perspective. To make the revolution successful, these forces create ideologies and practices that render the revolution incapable of restraint. This creates the conditions for a counterrevolt by the forces of experience and those who see relevance as defined in terms of identifying and communicating best current practice, forces that are similarly rendered incapable of restraint by the requirements for achieving a successful counterrevolution.

Both sides see themselves as disadvantaged in the struggle. In the perceptions of the advocates of academic knowledge, the advocates of experience have an enormous advantage in American business schools stemming from the way they are embedded in a system of business firms and business careers and from their control over the flow of financial resources essential to the schools. Faculties of business schools sometimes become antiacademic, pursuing careers as consultants to, or adulators for, business. As a result, advocates of academic knowledge believe that business school education and research, responsive to such imbalances in power, is inattentive to the limitations reflected in the time and space horizons manifested in experiential conceptions of relevance.

Early representatives for this view included G. Leland Bach (1958). Bach argued that business school research had to lead practice, rather than simply report it:

> I want to stress as strongly as I can my own belief that *fundamental* research is a major responsibility of every leading business school, especially those which offer graduate work. . . . The function of the university is to be ahead of best practice, not to be trailing a few steps behind the operating business world. (Bach, 1958, pp. 363–364)

A touchstone of academic knowledge is its denigration of experiential imaginations of reality and their tendencies toward superstition. Academic knowledge honors science, and science seeks to replace experience-based notions about the causal structure of phenomena with science-based ideas derived from the systematic observation of reality and the elaboration of abstract theories. Much of the claim of scholarship is that it penetrates the noise of normal experience and the temptations to erroneous inference that experience offers to provide an understanding of a true underlying reality. Insofar as they embrace academic knowledge, business schools confirmed a skepticism about the claims of experience (March, 2010).

Modern proponents of fundamental research and academic knowledge in business school include Pfeffer and Fong (2004), who also argued that business school today may be too much business and too little education. Other variations on this argument include Ghoshal (2005), who argued that business schools were at least in part responsible for bad management practices and that business schools, through both their teachings and focus on cases as well as other dimensions, have become overly focused on the bottom-line business (of business education) (Starkey and Tiratsoo, 2007).

In the perceptions of the advocates of experiential knowledge, on the other hand, American business schools are impervious to outside pressures. They are run by faculties for the benefit of themselves and academic knowledge. Although business schools secure a substantial part of their financial resources from the business community, they are seen as using those resources largely to pursue their own agendas of irrelevant research. As a result, advocates of experience believe that business school education, responsive to such imbalances in power, is devoid of knowledge that can be used to address the real problems of a business manager or firm.

Bennis and O'Toole are prime representatives of this view; they argued in a well-known article in the *Harvard Business Review* that business schools are "on the wrong track," essentially because they have "adopted an inappropriate—and ultimately self-defeating—model of academic excellence" (Bennis and O'Toole, 2005, p. 98). To "regain relevance," they argue that business schools must "come to grips with the reality that business management is not a scientific discipline but a profession" (Ibid., p. 102) and that "professions are oriented toward practice and focused on client needs" (Ibid.). Other similar arguments have been made by Ghoshal, who, although critical of management practices, often blamed bad theories for the unethical turns in the real world of business (Ghoshal, 2005). Speeches by presidents of the Academy of Management have also contributed to the debates about how (and whether) business schools are contributing to the real world of management (Hambrick, 1994; Huff, 2000).

10.3 THE UTILITARIAN BASIS
OF THE VALUE OF RELEVANCE

Debates about the proper place of experiential knowledge and academic knowledge in the education of managers proceed from an acceptance of the proposition that schools of management are creatures of a utilitarian morality. The time and resources devoted to the creation, retention, and transfer of knowledge are justified in instrumental ways. The fundamental expectation of the discourse is that the schools can and will justify themselves in terms of their contributions to individual and collective needs and desires. The undisputed criterion, shared across a wide variety of actors, interests, contexts, and commentators, is usefulness.

The conventional modern formulation emphasizes that in a world of scarce resources of time, energy, and money, investments in the development, refinement, and reproduction of knowledge should be rationalized by the returns they generate for individuals and for society. Knowledge activities are seen as having value by virtue of the ways they improve either the outcomes that can be achieved, the likelihood of achieving them, or the choices among alternatives. This broad utilitarian vision is embraced by the majority of those discussing the future of management education.

Utilitarianism in Business Schools

In its application to business schools, the catechism is quite familiar: Curricula should be relevant to students' needs and desires. Skills of graduates should be relevant to the needs and desires of employers and thereby to the needs of graduates (Bennis and O'Toole, 2005). Skills of faculty should be relevant to the needs and desires of organizations interested in employing them as consultants or their students as managers. Scholarship should be directed toward generating knowledge relevant to improving individual success, organizational efficiency, and economic growth (Daft and Lewin, 1990).

Scholarship in business schools has also been defended in terms of its usefulness for the institution, making the school "more attractive to better students, yielding a more qualified, as well as a larger, pool of applicants" (Becker, Lindsay, and Grizzle, 2003, p. 564). Both sides of the debate argue for "improvement" in business education so that schools can rise in rankings (for example, Adler and Harzig, 2009; Giacalone, 2009). A recent AACSB task force report on the Impact of Research (AACSB, 2008) evaluated business schools in terms of the value and usefulness for students, practicing managers, and society (AACSB, 2008). In that report, both rigor and relevance are praised for the impact (usefulness) that they can provide (Ibid., p. 15).

This utilitarian morality is the bedrock of contemporary enthusiasms and concerns over the introduction of markets to educational products. In the past few decades, business education—like education more generally—has become "commodified" and "marketized" through a sanctification of market-based allocations of resources as maximizing customer value. A utilitarian orientation is, however, broader, than a market orientation. Market formulations postulate that things should be useful to customers, but the conception of usefulness is pointedly subjective. Utility is determined by the user. Many participants in the educational debate would extend the idea of utility to include "objective" usefulness (as difficult as that is to specify) and thus would see a market implementation of usefulness as incomplete or misleading. These critics of markets and the "commodification" of education are, however, often thoroughly utilitarian in their opposition to markets. They question the usefulness of markets but accept the usefulness of the criterion of usefulness.

Complications and Limitations

A utilitarian frame for the pursuit of relevance is pervasive, but it suffers from two widely noted complications that threaten to make the pursuit unrewarding. *First, the definition of relevance is ambiguous, its measurement imprecise, and its meaning complex.* As in other discussions within a utilitarian culture, the definition of *utility* is often quite elastic when applied to management education. Relevance may reflect social as well as individual values, hedonistic as well as practical values, short-run as well as long-run values.

The dominance of a utilitarian morality induces efforts to provide utilitarian justifications, not only for such obviously practical items as bookkeeping but also for classical icons of literature, art, music, and metaphysics. On occasion, the morality has been twisted into such grotesquely convoluted specifications of usefulness as to become operationally meaningless. It becomes a language of argument more than a language of judgment.

Ambiguity and complexity are accentuated by the problems of uncertainty. Most of the significant values involved in education are hard to measure and predict. We value graduates who have developed a knowledge basis for lifelong capabilities, but there is little agreement on how to assess current students (or study programs) in those terms. We value knowledge that has a long-run impact on understanding, but there is little agreement on how to assess current research in those terms.

The values that humans profess appear often to be less consistent, less simple, less clear, and less precisely measured than expected value calculations demand. The result is that utilitarian arguments can easily degenerate into little more than variations of word games. "Costs" and "benefits" come to include abstractions not susceptible to calibration or comparison. Moreover, there is a well-known tendency to conflate measurability with significance, to assume that things that are difficult to measure can be ignored (Halberstam, 1972).

Second, the pursuit of relevance is often myopic in practice. Although the concept of usefulness can be interpreted to include an endless number of considerations, the ambiguities of relevance are ordinarily resolved in a way that overlooks consequences that are distant in time or space. In practice, consideration of relevance in discussions of both management education and management research often seems myopic (Knights, 2008). For example, any teacher in a modern business school is aware that the implicit time and space horizons of business students can be notably shorter and narrower than the implicit time and space horizons of scholarship.

Reasonable people can easily disagree about the appropriate spatial focus of a relevance criterion. What is relevant to top managers or society leaders is not necessarily relevant to actors in the immediate neighborhood of the action. To what extent should the teaching of a business school be based on perspectives relevant for workers, middle management, or top management? To stockholders or to political leaders? To what extent should a business school be relevant to its students? Its donors? Firms? Workers? Customers? The global economic and political system? The society?

The easy answer is that the school should be relevant to all of the various elements of a social system listed in the preceding paragraph, and to some extent contemporary business schools try to be. However, as a code word and as a primary criterion, *relevance* usually denotes attention to the concrete, practical concerns of immediate, local actors rather than more distant, less tangible, and more theoretical concerns. The focus is on relevance to managers or their masters. A system dedicated to the protection of "property rights" favors attention to the concerns of owners, however ownership of a business school may be defined.

As we will see in the discussion of professionalism in Chapter Eleven, there is considerable debate about the extent to which business and business managers should consciously seek to be useful to society. A generalized "invisible hand" argument has been interpreted as grounds for the conclusion that society is served best by business actions that are self-interested. Although an explicit adoption of such a pure position is eschewed by most business school leaders, some approximation to it is common. However, for many of those involved in the discussions, acknowledgment of direct business responsibility for actions intended to serve the interests of a broader society is obligatory.

Reasonable people also can disagree about the appropriate time perspective for relevance: Relevance carries a time subscript. Useful when? To what extent should a business school seek relevance in the near term? In the long run? Are managers to be educated for tomorrow, or for the decades to come? Are the things that matter in the long run different in important ways from the things that matter in the short run? Or is it true that the long run is merely a long string of short runs, thus that the long run will take care of itself if the short run is controlled?

Concern about too much attention to the short run was conspicuous in the arguments of the architects of the 1950s reform of North American business schools. G. Leland Bach wrote:

> My central proposition is both trite and revolutionary. It is that business education should be focused on training not for the business world of today but for that of tomorrow—for 1980 not for 1958. . . . surely anything we can do to develop flexibility of mind, openness and receptivity to new an changing ideas, habitual skills in learning for one's self, and other such mental characteristics must promise more use to the individual and to society over the quarter century of change ahead, than would comparable attention to descriptive information about today's institutions and today's best business practice. (Bach, 1958, pp. 351–352)

The issues are complicated by differences in certainty about consequences. Outcomes that are distant in time and space are systematically harder to predict than are outcomes that are local. Advocates of fundamental research and scholarship have to concede that the returns from such work are not only more distant but also more uncertain. The probability distribution over possible future outcomes has a relatively high variance. This makes investments in such things not only more "risky" in terms of the variance over possible outcomes but also more subject to biased errors of estimation. On average, scholars probably overestimate, and consultants probably underestimate, the possible returns from fundamental research, and this disparity in estimation probably increases as the temporal or spatial distance from the predicted outcomes increases.

Confidence that fundamental knowledge will ultimately yield practical return is characteristic of advocates of academic knowledge. For example, Simon (1991) noted,

> . . . when tests of relevance are applied, it is essential that they be applied by people who understand the tortuous, many-step process by which fundamental knowledge may gradually be brought to bear on management problems. (Simon, 1991, p. 10)

However, the evidence for the belief in the inexorability of practical return from fundamental scholarship is characteristically more anecdotal than systematic. Miner (1984, p. 296) analyzed thirty-two established organizational science theories in terms of their rated importance, validity, and usefulness. He found little evidence of any consistent relationships among these three attributes. And Kiechel (2010) argued that the "corporate strategy revolution" in the paradigm underlying the behavior of firms that occurred in the latter part of the twentieth century stemmed not from fundamental academic research but from the efforts of major consulting firms.

Myopia has been explored theoretically in the analysis of experience-based adaptive processes, such as problem solving, learning, evolution, and political competition. In problem solving, consequences in the long run are discounted relative to consequences in the short run. In learning, the mechanisms of learning from experience are local and immediate. They respond to local and immediate experience. In evolution, differential rates of survival and reproduction respond to local and immediate conditions. In political competition, groups advocating investments with usefulness that is local in time and space generally command greater resources and attention than do groups advocating investments with usefulness that is more distant in time and space. There is a systematic bias against activities that provide benefits at some temporal or spatial distance from the point at which adaptation takes place.

Because of the way they tend to ignore things that are distant in time and space to attend to things that are near, instrumentally adaptive processes are potentially self-defeating. Alternatives providing long-run, uncertain, and abstract benefits are at a disadvantage in competition with alternatives providing more immediate, more certain, and more concrete benefits. This disadvantage leads to pursuing a course that reduces long-run gains in the name of short-run gains. Exploitation tends to drive out exploration (March, 1991; Marengo, 1993). Although it is possible that an adaptive process will move too far toward exploration in pursuing a balance between exploitation and exploration, it is more likely that it will move too far toward exploitation.

It is an old story. Not always, but often enough to be worrisome, the explicit, calculated, fast-responding pursuit of a goal reduces the likelihood of reaching it. An explicitly "short-run" approach to pursuing self-interest may undermine longer-run credibility and trust. The repeated mobilization of adrenaline for a "fight-or-flight" response may undermine memory and learning. Pressure to respond quickly to feedback may undermine the patience essential to learning. The adverse consequences have been noted in child rearing, business strategy, economic policy, politics, and war. Similar propositions have been pronounced about many other important pursuits in life: The pursuit of virtue. The pursuit of love. The pursuit of glory. History offers copious evidence both for the ubiquity of the problem and for its intractability.

Activities with Returns That Are Uncertain, Indirect, or Delayed

The main thrust of advocates who stress the word *relevance* in business school debates is to be especially concerned with consequences for and problems of groups that are in the immediate neighborhood of the school. Thus, the relevance criterion exalts the importance of consequences for students, faculty, administrators, donors, and alumni of a particular school and diminishes the importance of consequences for those same groups in other schools and for more distant groups and individuals or broader concerns. The myopia of relevance favors teaching over research, teaching of interviewee technique over theories of information exchange, research on business problems over models for problem solving. It favors concrete knowledge over abstract knowledge. It favors casebooks over analytical models. It favors consideration of strategies for firms over strategies for public policy.

The myopia of relevance in business schools appears to support an expectation that adaptation in management education will be systematically biased against forms and practices having returns that are uncertain, indirect, or delayed. This feature of the pursuit suggests a utilitarian reason for caution about relevance.

Part of the problem lies in predictable biases. For example, program officers responsible for foundation or government grants, as well as grant recipients, have obvious positive biases that color their assessments of experiments. Because the program is not "theirs" subsequent program officers are likely to have negative biases. As a result, independent of the effectiveness of programs, turnover of support is likely to be affected by turnover of foundation officers and persistence in a program is likely to be associated with extended tenure of an officer.

Part of the problem, however, lies not with biased assessments but with the nature of learning from experience. Like rats in a T-maze, institutions can be seen as investing in various programs, monitoring their results, and modifying the investments on the basis of the results. It is classical learning. As has been pointed out by a number of modern observers, however, such learning is a form of sequential sampling in which the learner systematically increases experience with alternatives that have yielded good returns and decreases experience with alternatives that have yielded poor returns (Denrell 2007; Denrell and March 2001; March 1996).

Early experience with an alternative may be misleading because the sampling error due to small experience will be large. Early experience may show an alternative as better than it really is or worse than it really is. Mistakes of seeing an alternative as better than it is are likely to be corrected because learning increases sampling of alternatives that appear to be good. On the other hand, mistakes of seeing an alternative as worse than it is are less likely to be corrected because learning decreases sampling of alternatives that appear to be poor.

As experience (sample size) with an alternative accumulates, the implicit estimate of its return has smaller and smaller sampling error associated with it. The basic result is that the sample size of experience with "good" alternatives becomes much larger than the sample size of experience with "poor" alternatives. Thus, alternatives with initial results that are poorer than their long-term results are systematically disadvantaged by experiential learning. They are likely to be rejected prematurely.

This problem is well known. It has led to an extensive literature on two problems of experience-based adaptation that stem from the way experiential learning involves the endogenous, sequential sampling of possible experience and, therefore, the undersampling of alternatives for which early experience is poor. The first problem is the problem of stimulating *altruism*, a correction for spatial myopia. The second problem is the problem of encouraging *self-control*, a correction for temporal myopia. These are problems implicit in any form of adaptation to experience. They are problems in the pursuit of relevance.

The errors in estimation can be minimized by persisting in alternatives that yield poor early results, by slow learning. Such a strategy has, however, two obvious difficulties. First, in an institution in which actions have to be defended, it is hard to persist in early failures. Second, in fact, on average, alternatives that exhibit early failures will also exhibit long-run failures; so any strategy of persistence will incur the costs of persisting in poor programs.

There is no easy solution to the implicit optimization problem involved here (Denrell, 2007; Gittins, 1989). Learning strategies that respond quickly to feedback (fast learning) are likely to miss important opportunities, but they avoid persisting in folly. Learning strategies that ignore early feedback (slow learning) incur fewer costs of overlooked alternatives, but they invest relatively heavily in unproductive foolishness. The optimum is obscure, but it seems likely that most organizations, including foundations, probably are overly responsive to short-run feedback, thus make more mistakes of inadequate than of excessive persistence.

A possible illustration can be found in the history related here. The Ford Foundation program called for infusing business schools with foundational work in economics, decision theory, and behavioral science. The efforts in economics and decision science were relatively quickly successful and ultimately yielded important results that were recognized as major contributions not only to business but also to the academic disciplines. The efforts in behavioral science had a more mixed initial result. Early Ford Foundation–sponsored research on organizations became part of the canon of the disciplines and contributed to the movement of organizations' research to business schools, but attempts to increase business school involvement in fundamental behavioral science research foundered (Howell, 1966), and the effort was mostly abandoned. Although the behavioral sciences flourished in general (Berelson, 1963, pp. 10–11; Merton, 1963, pp. 267–268), they did not particularly flourish in business schools except to the degree that organization studies transformed itself into a quasi-discipline located in business schools (Argote and Greve, 2007; Augier et al., 2005).

Forty years later, it is possible to see how the teaching and practice of production management, accounting, and finance were transformed by fundamental research on topics underlying those fields. The teaching and practice of domains of management more closely linked to behavioral science have, however, not been similarly transformed. Although there has been some important organizations research in business schools, the impact of that research on the practice and teaching of management has been modest and reflected primarily in rather diffuse changes in the way in which organizations are seen. Concepts such as "bounded rationality," "absorptive capacity," "decision biases," "exploration and exploitation," "garbage cans," and "network centrality" have become common parts of the education, but their precise implications for practice have been generally less clear and less explored.

As a result, much of the teaching of topics such as leadership, innovation, and entrepreneurship that might have pointed to new ways of understanding such phenomena has become instead an echo of an earlier pursuit of "best practice," involving less fundamental research than wisdom extracted (with its usual mix of brilliance, superstition, erroneous inference, and hubris) from successful managers and their stories.

It is pure speculative fancy to say that greater persistence on the part of social institutions in supporting basic research on organizations and human behavior would have produced a knowledge base that would have made contemporary pursuits of fields like "leadership" more research based; but it appears that changes in the teaching and practice of management in fields in which there has been a substantial, fundamental, and persistent research effort in business schools are more significant than changes in the teaching and practice of management in fields in which the research effort has been less substantial, fundamental, or persistent.

10.4 ALTERNATIVE MORALITIES AND LOGICS

As is obvious in the history of North American business schools, a utilitarian context dictates the language of discussion. The argument within and around business schools is thoroughly Benthamite. The undisputed criterion, shared across a wide variety of actors, interests, contexts, and commentators, is usefulness. There is, however, a secondary theme. The pursuit of relevance and the utilitarian morality on which it is based overlook or reject moralities that emphasize education as an object of faith and beauty and its connection to humanity and human identities. Within such traditions, relevance is irrelevant.

The Essential Nature of Education

As John Stuart Mill pointed out in his famous critique, Bentham had "the completeness of a limited man":

> Man is never recognised by [Bentham] as a being capable of . . . desiring for its own sake, the conformity of his own character to his standard of excellence, without hope of good or evil from other source than his own inward consciousness. (Mill, 1862 [1950], p. 66)

Bentham failed to comprehend or represent a range of fundamental human sentiments that stem less from concerns about the usefulness of human institutions and practices than from demands that those institutions and practices identify, honor, and reproduce key elements of the human spirit. These demands lead to questions not about the usefulness of education and research but about the essential nature of education and research as components of a proper human existence about the definition and meaning of scholarly identities, and about contemplating and improving their beauties. Nietzsche wrote how our educational institutions must be rooted "in an inner renewal and excitation of the purest moral powers" (Nietzsche, 1909, p. 17).

Such issues and questions seem strange in a discourse organized around a utilitarian worldview, but they are at least as familiar in human history. Rather than Bentham and Mill, they conjure the voices of Plato, Kant, and Kierkegaard. The discussion is oriented not to what is useful but to what is "essential." What is it that is essential to education and research, without which it fails to fulfill the fundamental nature of its role in human existence? Education and research can be seen as lending grace, meaning, delicacy, and elegance to human life, not because those attributes can be shown to yield competitive advantage but because they are basic elements of an educational faith. A commitment to education can be seen as derived from a commitment to a philosophic conception of humanity and an aesthetic conception of beauty more than from a calculation of consequences.

Any recognition of the legitimacy of such issues in discussions of management education is necessarily a challenge to the dominant utilitarian argument. It is a challenge that is different from the challenge that "relevance" is usually defined in a too immediate local way, for it is a challenge to the relevance of relevance itself, even when given a broad and long-term meaning. It represents a point of view that is deeply antagonistic to a utilitarian worldview.

A Different Conversation

Questions of faith and beauty are difficult within institutions dedicated to utilitarian questions. They require a different kind of serious conversation. In the end, they are linked not to the consequences of education and research or of knowledge but to a sense of identity and aesthetic quality. What is essential to being human? And how is that essential nature reflected in an institution? They pursue not relevance but an appreciation of humanness and life and their manifestation in education and research and in universities. A condition for such an examination is a commitment to glorifying the human estate and, through that commitment, a commitment to sustaining grace and beauty in education and research.

Questions about what constitutes the essence of education and what constitutes its beauty are not easy questions to answer. They require a subtle combination of historical consciousness and philosophical elegance along with a relaxation of the utilitarian grip on argument. The relaxation is difficult. On the one hand, arguments about faith and beauty are always at risk of becoming masked variations of utilitarian arguments. Smart people learn to couch their arguments in a new language without commitment to the language. On the other hand, the technology of discussion of faith and beauty is much less developed (at least among students of management) than is the technology of utility with its economic superstructure.

From the point of view of those who pursue the meaning and beauty of education, the basic utilitarian framework is a mistake:

Higher education is a vision, not a calculation. It is a commitment, not a choice. Students are not customers; they are acolytes. Teaching is not a job; it is a sacrament. Research is not an investment; it is a testament. (March, 2003)

From such a perspective, commitment to a vision of what management education should be depends less on expectations of outcomes than on a sense of identity and its obligations.

If the pursuit of meaning and beauty is to complement the pursuit of relevance in business schools, the pursuit needs to become substantially less ordered by a calculation of consequences. In justifying action, debates need to be less concerned with expectations of good outcomes and more concerned with understanding and appreciating the appropriate fulfillment of meaningful identities, socially constructed senses of self and what is essential to being human. They need to involve a commitment to sustaining grace and beauty in education and research. The discussion needs to involve an articulation of the aesthetics of the elementary components of life.

Quixote said, "I know who I am." For management educators to know who they are, they would have to uncover what is essential to the aesthetics of a scholarly life. Presumably, knowledge achieves its beauty through precision of expression, through the simplification of complexity, through the generation of intellectual surprise. It augments the other beauties of life by providing interpretations of them. It glorifies consciousness and choice as indispensable conceits of human existence.

The words are brave (or foolish), but they are not easily made meaningful in any concrete way? At most, it is possible to imagine some crude guidelines for thinking about management education:

- First, it is possible to think of research and education as preeminently concerned with exposing, contemplating, and rejoicing in the beauties of ideas. The "winner's curse" has turned out to have some very practical uses, but it is the aesthetic of the idea that makes it particularly significant for management education.

- Second, it is possible to respect the aesthetics of competence. Bluster, chutzpah, and self-indulgent illusions of exceptional capabilities all have their place, but management honors the grace of the elementary skills that make an organization a work of art: The letters that are written with style; the pipes that are connected with delicate attention to fit; the motors that are tuned precisely; the abilities that are polished beyond all added usefulness. It is possible to introduce an artistry of elegance to the artifacts of efficiency—the opera of balance sheets and the sculpture of business plans.

- Third, it is possible to think of managers and management as icons of aspirations for humanity. The dilemmas of leadership can be seen as instances of the dilemmas of life and their human resolution in management as models for achieving humanness in life (March and Weil, 2005).

Those who emphasize seeking to realize the "essence" of education and to glorify its beauty match the catechism of utilitarianism with a catechism of their own: Ideas are not only instruments of purpose; they are objects for contemplation. Conversations about management contribute not only to the implementation of intentions; they are explorations of the beauties of words and their meanings. Education is not only a device for augmenting individual and social utilities; it is a sacred element of the human spirit. The essential manifesto: In the end, we are all dead, and the species is extinct; it is only the grace and beauty of the decoration that we provide to the realization of those outcomes that distinguishes us.

From the point of view of these advocates, business schools, like other educational institutions, create themselves through the persistence and imagination of their attempts to elaborate a sense of themselves that ennobles the human condition and glorifies the mind. They picture the performances and scripts of management education as refining the routines of reason into objects and instruments of beauty worthy of human aspirations. In such a world, it might be bearable if business schools were also occasionally useful, but that is a lesser aspiration.

Such a perspective sometimes borders on mysticism, and there is ample potential for pretentiousness in the invocation of meaning and beauty in a discussion of management education, as well as abundant dangers of nonsense. There are risks of forgetting the elementary requirements of education—that books be read, that curricula be specified, that papers be graded, that standards be imposed, that toilets and computers work. It is not only hard to deny that consequences matter, it is also stupid.

Constructing Management Education

We have described a short, incomplete history of argument over relevance in management education. It is a history of rhetoric, of attempts to provide elegant reasons for mundane actions. The rhetoric is often overblown, and the arguments often inconclusive, but they reflect a persistent desire to find justification for educational practice and institutions. Nothing in the history either of business schools or of the rhetoric about management education suggests progress toward resolution of the issues posed by the tension between experiential knowledge and academic knowledge. The histories are distinguished by their tendencies to cycle through shifting phases of emphases.

It is easy to despair at this cycling of argument in the pursuit of relevance and meaning for management education. It is natural to wish for some decisive resolution. It is, however, unreasonable to expect such an outcome. The implicit function of the unending debate between the believers in experience and the believers in scholarship is not to yield definitive answers but to encourage the keepers of institutions of management education to be cautious about embracing simple solutions stemming from glib presumptions that embrace either without attention to the other.

The argument, moreover, is not merely an argument between experience and scholarship; it is also an argument over the proper criteria by which to assess both. There is nobility in a utilitarian morality; there is nobility in a morality of identity and aesthetics; and there is nobility in weaving them together to create management education. In the best of all worlds, the unresolvable dialectic between the claims of experiential knowledge and the claims of academic knowledge provides an opportunity for making management education and business schools both more useful and more meaningful and beautiful as well. That happy result is not likely to be produced by some magical wand that eliminates conflict, but by unending confrontation of the inconsistent voices of a demanding soul. In the process, the management education that is constructed reflects both managers and educators, and the arguments they develop to justify that education define the kind of people they wish to imagine themselves to be.

10.5   Reasons and Interests

Not surprisingly given the academic arena, most descriptions of the history of the pursuit of relevance in management education have been couched primarily in the relatively antiseptic terms of intellectual debates. Although individual and group interests have obviously been implicated in relevance discussions, the terms of discourse have usually not been explicitly personal or group interest centered. Those who demand that business schools be instruments of the business community, that they be bastions of consulting, that they tie intelligence to practical problems, and that their speculations lead to practical implications, emphasize the general individual and social value of such arrangements. They speak in terms of strengthening management education, not in terms of serving interests.

Similarly, the voices that demand that business schools be institutions of fundamental scholarship, that they be bastions of research, that they embrace autonomous intellectual curiosity, and that they treat questions of immediate relevance as pernicious link their preferences to conceptions of general value. Like their brethren on the other side, they present themselves as advocates for improving management education, not for serving special groups. The implicit conception is one of a history that has evolved through a more or less reasoned conversation over policies couched in words and defended within philosophies.

Such an understanding is obviously an incomplete one. It confuses the tactical articulation of reasons by advocates with the political reality of the development of a living institution. A suppression of interests in developing the story makes business school history appear to be driven exclusively by a discourse on relevance. Like all such framings of history, it treats conflicts of interests as encapsulated in the arguments ornamenting them. It subordinates uncertainties with respect to whose interests are served to uncertainties with respect to what argument makes sense. A focus on discourse largely omits more brutal questions from political philosophy concerning whose interests should count, how the conflicting interests (welfare) of the various participants in a society (and future society) should be weighted in taking action. Who should be more relevant than whom? What should be more relevant than what?

It may be useful to recognize that individual and group interests are also implicated in, and lurk behind, the contending arguments. A twentieth-century history of North American business schools that was more interest based might well treat the debates over relevance on which we focus as minor rhetorical frosting for a serious political contest over control of business schools and management education. It would observe that relevance issues as they are discussed here are masks for issues of political power and that the obscuring of interests and their importance is not innocent in a struggle among interests. It gives advantages to some and disadvantages to others. At the most obvious level, advocates for experiential knowledge tend to be those with a comparative advantage in a world built around experience, and advocates for academic knowledge tend to be those with a comparative advantage in a world built around academic knowledge. There is no mystery in that, and the list of interests affected by business school choices is a long one.

Despite a recognition of the force of the argument, we persist in imagining that any characterization of words as epiphenomenal probably underestimates their significance, particularly in a political process in which academics are key players. In contemporary discussions of the role of words and ideas in history (Blyth, 2002; Goldstein and Keohane, 1993; Hall, 1989), we should be recorded on the side of those who think their effects are sometimes perceptible. Moreover, even if the content of the debate over relevance were of minor importance to the outcomes of business school history, it would be of major importance to the humanizing of that history. Reality is not always kind to the advocates of reason and discourse, but a commitment to reason and discourse is a hallmark of the romance of educated human existence.

Chapter Eleven

THE RHETORIC OF PROFESSIONALISM

In North American parlance, business schools are "professional" schools. They are grouped with other professional schools, such as architecture, education, engineering, law, medicine, and social work. Discussions of management education often refer to its "professional" nature, inviting imitation of other professional schools and exploring possibilities of alliances among them. The grouping leads to a certain amount of parallelism in the way the several schools are treated within the university. It also leads to a tendency to see professional schools as sharing common problems and professional school graduates as sharing common attributes. And it leads, at times, to symptoms of envy among some professional schools for the apparent successes of others.

Although the terminology of professional school sometimes appears in that respect to be overwhelmingly compelling, the role of professionalism in management and management education is by no means settled. The issue of "business as a profession" has been debated for decades. It has been implicated in various postwar discourses on whether business is, or can be, a profession (Khurana, 2007) and in discussions of professionalism in business education (Trank and Rynes, 2003). Is management a profession?

What difference does it make whether it is or is not? What are the implications of considering business schools as professional schools?

The most obvious aspect of a "profession" as the word is used in ordinary language practice (Cogan, 1955, p. 106) is that it enhances social status. Most of what are now considered "professions" were originally adjuncts of trades. Their "professionalization" was as much a claim of social status as it was a functional differentiation. As a result, the term *profession* has been applied in various contexts to almost every job as a form of flattery by outsiders or self-aggrandizement by insiders. As these various claims of status have been negotiated in social discourse, some modest agreements on legitimate labeling and status sorting have been achieved in which most occupations recognized as "professions" rank relatively high in measures of social approval.

Professional is, however, not a term of universal approbation. It identifies someone who receives remuneration for services. Remuneration may signify legitimacy and recognized value, but it may also signify the illegitimate substitution of pecuniary motivation for providing services that lose their value if they are procured through a market for services. According to some philosophies, virtue is compromised by being rewarded by anything other than itself (Kierkegaard, 2006 [1843]). Thus, calling a lover a "professional" is more likely to be an affront than praise. Nor is there any necessary reason why behavior following the rules of a professional identity will be "virtuous" in its consequences. Engineers using high standards of professionalism constructed the gas chambers of the Holocaust.

Nevertheless, *professional* is normally a positive term in the context of contemporary occupations. Being a professional normally confers status. So it is not surprising that numerous discussions of management education have evoked the image in a positive way. The advocates of change in business schools in the two decades after the Second World War generally supported the idea that management should aspire to a label of professional. In 1959, Gordon and Howell wrote, "Business is not yet a profession, but . . . it is beginning to resemble one" (p. 73). Most of the advocates of change believed that management education should be similar in important ways to education in professional schools such as those of medicine or law.

The postwar pursuit of professional status for business and business schools, however, encountered internal opposition that was not characteristic of experience in medicine, engineering, education, or law. Ideas of professionalism were associated with a view of management that was alien to some strong traditions of free market ideology. As a result, the efforts to have management take on the mantle of a profession were only partly successful and were somewhat transient. In the twenty-first century, the embrace of professionalism by business schools continues to be controversial.

11.1 THE IDEA OF PROFESSIONALISM

The idea of professionalism is a side product of the history of occupational specialization in the Western World. That history is a record of capability and status differentiation of categories of work and changing routes of access into them. Individuals have sought to enter and have been sorted into various work categories by social processes that regulate entry and enforce standards. The historical processes have been a mix of social class regulation, self-interested job protection, market self-management, and governmental intervention. Ultimately, they have led to relatively elaborate structures of rules.

The history of professionalization in the social and political systems of Western Europe and North America begins with the aristocracy. The aristocracy was a relatively well-defined group with rights of entry that were controlled partly by the group and partly by the state. Individual aristocrats recognized certain obligations of membership and were accorded certain rights as well as certain status by virtue of their certification as members of the group. In their behavior they were bound by a code of propriety that was maintained by tradition and was neither readily accessible nor viewed as applicable to those outside the aristocracy. That code was modified by a process of knowledge accumulation through experimentation and diffusion. The advantageous status position of the aristocracy and its rights were justified by their contribution to a stable, prosperous society.

This style of organizing useful, differentiated groups in a society has persisted. Beyond the aristocracy, some of the earliest recorded structures were those associated with the development of the trades as identifiable social groups drawn from nonaristocratic society and differentiated both from the aristocracy and from the masses of laborers. The trades recognized particular special skills (for example, scribes, conjurers, leatherworkers, butchers), recognitions that evolved into systems of apprentices, journeymen, and master tradesmen and the guilds surrounding them.

The guilds rather closely regulated entry into a trade, training in its special skills, and certification of skill. They also became allies of the merchant class in its struggles with the aristocracy, an alliance that eventually led to extensive governmental support for the guilds and their regulation of the trades. The advantageous status position of guild members and their rights were justified by their contribution to a stable, prosperous society. Whereas the basis for aristocratic rules lay in the experimentations and imitations of society, the basis for trade rules lay in the knowledge that was attributed to the accumulated learning of tradesmen and that was not easily accessible to outsiders.

This combination of group consciousness and organization, status, social responsibility, restricted access, and a linkage to an autonomous corpus of knowledge not readily accessible to outsiders is maintained in modern "professions." With the rise to preeminence of science as a basis for knowledge, however, professions based on the claims to knowledge from either inherited training or practical experience have given way, to a considerable extent, to those based on claims to knowledge derived from a codified corpus of knowledge derived from systematic research and learned through formal education.

There have been numerous attempts to specify the necessary criteria for profession. Although the various attempts differ, and there is no universal agreement, most treatments agree that a profession exhibits three major attributes.

The first attribute is *socially regulated selectivity*. Recognition as a professional is regulated by the profession, society, and state to ensure that only properly certified individuals are accorded the right to practice. The right to belong to the profession is restricted, and the restrictions are enforced by law and social expectations and implemented through impersonal rules.

Thus, lawyers are admitted to the bar, doctors are admitted to practice, engineers and teachers are licensed to serve through formal procedures that establish and certify their competence. Individuals engaging in practices that require those competences without the appropriate certification are subject to legal sanctions.

From a political point of view, the social and governmental regulation of entry to a profession and certification of professionals is certainly not innocent. It can be seen as reflecting the efforts of individuals within a trade to protect their positions and limit competition. However, the regulation of entry may also reflect a community response to the failure of markets to assure either competence or integrity on the part of practitioners. There is ample evidence that markets often have difficulty differentiating among peddlers of services in terms of either attribute.

The second attribute is an *autonomous knowledge basis*. Professionals rely on, and actively pursue, systematic knowledge not readily accessible to others. The practice of the profession depends on a body of codified knowledge stemming from experience and research. Whitehead wrote,

> The term Profession means an avocation whose activities are subjected to theoretical analysis, and are modified by theoretical conclusions derived from that analysis. . . . the practice of a profession cannot be disjoined from its theoretical understanding and vice versa. (Whitehead, 1933, p. 72)

Professionals (in this sense) are linked to specialized knowledge that is not readily accessible to, or interpretable by, nonprofessionals. Thus, the Gordon and Howell Report proclaimed:

> . . . the crucial criterion of a profession is . . . the existence of a systematic body of knowledge of substantial intellectual content and the development of personal skill in the conscious application of this knowledge to specific cases. (Gordon and Howell, 1959, pp. 71–72)

And G. Leland Bach, one of the prophets of the transformation of business schools, wrote:

> Business administration is a new profession. . . . It is a profession that is growing up rapidly. A crucial part of that growth must be the amassing of careful scientific analysis and research to lay bare what is hearsay in man-

agement, what is fundamental skill, and what is transient practice. (Bach, 1951, p. 7)

The link between professionalism and fundamental research-based knowledge underlies the tendency of professional schools to associate themselves with the keepers of fundamental knowledge—the universities, as well as the tendencies for the guardians of knowledge—the universities—to seek to control professional education.

The third attribute of a professon is *social trustworthiness*. Members of a profession are bound by autonomous rules of behavior that reflect the altruistic social demands of a professional identity, rather than the demands of an employer, client, or authority, or the temptations of individual self-interest. Thus, lawyers recognize obligations to justice that may conflict with the demands of clients; physicians recognize obligations to proper medical care that may conflict with the demands of health insurance companies; engineers recognize obligations to safe design that may conflict with the demands of clients; teachers recognize obligations to their pupils that may conflict with parental or bureaucratic pressures.

Mary Parker Follett wrote, "The word 'profession' connotes . . . a foundation of science and a motive of service" (1940, p. 117). Grayson characterized engineering as a form of

> . . . public service, aimed at meeting the needs of society by conceiving, developing and implementing solutions to technical problems of concern to society. (Grayson, 1977, p. 389)

In a similar vein, Flexner listed altruistic motivation as an essential component of professionalism (Flexner, 1915, p. 904).

A person is a professional by virtue of being able to command monetary reward for exercising abilities; and, simultaneously, a person is a professional by virtue of autonomy from monetary incentives. It is important for a professional to be able to make a valid claim to receiving payment for services; it is also important to be, to some degree, impervious to monetary incentives. The imperviousness of professionals to monetary incentives is sometimes described as a commitment to "service," to doing things that serve the community without necessary recompense.

The argument is that professionals should exhibit a commitment to social responsibility in conduct that takes precedence over personal or group gain. Social trustworthiness should be differentiated from the trustworthiness that is usually discussed in the modern economic and psychological literature, which deals primarily with interpersonal trust—the reliability with which people do what they say they will do. Social trustworthiness is the reliability with which a person acts with the community's interests at heart.

Early advocacy of professionalism in business was often linked to the importance of altruism in business (Flexner, 1915) and the idea of a "higher motive" (other than money) (Brandeis, 1914). Such a point of view is reflected in discussions of the role of business in society and the responsibilities of business schools in educating businesspeople for improving society, an argument that is clear in the statements of some of the leaders of the postwar changes in business schools (for example, Bach, 1958; Carroll, 1958), and even before (Donham, 1927).

11.2 THE HISTORY OF NORTH AMERICAN PROFESSIONAL EDUCATION

In 1945, most of the major professions recognized in the United States had links to institutions of higher education. In most cases, the links were represented by degree-granting programs located in colleges and universities, the more conspicuous partial counterexamples being in programs for the advanced training of professional performing artists (including musicians, artists, and actors). This arrangement, in which professional training was one of the functions of large multipurpose universities, evolved over roughly 150 years in the United States.

From Apprenticeships to Educational Institutions

The creation of formal programs for professional training grew out of and replaced earlier training that was primarily apprenticeship modeled after that developed within guilds. Although the formal training of medical practitioners existed to a modest extent in Europe earlier, their training in the United States was almost entirely apprenticeship training until the nineteenth century. The training of physicians resembled the training of barbers; indeed, the two trades overlapped. Early training for a career in the legal profession was largely apprentice based (Stevens, 1983 [2001]). A fledgling attorney worked with an established attorney to learn the trade. Engineering training was primarily apprenticeship training and practical experience. Teachers were selected for some elements of book learning, but their training in pedagogy took place on the job.

As one book about apprenticeships in medicine noted:

> In his education, the apprentice learned medicine as it was practiced in the community. He watched patients from the beginning to the end of their medical treatment. He observed the natural history of their illnesses, mostly infectious diseases, in the environment in which they occurred. He learned about the doctor's relationship with the patient and his family. He saw the family life and economic and social situation of the patient and learned what could and could not be done in that environment. Although the state of medical knowledge limited what he could learn about treatment, an observant apprentice could learn a great deal about illness.
>
> The apprentice also learned about the professional role of the physician in the community. He benefited or suffered from his perceptor's reputation. He became acquainted with other physicians in the region when they met with his preceptor on consultations or social occasions. He learned about the professional community of physicians and about differences in medical practices among physicians. (Rothstein, 1987, p. 26)

Until well into the nineteenth century, on-the-job training remained dominant; and the movement away from that practice and toward formal education for the professions encountered substantial resistance (Starr, 1984; Stevens, 1983). As the nineteenth century progressed, however, training for the professions gradually shifted from apprenticeship programs to formal educational programs located in schools. The institutionalization of legal education began in 1850 with the growth of law schools, some of them university based (Hurst, 1950, p. 268). For example, in 1900 there were 102 degree-conferring law schools in the United States; there were 146 in 1920 and 190 in 1940 (Hurst, 1950, p. 272). Medical schools too began to proliferate (Starr, 1984), as did schools to educate teachers (Geiger, 1999; Labaree,

1992). But whereas, in 1940, only six institutions had a medical curriculum that was not approved by the American Medical Association or the state medical exam boards, in 1936, only ninety-four of the existing 190 law schools were approved by the American Bar Association (Hurst, 1950).

Joseph Wharton, the founder of the business school at the University of Pennsylvania that assumed his name, is recorded as basing his efforts on a sense of the impossibility of sustaining an apprentice system for management. According to Sass:

> He knew that the practice of apprenticing young men to established business houses, the system that had trained him in business, no longer functioned. The pace of business had speeded up tremendously in the last forty years, and neither Wharton nor any of his successful peers had time to take on apprentices. If the next generation of business leaders were to receive a proper preparatory education, it would have to be done outside the business firm. (Sass, 1982, p. 19)

From Independent Schools to a University Base

In Western Europe by the end of the twentieth century, schools of medicine, law, engineering, education, and business were characteristically autonomous institutions dedicated solely to the education of individuals entering one kind of profession. In contrast, in the United States, such schools were characteristically situated within multipurpose universities. With few exceptions, American universities had one or more "professional schools" within their purviews.

The North American transition of professional schools to university-based status came as early as the late eighteenth century in some cases and took place more frequently during the nineteenth century, but in some cases (particularly in education) this didn't happen until the twentieth century. The first medical school in the United States was established in Philadelphia in 1765, and the first medical society was organized in New Jersey in 1766 (Starr, 1984, p. 40), and while the number of medical schools began to increase after the War of 1812, the reform of medical education and its integration into universities began around the 1870s (Starr, 1984, p. 112). Starr sees the development and then reform of medical education and the movement of medical schools into universities as "historically inseparable" and led by the same institutions and people.

The story in law schools was similar. Yale internalized a private law school in 1824. Tulane University "absorbed" the Louisiana Law School, which was otherwise privately run, when it wanted to establish a law school in 1847.

Schools for the training of teachers began as separate institutions (for example, academies, normal schools, teachers' colleges), originally with two-year programs that gradually were expanded to four years. They were absorbed by universities or converted to universities by the middle of the twentieth century.

Most engineering schools were similarly embedded in multipurpose universities by late in the nineteenth century, but the story in engineering was somewhat different from that of other fields. The demand for engineering talent came first from the military and quickly secured support from political leaders. The first North American schools for engineering were established early in the nineteenth century at West Point and the U.S. Naval Academy. Subsequently, engineering schools were established at several major North American universities, and, when the Land Grant Act of 1862 created a system of universities with special responsibilities in agriculture and mining, the idea of university-based engineering training was firmly established.

Small specialized schools focused on engineering, technology, and science also played an important role. Of the ones that survived, the more important were established in the latter part of the nineteenth century: Rensselaer Polytechnic Institute in 1824, Massachusetts Institute of Technology in 1861, Georgia School of Technology (predecessor to the Georgia Institute of Technology) in 1885, Throop Polytechnic Institute (predecessor to the California Institute of Technology) in 1891, and Carnegie Technical Schools (predecessor to the Carnegie Institute of Technology) in 1900.

Though professional schools in the United States came generally to be attached to universities or grew into universities (as in the case of the transition of the Carnegie Institute of Technology into Carnegie Mellon University), the relations between them and the rest of academe were never easy. Within multipurpose universities, professional schools were often seen as having systematically less-distinguished faculty and less-qualified students than those found in the major disciplines. They bore the onus of vocationalism within a culture of pedanticism. Grayson notes that in the mid-nineteenth century, students of engineering or science at Yale or Harvard "did not have equal status with the more elite students in the arts" (Grayson, 1980, p. 377). And Labaree describes schools of education as "the butt of jokes in the university, where professors portray it as an intellectual wasteland" (Labaree, 2004, p. 2). The "wasteland" description was also used by Simon (Simon, 1991, p. 139) to characterize impressions of business schools at the end of the Second World War.

North American professional schools were likely to operate relatively autonomously within their universities. The substantive links between the Harvard Business School and Harvard University, or between the University of California at San Francisco (a medical school) and the University of California, or between the Yale Law School and Yale University were continually being renegotiated, but they typically left the professional school with considerable autonomy.

Nevertheless, university administrators have sometimes struggled to assert control over the professional schools that were formally a part of their universities. A common theme was the effort to improve the academic respectability of professional schools. Beginning in 1869, President Eliot at Harvard was personally involved in a reorganization of the medical school that put the faculty into the university structure and added scientific classes to the curriculum (Starr, 1984, p. 115). As we have already seen in Chapter Eight, President Sterling at Stanford was similarly personally involved in the effort to make the Stanford Graduate School of Business more academically respectable in the 1960s. These efforts were sometimes supported by the professions involved, but outside professional groups often struggled with university administrations for control over professional schools.

The grouping of several different programs under a common label of "professional school" invites a presumption of similarity among them that is honored by procedures and institutional practice. Moreover, the parallelism in schools encourages a parallelism in conceptions of the professions involved. It is natural to see professionalism in the legal profession as having elements of similarity with professionalism in the practice of medicine. The location of both schools within a university, sharing a designation as "professional schools," encourages such thinking.

From Easy Entry to Credentials

University-based programs for professional education echoed the elitism of American colleges and universities. The earliest institutions of higher education in North America (such as Harvard University) were, in many respects, professional schools dedicated to providing training for the Protestant Christian ministry. Fairly quickly, however, they became sites for the proper education of gentlemen. As such, they specialized in variations on an Oxbridge theme of classical aristocratic education. Students were taught the kinds of things that identified a person of means and leisure. The American version never achieved the level of homogeneity and power that typified Oxford and Cambridge, but it became of marker of social status.

By its location within a university, a professional school created a certain presumption of the status superiority of its graduates. It encouraged the notion that professional training produced a person of superior capabilities, a person who was, simply by virtue of his or her special training, especially worthy. However, the idea of education as conferring special status or the notion that entry to a profession required a credential granted through formal education were ideas that were not always endorsed with enthusiasm in the United States. As the New World evolved with its rapid population and territorial growth, its substantially reduced class distinctions, its emphasis on accumulated wealth rather than bloodlines, and its increased emphasis on scientific and technological (rather than moral) progress, pragmatic concerns intruded on education-based social class distinctions.

This tendency was reflected in resistance to formal requirements for entry to the professions. For example, until about 1860 there were few academic professional standards for lawyers (Reed, 1921; Stevens, 1983 [2001]); even the bar exam (where required) was oral and easy. New York law provided that

> . . . any male citizen of the age of twenty-one years, of good moral character, and who possesses the requisite qualifications of learning and ability shall

be entitled to admission to practice in all the courts of this state. (Stevens, 2001, p. 33)

The lack of requirements led an early president of the American Social Science Association, Lewis Delafield, to bemoan the

> . . . prevalent notion among laymen, which is shared by many professional men and has found expression from certain judges, that the gates to the bar should be wide open, and easy admission allowed to all applicants. (Ibid., p. 27)

A similar situation existed in medicine. One physician who came to the United States in the 1870s from Europe noted the difference in how physicians treated their patients and pointed to the absence of social distance as a feature of the system:

> Physicians in America were more concerned with establishing a feeling of confidence and trust, hence of comfort in patients, than were our colleagues abroad. To a great extent, this was a natural consequence of the difference between the status of the physician in the United States and in Europe. Abroad, the medical degree per se invested the physician with a social standing and authority unknown in America, where, in 1874, the meager educational requirements made it easy to secure a diploma after "two sessions of so many weeks a year." With some exceptions, the rank and file of the professions were—as far as general education went—little, if any, above the level of the clientele. (Starr, 1984, p. 81)

By the end of the nineteenth century, however, the populism of American attitudes had surrendered to the pressures for university education for medical, engineering, educational, and legal professionals. Concerns about the superciliousness of educational pretense gave way to a recognition of the importance of the scientific and intellectual bases of professional practice. Dreams of a society without status distinctions were maintained in ideology but supplanted in reality by the functionally useful recognition of status differences based on distinctions in the access to useful knowledge as certified by formal educational certificates.

The dreams did not disappear, however, and the twentieth century was marked by the tension between the extensive democratization of higher education and the impulse toward education-based distinctions. As larger and larger numbers of people earned degrees from colleges and universities, the general status value of a baccalaureate degree was diminished. Marks of education distinction did not disappear, however. They came increasingly to be associated (a) with the ranking of the institution from which the degree was obtained and (b) with advanced degrees, including professional degrees. Entry to professional schools, once fairly routine for any reasonably animate college graduate, became more difficult, and the status conferred by such admission (and graduation) became notable. University-granted credentials of merit became increasingly vital.

Responding to Growing Demand

In the nineteenth century in the United States, education and professionalism were driven by social consciousness of the pressures coming from westward expansion, agricultural expansion, economic growth, and industrialization. In 1862, in the midst of the Civil War, Congress passed two acts that transformed the development of the country. One was the Homestead Act, which opened up enormous areas of land in the Midwest and West for individual farm development. The second was the Morrill Land Grant Act, which laid the foundations for a system of public higher education. These acts, along with generous subsidies, led to the construction of transcontinental railways, the rapid growth in the population of the West, and the proliferation of public universities.

Social and political concerns about furthering the effectiveness of vocations, particularly agricultural, mining, and engineering vocations, came to dominate the development of higher education. This was manifested most powerfully in the land grant universities that rather quickly came to be the primary higher educational engine of American economic and social development and one of the primary instruments for reducing inheritance-based social distinctions. In particular, engineering education became a major route for improving the social and economic position of working-class children and immigrants. While upper-class children migrated disproportionately to programs in humanities and social science at high-ranking institutions that provided the necessary veneer of culture and the practical usefulness of social connections, working-class children were more likely to pursue programs in science, technology, and engineering.

In the nineteenth century, the demand for doctors, lawyers, teachers, and engineers both grew substantially and was spread over the expanding country. Physicians, lawyers, engineers, and teachers were needed throughout the country; and the Morrill Act encouraged the notion that an appropriate response was the creation of vocational programs at land grant universities. Investments in infrastructure and equipment created additional demand for professional talents; the supply was helped by European immigration.

These developments and expansions of commerce, farming, and industry in the late nineteenth century stimulated the creation of professional training programs in universities. The demand for greater numbers of professionals, particularly in engineering and teaching, was a driving force. The minimal requirements for entry into the fields of the law and medicine in the early nineteenth century made the primary problem not so much increasing the supply as improving the quality of the supply, but the demand was strong.

To some extent, of course, the growth in demand and pressures for quality standards were self-stimulated. For example, a litigious society requires more lawyers; and more lawyers make a society more litigious. However, demand for more professionals grew exogenously as well. As standards of health rose, the demand for physicians rose. As industry grew more dependent on educated employees, the demand for education and educators rose.

Academic Respectability

As programs for professional education migrated to the universities and expanded in the twentieth century, they drew repeated criticism for their low academic standards. As we have seen in Chapter Three, the Flexner Report initiated major reforms in medical schools. Among the problems that Flexner identified in the medical schools was the failure to base the education of physicians on the underlying sciences of medicine. To facilitate the building of medical education on the underlying biomedical sciences, he found they needed to be affiliated with universities and to emphasize research (Flexner, 1910). After the Second World War, substantial funding allowed agencies such as the National Institutes of Health to become major players in efforts to tie medical schools to research. The changes fostered by such support resulted in a medical education that was much more firmly based on its underlying disciplines and sciences.

Legal education experienced a related phenomenon, but it proceeded from a different base. While engineering, medicine, and education were, at the time of the American Revolution, just beginning to be recognized, lawyers were already functioning in positions of power. Alexis de Tocqueville observed that the "aristocracy of America occupies the judicial bench and bar" and that "scarcely any political question arises in the United States that is not resolved, sooner or later, into a judicial question" (Tocqueville, 1831/1862, p. 282).

This made the pressures on law schools more directed to restricting entry than to making the schools more academic. The *Albany Law Journal* published a paper on why the legal profession

> ... should be so utterly regardless of its own fair name, and careless of the honors which ought to be connected with the practice of so noble a profession as to admit so readily horde upon horde ... within its precincts, with scarcely a voucher for the ability or worth, morally or intellectually, of such applicants as choose to present themselves. (Stevens, 1983 [2001], p. 24)

Shortly after the Flexner report was published, there was a call from the Committee on Legal Education that it was

> ... most anxious to have a similar investigation made by the Carnegie Foundation into the conditions under which the work of legal education is carried on in this country. (Ibid., p. 112)

The president of the foundation agreed and appointed a nonlawyer member of his staff (Alfred Reed) to conduct studies. Reed's first and most important report was published in 1921 and encountered considerable resistance from established groups within the legal profession (Ibid., pp. 114–118). Nevertheless, attempts to transform law schools followed, often moving the schools closer to academic roots. For example, the dean of Yale Law School,

Thomas Sawn, started building legal education on science and art because he found law schools to be both professional schools and academic scholarly places:

> It is the duty of a university law school to emphasize thought research and publication by its faculty and through the character of its instruction, this broader base of legal education, as well as to give the merely professional training. (Stevens, 1983 [2001], p. 135)

Similar pressures were evident in schools of engineering. A report on engineering education (sponsored by the Society for the Promotion of Engineering Education) took place during 1923 to 1929. Its recommendation of accreditation of curricula led to schools rapidly seeking accreditation. A primary theme was the forging of a more effective link between fundamental science and engineering training.

Schools of education were likewise induced to emphasize the values of academe. As argued by David Labaree:

> Teacher educators cannot professionalize unless they produce a solid body of research on teaching, and there cannot be a science of teaching unless there is an authoritative (that is, university based) interest group with an incentive to generate it. (Labaree, 1997, p. 143).

The movement of professional schools to universities and the ensuing attempts to make them more conspicuously academic encountered resistance in every profession. Consistently, reforms to make professional schools attend more to fundamental knowledge and research led to complaints. The charge was that the schools were neglecting their links to the profession. For example, Geraldine Clifford and James Guthrie, writing about university-based professional education of educators, argued,

> Our thesis is that schools of education, particularly those located on the campuses of prestigious research universities, have become ensnared improvidently in the academic and political cultures of their institutions and have neglected their professional allegiances. (Clifford and Guthrie, 1988, p. 3)

The complaints reflected a continuing debate in professional schools that has by no means abated in the twenty-first century.

Four Issues

Thus, as we examine management as a profession and the development of collegiate schools of business, it may be well to keep in mind four closely related issues that have been reflected in the histories of other kinds of professional schools:

- *Populism*: The history of professional schools is a microcosm of the tensions between populism and elitism that infuse North American life. The populist position is that all human beings are equal or at least that the only legitimate differentiations among people are differentiations made by ordinary people on the basis of their own judgment and knowledge. The distinctions of social class, by which some people are known to be more appropriately identified as social and political leaders than others, are anathema. So also are the distinctions of certified knowledge, by which some people are authoritatively defined as being more appropriately identified as doctors, plumbers, engineers, teachers, or lawyers, thereby excluding others from practice. Professional education, with its standards of admission and graduation, flies in the face of populist traditions in every professional domain. Distinctions that disqualify the ordinary citizen from the practice of medicine or law, from the position of teacher, or from a job as an engineer fly in the face of the populist egalitarian instinct.

- *Separatism*. Every profession demands both knowledge that is idiosyncratic to the particular profession and knowledge that is more general. Is this mix better achieved in a separate institution specialized to the particular needs of the particular profession? Or is it better achieved in an institution that considers itself the guardian of more general knowledge? The answer is not obvious, and the history of professional schools in North America involves considerable debate over the advantages and disadvantages of maintaining professional education separate from other education. In every profession, the earliest schools were separate institutions. In all the major professions, those separate schools have been largely merged into, or supplanted by, schools embedded in larger universities. In all of the university-based professional schools, there are continuing disputes over the extent to which a professional school should be integrated into the university with which it is associated.

- *Authentication.* A profession offers authentic competence. A professional is one who has access to and dispenses genuine capabilities. How are professional competence and integrity authenticated? Every profession offers services to others who pay for the services. There is a market. Under some circumstances, the market operates to differentiate competent, honest professionals from incompetent, dishonest ones and to eliminate the former in favor of the latter. It does so at relatively modest cost. Unfortunately, markets for professional services do not always work well. Beliefs in the inability of markets to authenticate professionals are common, so they are regulated. Licenses are granted and withdrawn. Credentials are certified. Rules of behavior are promulgated. Market judgments about the competence of professionals are augmented by the judgments of experts. These experts may be organized by the profession, or by a public agency, or by some combination of both. Professions differ considerably in the ways in which this process of authentication takes place; on the extent to which the process relies on the market or on regulation and if on regulation whether it is regulation by the profession or by the state; and on the role of professional schools in the process.

- *Fundamental knowledge.* A profession is based on competence that is not easily accessible to nonprofessionals. To what extent is that competence built on fundamental research-based knowledge? Professional competence includes routines for dealing with specific problems that fall within the profession's purview. It includes information on the history of correlations between choices and successes within the domain of expertise. It includes a repertoire of explanations for professional actions. It includes awareness of theories bearing on the domain of professional activities, theories drawn from scientific research, professional memories and conversations, and personal speculations based on personal experiences. For some professions and professionals, the role of fundamental research-based knowledge is relatively minor. Relatively few professional soccer players know much about the physics of movement of objects through space that underlie the trajectory of a ball propelled by a foot or head. For other professions and professionals, fundamental research-based knowledge is essential. Modern treatment of most diseases depends on knowledge of at least the rudiments of scientific theories. Professions also differ in the ways in which they organize the retrieval of such knowledge and the extent to which there are specializations or cascades of expertise.

11.3 MANAGEMENT AS A PROFESSION

Defining management as a profession is, in part, an attempt to raise the social status of the occupation. According to some studies (Ganzeboom and Treiman, 1996; Hauser and Featherman, 1977; Reiss, 1961) business managers in the United States, despite their relatively high economic rewards, persistently rank lower in the social status hierarchy than do such professionals as physicians, scientists, and professors; sometimes they rank even lower than politicians. Thus, it is natural for those involved in the education of executives to consider the possibility of negotiating social recognition of professional status for managers as part of a general claim of social rank.

Early discussions of business becoming a profession proudly spoke of the "special class" to which they belonged. In a speech at the opening of the University of Michigan School of Business in 1913, Edward Jones proclaimed:

> There has begun to merge a special class of administrators, who are not capitalists, but stand midway between the multitude of stock and bond owners on the one side, and the wage-earning classes and the public as consumers on the other. This special class is more and more becoming responsible for the inauguration and execution of industrial and commercial policies. It is a great opportunity of this college to assist this rising profession to a consciousness of itself, to help it realize its trusteeship, and to stimulate it to conceive itself as an intellectual aristocracy in the world of affairs. (Jones, 1913, p. 187)

However, such an elevation encounters expectations of socially regulated entry, autonomous knowledge basis, and social trustworthiness that are more problematic with respect to management than with respect to professions such as law, engineering, teaching, or medicine. For example, in 1930, Abraham Flexner argued that business was not a profession because it was

> . . . shrewd, energetic, and clever, rather than intellectual in character; it aims . . . at its own advantage, rather than at noble purpose within itself. (Flexner, 1930, p. 164)

Flexner's prejudices led him to view the business schools of his time (most specifically the Harvard Business School) as unfit for university recognition.

As long ago as 1927, the then dean at Harvard Business School noted the lack of entry barriers to business, compared to other professions:

> Young men enter business too frequently because they do not feel competent or inclined to enter any of the so-called learned professions, rather than from a positive desire to enter upon a business career. Business has thus become in part a catch-all and a dumping ground into which in the case of many families inferior sons are advised to go. (Donham, 1927, p. 417)

Although the MBA degree has become subsequently almost a de facto requirement for a management career in North America, management is far from exhibiting socially regulated entry. There are no public licensing requirements, no public examinations, no public agencies enforcing rules; and if there is currently any group advocating such things, it is tiny in size and miniscule in influence. In that sense, at least, management is no closer to being a profession than it was in 1945.

The proponents of managerial professionalism generally limit their advocacy to the other two requirements. For them, recognizing management as a profession implies giving credence to two powerful assertions. First, management must be based on a body of fundamental knowledge that informs actions, and management must be connected to the research community in such a way as to be continually responsive to the augmentation of knowledge through fundamental scholarship. The partnership between management and academic knowledge must be strong and ongoing. In practice, attitudes toward the idea that management should be based on research-grounded knowledge are decidedly ambivalent. Experiential knowledge is often honored at least as much as knowledge based on research.

Second, management must be embedded in a social system that defines and enforces a set of professional rules of conduct. In a dedication address at the opening of Harvard Business School (published in the *Harvard Business Review*), the former chairman of the General Electric Corporation noted,

> Today and here business formally assumes the obligations of a profession, which means responsible action as a group, devotion to its own ideals, the creation of its own codes, the capacity for its honors and the responsibility for its own disciplines; the awards of its own service. (Young, 1927, p. 394)

Those codes of conduct and rules reflect judgments about what it means to be a proper manager, thus an ethical code that is independent of individual self-interest, an organizational hierarchy, the demands of clients, or the impositions of government. Professional managers doubtless identify with the organizations that employ them; but, by this criterion, they should also identify with a profession and its standards. They should be prepared, under some circumstances, to sacrifice their own self-interest and the interests of those who hire them to the rules of proper professional behavior.

Like the demands for an autonomous knowledge base grounded in research, the demands for social trustworthiness pose problems for the rhetoricians of management. Most conspicuously, they conflict with an ideology that venerates market determinations of value and the social role of self-seeking arbitrage. The teachings of business schools tend to subordinate formulations of virtue based on moral codes and social responsibilities to formulations that picture maximizing personal income, corporate profit, or shareholder value as the highest social virtue for management.

Postwar Changes in the Knowledge Base of Management

The main thrust of the reforms of the 1950s and 1960s was to move the locus of knowledge about management further from experience and closer to scholarship. Prior to the war, most of the knowledge that was communicated in management education was drawn from the experience reflected in standard good practice. A standard route to a professorship was a prior career in management; such research as there was tended to involve efforts to observe and report business practice. After the war, the knowledge bases for virtually all aspects of management became notably more academic.

The knowledge base for the management of production, orders, and inventories was moved from experience to the scholarship of operations research—linear and dynamic programming, queuing theory, artificial intelligence. The knowledge base for the management of finance was moved from experience to the scholarship of efficient markets—derivatives and other financial instruments of cleverness in efficient markets. The knowledge base for accounting was moved from experience to the scholarship of game theory and agency theory. The knowledge base for the management of human factors was moved from experience to the scholarship of economic incentives, group dynamics, and organization theory.

The trend was extended to business functions that were traditionally seen as almost entirely experience based. Business strategy and leadership became topics for research with the full panoply of scholarly accoutrements, including scholarly journals. And when entrepreneurship emerged as an important business phenomenon, business schools rushed to include it in their curricula, first by hiring successful entrepreneurs as instructors and then by gradually replacing them with scholars doing research on the topic.

Postwar increases in the scholarly bases for business education were more extensive in some schools than in others, being particularly evident in schools attached to major research universities and in schools primarily engaged in postbaccalaureate programs. The counterreformation of the 1980s and 1990s slowed the process but did not entirely reverse it. In numerous ways, management became more professional in the sense of being more profoundly connected to a research community built around technical, academic knowledge.

The Issue of Social Trustworthiness

Social trustworthiness is often seen as a component of professionalism. It is also frequently seen as an element of virtue. In that spirit, advocates of the "professionalization" of management tend to picture professional codes as reflecting ethical standards that are higher than those enforced by markets, clients, or bosses and to associate managerial professionalism with the triumph of virtue over greed.

Wallace Donham, the second dean of the Harvard Business School, noted the importance of educating "socially minded businessmen" and endorsed the idea of the "social responsibilities of business" (Donham, 1927). Donham argued that if business schools focused only on individuals and on selfishness and gave their students a "typically selfish and materialistic point of view," it would be better to "sink the schools of business at the bottom of the ocean" (Ibid., p. 407). The Donham perspective was extended by Donald K. David, a dean of HBS after the Second World War, who sought to instill a sense of corporate social responsibility (Spector, 2008).

An early dean of the Chicago School of Commerce and Administration, Leon Marshall, laid a similar charge on that school:

> The college assumes that . . . its justification must be a social justification; that, however important it may be to turn out business men who can make money, social workers who can command good salaries, civic workers who can rise to positions of influence and affluence, the most important task of all is to aid in promoting the progress and welfare of society. Our medical schools are demanded not primarily that physicians may command good fees but that society may be served. Our law schools may aid in making lawyers who will be wealthy, but the mere fact that we impose a bar examination shows that the interest of society, not that of the individual, is dominant. So our schools of commerce will miss their purpose if, either by intention or through neglect, the individual, money making side is permitted to have the ruling hand. (Marshall, 1913, p. 101)

Such views, however, conflicted with the rhetoric of self-interest and markets that permeated (and still permeate) business school life. In fact, modern North American society both loves markets and abhors them. It associates social value with market value yet venerates actions that substitute moral and social values for market values. It glorifies those who command high prices in the market but elevates to an even higher status those who, though capable of market success, forego it or moderate it in the name of moral values. It honors both the accumulation of great wealth and its philanthropic divestiture in socially useful ways.

It was in such a context of ambivalence that the efforts to ground management in fundamental research produced an important secondary effect. Peter Drucker, the doyen of management gurus in the United States, noted the change, but also the danger, in pursuing academic respectability at the expense of social concern:

> The business schools no longer see themselves as social instruments. They want to be "respectable" as, say, mathematics department are respectable. But this is wrong. Professional schools are . . . social institutions. (quoted in Zalanznick, 1986)

Drucker was prescient, but he may not fully have anticipated the way in which the pursuit of academic respectability by business schools would come to conflict with social concerns. Most of the academic research on which the new management was built had its primary intellectual roots in decision theory, game theory, and neoclassical economics. Explicitly or implicitly, the research and the research community accepted the dictum that society is best served by, and morality best represented by, allowing markets to make allocations among self-interested actors. Even some of those most committed to the reforms of the 1950s and 1960s saw the social good as being served more by the use of fundamental knowledge to improve managerial efficiency than through modifying the self-interest incentives underlying managerial behavior. As Cyert and Dill (1964) noted,

> Our economic system is essentially a decentralized one in which the resources of society are allocated by a myriad of managers. If these managers and the students who will succeed them can be taught to make and evaluate decisions in a more valid and scientific manner, the use of our resources will be improved and our society will be strengthened. (p. 237)

One of the more eloquent spokespeople of the position was Milton Friedman, who labored to persuade corporation managers that, when they talked of "social responsibility," they were speaking about socialism:

> . . . businessmen believe that they are defending free enterprise when they declaim that business is not concerned "merely" with profit but also with promoting desirable "social" ends; that business has a "social conscience"

and takes seriously its responsibilities for providing employment, eliminating discrimination, avoiding pollution and whatever else may be the catchwords of the contemporary crop of reformers. In fact they are—or would be if they or anyone else took them seriously—preaching pure and unadulterated socialism. Businessmen who talk this way are unwitting puppets of the intellectual forces that have been undermining the basis of a free society these past decades. (Friedman, 1970, p. 125)

For those who decried the invocation of social responsibility, a business manager was bound to pursue the interests of the firm's owners without recourse to personal ethics or personal judgments of social needs. It was a position that seemed to those on the other side to echo the arguments of the defendants in the Nuremberg Trials who were "just following orders," but it was a position that secured considerable support in business schools and in the business press.

Within such an orientation, market failures are best accommodated by modest social interventions in the market, not by controlling self-interest through codes of proper behavior. As the rules of business practice that had been developed through experience were replaced by rules derived from neoclassical economic or decision theory assumptions, independent codes of proper behavior were eroded. Focus became more and more on personal or shareholder maximization, in the spirit of the argument that the social responsibility of business was to increase profits (Friedman, 1970; Henderson, 2001; Desrochers, 2010). As management became more professional by virtue of its links with a research community, it simultaneously became less professional by virtue of being not as well embedded in an ethical standards community enforcing a set of ethical rules other than the pursuit of self-interest.

The process can be illustrated in education for the profession of accounting, a component of business education with a history that largely antedated other business school efforts. By the criteria we have identified, traditional accounting qualified as a profession, though its embedding in a fundamental research community might have been questioned. Admission to the ranks of Certified Public Accountants has been regulated by law and examining agencies, and accountants have been bound by a set of rules that qualifies them as proper accountants and often frustrates the profit-maximizing ambitions of managers.

After the Second World War, accounting became increasingly connected to a research community (primarily microeconomics and game theory) but simultaneously increasingly disconnected from an accounting standards community that imposed rules that could not be rationalized within economic theory. The changes were fought in several places but most dramatically within the Financial Accounting Standards Board, which gradually substituted ideas drawn from academic economists for rules defended by traditional accountants (Jackson and Cook, 1998; Zeff, 1999).[1] Accounting firms became consulting firms using modern economic analysis in the service of managerial desires. Independent audits as rule-based, tough-minded assessments of managerial actions according to independent rules and sentiments were significantly compromised.

Popular outrage at the events at Enron and in American financial institutions stimulated demands for rethinking the possible role of a code of professional ethics for a profession of accounting and a profession of management. For example, Robert Shiller wrote in a *Wall Street Journal* op-ed column that the business curriculum could lead to an "ethical disconnect" and that the courses "often encourage a view of human nature that does not inspire high-mindedness."[2]

In recent years, business schools have been asked once again to reform their curricula, often with explicit reference to professionalism and social trustworthiness. The AACSB, the Aspen Institute, and various other institutions have joined the voices of change and the call for "responsible management education" in the wake of financial and corporate scandals. For instance, the founding dean of the Carey School of Business at Johns Hopkins University, Yash Gupta, noted in 2008 that the purpose of the school was to

> . . . restore the ideals of professionalism and instill a humanistic spirit that turns business into an engine of positive transformation. Yes, we are about a healthy bottom line, but we care even more about a healthy planet populated by healthy people. If, indeed your goal is to serve, then you will

identify opportunities—with your passion, your perseverance, your sense of purpose.[3]

The cry has sometimes become strident, as found in the comments of the noted student of organizations, Henry Mintzberg. MBAs, he finds, tend to be arrogant and with a narrow focus on shareholder maximization. Mintzberg attributes the lack of social responsibility in business organizations to a focus on individual interests rather than social values and ethics, a focus attributable to unfortunate elements in MBA education. He assigns particular blame to the tendency of business schools to emphasize maximizing shareholder value. Business schools, he intones, are part of the problem, not the solution. A corrupt system, with corrupt and corrupting students, produces a "society of meanness" (Mintzberg, 2004, p. 153). Such sentiments have occasionally stimulated the rethinking of students who already had their MBA degree; one recently wrote in the *London Times*:

> I write as the holder of an MBA from Harvard Business School—once regarded as a golden ticket to riches, but these days more like a scarlet letter of shame.[4]

In this context, former students, business school leaders, and managers who describe management as a profession are, in effect, proclaiming a desire for a change that would bring business schools much more forcefully to embrace the goal of social trustworthiness in management and to forge the social institutions required to maintain those bases. Thus, Gordon and Howell proclaimed that a profession "must set up standards of professional conduct, which take precedence over the goal of personal gain" (Gordan and Howell, 1959, p. 73). And, by 2009, several hundred MBA students at the Harvard Business School (but less than a majority) were signing pledges to guard "against decisions and behavior that advance my own narrow ambitions but harm the enterprise and the societies it serves."[5]

Such sentiments are challenges to one of the central themes of business school education—maximizing self-interest (or perhaps the self-interest of the firm) as the essential criterion of managerial quality. And they confront directly some of the more hallowed principles of the social philosophy of economics as pronounced by Friedrich Hayek, Milton Friedman, and George Stigler—the patron saints of modern business economics.

Academic Independence

A professional education is necessarily tied to the profession for which it prepares graduates. A professional school is part of a community of professionals that evolves and enforces the standards of the profession and socializes the novice into obedience to them. The school serves the profession. In a fully developed profession, the professional community connects practitioners, educators, and researchers and subordinates the autonomy of each to community understandings, including political, social, and economic understandings.

Therein lies a problem for some academicians. The school serves the profession, but it exists in a university that is dedicated to the independent pursuit of knowledge. If management were to become a profession, business schools and the business community would be linked to a degree that might be uncomfortable for faculty with strong commitments to academic independence. The ties between medical schools and the medical profession or between engineering schools and the practice of engineering have led to practices of collaboration that have been condemned (for example, Kleinman, Eisenberg, and Good, 1978; Sox, 2007; Starr, 1984; Thompson, 1993; Walker, 1971; Whitehouse, 2008) as well as praised. Where professional schools are located in universities, as they are in the United States, the conflicts are accentuated by traditions of university autonomy.

Some of the problems are manifest in the mixed reactions to close association between medical schools and the pharmaceutical industry and between engineering schools and the information technology industry. For example, a 2008 article in *Culture, Medicine and Psychiatry* written by a doctor and a long-time consultant to the pharmaceutical industry, about "Why I No Longer Consult for Drug Companies," argues that the close linkage between medical schools and the peddling of drugs corrupted the development of medicines:

> I . . . saw that while we formerly developed drugs for diseases, the pharmaceutical industry had in fact switched to creating diseases for drugs . . .

I began to realize that they [drug companies] were trying to manipulate my opinion as much as I was trying to give them mine. I came to see that marketing was replacing science as the dominant conversation . . . I have stopped consulting for the pharmaceutical industry because I do not want to help them control not only our health but our very conceptions of health and illth. (Whitehouse, 2008, pp. 6, 9)

Other contributors to these debates have described how the medical profession did not formally address issues of conflict of interest until the 1980s (Thompson, 1993) and even then relied often on the moral character of the individual physicians at a time of the rise and growing power of the "new medical-industrial complex" (Relman, 1980, 1997, 2007). The problems of medical education and possible conflict of interests also include issues of the increasing neglect of the patients with the growing market for health care and the difficulties of maintaining medical professionalism in a commercialized health care market (Johns, Barnes, and Florencio, 2003; Relman, 1997, 2007). Relman (2007), in the *Journal of the American Medical Association*, describes the crisis of the medical professionalism as being as severe as the crisis in the health care system. He attributes these problems to the endangered "ethical foundations" for medicine, which include the commitment of physicians to put the needs of others ahead of their own and the erosion of the "soul" of medical education (p. 2668). He decries the growing commercialization of health care and the view that medicine can be seen as a "business" (Ibid.).

Similarly, it has been argued, the intertwining of business schools and business can result in a dysfunctional enthusiasm in the schools for business practice (Ghoshal, 2003; Shugan, 2006; Tinker, 2004; Zimmerman, 2001). The argument touches most directly on the tendency of business school faculty to have their research funded by business enterprises and to be heavily involved in well-paid consulting activities that sometimes seem to make them less students of business than apologists for it. It has been suggested that business school faculty, entwined with business firms through their consulting and research, are in danger of becoming publicists for firms. An example reached the pages of the *CFO Magazine* in an article called "The Case against Cases." The article details how a business school professor engaged in consulting with Enron wrote a profoundly positive case about the company illustrating the importance of "entrepreneurial energy" (Harris, 2003). After the Enron scandal, the case was revised.

As James Howell, one of the authors of the Gordon and Howell report, later observed:

> A business school has to serve the profession, but that doesn't mean that it should always do what the profession wants it to do. Its obligations are to its students and to the profession as it is emerging, not necessarily as it exists today. I think it's important that business schools stay some distance away from the business community. Their primary responsibility is not to today's business community, it's to the business community of the future and, in a more abstract sense, to society. (Howell, 1984)

The problems permeate a business school. Although business school scholars who are funded by business firms steadfastly proclaim their independence, the correlation between funding and a positive picture of business practice seems high. Contemplating the tendency of research studies to become marketing brochures, one essay in the Dow Jones publication *Smart Money* noted the criticism of:

> ... the idea of the financial sector tapping into academia to create market-driven research, whether it's designed to lobby government agencies and shape the national debate over financial reform or influence brokers and advisers who recommend financial products to millions of clients. (Parmar, 2010, pp. 64–65)

The problem is not limited exclusively to funding patterns. The research foci of business schools tend to follow business practice rather than anticipate or lead them. When mergers and acquisitions were popular in business, research on mergers and acquisitions flourished. When outsourcing became common in business, research on outsourcing became common. When the growth of new firms in the computer and software industries became manifest, business schools rushed to do research on entrepreneurship. This orientation tends to make business schools the publicity departments of business firms and industries rather than institutes for independent study.

Moreover, the overwhelming orientation in a business school is to the problems and successes of individual business firms. Research studies examine how to improve firm profitability and try to identify the correlates of firm survival. Publications relate conclusions about strategies and practices associated with success of firms. Relatively few business schools devote significant resources to examining how to maximize returns to other participants in the economic system (such as workers, consumers, and governments) or to exploring how to further the more general interests of the industry or society, which may, for example, be better served by turnover in firms than by their endurance.

In such a spirit, some commentators on business schools make a distinction between the role of academic research in improving business practice and the role of academic research in understanding business:

> Research in business, for business or by business is conducted for the purpose of immediate gain, such as the sales or marketing research carried on by some particular corporation, or . . . the broader studies of business problems pertaining to a whole industry which are conducted by an organization of the businessmen in that industry. Research about business, on the other hand, is not concerned with immediate gain. Its object is to gather basic facts about business as a whole for the purpose of deducting general principles. (Mayer, 1925, p. 258)

There is no question that business school teaching and research subordinate concern with the social and economic effects of the institutions of business (particularly business firms) to concern with improving the successes of individual firms or members of firms. The former are taken as self-evidently positive within a capitalist, neoeconomic ideological faith; the latter are taken as projects for investigation. As a result, the contributions of business schools to understanding how businesses fit, or might fit, into the social and economic system of a country or the world tend to be quite modest.

The Pursuit of a Managerial Identity

In pursuit of improved business efficiency, much of management education involves training in technical skills. These skills include a wide variety of technologies: accounting, budgeting, finance, business law, marketing, operations management, negotiation, group processes, persuasion, product development, research management, information technology, business plans, decision making, strategic management. Each of these technologies draws from a mixture of experiential knowledge and academic knowledge, and teaching in business schools similarly reflects such a mixture. The curricula in different schools and in different areas reflect different judgments about the appropriate mix of experiential and academic knowledge, with some domains in some schools being taught almost entirely from the point of view of experiential judgments about "best practice" and other domains in other schools being taught almost entirely from the point of view of academic knowledge.

The teaching of these technologies is, however, embedded in a somewhat different set of lessons that permeate the classrooms and cultures of business schools. These lessons comprise the socialization of business school students into one or more identities of critical importance to modern business organizations. Like the technologies of management, the identities of management are constantly evolving even as they are being learned. The identity of manager is negotiated and adapted every day in the workplace and in the classroom; and the identities of the twenty-first century are different in many important ways from the identities of the nineteenth century. Nevertheless, some of the more important things learned in business school are the enduring rules of proper managerial behavior.

These identities are important. As has frequently been observed, there are two grand theories of how individuals act and justify their actions. The first theory emphasizes choices based on anticipation of their consequences. Such a theory underlies most of modern economics, decision theory, and much of what is taught explicitly in modern business schools. This logic of consequences leads to self-interest theories of individual behavior and exchange theories of social control and governance (Hirschman, 1977; March and Olsen, 1995, Chapter 2).

The second theory emphasizes choices based on fulfilling the rules of an identity and matching appropriate behavior to a situation. Such a theory underlies important parts of modern sociology and psychology, as well as much of what is taught implicitly in modern business schools. The logic of appropriateness leads to identity-based theories of individual behavior and of social control and governance (Ibid.).

No one who has participated in modern business schools would doubt that some of the more conspicuous things that are learned in those schools are the rules of managerial identity. The schools tend to be powerful socializing instruments, particularly within MBA programs. They socialize students into the MBA role as a route to socialization into the managerial role. Business school students learn how to dress, act, speak, think, and experience life as an MBA, manager, consultant, or entrepreneur. They are shaped in their manners and their thoughts as thoroughly as military cadets are shaped in a military academy, priests are shaped in a seminary, lawyers are shaped in law school, engineers are shaped in a school of engineering, teachers are shaped in a school of education, and physicians are shaped in a medical school. They come to speak a distinctive language, approach problems in a distinctive way, and value distinctive abilities.

Much of identity learning involves modeling. Exemplars of proper managers are displayed and described. Peers, instructors, and visitors exhibit appropriate attitudes, styles, and behaviors. Classroom exercises give training not only in the techniques of management but also in the ways in which those techniques are used so as to fit into a managerial culture. Inappropriate behavior is scorned; proper behavior is rewarded. The characteristic MBA identity—and thereby the managerial identity—is accepted and executed by the vast majority of MBA students.

The socialization is reliable enough to invite lampoons on the part of outsiders. A standard perception on a university campus (outside of the business school) is that MBA students arrive on a campus looking and acting more or less like people; within two weeks, they are easily recognizable as MBA students, using MBA-speak to communicate and sharing mannerisms, dress, and understandings that decisively distinguish them from others. Business schools differ in the degree of conscious attention to socialization into identities, but they all serve as critical institutions not only for learning how to be an MBA but also for learning how to be a manager, a consultant, or an entrepreneur.

The identity is, however, substantially devoid of elements of social consciousness in the sense of obligations to a code that specifies broad social responsibilities and awareness. A dominant theme within the ideology of business and management and the identities associated with them is the idea that life is best managed by self-interested incentives, particularly monetary incentives. A good manager pursues his or her own self-interest and anticipates that others will do the same. A business manager (principal) aligns incentives within the firm in such a way that the pursuit of self-interest on the part of others (agents) leads to maximal achievement of managerial or shareholder self-interest. Everyone seeks to maximize individual monetary wealth, and the presumed result (if organized properly) is maximal gain for the organization and society. Any less self-interested motives that may survive the training are expected to be justified by reference to some perturbation of self-interest.

A standard critique of management education in this respect is that the identity-based rules of proper behavior learned in business schools are unattractively linked to a conception of proper behavior that is excessively egocentric. The argument is that, in the name of an ideology that associates social virtue with personal selfishness, management education actively discourages social trustworthiness. Ideas of social trustworthiness as a component of individual managerial identities are not easily reconciled with contemporary economic ideologies or contemporary business education based on them.

This is not to say that individual managers are devoid of social trustworthiness. Many are deeply committed to altruistic goals; but such an orientation is not normally seen as a significant part of the managerial identity. A 2000 study comparing the motivation in choosing a school reported by business school and law school students found that only 2 percent of business school students stressed altruism or doing something for social justice or society as part of their motivation, compared to 19 percent of law school students (Schleef, 2000). To many outside observers, the 19 percent seems discouragingly low, but the 2 percent seems obscene. Indeed, management education and business school culture are more likely to denigrate altruistic motives than to encourage them, for example in discussions of layoffs, downsizing firms, outsourcing business tasks, or engaging in political lobbying.

11.4 FINDING A WAY TO PROFESSIONALISM

The reforms in business education of the 1950s and 1960s went a long way toward embedding management in a research-based body of knowledge. Those reforms were eroded in the last two decades of the twentieth century, but they remain significant. In that sense, management has become more professional. At the same time, although there was no movement toward formal licensing requirements for managers, the MBA degree was elevated to a quasi-required certificate.

The reforms, however, did little or nothing toward making management more socially trustworthy. Indeed, by virtue of the turn in North American economics toward a particular interpretation of neoclassical assumptions about the efficacy of markets, academic scholars came to rationalize individual selfishness as socially advantageous, a turn that was enthusiastically embraced by the selfish and that relegated defenders of social trustworthiness to the meager crumbs of reputation in repeated games.

There is no easy way out of such a hole for those who find the results unacceptable. The kind of "professional" vision of managerial identity that animated many of the leaders of the postwar reforms conflicts with an alternative "rational actor" vision that sees a manager as a self-interested manipulator of self-interested collaborators and competitors in a world convinced of the postulated morality of the "invisible hand." And the latter vision, without any doubt, dominates contemporary business schools and the research on which the teachings of management are based. Discussion of the role of management as a profession in the creating of a better world has been made largely irrelevant, as has discussion of the role of the business school in improving society.

As long as business schools are dominated by economics and economics is dominated by the ideologies of the Chicago School, there can be no significant professionalization of management education insofar as professionalization implies acceptance of the virtue of social trustworthiness.

The economic theory underlying most research on management and most teaching of management is a theory of self-interest seen as a route to social well-being. It is not neutral with respect to a conscious commitment to a social conscience; it sees such a commitment as both self-destructive and socially disadvantageous.

Significant change in business schools in this respect would require either that economics change or that business schools veer away from dominance by economists. Either change is imaginable, but neither seems immediately likely. It is possible that economics might shift from a consequentialist-based theory to an identity-based theory, but that possibility seems unlikely. Neither the academic community nor the business community seems particularly disposed to go in that direction.

Business schools are professional schools by categorization edicts of North American universities, but they do not train professionals as that term is normally understood. Periodically, someone raises the hope that they might change in this respect; but the press toward professionalization has foundered on a deep inconsistency between expectations that a professional will exhibit social trustworthiness and the market-based ideological and intellectual bases of management education and research.

Chapter Twelve

The Lessons of History

Fascination with history is a mark of modern civilization. It is manifest in books that are published, in theories that are proposed, and in stories that are told, including the ones told in this volume. The telling of stories and the construction of theories of history involve the pursuit of pure aesthetic or emotional gratification, as well as the status associated with exhibiting knowledge, but they also typically reflect a desire to learn from experience. Humans are encouraged not only to tell elegant stories of history but also to act intelligently on the basis of what they have learned.

Unfortunately, anyone who seeks to learn from history encounters the great reluctance of history to divulge unambiguously the lessons to be learned. Humans extract meaning from history both by reproducing actions, technologies, and procedures associated with success and by developing stories and models of the causal structure revealed by experience. In both cases, the extractions are subject to profound limitations (March, 2010). History provides only small, uncontrolled samples as a basis for understanding complex causal relations, and interpretations of history are subject both to the inherent difficulties of the task and to human habits of historical myth building by which they generate legends that are widely shared but difficult to assess.

We are confronted with the great dilemma of historical understanding: An understanding of history seems vital to human intelligence, but it also seems resistant to human comprehension. The history of North American business schools in the twenty-five years after the conclusion of the Second World War is no less opaque than other histories, and we have no special abilities for avoiding the difficulties that are faced in learning from that history. Nevertheless, we think it may be possible to draw some limited and tentative understandings from the tales we have told.

12.1   A Revolution of Sorts

The years we have examined represent only a short period in the history of North American business schools, but the period covers a time in which the character and position of many of those schools appear to have changed significantly. None of the changes took place overnight, and, to some extent, the 1950s and 1960s simply accelerated trends that were begun earlier. But the acceleration was significant, and business schools and their relations with universities and society changed perceptibly. The changes were not violent; they were shaped by the previous histories of business schools; they were not completely implemented; they were subsequently rescinded to some extent; but they were notable.

Four elements of the social organization of business and the role of business schools were sharpened and accentuated:

- First, a socially approved, differentiated managerial class was increasingly delineated. Management, which had historically been a relatively open occupational category with access primarily from the ranks of workers and owners, became much more defined as an academically based and certified class. The social understanding that an appropriate manager should hold an MBA degree was created to a large extent during this period.

- Second, the terms of professional managerial discourse were codified and disseminated. The language of management became both specialized to managers and shared by them. Spreadsheets became the language of discourse. Aligning incentives became the terminology of management. A proper manager could talk to another proper manager with considerable confidence that the terms and prejudices involved in management would be shared.

- Third, business schools were confirmed as gatekeepers to the managerial class and to managerial rhetoric, certifying the first through the MBA degree and the second through their teaching and consulting, academic journals, and contacts with the media. The schools and the education they provided became conspicuous links joining scholarship, mentorship, reporting, and consulting.

- Fourth, business schools came to accept responsibility for generating new fundamental knowledge relevant to management. It came to be believed that knowledge essential to management existed and that its depositories were business schools, which developed knowledge through their programs of scientific research and dispensed it through their teachings, writings, and consultations.

These effects were conspicuous; they were important; and they have to some extent endured. Inconsistently in some respects but noticeably, the world of management joined the worlds of such domains as medicine, law, science, and theology by becoming certified as differentiated by academic credentials, by using a specialized language, by having a basis in fundamental knowledge inaccessible to others, and by claiming standing as a profession with regulated entry.

12.2   UNREALIZED HISTORIES

What actually happened in the history on North American business schools can be seen as a draw from possible histories. As a representation of the causal structure of history, it is a sample of one. In principle, we might like to learn from a larger sample of possible histories and their likelihoods, not just from the particular history that was observed. Unfortunately, promoting possible histories to the status of "facts" exposes the fragility of the distinction between theories and evidence for them and might extend the present volume into a library of volumes.

Nevertheless, counterfactual histories are useful in understanding the true causal structure of history. They are the pasts that might have happened, the paths not taken (Ferguson, 1997; Tetlock and Belkin, 1996). Exploring many of the unrealized branches of postwar business school history is well beyond the will and capabilities of the present authors, but we will note two particular directions in which the history might have gone but did not, possible histories that were not realized. Both their possibilities and their failure to be realized illuminate the bases of business school history.

Engineering Management

The first unrealized history involves the role of schools of engineering in management education. We have already told the story of the Graduate School of Industrial Administration at the Carnegie Institute of Technology (see Chapter Seven). GSIA became a model of reform of both management education and business schools. It was located at an engineering school and included in its original formulation a requirement that candidates for the master's degree in management should already have a baccalaureate in engineering. The formulation reflected, in part, a belief that the kind of quantitative skills that would be required by the new managerial technology were unlikely to be found in the usual business school applicant pool.

The establishment in 1952 of the Sloan School of Management at the Massachusetts Institute of Technology came from similar sentiments. A course in engineering administration was offered at MIT in 1914. Beginning in 1931, the Department of Business and Engineering Administration co-offered a course with the Department of Economics on fundamentals in management decision making. Alfred Sloan began funding the school in 1938 with endowed professorships and a fellowship program for engineering managers. Sloan was convinced that individuals with an engineering background were more likely to be successful in management than those without such a background. Subsequently, on September 5, 1950, during a conversation with Karl T. Compton, then the president of MIT, Sloan asked if the initial professorship was accomplishing a good purpose and if MIT was interested in developing the field further.[1]

Compton's response was favorable, and he developed the idea with an eye to differentiating the product. He resisted naming the new school at MIT as a "School of Business Administration," eager that the school present itself in a way distinct from the Harvard Business School. He thought that talking about "industrial management" was a way for MIT to differentiate itself from Harvard and to associate itself with the engineering and science overtones of "industrial."

Clearly, many of the early actors at MIT saw the Sloan School as particularly well positioned to build on science and technology in constructing a program in management. A 1950 memorandum on the "Proposal to Establish a School on Technology and Business Management at MIT" trumpeted the MIT role in combining engineering and business knowledge:

> The grant is intended to permit MIT to develop a school or special division in which students with a scientific and technical background would be given an opportunity to study business administration and become familiar with the problems of business management. The broad idea would be to train future business leaders, giving them not only an understanding of managerial problems per se but encouraging them to combine such administrative responsibility with the foundation of technical knowledge which is so important to the process of modern enterprise.[2]

The sentiments echo strongly the sentiments of the founders of GSIA at another engineering school, the Carnegie Institute of Technology.

After the Second World War, engineering schools, in general, did not rise to the opportunities that were perceived by Sloan, GSIA, and others. If they had, management education might have developed in a different way. Operations research might have become more central to management education; financial economics less central. Theories of choice and of teams might have become more important; theories of markets less so. Research on the design and implementation of information technology might have become more developed; research on the theory of games and agency theory less so.

There undoubtedly were elements of chance and basic positive feedback loops that affected the direction management education took. Nevertheless, it is possible to identify some possible reasons why engineering management did not come to occupy a larger role in management education despite the apparent plausibility of such an outcome.

Partly, management education in schools of engineering was bypassed because the activists at the Ford Foundation were much better linked to existing schools of business than they were to engineering schools. They were conscious of the potential inconsistency between business schools as they existed in the 1950s and a program of management education that emphasized quantitative skills, but they turned their attention to correcting deficiencies in business schools rather than to exploiting the comparative advantage of engineering schools with respect to quantitative preparation.

At the same time, the nature of "management" was changing. The forms of industry and management that animated Alfred Sloan and others and that typified the successes of the Second World War were in the process of disappearing in the United States. The heavy engineering, large factory production processes of the steel, automobile, aluminum, and chemical products industries were being replaced by a business world that was much more dominated by issues of finance, by service industries, and by small entrepreneurs. As it turned out, although discussions of "management" education failed for a long time to recognize the significance of the fact, North American business schools drifted away from the education of industrial managers largely because the North American world of business drifted away from industrial organizations.

Ultimately, a disproportionate share of the top graduates of elite business schools went to work for the financial industry or for consulting firms. Labor markets paid the highest salaries to graduating MBAs who had talents in finance or consulting. Those graduates did not become managers of firms that produce physical products. They became experts in the management of speculation or in the management of advice. Both are potentially noble callings, but they are not particularly close to the image conjured by most discussions of "managers." Though it is imaginable that they might have done so, engineering schools were not particularly well positioned to develop the strengths in finance and strategic management that became the strengths of business schools.

Also of importance in deflecting schools of engineering from management education were the other opportunities that tempted engineering schools at the same time. In the decades immediately after the Second World War, electrical engineering grew dramatically in scale and importance relative to mechanical engineering. The energies of schools of engineering were overwhelmingly devoted to building strength in electrical (and subsequently in computer) engineering. There was very little extra entrepreneurial energy left to devote to the field of engineering management. The small programs at most schools remained small and on the periphery of the excitements that affected business schools or engineering schools. If the onset of electrical engineering had been delayed, if the visions of Alfred Sloan had been more general than MIT, and if the staff at Ford had been drawn more from engineering backgrounds, it is possible that history would have been different.

Finally, the sheer size of the demand for certified managers and for management education militated against engineering management. Management training programs in engineering schools would either have created entry barriers that excluded the large number of quantitatively challenged aspirants for business education or would have considerably transformed engineering schools. The Ford Foundation programs faced the same problem but succeeded in imagining it could be solved by a long-term change in North American higher education and a short-term expedient of remedial education in quantitative skills for students in business schools. The elements of wishful thinking and imaginative evaluation of results that were involved in assessing progress in business schools would probably have been more difficult to sustain in engineering schools.

Information Technology

A second unrealized course of history involved the development of information technology and computer science. In the early days of information technology, it was not clear where the field "belonged" in academe. Its pioneers were drawn for the most part from mathematics and engineering, but they had difficulty securing disciplinary acceptance of the field in those domains. Some important contributions were drawn from IT enthusiasts in business schools. People such as Herbert Simon and Allen Newell and their early students, such as Julian Feldman and Edward Feigenbaum, were heavily involved in the development of the field of artificial intelligence.

However, it proved hard to gain legitimacy as a distinct field within business schools. As late as the 1970s, the faculty of the Stanford Graduate School of Business decided to eliminate its information systems group in large part because it found it difficult to grant tenure in that field. By the standards of the established fields, the work published in information system journals was assessed as inadequate. Similar judgments were made in other business schools, as in many engineering and science departments.

Ultimately, of course, the field of computer science came to be fully accepted and found a proper academic location, usually in a school of engineering. By the end of the century, the field was viewed as one of the premier fields in contemporary science and engineering. Simon, Newell, Feldman, and Feigenbaum all abandoned their links with business schools and took up residence in computer science (or similar) departments. Business schools, on their part, abandoned any significant role in the development of information technology or computers relevant to business and became exclusively consumers of such products.

It seems likely that if information science had become lodged in business schools, both the science and the schools might have developed differently. Information science has developed formidable human–machine systems with only limited access to contributions from economics or behavioral science. For the most part, the technology has transformed human habits and social organization to fit the machines, rather than fitting the machines to humans and their social structures. To argue that a location within business schools would have altered that course is difficult, but some slight course adjustment might have been observed.

If information science had remained as a major presence in business schools, would it have changed the course of business education? Possibly not, although the separation of information science from management education certainly made it difficult for a business school to maintain competence in a rapidly developing scientific and engineering field. The slowness of North American management in adapting information technology to managerial and production functions may relate in part to the limited engineering knowledge in business school–trained managers and to the persistent position of business school faculty as technological followers rather than leaders.

Using Hypothetical History

There are good reasons why engineering schools did not become the site for the growth of management training, but they might have done so. There are good reasons why business schools did not become the locale for developments in information technology, but they might have done so. If either outcome had been realized, the story we have told would have been different in important ways. However, neither hypothetical history suggests any major modification in the basic outcomes we have outlined beyond substituting engineering schools for business schools as the carriers of the new management education.

Nor do the histories that might have happened suggest any major modifications in the basic processes that we have described. The story is one of possible changes seeking vulnerable institutions as well as institutions seeking change. Understanding the particular marriages between changes and institutions and the particular orchestrations of those marriages that were observed requires tracing developments in fine detail, but the global outcomes were probably implicit in the context and would not have been significantly different even if history had meandered in somewhat different ways.

12.3   UNDERSTANDING A REVOLUTION

We have tried to identify some of the factors that produced the changes in North American schools of business in the two decades after the Second World War and to articulate some possible general implications for institutional change. In particular, we have emphasized the importance of a powerful diffuse worldview, several important historical threads, linkages among institutions containing elements of change, and features of social disorder both in business schools and in other involved institutions.

A Powerful Diffuse Worldview

Business schools evolved into their 1970 forms through a mix of entrepreneurial imagination, diffusion of prejudices and language, shifts in attention, visionary planning, networks of ambition, flows of resources, academic discourse, conflicts among interests, and the happenstance of opportunities.

There were established institutions; there were interests; there were people. The changes were championed by various individuals and groups in business schools. However, the transformation was not entirely, or even primarily, a business school phenomenon. This is not a story that can be told adequately in terms of business schools alone. Nor is it a story that can be told as stemming simply from the pressures of powerful interests or the machinations of a small cabal. The changes that reshaped the paradigm in North American management education were embedded in and took much of their character from a broader climate surrounding economic, political, and social life in the United States. Most of the coherence that can be detected came from a powerful, diffuse worldview associated with postwar opinion leaders in many interlocked institutions. While the influence of business schools on this worldview context was negligible, the influence of the context on business schools was profound.

The story we have told honors the important contributions of several key actors who belonged to that community, people such as Ernest Arbuckle, G. Leland Bach, Thomas Carroll, Donald David, H. Rowan Gaither, Aaron Gordon, James Howell, F. Cyril James, George Schultz, Herbert A. Simon, Alfred P. Sloan Jr., and W. Allen Wallis. Their foresight and effective involvement in the reform of business schools contributed considerably to the ways in which the story unfolded. Those leaders, however, were shaped in their sentiments by their involvement in a particular period of time and a broad social consensus that the times produced. This is a story of change that came naturally out of a set of beliefs that were widely shared among key actors and institutions in the postwar period. The business school leaders involved in the process belonged to a large cadre of like-minded individuals.

This diffuse world view produced a string of memoranda, speeches, and reports (of which the Pierson Report and the Gordon and Howell Report were two) on many topics. There were disagreements over important issues, and some of those disagreements produced differences in the ways the reformation unfolded in different institutions, but the central core aspirations and judgments were remarkably similar. They were similar because there were numerous arenas for discussions in which the sentiments were shaped and shared and because a distinctive historical period of a depression and a war and its aftermath created a confluence of understandings. The understandings were not planned to provide a basis for the reform of business schools, but they became a basis.

We have tried to show how widely shared optimistic beliefs about the role of fundamental knowledge, interdisciplinarity, and mindful social intelligence in social progress permeated various institutions and contemporary themes. Key institutions and individuals were tied together through extensive interpersonal and interinstitutional linkages. The ideas flooded the speeches and writings of the time, blanketing the business school community with a consistent worldview. It was not the only worldview, of course, but it was dominant. It was reflected in many places in many ways.

The members of the group did not form a cabal of plotters, but they existed in a community of like-mindedness. Their prejudices became the effective dogma of a generation of policy makers, academics, and quasi-academics. The like-mindedness ultimately dissipated, and some signs of the dissipation can be seen early—but for a time it was pervasive. This loosely organized but tightly connected group shared a set of prejudices about the importance of basic research to policy making and professional practice, about social science, about mathematics and mathematical models, and about professionalism.

The community of like-mindedness involved leading academics, business leaders, foundation officers, and public policy makers. The boundaries of the community were imprecise but defined clearly enough so that identifying community members was not difficult, and the normal practices of life brought members together frequently in various guises. They arranged for each other's participation in committees, commissions, and conferences. They nominated each other for positions of authority; they cited each other; they sought each other's counsel and suggested each other as consultants to others.

Without any significant central coordination and with little consciousness beyond a shared commitment to a set of visions, the members of the group supported each other. When, in the 1950s, Wallace Sterling, the president of Stanford University, sought ideas for strengthening the Graduate School of Business at Stanford, he was immediately led to a group of people and institutions who not only could tell him what questions he should ask but also what answers he should accept.

No one planned that network; it had leadership, but it was far from hierarchical. Like the Florentine banking and family networks that evolved around Cosimo de' Medici without clear political intention and then were used to build a political regime (Padgett and Ansell, 1993), the postwar social science network grew out of wartime experience and standard academic and policy-making proclivities toward professional conversations around scholarly and public policy concerns. The capability for coordinated action developed first; awareness of its usefulness for affecting social policy and business schools came later.

Threads of History

History unfolds in a way that makes it more a meander than a planned tour. It connects to elements of the past in ways that make the present dependent on the past yet persistently unpredictable from it. Looking backward, it is relatively easy to see some of the ways in which the course of history has connected the present to certain features of the past; it is much harder to see why the present has not been connected to other features of the past. This feature of history makes telling the story of history fairly simple relative to the true understanding of it.

We confess the problem without having much of any solution to it. We have tried to identify some threads of history and some institutions that provided important roots for the shared view that permeated reform. Business school reform had a genealogy that flowed naturally from the history of the United States and North American higher education.

Depression and War The attitudes that guided the reform of business schools were shaped by the experiences of individuals in two extraordinarily compelling historical periods—the Great Depression of the 1930s and the Second World War. Almost all of the key figures involved in the reform of business schools after the war were born in the decade between 1909 and 1918. The depression of the 1930s and the Second World War (1939–1945) were decisive features of formative periods of their lives, as they were in the lives of most of their younger followers born between 1919 and 1935.

These were periods in which pervasive threats to American life seemed to summon collective social action. They were periods in which ideas of individual obligations to society and the necessity of collective action to solve collective problems were taken as given. They were periods in which it came to be accepted that planning and social policy had a role to play in mitigating the pains of economic cycles and threats to American sovereignty and power. They were periods in which the apparent success of deliberate, mindful intelligence in inventing strategies and tactics for decisive action in war reinforced confidence in the application of knowledge and trained capabilities in solving peacetime problems of economic growth and prosperity, disparities in wealth and income, unemployment, social security, health care, and threats of nuclear warfare.

Collective action presumed collective goals and was guided to intelligent choices by systematic analysis that drew on science, mathematics, and the other paraphernalia of analytical power. The point was not just to interpret or understand the world but ultimately to change the world and make it a better place. Social objectives seemed clear. The possibilities for using intelligence to further those objectives seemed myriad. The experience of the depression and the war, as that experience was interpreted after the war, sustained confidence in the possibilities.

The emphasis on seeking deliberate social control over the destiny of human institutions was accentuated by anxiety about maintaining the preeminence that had been realized by the United States in the postwar military, political, and economic world, an anxiety that was increased by the success of the Soviet Union in placing a satellite into space. Sputnik and other symptoms of American vulnerability or weakness in science, technology, and organized capabilities were used to justify efforts to expand or reform the American research and educational effort, including that provided by business schools (David, 1949).[3]

The Legend of Abraham Flexner The legend of Abraham Flexner, as that legend came to be understood, provided both hope for institutional change in higher education and a model of how to produce it. The Flexner Report was credited with leading to a massive transformation of medical schools, one that embedded medical education firmly in scientific knowledge. Those reforms were sanctified as major contributions to national (and international) well-being. The postwar reformers of business schools explicitly saw Flexner as a model of what needed to be done for management education. They saw themselves as replicating the transformation of medical education.

The Flexner reforms in medical education had been credited with eliminating weak schools and greatly increasing the links between medical training and the sciences underlying medical knowledge. They were associated with substantial improvements in the talent and prior preparation of medical students, in the quality of medical school faculty, and in the establishment of fundamental research as an essential part of medical school responsibility.

By the 1950s and 1960s, few individuals involved in business schools had any direct knowledge of the Flexner experience. Direct knowledge about the medical school transformation was less significant in molding sentiment than was the legend of Flexner. The legend subordinated any doubts about the importance or effects of the Flexner Report to a story of a glorious reformation accomplished by intelligence and energy. It painted a heroic picture of how a moribund set of educational institutions could be improved by the determined intervention of a few, dedicated individuals in pursuit of a systematic program of reform. The business school activists of the 1950s and 1960s sought to emulate the legend as they understood it.

The Aura of Robert Maynard Hutchins The spirit of the University of Chicago as it had been shaped particularly by the fulminations of Robert Maynard Hutchins produced a widely shared group of beliefs within elite elements of universities. Those beliefs emphasized the role of fundamental knowledge and intellectuality in higher education. Hutchins's attitudes of disdain toward vocationalism and about the importance of fundamental knowledge shaped thinking in academia, particularly among individuals who had been at the University of Chicago but extending beyond them to a large fraction of intellectual leaders in North American universities.

Those attitudes were conspicuous in the reform of business schools. Hutchins had little tolerance for business schools, seeing them as vocational institutions inconsistent with the aspirations of a university. By the time the changes in business schools were underway, Hutchins himself was a minor figure, more likely to be reviled than praised, but mostly ignored. However, the aura he created at the University of Chicago permeated the reform of business schools. Many of the key actors in the reform had links to Hutchins's Chicago and shared many of the prejudices that were associated with him, including negative attitudes about the inferior state of education and research in business schools. To a substantial extent, their enthusiasm for reform stemmed not from love or admiration of business schools but from distaste for their weaknesses.

Just as Hutchins in many ways envied the intellectuality he associated with European and classical education and bemoaned the intellectual poverty of contemporary North American education, the business school reformers envied the academic core of the disciplines. They were discomforted by the limited academic standing of business schools and sought to emulate the scholarly standards and research productivity of the disciplines. Many of the key actors identified more with a discipline than with a business school and sought to create a world in which their association with the latter would be less of an intellectual embarrassment.

The Hutchins credo embraced an intellect based on fundamental knowledge and multidisciplinary problem solving. It welcomed experimental deviance and rational discourse grounded in an understanding of philosophy, science, and history. It saw higher education as an exaltation of the power of the mind. It sustained impulses toward radical change in education by unremitting criticism of existing practice. The major figures in business school reform used calmer language to communicate a similar perspective.

The RAND Corporation The RAND Corporation incubated a wartime idea about the mobilization of academic expertise in the service of the nation into a peacetime cluster of beliefs. Originally conceived as a "think tank" for the U.S. Air Force, focused on generating ideas about military strategy, weaponry, and tactics, RAND became a focus for academicians interested in understanding and improving decision making in complex systems.

RAND provided an arena in which a permeable and changing group of concerned and influential individuals met and talked, as well as ample illustrations of the possibilities for using mathematics, formal analysis, interdisciplinary collaboration, and educated intelligence in the solution of modern problems. RAND was both the core of an intellectual network and an example of postwar social engineering. It attracted and affected the best and the brightest, including many of those who would be active in the reform of business schools. It was the Viennese coffeehouse of the postwar social science and management intelligentsia.

Over time, RAND suffered from the insistent pathologies of success, from being associated with the egregious self-assurance and mistakes of rational analysis, and from excessive aspirations for applying RAND methods to peacetime social problems. However, for two decades after the Second World War, the RAND community of social scientists, statisticians, economists, and mathematical modelers overlapped considerably with the intellectual leaders of the business school reforms.

The Ford Foundation The Ford Foundation provided the resources and leadership that propelled the reforms. Ford was in the process of evolving from a relatively small family foundation to a major social force. In the process, it was looking for leadership and for programs. The efforts were complicated by the variety of possibilities that might be considered and by the clamor of Joseph McCarthy and his associates who were eager to lead tax-exempt foundations into domains and practices that minimized exposure to possible communist subversion of American democracy and capitalism, in which category they included a large fraction of what academic social scientists did and professed.

Before it finally settled down, the foundation was led through several changes in its board and management and through substantial turmoil in its organization. The turbulence provided unstable opportunities for initiative and brought the foundation briefly to the reform of management education and business schools and echoes of Flexner, RAND, and Hutchins's

University of Chicago. In the process of redefining itself, the foundation, as a minor part of its activities, provided coherence, money, and a manifesto to the reform of business schools.

Changing the Rhetorical Balance of Power

As we have noted in Chapters Nine, Ten, and Eleven, the period after the Second World War witnessed the expenditure of considerable rhetorical energy in business schools. It would be hard to argue that any of the issues around which the arguments over changes were organized were significantly resolved by the rhetoric or the debate, but it is clear that the changes in business schools reflected unambiguous modification in the rhetorical balance of power.

The supremacy of business cases as instruments for introducing reality into the classroom was challenged. Case instruction remained the dominant form of teaching, but its dominance became less overwhelming. Academic knowledge was granted an enhanced role in management education, relative to experiential knowledge. It did not displace experiential knowledge, nor even achieve clear preeminence, but its role was augmented. The idea of management as a profession with a grounding in special knowledge and having regulated qualifications for entry became more respectable, although there remained clear and powerful voices in resistance to the idea of professionalization, particularly ideas of social responsibilities beyond share-price maximization.

All of these rhetorical developments were significant in two senses. First, the case method of instruction, the ideological dominance of experiential knowledge, and the limited professional standing of managers were all dislodged somewhat from their "taken for granted" position in business education. They did not disappear, nor did they concede primacy, but they became subject to debate. Second, this rhetorical challenge facilitated the political and institutional challenges in individual business schools that led to a new mix of business education. The changes were provided with a litany that offered a counterweight to traditional rhetoric. Nothing was "settled," but the balance shifted, at least temporarily.

Vanity, Vision, and Self-Delusion

Any story of institutional change as substantial as that discussed in this book has to confront the fundamental dilemma of innovation: Some innovation is normally essential to long-run institutional survival, but most innovations are disasters. As a result, most viable institutions are cautious about change (Hodgson and Knudsen, 2010). Any enthusiasm for reform has to be tempered by awareness of two fundamental complications involved in embracing new ideas:

- First, most new ideas are bad ideas. The tendency of history to dwell longer on the few successes with new ideas and programs than on the many failures often obscures the poor odds involved, but any institution that specializes in innovation will specialize in failure.

- Second, distinguishing good new ideas from bad new ideas is ordinarily possible only after considerable time. Most new things require experience, practice, and modification to realize their potential, and early experience provides an unreliable stream of information for judging a new idea. As a result, revolutions require persistence in the face of early negative feedback.

Adopting new ideas and persisting in them in the face of negative feedback are ordinarily routes to disaster (March, 2010). Most effective social systems achieve their effectiveness in large part by avoiding novelty and responding to negative feedback by revising course. As they gain knowledge about the world, business schools, foundations, and other legitimate institutions become less likely to adopt or sustain novel ideas. The better they understand the world and the better they are connected to cultural understandings, the more their programs will be viewed favorably by the world, the more likely they are to do something moderately positive, and the less likely they are to have a revolutionary impact. Programs that might possibly make large improvements will have difficulty gaining support; if they are undertaken, they will usually make things worse, possibly dramatically (March, 2006).

Successful integration into the establishment helps assure survival for institutions; it also makes them conservative. When institutions are well integrated into the societies they serve, when they are internally stable, and when their procedures are systematic and careful, they are not likely to take actions challenging the status quo. The programs that they pursue will, on average, provide positive results, but they will exhibit only modest risk taking. Established, well-organized institutions are generally poor instruments for making the truly foolish investments that combine a small chance of genius with a large likelihood of idiocy (Embree, 1949).

Any investigation of a successful innovation within successful institutions confronts these complications. Business schools, foundations, and government agencies are creatures of the same society that they seek to change. They are instruments recruited and guided by established interests. They are receptacles for conventional ideas and ideologies. They are megaphones for the powerful and well connected. No social institution is a precise mirror of society; but no institution is separate from the conversations and concerns that permeate the institutions surrounding it, from the sources of its funds, nor from the sentiments of the interests that have gained authority to control it.

Because a new direction is more likely to be a progenitor of a new disaster than of a new golden age, and established organizations are more likely to resist than to embrace novelty, it is a paradox that innovations and change are nonetheless common in organizations. Although the poor prospects of new ideas normally make them unattractive to sensible actors, organizations seem frequently to adopt them, most often to their regret, but occasionally with exceptionally good results. Persuading an organization to pursue any particular innovation is ordinarily difficult, but novelty—often uninvited or unintended—is an endemic feature of organizational life.

Novelty is common in large part because organizations are ignorant of the risks or inefficient in avoiding them (March, 2010). The "errors" they make occasionally turn out to be credited later as brilliant. The result is that organizational genius at innovative ideas and organizational disasters are remarkably closely related. A. O. Scott commented on what he saw as the positive correlation between the number of truly awful films from a particular group in the film industry and the number of truly great ones:

> Disasters and masterpieces, after all, often arise from the same impulses: extravagant ambition, irrational risk, pure chutzpah, a synergistic blend of vanity, vision and self-delusion. (Scott, 2005)

The business school reformers of the 1950s and 1960s probably profited from their own "extravagant ambition, irrational risk, pure chutzpah, a synergistic blend of vanity, vision, and self-delusion." They believed in the existence and achievability of progress and believed that they were instruments of that progress.

Institutional Vulnerability

It would, however, be a mistake to attribute these reforms simply to quixotic heroes, to visions pursued passionately by true believers against all odds. There are elements of the present history that can be interpreted in that way, but such a frame would misrepresent most of the story. The history of the business school revolution of the 1950s and 1960s is probably better seen as reflecting a process in which various groups developed capabilities and beliefs during and after the Second World War, capabilities and beliefs that they opportunistically directed toward vulnerable institutions when the opportunities arose in the 1950s and 1960s.

Changes were facilitated by a breakdown in the internal social order and power structures of the institutions involved. That breakdown made those institutions into inviting opportunities. The disorder within business schools stemmed from several things but most conspicuously from the long-term erosion of academic support for business schools and a short-term disruption in the academic labor market. If business schools had had a more stable or more quiescent labor force and a more solidified position within academe, they would have been less vulnerable to the changes.

Unlike many of their European counterparts, North American business schools were integral parts of universities in which they played a minor, and little-valued, role. They were tolerated as a necessary response to external pressures; they were not admired. Their faculties were viewed as lacking in intellectual power and research capabilities; their students were viewed as inferior; their curricula were viewed as vocational rather than academic.

As North American universities recovered from the dislocations of the Second World War and experienced growth in size and prestige, the academic establishment within universities reasserted itself. Business schools found themselves under attack within the university community on which they depended.

As the Gordon and Howell manifesto reflected:

[The business school] is an uncertain giant, gnawed by doubt and harassed by the barbs of unfriendly critics. It seeks to serve several masters and is assured by its critics that it serves none well. The business world takes its students but deprecates the value of their training, extolling instead the virtues of science and the liberal arts. It finds itself at the foot of the academic table uncomfortably nudging those other two stepchildren, Education and Agriculture. (Gordon and Howell, 1959, p. 4)

In addition, the demand for faculty with PhDs from good universities exceeded the supply. Business schools found themselves in competition for faculty not only with other business schools but also with expanding arts and science departments, expanding engineering schools, and expanding private-sector employers. The business school faculty social order, which had been based on a different kind of labor market, was disrupted. New faculty members, and senior faculty who had academic reputations, many of them with disciplinary backgrounds, used their market positions within these unstable times to extract commitments from business schools with respect to research support and the nature of business school curricula and programs.

Not all foundations (or other institutions) were equally able to take advantage of such opportunities. Those that were stable, socially integrated, well organized, and effectively managed were unlikely to do so. At another time or in a foundation other than the Ford Foundation, the program of financial support for reform in management education would have been abandoned or made a good deal less revolutionary. Ford pursued this set of programs for reasons that do not occur every day.

The foundation was trying to get its act together. Henry Ford II was an icon who was in the process of abandoning, mostly by choice but with some regrets, his dominant role. The board was trying to exercise leadership without itself having strong, stable leadership. The foundation needed to make grants, but its procedures for doing so were not effectively routinized.

The major personalities and officers were jockeying for position. They were moving in and out of jobs and in and out of the foundation. Initiatives were started without clear conceptions of what they required. They were stopped or changed without clear understandings of why. Amid all of this, the foundation found itself under attack by some members of the U.S. Congress for symptoms of inadequate anticommunism.

The putative leaders of the Ford Foundation identified huge problems of economic growth and development (as well as problems of peace and so on). For the most part, their resulting efforts to mitigate these huge problems have had disappointing returns. Amid all of these grand problems and the attention directed to them, a small group at the foundation briefly saw a small opportunity to do something moderately useful on a tiny aspect of something that might be connected slightly to a few of those problems—business schools and management education.

If the foundation had been less in transition, it would probably have neither undertaken nor persisted in a program of reform that required such a significant change in such an insignificant domain; nor would it have been successful if it had tried. This suggests that institutional vulnerability is as valuable in the instruments of change as in the objects of change. Institutions that are in modest turmoil, somewhat poorly connected to the social establishment, somewhat poorly organized, somewhat distracted by "important" problems, and somewhat poorly managed are more likely to support minor initiatives for social change (such as reform of business schools), most of which will turn out to be either disasters or transitory victories, but some of which may become turning points in minor parts of social history. Their lack of organizational coherence and the distractions of major issues provide opportunities for innovation that better organized systems would shun.

The opportunity did not arise because management education and research were much more salient issues than they had been previously. It arose because the business school social order was vulnerable, because management education could be linked to some dimensions of postwar academic research ideology, because the Ford Foundation was trying to figure out what it would be when it grew up, because business school reform was po-

litically safe in an era of McCarthyism, because elements of potential opposition and competition were momentarily disorganized and distracted by
grander questions, and because a handful of people were ambitious enough,
both for their own careers and for social progress, to try to do something.

The story suggests that there are unpredictable moments in history when
external support may make a difference in institutional change. These moments are typified by the existence of strong, but disorganized, forces for
change within the institutions and elements of disorganization or change
within the external group so that the deviant (poorly socialized) groups
within the latter can enter into an alliance with deviant (poorly socialized)
groups in the former. Because most such alliances are doomed by the disorganization of their supporters and the foolishness of their programs, moments of success are also typified by the good fortune of having pursued
one of the rare new initiatives that turn out to be based on good ideas.

Conventionality and Change

The reforms of business schools were substantial enough that they might
possibly warrant the label "revolutionary," but it should be observed that
the reforms also had a distinct aura of conventionality. The "revolution" had
extensive support within the postwar establishment. It was not a wild idea
concocted in some place far removed from respectability but a program
based on a set of beliefs that had secured wide acceptance among postwar
leaders in social science. The institutions involved were thoroughly respectable and socially conservative; but, in this instance, in addition to having a
somewhat uncertain social order, they were tied to a strong (and respectable) group of "revolutionaries." Insofar as the changes in business schools
constituted a revolution, it was a revolution analogous more to the American Revolution of 1776 than to the French Revolution of 1789.

Moreover, the leaders of the reform of business schools did not create
the shared understandings that justified the changes. Leaders were created
by the understandings. As the postwar groups met and discussed postwar
needs, they came to some understandings—and, within those understandings, they identified some individuals who were capable of taking the lead
and had personal incentives to do so. These individuals were effective in

furthering the cause, but they did not invent it. They differed with each other with respect to some educational, scholarly, and political issues, but they were all easily recognized as part of an established religion of postwar social policy. They were not unconventional thinkers who changed people's ideas. They were thoroughly conventional within the community of postwar leaders within which they lived.

Thus, conventionality was mobilized in the service of revolution. Most of the soldiers of this revolution were surrounded by other soldiers of similar faiths. They were conscious of being a vanguard deviating from elements of an older establishment as they conceived it, but they never felt lonely. The beliefs that distinguished their cause were widely shared among the people they respected. Like juvenile delinquents surrounded by peers who reinforce their delinquency, they enjoyed the sense of being innovative while conforming comfortably to the attitudes of their group. This is, of course, a characteristic of most successful revolutions.

12.4   A CHANGING WORLD

The processes and forces that produced the flow of events in business schools after the Second World War were reconstituted subsequently. The world did not stand still. Much of the drift of business schools from the postwar visions can be attributed to powerful challenges to the postwar consensus, in particular generated by the hubris of managers after a long period of economic successes, and the glorification of the individual self that emanated from the counterculture movement associated with the student protests of the 1960s and 1970s; this drift was reinforced by the global triumph of free-market capitalism and its associated economic ideology in the 1980s and 1990s.

The End of the Postwar Consensus and the Triumph of the Self

During the quarter-century after the Second World War, there was a widely shared consensus that reflected optimism about the possibilities for social change through knowledge, enthusiasm for fundamental scientific knowledge as a basis for collective management and social policy, and commitment to multidisciplinary approaches to social problems.

Among other things, this postwar consensus powered changes in business schools. It persisted into the 1960s. However, it suffered grievous blows beginning in the last half of the 1960s. The consensus collapsed in the face of the worldview challenges associated with the student protests of the period from 1965 to 1975 and the parallel emergence of radical free-market economic challenges associated with the international triumph of capitalism. The worldview that powered the reforms was left considerably weakened.

In the late 1960s and early 1970s, universities became primary sites for protests against the Vietnam War, against racial and gender discrimination, against the draft, and against older generations (DeBenedetti, 1990; Garfinkle, 1995). The protests became violent in many instances and were often met by responses from university and public authorities that seemed to fuel the protests rather than extinguish them. For a decade, these protests occupied a major share of the attention of university administrators and were the most compelling guise under which universities appeared in the media.

Ultimately, the protests ceased, but they left an indelible mark on business schools. The mark did not stem from direct involvement of business schools in the agitations. Business schools were relatively untouched directly by the protests. Business school students tended not to join the protests, indeed to distance themselves in dress and manners from the protesters; business school faculty tended to side with the university administration against the protesters; the business community and alumni supporters of business schools were overwhelmingly opposed to the protests.

The effects were not direct but came from a rather dramatic shift in the ideological context of university and business school life. The basic principles on which the postwar consensus was built became problematic. A new generation of intellectuals, student radicals, and social scientists reshaped the academic worldview. The optimism about social progress through research, as well as the glorification of fundamental research, interdisciplinarity, mathematics, and mindful social intelligence in the service of collective action, were all challenged.

The optimism about long–term social change and social progress as driven by research and the thoughtful knowledge generated by research was replaced by enthusiasm for relatively short-run change precipitated by the instinctive emotions of direct social activism. The Vietnam War came to be defined as a refutation of analytically based intelligence (Halberstam, 1972). The integration of social science and the establishment, especially with the military establishment, as reflected particularly in the involvement of leading social scientists with RAND, the Office of Naval Research (ONR), and the Advanced Research Projects Agency (ARPA), was transformed from a laudable example of engagement of social science in solving social problems to an anathema.

Dominant groups in social science moved away from an emphasis on planning and analysis derived from science, mathematics, and interdisciplinarity as the foundations of social progress. In the debates within social science, the balance between science and the humanities, which the postwar consensus had moved sharply toward science, now moved perceptibly away from science. Social science legitimized conceptions of knowledge and progress as more socially constructed (thus as relatively arbitrary), and of academic knowledge as having little defensible claim to objective validity. History became explicitly a domain of politics.

Perhaps most importantly, however, the protests spawned an emphasis on the self that was portrayed as the reemergence of a spirit of individual freedom. The protests elicited countercultural movements that worked to encourage individuals to differentiate themselves from the establishment in their conceptions of attire, food preferences, sexual organization, political involvement, and social ideology. Mindful intelligence, with its overtones of collective planning and distinctive expertise, was contrasted with the free, individual spirit. Nurturing the self became a central concern, reinforced by myriads of schemes for recognizing, discovering, developing, and honoring the individual psychic and spiritual core. Defending the self against threats from institutions, traditions, and history became a paramount endeavor and a new religion.

Rethinking Economics

As North American society was coping with, and in many respects embracing, the causes endorsed by the student activists, the postwar consensus was assaulted on another front by a politically quite different but philosophically quite similar shift in sentiments about the nature and role of markets. Capitalism as an economic system and neoclassical economics as an ideology were embraced, particularly with the collapse of the Soviet Union and its Eastern European empire. Enthusiasms for the permissive anarchies of countercultures, free love, recreational drugs, and rock music merged easily into enthusiasms for the permissive anarchies of free-market economics.

The ideological shift had very substantial effects on the discipline of economics. At least since Adam Smith, economics had been built around widely accepted theorems about the efficiency of markets in reaching Pareto-optimal allocations. However, depression, wartime, and postwar establishment economics elaborated that acceptance by focusing on a set of perceived limitations of markets and of Pareto optimality, and the appropriateness of governmental intervention to rectify them:

- *Instability.* The tendency of markets to fluctuate in ways that created problems for individuals, firms, and societies without compensating efficiency benefits.
- *Monopoly.* The tendency of markets to stimulate and support coalitions of actors who are able to frustrate competition in order to extract personal benefits.
- *Inequality.* The tendency of markets to produce and sustain socially unacceptable disparities in the distribution of wealth among individuals.
- *Corruption.* The tendency for the wealth generated by markets to be used to corrupt democratic equality in political processes.

Both in Europe and in North America, postwar establishment economics provided intellectual justifications for social democratic policies that were designed to stabilize economies, inhibit monopolies, redistribute wealth, and limit political corruption. Leading economic theorists were simultaneously enthusiasts for the efficiencies of markets and advocates of methods for the social management of markets.

These justifications for social interventions into markets and the economic sensibilities on which they rested gradually came under attack. The voices of the opposition came to be heard increasingly after 1970 as the political systems of North America and Europe veered to the right. The new libertarian radicals merged the 1970s ideologies of counterculture free expression and the 1980s ideologies of free-market greed. Their successes offended the defenders of the 1950s and 1960s establishment, particularly with the elements of individual self-indulgence that they stimulated, but they inflicted substantial wounds on the postwar consensus, particularly within business schools with their other natural linkages to business and the political right.

In the course of these realignments, departments of economics and schools of business differentiated themselves politically and ideologically from the rest of social science. The subsequent large salaries and independent resources of business schools combined with their political and ideological distinctiveness to make them the envy and the enemy of other scholars and fueled academic revulsion at the perceived role of business schools in the 2008 meltdown of financial institutions.

Rethinking the Balance between Academic and Experiential Knowledge

The postwar period was a period of considerable change in business schools, but the changes were hardly installed before they were challenged by a resurgence of the forces they had overcome and by changes in the temper of the times. The postwar era of science and optimism about intelligent social analysis and planning was succeeded by the burst of information technology in all its forms, the explosion of the civil rights movement, the flourishing of women's liberation with a newly reinstated feminist ideology, and the emergence of ideologies of the self associated first with recreational drugs, relaxed sexual regulations, and cultures of personal gratification, and subsequently reconfirmed by the exaltation of personal self-interest as an engine of efficiency and social welfare through free markets.

Beginning as early as 1970 and clearly after 1980, business schools became less academic. They reduced their emphasis on academic prowess and satisfying the academic faculty establishment and increased their attention to the desires of their consulting and financial constituents. The business clients of business schools reasserted their claims to control. The operational rankings of business schools ceased to be those of academic colleagues and became those of the business press. Management education was reoriented toward greater attention to experiential knowledge and less attention to academic knowledge, and business school discourse included direct assaults on the ideology of fundamental knowledge and the exaltation of basic research (Bennis and O'Toole, 2005; Ghoshal 2005).

The change stemmed partly from a relatively long period of economic growth and business prosperity. North American business thrived for almost the entire last half of the twentieth century. In constant dollars, both the gross domestic product (GDP) and the Dow Jones Industrial Average increased more than sixfold between 1945 and 2000. During most of that period it was relatively difficult for a reasonably prudent person to lose money on the market or in business. The times reinforced confidence that experience yielded lessons of how to be successful. The hubris generated by business successes manifested itself in a plethora of books by successful business executives offering advice on how to replicate their personal and organizational successes. The business press thrived and sought to influence business schools to devote closer attention to the experiential knowledge validated by success.

In much the same way that postwar leaders had gained confidence in the validity of their beliefs from their involvement in the successes of the war, business leaders gained confidence in their beliefs from their postwar economic successes. In both cases, the subjective confidence in learning was probably greater than the validity of the beliefs that resulted, but it was the former that influenced behavior, not the latter. Although the lessons extracted from experience by different executives were often disconcertingly inconsistent, they seemed patently more directly useful and conspicuously more expansively and unconditionally proclaimed than the lessons from academic research.

In parallel with this change came a redefinition of the route to academic standing for business schools. An important driving force of the transformation in the 1950s and 1960s was the desire of business schools, their administrations, and their faculties to achieve the academic respectability that they clearly did not enjoy prior to 1950. They sought to do that by building a record of faculty fundamental research contributions comparable to those of other parts of the university and by significantly increasing the rigor of their courses. To a perceptible extent, they succeeded.

In the 1980s and 1990s, however, an alternative route to respectability arose. Business schools continued to seek legitimacy within universities, but there was a profound shift in the bases and locus of legitimacy. Rather than legitimacy among academic colleagues in other parts of the university, the schools increasingly sought legitimacy among administrators and trustees. Business school leaders increasingly saw the road to legitimacy as being less the development of fundamental research and a contribution to knowledge than the cultivation of financial support, including support from conservative foundations. University presidents moved in the same direction. It was a time of great personal fortunes obtained through business adventures, and universities became captivated by the possibilities for extracting significant resources from private fortunes. In an era in which top administrators of the university as a whole were heavily concerned with raising money from private donors to support their universities, business schools had easier access to outside wealth than did many other parts of the university and extracted standing from their money-raising successes.

Whereas the respectability of the 1950s and 1960s was respectability with the academic faculty and was secured through research contributions, the respectability of the 1980s and 1990s shifted to respectability with top university administrators and boards and was secured through gathering financial resources. Business school endowments and reputations among donors and boards grew dramatically; business schools separated themselves from their relatively modest involvement with high-prestige sources of research support (such as the National Science Foundation), along with the external validation they provided, in favor of more local, less demanding (in the sense of disciplinary rigor) private sources.

Business schools became richer and were able to pay the large salaries required to overcome the differential in their attractiveness to top academic researchers that stemmed from a deficit in their academic position. By the start of the twenty-first century, business schools were increasingly basing their positions on financial, rather than academic, strength and trusting that in a market-based world the former would allow them either to purchase or to ignore the latter.

Rethinking Interdisciplinarity

The postwar business school reformers had endorsed the twin virtues of fundamental research and interdisciplinarity. In practice, the two proved to be largely incompatible. The clear auditors of fundamental research were found in the disciplines, and schools that sought to maintain a presence in fundamental research that gained approval from the disciplines were driven to become more explicitly linked to the disciplines, particularly economics. In a standard positive feedback way, interdisciplinary programs grew to attract groups of scholars with lower means and higher variances of talent than found in disciplinary programs.

Moreover, insofar as the theoretical, ideological, and political views of the new (Chicago) economics became the dogma of the economics discipline, as they did to a substantial extent, a commitment to fundamental disciplinary knowledge in economics precluded most efforts toward interdisciplinary collaboration with other social science disciplines. At even such an outpost of the postwar reforms in business schools as the Graduate School of Industrial Administration at Carnegie Mellon University, interdisciplinary efforts tended to migrate out of the school either to other departments at Carnegie Mellon, such as Decision Sciences, Public Policy, or Computer Science, or to other institutions. GSIA became a business school that emphasized disciplinary economics to a much greater degree than it had earlier.

To some extent, interdisciplinary work was replaced by economic intellectual imperialism as economists invaded other fields with economic tools. This resulted in substantial invasions of sociology, psychology, political science, and law by economic models, much of it stimulated by the imagination of Gary Becker (for example, see Becker, 1968, 1976). In such a spirit, for example, the Stanford Graduate School of Business created a program dedicated to economic models of political processes.

The rethinking of interdisciplinarity can be seen not only in the tendency for the functional fields of business as well as business schools as a whole to become more tightly linked to disciplinary economics but also within fields, such as organization studies, that were established as inter-disciplinary domains during the 1950s and 1960s and that tended to divide into separate discipline-connected subdomains. Conversations among organizational economists, organizational psychologists, and organizational sociologists became less common than conversations between each group and its associated disciplinary colleagues.

Rethinking Social Responsibility

The leaders of business schools in their early days and their successors after the Second World War shared a profound sense of the role of business in organizations and in a society of shared purposes. Harvard Business School leaders long emphasized the need for social consciousness in business. Donald David, who later was involved in the Ford Foundation's efforts to reform business schools, spoke to the incoming MBA class in 1946 on the need for future businessmen (that is, the students to whom he spoke) to take "responsibilities" that now were resting on the shoulders of "the business leaders of the country" (cited in Spector, 2008, p. 319).

Years earlier, another Harvard dean, Wallace Donham, had made it a key in his request for a new curriculum when he took over as dean, that there be a focus on the "public responsibilities" of business in society (Cruickshank, 1987, p. 270). He argued,

> Unless more of our business leaders learn to exercise their powers and responsibilities with a definitely increased sense of responsibility toward other groups in the community, unless without great lapse in time there is through initiative of such men an important socializing of business, our civilization may well head for one of its periods of decline. (Donham, 1927, p. 406)

These early deans saw business and managers as part of a nested set of integrated communities whose collective interests they served. They saw business schools as inculcating a commitment to social responsibilities. They embraced the idea that the conscious pursuit of social goals through socialization of the young, analysis, thoughtful choice, and planning was an obligation of intelligent, well-trained citizens. When Rowan Gaither spoke at the Stanford University Conference organized to attract Ford Foundation support for the reorganization of the Stanford Graduate School of Business (see Chapter Eight) in 1958, he identified some important rules for management thinking in meeting the challenges of the future. "Above all," he said, "it must be an attitude of selfless dedication to our national purposes" (Gaither, 1958, p. 6).

After about 1970, the external intellectual and social forces that had pushed the postwar revolution toward a commitment to social responsibility in North American business schools were increasingly on the defensive. The glorification of the individual self by the counterculture movement and by free-market economics elevated greed, self-indulgence, selfishness, and narrow self-interest to status as virtues and made ideas of collective goals and social responsibility seem old-fashioned and naïve, even—in the North American vernacular—unpatriotically socialist.

The key to management became the alignment of incentives for self-interested others to serve the self-interests of the manager (or his or her master). Business ethics became an esoteric and not conspicuously valued subject rather than part of basic socialization. When the excesses of the early twenty-first century provoked outside criticism of business school ethics and demands that business schools introduce a stronger sense of social responsibility into the curriculum, the response of the schools was, in general, minimal and often explicitly antagonistic. Significant voices, echoing the litanies of Woodstock and Chicago, maintained that the only social obligation of managers was unremitting masturbation, and social systems worked best when individuals pursued their own self-interests without recourse to vague contrary ideas of "social good" or "public interest."

A Fragile Revolution

The reformers of the 1950s and 1960s saw themselves as creating a new era in North American business schools, and by 1970 they could take some credit for having accomplished that objective. Business schools had changed. The students were better prepared. The faculties had stronger research reputations. The curricula were more demanding. Business schools laid claim to recognition as serious academic institutions with substantial commitments to fundamental research. The postwar changes exhibited some resilience. Largely because a generation of administrators and faculty members carried forward the sentiments and practices of the reforms, they left some marks in North American business schools that seemed to endure even as late as the first decade of the twenty-first century.

However, when the social, ideological, intellectual, and political context of North American universities changed in the latter part of the 1960s and the early 1970s, the changes proved somewhat fragile. The postwar revolution faltered as the consensus that formed a key context for the reforms of the 1950s and 1960s disintegrated. Driven in large part by the changing social context and accentuated by the diminishing joys of flagellation, a counterreformation in North American business schools enveloped business schools in the 1980s and 1990s.

The counterreformation focused on three key aspects of the postwar reforms: the substitution of academic knowledge for experiential knowledge, the stimulation of interdisciplinarity, and the emphasis on professionalism with its element of social responsibility. In the 1980s and 1990s, the role of experiential knowledge grew relative to academic knowledge; interdisciplinarity was increasingly subordinated to the discipline of economics; and the idea of managerial social responsibility was largely converted to a sanctification of self-interested action. As the twenty-first century began, the strains generated by the earlier reforms and the counterreformation became conspicuous with a cascade of essays bemoaning either the postwar changes or their abandonment (Mintzberg, 2004; Pfeffer and Fong, 2004).

As we have noted before, these philosophical and rhetorical issues decorated, and to some extent influenced, the underlying political conflicts in business schools. Although actual conflicts in any particular school were normally characterized by a more nuanced arrangement that obscured and moderated the main conflicts, the latter were typically relatively simple. To a substantial extent they arrayed the forces of academe, including particularly the faculty and its allies, against the forces of donors, business groups, alumni, and their allies. All of the groups recognized the value of collaboration, rather than conflict, and each of them tried to form alliances with groups on the "other" side. As a result, they tended to avoid outright warfare most of the time, though the tensions remained.

One of the devices for avoiding warfare was ceremonial. The names of donors decorated the schools, their buildings, and their honorary degrees. Business and alumni leaders were routinely invited to address students. Alumni were courted for donations and encouraged to maintain contact with the schools. Academic names were associated with the recommendations of consultants. One of the devices was rhetorical. The proclamations are familiar: Academic knowledge thrives in juxtaposition with experiential knowledge. Practical prescriptions must be grounded in fundamental knowledge. Profound theoretical ideas are generated by working on mundane practical problems. The proclamations contained elements of truth.

The opportunities for ceremonial and rhetorical agreement moderated overt conflict. Nevertheless, the last half of the twentieth century saw shifts in the balance of power among the groups contending for control of management education and research. In many business schools, the 1950s and 1960s saw a shift from attending primarily to business groups to attending more to academic groups. In many business schools, the 1980s and 1990s saw a shift in the other direction.

12.5   PRESENT SEEDS OF FUTURE DISRUPTIONS

The Great Depression and the Second World War produced a particular collection of beliefs among social scientists and social activists about mindful collective action as a response to social problems. This collection of beliefs was as vital to the changes of the 1950s and 1960s as its replacement by the glorification of the self was to the changes of the 1980s and 1990s. There is no reason to suppose that the cultural and intellectual contexts that we have associated with the protest movements of the late 1960s and early 1970s or later contexts associated particularly with enthusiasm for the self and for markets are the final twists in the social and ideological context of business schools.

As North American business schools are propelled well into the twenty-first century, both the reformation of the 1950s and 1960s and the counter-reformation of the 1980s and 1990s have begun to fade into the dim memories and enduring inexplicabilities of educational practice. The collapse of financial markets in 2008 and the economic vitality of the Chinese version of a socialist capitalism reduced somewhat the free market and in-dividual self-enthusiasms of the last decade of the twentieth century but without immediately substituting another creed.

Business schools struggled to meet new financial constraints and to deal with the effects of an economic recession that reduced the demand for business school graduates while increasing the demand for business school admission. As more and more schools successfully solicited huge gifts from immensely rich individuals, more and more schools assumed the proper names of their benefactors and drifted toward the business, economic, and political prejudices that the donors embraced. This drift and the wealth from which it stemmed tended to alienate important parts of the academic community. Business schools struggled to maintain both academic respectability and the approbation of the business community and business press. They struggled to expand their presence internationally and in executive education without undermining their North American and MBA cores.

Predicting the Future

If the past is any indication, the future of business schools depends on major unpredictable events that will unfold over the coming years. There are many things that might happen in the coming decades, any one of which would radically change the schools. Unfortunately, although we know with certainty that some event of dramatic importance will occur, the likelihood of any specific event is too small to warrant anticipating it.

Business schools will change in the future, as they have in the past, in response to the pressures of their environments and the vulnerabilities produced by uncertainties about their social structures and conventions. They will not be changed in any particular arbitrary direction simply by virtue of the desires of their current inhabitants or constituents, and anyone who sets out on such a crusade is embarking on a foolish adventure. Foolishness is, of course, a common attribute of successful reforms, but the odds for success for any particular instance of foolishness are not good.

Changes in organizations depend on a combination of the persistent pursuit of apparently irrelevant competences and ambitions with an opportunistic practical imagination, recognizing occasions when something can be done and lending timely support to the effort. Change has come in the past, and we assume it will in the future, when a relatively prepared movement exploits a relatively random opportunity to tweak a relatively disorganized institution and develops a relatively coherent rhetoric that sustains the effort and decorates its success. The resulting successes are fragile, for they must confront their own subsequent vulnerability to other relatively prepared movements encountering relatively random opportunities to move history along its path. These elements of opportunism in effective action are as difficult to predict as are the sporadic presentations of occasions for its exercise.

New directions are associated particularly with periods of disruption in the social order of the institutions involved. As a result, it may be useful to identify current features of business school life that have created or will create tensions capable of making the schools vulnerable to change, even though specifying the precise changes that will occur is impossible. These are sources of disorder in the social institutions surrounding business schools (including the schools themselves). Identifying such features of business schools or their contexts is, of course, somewhat fanciful. The major surprises will come from changes in contexts that are themselves surprising. Nevertheless, we can recognize a few rather obvious sources of possible future vulnerabilities in the social order of North American business schools.

The Decline of the American Empire

The most obvious new twist in the context is the end of the North American political and economic hegemony. Just as the character of Oxford University in the nineteenth century was linked to the power and glory of the British Empire, a large fraction of the character of North American business schools in the last half of the twentieth century was derived from their location in a political and economic hegemon. It was a location that yielded the power and resources that propelled the schools to dominance. It also yielded arrogance, parochialism, and rigidity, all of which make the schools vulnerable to threats from Europe and Asia as the hegemony is broken or reduced.

Although the details and timing of the changes are difficult to predict and dependent on military, political, and economic developments that by no means seem obvious to envision, Asian economic and political power seem likely to grow in coming decades in the absence of some major demographic catastrophes. The domestic problems and political habits accumulated through years of profligacy seem to portend difficulties for the United States. Without engaging in extravagant prophecies of doom, it does not require extraordinary perceptiveness to anticipate a decline in North American power and influence.

It seems more or less axiomatic that any such decline will extend to the hegemonic position of North American business schools. Competition from outside North America will erode the position of the business schools in their competition for students, faculty, and reputations. What is somewhat harder to anticipate is the response of North American business schools to the decline of the American Empire. The rapidity with which the schools changed after the Second World War offers some basis for imagining that they may respond quickly again in the future, but the rigidities produced by success erode the capabilities of business schools for substantial change.

The response is particularly difficult to predict because of the scale and heterogeneity of business education in the United States. Undoubtedly, the premier business schools will seek to tie themselves to the world economy by attracting international students and faculty and by establishing presences in booming economies—but, insofar as their claim to excellence rests on claims of excellence in North American business, it may be difficult to sustain. A possible route would be to re-create the 1950s and 1960s emphasis on fundamental research and establish a reputation that is independent of the reputation of North American business, but that would require a major reorientation for most schools and support for the change from their major financial angels. Such support seems unlikely in the present climate but might become more likely if American society as a whole comes to be concerned about a general failure to maintain the fundamental research assets of the country.

The Reconstruction of "Management"

The postwar reformers of business schools had a conception of business management and managers that was built around a particular conception of business. For the most part, that conception pictured business as consisting in the production and distribution of physical products—steel, automobiles, oil, and the like. The production and distribution was accomplished through large, hierarchical organizations employing managers who were responsible for making and implementing efficient resource allocations in these operations. Successful managers normally spent most of their careers in a single firm, advancing upward in the hierarchy at speeds that depended on their productivity, good fortune, or connections. The reformers sought to make business school training more relevant to such careers.

As the twentieth century wound to a close, MBAs were increasingly employed in quite different ways. Many of them had become part-time contract laborers called "consultants." They were employed by consulting firms to provide managerial advice to other firms. Others of them had secured employment in the financial industry, managing funds and inventing gambles. Although some became managers of firms that produced physical products and offered extended careers, those opportunities seemed to be shrinking in numbers and in perquisites. To a substantial extent, as North American industry outsourced its production, it greatly reduced the demand for production management in North America. The functional fields of management—production, personnel, marketing, accounting—lost some of their stability as corporations became more fluid in their compositions, structures, and commitments.

The change was gradual and was felt particularly in the increased demand for students trained in finance, but business schools found their conception of management no longer well aligned with the realities of what their graduates did. For the elite schools, this probably made little immediate difference; at least to some extent they had settled comfortably into a screening role by which their primary contribution was in signaling the intelligence of potential "managers" rather than any profoundly distinctive competence their schooling provided (Spence, 1973). However, the disjunction between the view of management on which the MBA was constructed and the reality of MBA employment creates a certain amount of stress on MBA programs that is more likely to increase than decrease over the next few decades.

The Mismatch between University Structures and Educational Demands

In a world characterized by rapid changes in knowledge, a conception of education as occurring for a brief time early in a career has become exotic. North American universities are huge physical presences in particular places. They are built on a conception of higher education that presumes a student attends the university full time for several years at an early stage in his or her life. That student gathers knowledge from a full-time resident faculty, knowledge that will serve for the rest of his or her life. The practices and structures of higher education are based on a presumption that the knowledge basis imparted during attendance at a university will serve as useful knowledge indefinitely or will initiate a process of learning that will update itself continuously over many years.

In most respects, such universities make very little educational sense in a world of changing knowledge. Necessarily, they teach knowledge, much of which rather quickly becomes irrelevant. As a result, they find most of their educational justification as systems for sorting people according to talent, as playgrounds for the maturation of individuals drawn from a society that delays maturation until the ages of twenty to thirty, as social welfare programs for the young unemployed, and as mobilization centers for part-time, temporary revolutionaries before they revert to respectability.

At some level, most universities recognize the disjunction between traditional university education and the realities of knowledge expansion and change. They try to participate in "lifelong learning." Most universities offer a variety of educational opportunities for individuals who are not part of their regular student communities. Whatever merit such efforts have, they involve a tiny fraction of the central university's resources and, at least within the core disciplinary parts of the university, are viewed more as public relations efforts than as essential elements of a university's educational charge.

Some of the programs are efforts to provide culture to middle-class grad-uates who enjoy reading novels, listening to good music, or admiring fine art. Some of the programs are efforts to provide post hoc remedial training in first-level technical skills that grandchildren have but their grandparents do not. Some of the programs are efforts to provide an opportunity for po-lite exposure to current events for people who are not disposed to read a good newspaper or who enjoy the stimulation of discussions with others of similar backgrounds and inclinations.

In principle, the disciplines might take the lead in updating their gradu-ates in the results of new research, but in practice that is not what we ob-serve. The primary places for significant efforts in this direction are not in the liberal arts disciplines but in professional schools. Every profession based on knowledge has had to face the problem of continuing education, and every professional school has struggled with how to provide such edu-cation. Schools of medicine undertake continuing education for physicians. Schools of engineering undertake continuing education for engineers. Schools of architecture undertake continuing education for architects. And so on. The efforts are serious. They are often substantial. Many of them seek to exploit the distributed knowledge possibilities of the Internet. They are, however, persistently hard to fit into the same academic structure that houses conventional degree-granting programs.

In this spirit, business schools have increasingly devoted resources and energy to developing and marketing programs of executive educa-tion. Some of these have been variations on a traditional business school activity—part-time degree programs for working managers. The "executive MBA" has increased its presence. In many ways more significant, however, has been the growth in programs of executive education that are not tied to any traditional degree. Advanced management programs have become important parts of the business school repertoire. They are often significant contributors to business school cash flow.

Programs in continuing education for engineers or physicians are fre-quently tied explicitly to research developments. Advanced management programs are less likely to be research based, and programs in executive education fit better into a school that is linked to consulting than into a school that is linked to research. As these programs have developed to date in most business schools, they represent firm commitments to the elements in the school and among its clientele who are least concerned with research or research knowledge. They tend to become autonomous activities separate from the research activities of the schools. The schools struggle with this separation, but it is persistent.

Although it is possible to imagine designing a program in executive education that is directed toward strengthening and drawing from academic research, there is little sign that such a program would secure much sustained enthusiasm either among the administrators of executive education or among its customers. Although the reformers of the postwar period undoubtedly would have endorsed such programs, it would require considerable entrepreneurial imagination to make a serious link between continuing education in management as it has developed in business schools and an orientation to fundamental scholarship.

The Unbundling of Research and Education in North American Universities

North American universities treasure their position as core institutions for the nation's fundamental research activities. Research universities collectively provide the United States with research capabilities that are the envy of other countries. North American universities are, however, continually at risk of losing the political and social support that is essential to their research programs. For most of modern North American history, research (and particularly research that is not linked to immediate uses) has been a political orphan.

For the most part, North American universities are justified politically not by their research prowess but by their role in the education of young students. Overwhelmingly, universities, even those universities that form the core basis of North American research capabilities, seek financial and political support in the name of their educational programs. The North American social and political system finds it much easier to support higher education for its degree-granting activities than for its research activities. North American institutions of higher education have evolved into systems that both produce and dispense knowledge (as well as athletic teams, but that is another, not totally unrelated, story). By bundling the two kinds of activities into a single package, called a university, research is subsidized by the political strength of education.

Policy makers persistently try to separate the production of knowledge from its dispensing to take advantage of the enormous cost differences between the two. Knowledge can be dispensed at only a fraction of the cost of producing it. It seems rather obvious that the education functions of major North American universities could be accomplished at a much lower cost if they did not have to bear the costs of a research function. Thus, the state of California has a master plan for higher education that limits the support of research to only a few of the many collegiate institutions given public resources, and some other countries have long concentrated research activities in institutes or academies separate from educational institutions.

There is, however, a complication: It appears to be true, and is certainly widely believed by the North American consumers of education, that the more the dispensing of knowledge is separated from its production, the greater the difficulty in avoiding a steady decay in the quality of knowledge dispensed. Harvard, Yale, Princeton, Chicago, Stanford, and Berkeley undoubtedly have many fine teachers, but their attraction to outstanding students comes primarily from the research reputation of their faculties and the quality of the students attracted by those reputations.

Nevertheless, it is not hard to anticipate a political shift in the direction of separating the teaching and research functions of North American universities under pressure from attempts to "rationalize" higher education. The ways by which these pressures are accommodated within universities will significantly affect university-based business schools and research in those schools. Most North American business schools are likely to be driven increasingly to a more vocational orientation that would make them a significant contributor to "cost-effective" professional education but would tend to remove them from a role in fundamental research.

The Limited Academic Respectability of Business Schools

A primary premise of the reforms of the 1950s and 1960s was that business schools were parts of multipurpose universities that sought to enforce the standards and culture of academe. A primary result of the reforms was that business schools became academically more respectable. To an extent that considerably exceeded the situation before the war, business schools came to be accepted as legitimate academic institutions within universities.

The acceptance was less than total. North American business schools achieved greater academic legitimacy in the 1950s and 1960s, and some individual business school scholars were clearly recognized as outstanding within the disciplines, but business school researchers tended to be systematically valued less by the academic research establishment than researchers elsewhere. Domains of research that came to be housed primarily in business schools (for example, economics of finance, organizational psychology) found that their disciplinary standing tended to be reduced.

Whether the valuations reflect a persistent unjustified bias in recognition or a persistent quality deficit in business school research is subject to debate, but the fact that business schools in the twenty-first century pay a significant premium to obtain highly regarded scholars who have disciplinary employment options suggests that business schools are still judged (on average) to be deficient as locales for serious academic research. Enthusiasm for business schools continues to be greater among university administrators, money raisers, and trustees than among research faculty. This difference was accentuated by the counterreformation of the 1980s and 1990s in which the commitment to academic research wavered in business schools.

Business schools make more or less continual choices between satisfying their academic constituents and satisfying their business constituents. A distinctive feature of the postwar period was that these pressures were briefly aligned. Major business leaders championed an academic business school. When this alignment was upset, as it was later in the twentieth century, business schools could maintain support from the academic community only at the cost of reduced support from the business community and vice versa. The history of business schools prior to the Second World War suggests that, when such a choice is forced, most business schools will feel compelled to turn toward the business community. As long as this is true, academic respectability is likely to decline unless some combination of factors elicits organized business support for university-based fundamental research on business.

The tensions extend into the teaching function of business schools. Most of the leading business schools view their MBA programs as essential cores of the schools. They set the tone. They define the "quality" of the school. They provide a large share of the tuition revenue and alumni support for the school. In large part, "management education" means the MBA program. An essential feature of the reforms of the 1950s and 1960s was strengthening the link between research and management education in the MBA program. Faculty members were invited to excite students with research results without necessary immediate links to management practice. Students were invited to appreciate the beauty of research and to establish links to researchers that might continue in their future activities.

As the stridency and effectiveness of pressures toward "relevance" increased in the 1980s and 1990s, this community based on research involvement and enthusiasm disintegrated to a substantial degree. Faculty engaged in relatively fundamental research found the gap between their research and their teaching increased to such a degree that the content of their teaching sometimes seemed to become largely disconnected from the content of their research. They found students to be impatient with research and insistent on certified relevance and administrators as supportive of the student orientation.

Although no firm data exist on the phenomenon, there are signs that this has led to an alienation of many research faculty from the primary teaching program of the business school. The phenomenon is not unique to business schools. It is common in other parts of the university as well. However, business schools suffer particularly from the process. Teaching tends to become not an adjunct to the pursuit of fundamental knowledge but a drag on it. In many business schools toward the end of the twentieth century, the fraction of MBA teaching done by faculty members without involvement in research increased. Faculty members involved in research reduced the time and energy they devoted to MBA teaching. The MBA teaching faculty and the research faculty became differentiated. It seems possible that the research functions may well wither in time as research-oriented faculty members seek more congenial locales and outside supporters tie financial support increasingly to teaching functions.

12.6 A Golden Age

The reforms of the 1950s and 1960s define, from some points of view, a golden age in business schools. "Golden ages" are figments of nostalgia. They are to be contemplated with envy of their gratuitous self-adulation and with mockery of their self-indulgent pretense. The beauties of the 1950s and 1960s were partly illusory. Insofar as they were real, they were produced with the usual doses of chicanery, self-aggrandizement, fantasy, and historical reconstruction.

Nevertheless, it was a time when a relatively fortuitous combination of ideas and people encountered a relatively fortuitously vulnerable set of institutions and produced a relatively substantial change. Business schools were changed. By most of the terms by which the schools were seen as deficient in 1950, they became better by 1970. They became more committed to fundamental research and to managerial professionalism. They increased their esteem within university cultures. They produced a generation of new scholars committed to academic, research-based schools of business.

To the misfortune of those scholars and their teachers, the world changed. It did not change as a reaction to the reforms, although there was some of that. The world changed for its own reasons, and the changes altered the landscape of business school life. As the scholars and policy makers who grew up during the Great Depression and the Second World War and launched their careers in the 1950s and 1960s were gradually removed from the scene, they were replaced by individuals who grew up in different times and were imbued with different, less academic, and more self-interest-oriented perspectives. The "golden age" was transformed to a significant extent into an era of the glorification of huge fortunes and of those who accumulated them, the anointing of greed as a social virtue, and the substitution of the lessons of experience for the lessons of analysis and research.

But, briefly, there was Camelot.

Notes

Chapter One

1. Throughout the book, we have adopted a convention for dealing with citations. Items that are available publically through normal library or publishing channels are cited in the text by author and date, with the full reference provided in the references at the end of the book. Items that are not so available, including those available only in specialized archives, are cited in footnotes.

2. Ford Foundation Archives. J. E. Howell, Discussion paper, dated March 23, 1962, "A Terminal Program in Business Education: GCT."

3. Reed, J. Remarks at the RAND Graduate School Graduation, 2004, Marina Del Rey, CA (unpublished transcript).

Chapter Two

1. This is according to a 1965 report by John Wheeler to the Ford Foundation, entitled "Report to the Ford Foundation on Changes in Collegiate Business Education in the United States 1954–1964 and the Role of the Ford Foundation in These Changes," p. 91. Ford Foundation Archives. Located in the General Manuscript section in the Archives.

2. Stanford Graduate School of Business Archives, Jackson Library, Stanford University. Paper dated July 30, 1963.

Chapter Three

1. A statement of the AMA's current purpose is available at www.ama-assn.org/ama/pub/about-ama/our-people/member-groups-sections/organized-medical-staff-section/about-us/purpose-mission-commitment.shtml.

2. A reproduced version of the original report is available online at the Carnegie Foundation's home page, available at: www.carnegiefoundation.org/sites/default/files/elibrary/Carnegie_Flexner_Report.pdf.

3. This document is titled "Quotations Relevant for Planning the Center for Advanced Study." November 19, 1952. Herbert Simon papers, Carnegie Mellon University Library Archives.

CHAPTER FOUR

1. Office of the President, Hutchins Administration Records, Special Collections Research Center, The University of Chicago Library, Series I, General Files, Box 43, Folder 3, untitled document beginning, "I fully agree with you that at this time . . ."

CHAPTER FIVE

1. The connections are detailed in the following documents from the RAND Corporation Archives: "Statement by Frank Collbohm, Director, the RAND Corporation, on the Origins and History of RAND, with special reference to the roles played by Mr. Rowan Gaither, the Ford Foundation, and by Mr. Collbohm," April 12, 1954; and "Memorandum to Frank Collbohm from Rowan Gaither: Comments on and Supplement to Frank Collbohm's Memorandum of April 12, 1954." Located in the RAND Corporation Archives.

2. John Williams, "An Overview of RAND." RAND D-10053, 1962, pp. 1–2. RAND Corporation Archives.

3. Warren Weaver, "Opening Remarks." RAND conference of Social Scientists, New York, September 1947, Plenary session. RAND D-paper, RAND Corporation Archives.

4. John Williams Interview, RAND Corporation Archives, Williams Folders, p. 2.

5. John Williams Interview, RAND Corporation Archives, p. 3.

6. Letter from John Williams to John von Neumann, December 14, 1947, RAND Corporation Archives.

7. O. Helmer, "The Conference on Applications of Game Theory to Tactics." RAND D-444, 1949, p. 1. Rand Corporation Archives.

8. See also Merrill Flood, "Report on a Seminar on Organization Science," RAND P-7857, 1951. RAND Corporation Archives.

9. B. Brodie, C. Hitch, and A. W. Marshall, "The Next Ten Years," RAND D-2700, 1954. RAND Corporation Archives.

10. O. Helmer, The Game Theoretical Approach to Organization Theory. RAND P– 026, 1957, p. 1. RAND Corporation Archives.

11. O. Morgenstern, Prolegomena to a Theory of Organization. RAND RM–734. December 10, 1951. RAND Corporation Archives.

12. Merrill Flood, *Report of a Seminar on Organization Science*. Research Memorandum RM-709, 1951. RAND Corporation Archives.

13. S. Winter, "Toward a Neo-Schumpeterian Theory of the Firm." RAND Working Paper P-3802, 1968. Rand Corporation Archives.

14. See, for example, Andrew W. Marshall, "Improving Intelligence Estimates through the Study of Organizational Behavior." RAND paper for the Board of Trustees, March 15, 1968; and Andrew W. Marshall, "Bureaucratic Behavior and the Strategic Arms Competition." Southern California Arms Control and Foreign Policy Seminar (1971); both located in the RAND Corporation Archives.

15. But see J. Loftus and A. Marshall, "RAND Research on the Soviet Military," D-4943-PR, 1958; J. Loftus and A. Marshall, "Forecasting Soviet Force Structure: The Importance of Bureaucratic and Budgetary Constraints." RAND RM-3612-PR, 1963.

RAND Corporation Archives; and A. W. Marshall, "Improving Intelligence Estimates through the Study of Organizational Behavior." RAND paper for the Board of Trustees, March 15, 1968.

16. Richard Nelson and James Schlesinger, "A Long-Range Basic Research Program for the Department," RAND M-6527, 1963. RAND Corporation Archives.

17. A. W. Marshall and S. Winter, "Memorandum to Rowen, A RAND Department of 'Management Science'—the Case in Brief," December 29, 1967, memo no. 8668. RAND Corporation Archives; A. W. Marshall and S. G. Winter, "Program of Studies in the Analysis of Organizational Behavior," RAND internal letter L-4277, March 3, 1967.

18. See M. Augier and B. Watts, *Conference Report on the Past, Present and Future of Net Assessment*. Office of the Secretary of Defense: Office of Net Assessment, 2008; and B. Watts and M. Augier, Reflections on Strategy. Unpublished Report for the Office of Net Assessment, Office of the Secretary of Defense, 2009.

19. Interview with John Williams. RAND Corporation Archives, p. 10.

20. Allen Newell Interview, Carnegie Mellon University Library Archives, p. 12.

21. Allen Newell, "The Capacity of a Railroad Freight Yard: A Survey of the Problem—Not a Solution." RAND RM—555, June 14, 1950. RAND Corporation Archives.

22. A. Newell, Observations on the Science of Supply. Technical Report D-926, 1951. Rand Corporation Archives.

CHAPTER SIX

1. This 1951 report by Gaither was titled *Report of the Study for the Ford Foundation on Policy and Program*. It is located in the Ford Foundation Archives.

2. Ibid.

3. Ibid.

4. Ibid.

5. Ibid.

6. Ibid.

7. Ibid.

8. Ibid.

9. "The Ford Foundation: Behavioral Science Division Report," 1953, p. 1. Herbert Simon Archive papers, Carnegie Mellon University Archives.

10. Gaither, 1951, p. 4.

11. "The Ford Foundation Behavioral Science Program: Proposed Plan for the Development of the Behavioral Sciences Program," 1951, Carnegie Mellon University Archives, Herbert Simon Collection.

12. Ibid.

13. Gaither, 1951, p. 96.

14. Oral history interview with Robert Hutchins, p. 9, Ford Foundation Archives.

15. Oral history interviews with Bernard Berelson, pp. 6–7, and Joseph McDaniel, p. 123, Ford Foundation Archives.

16. Oral history interview with Donald Marquis, p. 7, Ford Foundation Archives.

17. "The Ford Foundation Behavioral Sciences Program. Final Report, 1951–1957," p. 5. Ford Foundation Archives.

18. "Report of Three One-Day Conferences on 'Economics and the Behavioral Sciences,'" Herbert A. Simon papers, Carnegie Mellon University Library Archives.

19. "The Ford Foundation, Behavioral Science Division: Advisory Group on Economics and the Behavioral Sciences," July 1952. Herbert A. Simon papers, Carnegie Mellon University Library Archives.

20. See the 1966 report written by James E. Howell and titled, "The Ford Foundation and the Revolution in Business Education: A Case Study in Philanthropy." Ford Foundation Archives.

21. Hearings before the Select Committee to Investigate Tax-Exempt Foundations and Comparable Organizations, House of Representatives, 82nd Congress, Second Session, on House Resolution 561. Washington, DC, November 18, 19, 20, 21, 24, and 25, and December 2, 3, 5,8, 9, 10, 11, 15, 22, 13, and 30, 1952, p. 1.

22. Howell, 1966.

23. Oral history interview with Robert McNamara, p. 4. Ford Foundation Archives.

24. "Program for Area III on Economic Development and Administration: A Report Submitted by the Advisory Group to the Ford Foundation," staff report number 005047, January 15, 1954, p. 4. Ford Foundation Archives.

25. Ibid., p. 30. They also explicitly encouraged interdisciplinary research and noted that "support is not given to disciplines as such," seeking instead the collaboration of psychologists, political scientists, business scholars, and others to help extend the scope of economics because understanding the big issues in society requires collaboration of "several social sciences and administration" and thus needs "cooperation among the intellectual disciplines" (p. 8).

26. "General Objectives and Basic Problems," Wyman Fiske, staff report number 010620, March 1947. Ford Foundation Archives.

27. "Program for Area III on Economic Development and Administration: A Report Submitted by the Advisory Group to the Ford Foundation," staff report number 005047, January 15, 1954, p. 4. Ford Foundation Archives.

28. Memorandum to the Program Committee from Thomas Carroll, November 3, 1953, p.1. Ford Foundation Archives. Gaither Papers, Box 4.

29. "1957 Annual Report of the Ford Foundation," p. 25. Ford Foundation Archives.

30. "Program for Area III on Economic Development and Administration," Report by the Advisory Group to the Ford Foundation, staff report number 005047, January 15, 1954, p. 11. Ford Foundation Archives.

31. Memorandum from G. Leland Bach, 1960. Ford Foundation Archives.

32. Howell, 1966, pp 5–6.

33. Report from "The Special Committee": "Program in Economic Development and Administration (including Population and Aging), Evaluation (1953–1961) and Statement of Current Objectives and Policies." December, 1961, p. 10. Ford Foundation Archives.

34. Ibid., pp. 10–11.

35. Bach, 1960.

CHAPTER SEVEN

1. Press release about the Ford Foundation grant. In *The New York Times*, December 14, 1952, page E9.

2. J. E. Howell, The Ford Foundation and the Revolution in Business Education: A Case Study in Philanthropy, 1966, p. 9. Ford Foundation Archives.

3. Alfred Sloan in "Memo for Release, from MIT," December 20, 1950, p. 2–3. MIT Sloan Archives.

4. "The Carnegie Plan," Doherty Papers, Carnegie Mellon University Library Archives.

5. See F. Modigliani and H. A. Simon. "On the Relation between a Heuristic and an Exact Production Decision Rule." Unpublished working paper, 1954, Carnegie Mellon University. Herbert Simon Papers, Carnegie Mellon University Archives.

6. From Modigliani to Simon, November 22, 1990. Herbert Simon Paper, Carnegie Mellon University Archives.

7. Letter (n.d.), Cooper to Simon: "Lee Bach . . . has approached me with an offer at Carnegie Tech where he's just been made chairman. . . . What do you think?" Herbert Simon Papers, Carnegie Mellon University Archives.

8. Interview with W. W. Cooper, conducted March 30, 2001, unpublished transcript.

9. Letter from Simon to Cooper, December 15, 1942. Herbert Simon Papers, Carnegie Mellon University Archives.

10. Letter from Simon to Cooper, April 24, 1946. Herbert Simon Papers, Carnegie Mellon University Archives.

11. Letter from Cooper to Simon, November 1, 1946; Letter from Cooper to Simon, February 16, 1948; Letter from Simon to Cooper, February 24, 1948. Herbert Simon Papers, Carnegie Mellon University Archives.

12. Letter from Bach to Simon, March 14, 1949. Herbert Simon Papers, Carnegie Mellon University Archives.

13. Interview with William Cooper, March 30, 2001. Unpublished transcript.

14. Memo, Lee Bach, "A Computer for Carnegie," 1984. Herbert Simon Papers, Carnegie Mellon University Archives.

15. Letter from Simon to Berelson, September 13, 1952. Herbert Simon Papers, Carnegie Mellon University Archives.

16. Letter from Simon to Marschak, November 11, 1952. Herbert Simon Papers, Carnegie Mellon University Archives.

17. Letter from Simon to Clifford Hildreth, August 3, 1982. Herbert Simon papers, Carnegie Mellon University Archives.

18. Miller, in personal conversation, and at a Lee Bach Memorial session at Stanford University, May 29, 2009. Stanford Graduate School of Business.

19. Interview with Charles Holt, March 2001, unpublished.

20. Letter from Simon to William Simpson, November 20, 1950; Letter from Simpson to Hitch, November 28, 1950; Letter from Simon to Simpson, December 22, 1950. All in the Herbert Simon Paper Collections, Carnegie Mellon University Archives.

21. Oral history interview with Kermit Gordon (December 1972), p. 18. Ford Foundation Oral History Interviews. Ford Foundation Archives.

22. Remarks by Herbert Simon prepared for a panel at the Annual ASSA conference, New Orleans, January, 2001. See also Williamson, 1996; 2002.

23. Julian Feldman, Remarks at an ASSA panel on Carnegie, New Orleans, January 2001.

24. Herbert Simon, Remarks prepared for an ASSA panel, New Orleans, January 2001.

Chapter Eight

1. J. E. Howell. "The Ford Foundation and the Revolution in Business Education: A Case Study in Philanthropy," 1966, p. 8. Ford Foundation Archives.

2. Michael Watkins, "Open Letter to the Alumni and Students of the Harvard Business School." Posted on March 22, 2004, at http://media.www.harbus.org/media/storage/paper343/news/2004/03/22/News/Open-Letter.To.The.Alumni.And.Students.Of.The.Harvard.Business.School-638061.shtml.

3. Memo to trustees, Minutes of the University Trustees, March 24, 1881. University of Pennsylvania Archives.

4. Ibid.

5. "Research in a Graduate School," by J. Willitz, p. 10. University of Pennsylvania, Wharton Archives.

6. Minutes of the Wharton faculty, Dec. 1, 1959. University of Pennsylvania, Wharton Archives.

7. "Report of the Wharton School Pre-Survey Committee," November 8, 1956, UPB5.4:0019A. Wharton Archives: UPB5.4:C071A.

8. The other members of the board included Albert J. Hettinger Jr., formerly a member of the faculty of the Harvard Business School but at the time a partner in an outside firm; John S. Keir, formerly on the Wharton faculty but at the time chairman of the board of Dennison Manufacturing Company; Maurice W. Lee, dean of the School of Business Administration at the University of North Carolina; and William H. Newman, formerly a member of the Wharton faculty but at the time a faculty member at the Columbia University Graduate School of Business.

9. Submission to President Harnwell by Joseph Willits, dated March 9, 1959, UPB5.4:0019A. Wharton Archives Box UPB5.4:0019A., p. 6.

10. Ibid., p. 1.

11. Horlacher et al.: "A Program for the Wharton School" memo, November 1957. University of Pennsylvania, Wharton Archives.

12. Wharton Archives of the Educational Survey at Wharton, p. 7.

13. Ibid., p. 10.

14. Ibid., pp. 19–20. The report includes a footnote to Dr. Gladys L. Palmer, "The Role of Research in the Wharton School of the Future" (Educational Survey Report R-1), June 1957.

15. "Statement on the Wharton School of Finance and Commerce, Comments by Joseph Willits," p. 13. Wharton Archives.

16. The Ford Foundation was aware of the Wharton efforts, of course. A report from 1956 noted (in discussing the efforts at improving management education) that "the operation of the Wharton School at the University of Pennsylvania is presently being reviewed by both inside and outside advisors as par of a broader study of the entire university which is being directed by Dr. Joseph Willitz"; then they note that the $50,000 grant made available "for the support of the Wharton School re-study, which it is hoped may both strengthen the School and yield results applicable to other schools of administration as well" (Meeting of Consultants to Program in Economic Development and Administration, September 29, 1956, p. 3). Ford Foundation Archives.

17. Interview with Albert Bowker in 1991, available in online archive at the University of California, Berkeley: "Statistics Taught as a Serious Subject," p. 121: http://content .cdlib.org/ark:/13030/hb1p3001qq/

18. Ford Foundation Annual Report, 1953, p. 68. Ford Foundation Archives.

19. John Wheeler, "Report to Ford Foundation on Changes in Collegiate Business Education in the United States 1954–1964 and the Role of Ford Foundation in These Changes," 1965, p. 118. Ford Foundation Archives.

20. Robert Gordon, 1957, Memo to Chamberlein. Ford Foundation Archives.

21. George Stigler, "The Chicago School of Economics," p. 4. Paper located in the Special Collections Research Center, The University of Chicago Library, George Stigler Papers.

22. All letters from the Stigler Archives in the University of Chicago Library.

23. George Stigler, "The Chicago School of Economics," p. 4. Paper located in the Special Collections Research Center, The University of Chicago Library, George Stigler Papers.

24. The correspondence between Wilbur and Hoover (and others) relating to these early meetings is located in the Stanford University Archives, Special Collection 216.

25. See the 2005 report on Stanford History available at http://histsoc.stanford.edu/ hh3/hh3p33-66.pdf.

26. See "Interview with Herbert Hoover" by Ferris Miles, January 20, 1952, Collection 216, Box 36. Folder: Interview. Stanford University Archives.

27. An early version of the plan was submitted in 1951 (letter from Ferris Miles to Wallace Sterling, cover letter and draft of plan, dated April 16, 1952). Stanford University Archives.

28. Letter from J. Hugh Jackson to Sterling, November 20, 1951. SC collection 216, box 26, Folder 4. Stanford University Archives.

29. See the correspondence between Sterling and Gaither, 1957, Collection 216, Box A20. Stanford University Archives.

30. Letter from Wallace Sterling to George L. Bach, April 3, 1956. Sterling wrote: "A committee of the Graduate School of Business here joins me in the hope that you will have interest in the deanship of the school" (Collection 502, Lee Bach Papers, Stanford University Archives). Bach responded that, although he found the possibility of being dean at GSB an "attractive one," he declined, mentioning that GSIA was still developing and he was busy shaping all aspects of that program. (Letter from Lee Bach to Sterling, April 6, 1956. Collection 502, Lee Bach Papers, Stanford University Archives).

31. For example, Berelson wrote to Sterling noting a recent meeting among him (Berelson), Sterling, and Terman, discussing the problems of graduate education (Berelson at the time was director of the behavioral science program at Ford) (Letter from Berelson to Sterling, July 23, 1956. Stanford University Archives, Special Collections). That same year, correspondence between Sterling and Gaither shows that Sterling met Gaither several times in those years (for example, Letter from Sterling to Gaither, October 19, 1955; Letter from Gaither to Sterling, March 12, 1956), Stanford University Archives.

32. "Long Range Program. Graduate School of Business. A Statement of Philosophy, Objectives and Needs," June 15, 1959. Stanford University Archives, Special Collection, Stanford University.

33. Ibid., p. 7.

34. Office memorandum, from Lee Bach, subject: "Where does business education stand now? How well does it meet society's needs? What can be done? By whom? How? When? (June 25, 1984. Collection SC 502. Bach Papers, Stanford University Library Archives.)

35. Letter from Carroll to Sterling, July 8, 1959, Stanford University Library Archives, Special Collection.

36. Paper found in Bach's papers titled "The GSB Change Environment: Some Eras Have It—Some Eras Don't" (dated December 1, 1983; it was a paper written for Professor Leavitt's class but is in Bach's files) (pp. 6–7). Stanford University Library Archives, Lee Bach Papers.

37. Ford Foundation Archives, "The Special Committee: Program in Economic Development and Administration. Evaluation (1953–61) and Statement of Current Objectives and Policies," p. 7. They also mention Wharton as an example.

38. J. Wheeler, Report to the Ford Foundation on Changes in Collegiate Business Education in the United States, 1954–1964, and the Role of the Ford Foundation in These Changes. Unpublished Report, 1965. Ford Foundation Archives. Located in the General Manuscript section in the Ford Foundation Archives.

39. Ibid.

40. Ibid., p. 181.

41. Ibid., p. 183.

42. Ibid., p. 187

43. Ibid., p. 87.

44. Ibid., p. 193.

45. Ibid., p. 195.

46. "This Is Wharton," School Brochure dated October 5, 1964. University of Pennsylvania, Wharton Archives, dean's collection boxes.

47. Unpublished 1990 conversation with John W. March, former member (1978–1982) of the FASB.

CHAPTER NINE

1. Available at www.businessschooladmission.com/teaching_methods.php; date of creation is 2008.

2. The annual report for 2008 is available at: www.hbs.edu/about/annualreport/2008/pdf/02%20hbs08_5_year_summary.pdf.

3. Herbert A. Simon, "Observations and Comments on the Organization Studies of the Systems Research Laboratory," RAND RM-922, August 29, 1952. RAND Archives.

4. J. Kruskal and A. Newell, *Organization Theory in Miniature*. RAND Report, 1951. Located in the RAND Archives (and in the Allen Newell Archives, Carnegie Mellon University Library).

5. Robert L. Chapman. "A Theory of Organizational Behavior Deriving from Systems Research Laboratory Studies." RAND P-802, 1956. RAND Archives.

Chapter Eleven

1. Unpublished 1990 conversation with John W. March, former member (1978–1982) of the FASB.

2. R. Shiller, "How Wall Street Learns to Look the Other Way." *Wall Street Journal* Op-Ed, February 8, 2005.

3. Cited in Johns Hopkins University brochure (2008), available at http://carey.jhu .edu/bin/o/q/Johns_Hopkins_Global_MBA.pdf.

4. Philip Brougthon, "Harvard's Masters of the Apocalypse," *The Times of London*, March 1, 2009.

5. Leslie Wayne, "A Promise to Be Ethical in an Era of Immortality." *New York Times*, May 29, 2009.

Chapter Twelve

1. "Proposal of Gift from Alfred Sloan," September 7, 1950. MIT Sloan Archives, MIT Library, p. 1. For a brief overview of the Sloan School history, see http://mitsloan.mit .edu/50th/s-main.php.

2. "Proposal to Establish School on Technology and Business Management at MIT." Dated September 18, 1950. MIT, Sloan Archives., MIT Library.

3. See R. Gaither, *Report of the Study for the Ford Foundation on Policy and Program*, 1951. Ford Foundation Archives.

References

AACSB. (2008). *Task for Research, Impact of Research*. Tampa, FL: AACSB International, 2008.

Adam, J. D., and P. F. Salipante. (2003). Bridging scholarship in management: Epistemological reflections. *British Journal of Management*, 14(3): 189–206.

Adler, N., and A. W. K. Harzing. (2009). When knowledge wins: Transcending the sense and nonsense of academic rankings. *The Academy of Management Learning and Education*, 8(1): 72–95.

Allison, G. (1971). *Essence of Decision: Explaining the Cuban Missile Crisis*. Boston: Little, Brown.

Amabile, T. M., C. Patterson, J. Mueller, T. Wojcik, P. Odomirok, M. Marsh, and S. Kramer. (2001). Academic-practitioner collaboration in management research: A case of cross-profession collaboration. *Academy of Management Journal*, 44(2): 418–431.

American Medicine (1910). Vol. 5, pp. 441–442.

Andrews, K. R., ed. (1951). *The Case Method of Teaching Human Relations and Administration*. Cambridge, MA: Harvard University Press.

Arbuckle, E. (1959). Looking ahead. *Stanford Alumni Bulletin*, 28(1): 5–7.

Arbuckle, E. (1960). Training men to solve problems of the future. *Stanford Alumni Bulletin*, Special Supplement.

Argote, L., and H. Greve. (2007). A behavioral theory of the firm—40 years and counting: Introduction and impact. *Organization Science*, 18: 337–349.

Argyris, C. (1980). Some limitations on the case method. *Academy of Management Review*, 5(2): 291–298.

Arky, R. A. (2007). Abe Flexner, where are you? We need you! *Transactions— American Clinical and Climatological Association*, 118: 89–96.

Arrow, K. (1964). Control in large organizations. *Management Science*, 10(3): 397–408.

Arrow, K. (1983). *Social Choice and Justice. Collected Papers of Kenneth Arrow, Vol. 1*. Cambridge, MA: Harvard University Press.

Augier, M., and J. G. March. (2007). The pursuit of relevance in management education. *California Management Review*, 49(3): 129–146.

Augier, M., J. G. March, and B. Sullivan. (2005). Notes on the evolution of a research community: Organization studies in Anglophone North America, 1945–2000. *Organization Science*, 16(1): 85–95.

Augier, M. and M. Prietula (2007). Historical roots of the behavioral theory of the firm model at GSIA. *Organization Science*, 18(3): 507–522.

Ayers, S. (1996). *Health Care in the United States: The Facts and the Choices.* Chicago: American Library Association.

Babb, E., M. Leslie, and M. D. van Slyke. (1966). The potential of business gaming methods in research. *Journal of Business*, 39: 465–472.

Bach, G. L. (1951). Education for management in a mobilizing economy. *Advanced Management*, May: 7–9.

Bach, G. L. (1958). Some observations on the business school of tomorrow. *Management Science*, 4: 351–364.

Bach, G. L. (1986). A computer for Carnegie. *Annals of the History of Computing*, 6(1): 39–41.

Baillie, A. (1993). Mixing case method with business games: Student evaluations. *Simulation and Gaming*, 24: 336–355.

Bane, R. (1959). *Physicians for a Growing America: Report of the Surgeon General's Consultant Group on Medical Education.* Washington, DC: U.S. Government Printing Office.

Banta, H. D. (1971). Abraham Flexner: A reappraisal. *Social Science and Medicine*, 5(6): 655–661.

Beck, A. (2004). The Flexner Report and the standardization of American medical education. *The Journal of the American Medical Association*, 291: 2139–2140.

Becker, E., C. M. Lindsay, and G. Grizzle. (2003). The derived demand for faculty research. *Managerial and Decision Economics*, 24: 549–567.

Becker, G. S. (1968). Crime and punishment: An economic approach. *Journal of Political Economy*, 76(2): 169–217.

Becker, G. S. (1976). *The Economic Approach to Human Behavior.* Chicago: University of Chicago Press.

Behrman, J. N., and R. I. Levin. (1984). Are business schools doing their job? *Harvard Business Review*, 62(1): 140–147.

Bellman, R. (1984). *Eye of the Hurricane: An Autobiography.* Singapore: World Scientific Publishing Company.

Bennis, W., and J. O'Toole. (2005). How business schools lost their way. *Harvard Business Review*, 83(5): 96–104.

Berelson, B. (1961). Graduate education in the United States. *American Behavioral Scientist*, 4(5): 25–29.

Berelson, B. (1963). Introduction to the behavioral sciences. In B. Berelson, ed., *The Behavioral Sciences Today*, pp. 1–11. New York: Basic Books.

Blyth, M. (2002). *Great Transformations: Economic Ideas and Institutional Change in the Twentieth Century*. Cambridge, UK: Cambridge University Press.

Boelen, C. (2002). A new paradigm for medical schools a century after Flexner's report. *Bulletin of the World Health Organization, Geneva*, 80 (7): 592–593.

Bonner, T. (1998). Searching for Abraham Flexner. *Academic Medicine*, 73(2): 160–166.

Borden, S. (1998). Avoiding the pitfalls of case studies. *Journal of Mass Media Ethics*, 13(1): 5–13.

Bornet, V. (1961). *RAND: The First Fifteen Years* (RAND D-9461-RC). Santa Monica, CA: Rand Corporation.

Bossard, J., and J. Dewhurst. (1931). *University Education for Business*. Philadelphia: University of Pennsylvania Press.

Brandeis, L. (1914). *Business: A Profession*. Boston: Small, Maynard & Company.

Brown, R. (1979). *Rockefeller Medicine Man: Medicine and Capitalism in America*. Berkeley: University of California Press.

Bush, V. (1970). *Pieces of the Action*. New York: Morrow.

Calkins, R. (1961). The problem of business education. *Journal of Business*, 34(1): 1–9.

Carroll, T. (1958). Education for business: A dynamic concept and process. *The Accounting Review*, 33: 3–10.

Carroll, T. (1959). A foundation expresses its interest in higher education for business management. *Journal of the Academy of Management*, 2(3): 155–165.

Carson, W. W. (1954). Development of a student under the case method. In M. P. McNair, ed., *The Case Method at the Harvard Business School*, pp. 82–86. New York: McGraw Hill.

Chapman, C. (1974). The Flexner Report by Abraham Flexner. *Daedelus*, 103 (Winter): 105–117.

Chapman, R., J. Kennedy, A. Newell, and W. Biel. (1958). The System Research Laboratory's air defense experiments. *Management Science*, 5: 250–269.

Charnes, A., and W. W. Cooper. (1962). On some works of Kantorovich, Koopmans and others. *Management Science*, 8: 246–263.

Chesney, A. (1963). *The Johns Hopkins Hospital and the Johns Hopkins University: A Chronicle*. Volume II, 1893–1905. Baltimore: The Johns Hopkins University Press.

Chia, R., and R. Holt. (2008). The nature of knowledge in business schools. *Academy of Management Learning & Education*, 7: 471–486.

Christ, C. (1952). History of the Cowles Commission, 1932–1952. In *Economic Theory and Measurement, a Twenty Year Research Report, 1932–1952*. New Haven, CT: The Cowles Commission.

Cleeton, G. U. (1965). *The Story of Carnegie Tech*. Pittsburgh: Carnegie Mellon University Press.

Clifford, G. J., and J. W. Guthrie. (1988). *Ed School: A Brief for Professional Education*. Chicago: University of Chicago Press.

Cogan, M. L. (1955). The problem of defining a profession. *Annals of the American Academy of Political and Social Science*, 297: 105–111.

Coggeshall, L. (1965). *Planning for Medical Progress through Education*. Evanston, IL: Association of American Medical Colleges.

Cohen, K. J., and E. Rhenman. (1961). The role of management education games in education and research. *Management Science*, 7(2): 131–166.

Cooke M., D. Irby, W. Sullivan, and K. Ludmerer. (2006). Medical education: American medical education 100 years after the Flexner Report. *New England Journal of Medicine*, 355 (September): 1339–1344.

Cooper, W. W. (2002). Auditing and accounting: Impacts and aftermaths of R. M. Cyert's research in statistical sampling. In M. Augier and J. G. March, eds., *The Economics of Choice, Change and Organization*, pp. 99–108. Altershot, UK: Edward Elgar.

Cooper, W. W. (2004). Memorial to Herbert A. Simon. In M. Augier and J. G. March, eds., *Models of a Man: Essays in Memory of Herbert A. Simon*, pp. 67–74. Cambridge, MA: MIT Press.

Copeland, M. (1920). *Problems in Marketing*. Chicago: A. W. Shaw Company.

Copeland, M. (1954). The genesis of the case method in business administration. In M. P. McNair, ed., *The Case Method at the Harvard Business School*, pp. 25–33. New York: McGraw-Hill.

Copeland, M. (1958). *And Mark an Era: The Story of the Harvard Business School*. Boston, MA: Little, Brown.

Corner, G. (1965). *Two Centuries of Medicine*. Philadelphia: Lippincott.

Cragg, C. I. (1954). Because wisdom can't be told. In M. P. McNair, ed., *The Case Method at the Harvard Business School*, pp. 6–14. Cambridge, MA: Harvard University Press.

Cruickshank, J. (1987). *A Delicate Experiment: The Harvard Business School 1908–1945*. Boston: Harvard Business School Press.

Currie, B. (1951). The materials of law study. *Journal of Legal Education*, 3(3): 331–383.

Cyert, R. M., and W. Dill. (1964). The future of business education. *The Journal of Business*, 37(3): 221–237.

Cyert, R. M., and J. G. March. (1963). *A Behavioral Theory of the Firm*. Englewood Cliffs, NJ: Prentice Hall.

Czarniawska, B., and B. Joerges. (1996). Travels of ideas. In B. Czarniawska and G. Sevón, eds., *Translating Organizational Change*, pp. 13–48. Berlin: de Gruyter.

Daft, R. L., and Lewin, A. Y. (1990). Can organization studies begin to break out of the normal science straitjacket? An editorial essay. *Organization Science*, 1(1), 1–9.

Daniel, C. (1998). *MBA: The First Century*. Lewisburg, PA: Bucknell University Press.

David, D. (1949). Business responsibilities in an uncertain world. *Harvard Business Review*, 29 (May 1949 Supplement): 1–9.

Davis, N. (1856). *History of the American Medical Association*. Philadelphia: Lippincott.

Day, R. (1968). Beyond the marketing game—New educational uses for simulation. In A. W. Shaw (Ed.), *Proceedings of the American Marketing Association*, pp. 581–588. Chicago: American Marketing Association.

DeBenedetti, C. (1990). *An American Ordeal: The Antiwar Movement of the Vietnam Era*. Syracuse, NY: Syracuse University Press.

Denrell, J. (2007). Adaptive learning and risk taking. *Psychological Review*, 114: 177–187.

Denrell, J., and J. G. March. (2001). Adaptation as information restriction: The hot stove effect. *Organization Science*, 12: 523–538.

Desrochers, P. (2010). The environmental responsibility of business is to increase profits (by creating value within the bounds of private property rights). *Industrial and Corporate Change*, 12: 161–204.

Dewing A. S. (1954). An introduction to the use of cases. In M. P. McNair, ed., *The Case Method at the Harvard Business School*, pp. 1–5. New York: McGraw-Hill.

Dill, W. R., and N. Doppelt. (1963). The acquisition of experience in a complex management game. *Management Science*, 10: 30–46.

Djelic, M. (1998). *Exporting the American Model*. Oxford, UK: Oxford University Press.

Doherty, R. (1950). *The Development of Professional Education: The Principles Which Have Guided the Reconstruction of Education at Carnegie Institute of Technology, 1936–1950*. Pittsburgh: Carnegie Institute of Technology.

Donham, W. B. (1922). Business teaching by the case system. *American Economic Review*, 12(1): 53–65.

Donham, W. B. (1927). Social significance of business. *Harvard Business* Review 5: 406–419.

Donham, W. B. (1933). The failure of business leadership and the responsibility of universities. *Harvard Business Review*, 11: 418–435.

Drake, D. (1832). *Practical Essays on Medical Education and the Medical Profession in the United States*. Baltimore: The Johns Hopkins University Press.

Durand, T., and S. Dameron, eds. (2008). *The Future of Business Schools: Scenarios and Strategies for 2020*. London: Palgrave MacMillan.

Dzuback, M. A. (1991). *Robert M. Hutchins*. Chicago: University of Chicago Press.

Edelfelt, R. (1988). US management education in comparative perspective. *Comparative Education Review*, 32(3): 334–354.

Embree, E. R. (1949, March). Timid billions: Are the foundations doing their job? *Harper's Magazine*: 28–37.

Engwall, L. (1992). *Mercury Meets Minerva*. Oxford, UK: Pergamon Press.

Fama, E. (1980). Agency problems and the theory of the firm. *Journal of Political Economy*, 88: 288–307.

Faria, A. J. (1990). Business simulation games after thirty years: Current usage levels in the United States. In J. W. Gentry, ed., *Guide to Business Gaming and Experiential Learning*, pp. 36–47. London: Nichols/GP Publishing.

Faria, A. J. (2004). A survey of simulation games users, former-users, and never-users. *Simulation and Gaming*, 35(2): 178–207.

Faria, A. J., and R. Nulsen. (1996). Business simulation games: current usage levels a ten year update. In A. L. Patz and J. K. Butler, eds., *Developments in Business Simulation and Experiential Exercises*, pp. 22–28. Madison, WI: Omnipress.

Fenton, E. (2000). *Carnegie Mellon 1900–2000: A Centennial History*. Pittsburgh: Carnegie Mellon University Press.

Ferguson, N. (1997). *Virtual History: Alternatives and Counterfactuals*. New York: Basic Books.

Financial Times. (2005, April 29). Comment and analysis: Shredded credibility?

Fitz, E. (1884 [2009]). *The High School in Its Relation to Business Life*. Ann Arbor: University of Michigan Library.

Fleming, D. (1954). *William Welch and the Rise of Modern Medicine*. Baltimore: Johns Hopkins University Press.

Flexner, A. (1909). Adjusting the college to American life. *Science Magazine*, March 5, 361–372.

Flexner, A. (1910). *Medical Education in the United States and Canada: A Report to the Carnegie Foundation for the Advancement of Teaching*. New York: Carnegie Foundation for the Advancement of Teaching.

Flexner, A. (1915). Is social work a profession? *Proceedings of the National Conference of Charities and Corrections*. Chicago: Hildmann Printing.

Flexner, A. (1925). *Medical Education: A Comparative Study*. New York: Macmillan.

Flexner, A. (1930). *Universities: American, English, German*. Oxford, UK: Oxford University Press.

Flexner, A. (1932, April). Failings of our graduate schools. *Atlantic Monthly*, 149: 441–452.

Flexner, A. (1938). The usefulness of useless knowledge. *Harper's Magazine* (October): 544–552.

Flexner, A. (1940). *I Remember: The Autobiography of Abraham Flexner*. New York: Simon and Schuster.

Flexner, A. (1960). *Abraham Flexner: An Autobiography* [revised and expanded edition]. New York: Simon and Schuster.

Flood, M. (1958). Some experimental games. *Management Science*, 5: 5–26.

Follet, M. P. (1940). *Dynamic Administration. The Collected Papers of Mary Parker Follet*. New York: Harper and Brothers.

Friedman, M. (1970, September 13). The social responsibility of business is to increase its profits. *New York Times Magazine*, 33(30): 122–125.

Gaither, R. (1958). Speech at Stanford Conference on "Growing Dimensions of Management." Printed in: Report from the 17th Stanford business conference. Stanford University Library.

Ganzeboom, H. B. G., and D. J. Treiman. (1996). Internationally comparable measures of occupational status for the 1988 International Standard Classification of Occupations. *Social Science Research*, 25: 201–239.

Garfinkle, A. (1995). *Telltale Hearts: The Origins and Impact of the Vietnam Antiwar Movement*. New York: St. Martin's Press.

Geiger, R. (1999). The ten generations of American higher education. In P. G. Altbach, R. O. Berdahl, and P. J. Gumport, eds., *American Higher Education in the Twenty-First Century*, pp. 38–70. Baltimore: The Johns Hopkins University Press.

Ghoshal, S. (2003). Business schools share the blame for Enron. *Financial Times*, July 18.

Ghoshal, S. (2005). Bad management theories are destroying good management practices. *Academy of Management Learning and Education*, 4(1): 75–91.

Giacalone, R. (2009). Academic rankings in research institutions: A case of skewed mind-sets and professional amnesia. *Academy of Management Learning and Education*, 8(1): 122–126.

Gilbert, J. (2008). Abraham Flexner and the roots of interprofessional education. *Journal of Continuing Education in the Health Professions*, 28(S1): 11–14.

Gillmore, C. S. (2004). *Fred Terman at Stanford: Building a Discipline, a University, and Silicon Valley*. Stanford, CA: Stanford University Press.

Ginsberg, A. D. (1984). Restoring the balance between research and medical education. *Canadian Medical Association Journal*, 131: 1195–1196.

Gittins, J. C. (1989). *Multi-Armed Bandit Allocation Indices*. New York: Wiley.

Goffman, E. (1959). *The Presentation of Self in Everyday Life*. Garden City, NY: Doubleday Anchor.

Goldstein, J., and R. O. Keohane, eds. (1993). *Ideas and Foreign Policy*. Ithaca, NY: Cornell University Press

Goldstein, R. (1961). RAND: The History, Operations, and Goals of a Nonprofit Corporation. RAND Paper. P-2236. Santa Monica, CA: The RAND Corporation.

Gordon, R. A. (1945). *Business Leadership in the Large Corporation*. Washington, DC: Brookings Institution.

Gordon, R. A., and J. E. Howell. (1959). *Higher Education for Business*. New York: Columbia University Press.

Graham, R. G., and C. F. Gray. (1969). *Business Games Handbook*. New York: American Management Association.

Grayson, L. (1977). A brief history of engineering education in the United States. *IEEE Transactions on Aerospace and Electronic Systems*, AES-16(3): 373–392.

Halberstam, D. (1972). *The Best and the Brightest*. New York: Random House.

Hall, P. A. (1989). *The Political Power of Economic Ideas*. Princeton, NJ: Princeton University Press.

Hambrick, D. (1994). What if the academy actually mattered? *Academy of Management Review*, 19(1): 11–16.

Harris, R. (2003). The case against cases. *CFO Magazine*, April.

Harsanyi, J. (1962). Bargaining and ignorance of the opponent's utility function. *Journal of Conflict Resolution*, 6: 29–38.

Haskell, T. (1977). *The Emergence of a Professional Social Science: The American Social Science Association and the Nineteenth Century Crisis of Authority*. Urbana: University of Illinois Press.

Hauser, R. M., and D. L. Featherman. (1977). *The Process of Stratification: Trends and Analyses*. New York: Academic Press.

Hawkins, H. (1972). *Between Harvard and America: The Educational Leadership of Charles W. Eliot*. New York: Oxford University Press.

Henderson, D. (2001). *Misguided Virtue: False Notions of Corporate Social Responsibility*. London: Institute of Economic Affairs.

Hertz, D. (1965). The unity of science and management. *Management Science*, 11(6), Series B (April): B 89–B 97.

Hiatt, M., and C. Stockton (2003). The impact of the Flexner Report on the fate of American medical schools in North America after 1909. *Journal of American Physicians and Surgeons*, 8: 37–40.

Hildredt, C. (1986). *The Cowles Commission in Chicago, 1939–1955*. New York: Springer.

Hirschman, A. O. (1977). *The Passions and the Interests: Political Arguments for Capitalism before Its Triumph*. Princeton, NJ: Princeton University Press.

Hodges, B. (2005). The many and conflicting histories of medical education in Canada and the USA: An introduction to the paradigm wars. *Medical Education*, 39(6): 613–621.

Hodgson, G. M., and T. Knudsen. (2010). *Darwin's Conjecture: The Search for General Principles of Social and Economic Evolution*. Chicago: University of Chicago Press.

Holt, C. C., and F. Modigliani. (1961). Firm cost structures and the dynamic responses of inventories, production, work force, and orders to sales fluctuations. In *Inventory Fluctuations and Economic Stabilization. Part 2, Causative Factors in Movements of Business Inventories*, pp. 1–55. Washington, DC: U.S. Government Printing Office.

Holt, C. C., F. Modigliani, J. F. Muth, and H. A. Simon. (1960). *Planning Production, Inventories, and Work Force.* Englewood Cliffs, NJ: Prentice Hall.

Hotchkiss, W. (1920). The basic elements and their proper balance in the curriculum of a collegiate business school. *Journal of Political Economy*, 28(2): 89–107.

Howell, J. E. (1984). In J. Schmotter, An interview with Professor James E. Howell. *Selections* (spring, 1984): 9–13.

Huff, A. S. (2000). Citigroup's John Reed and Stanford's James March on management research and practice. *Academy of Management Executive*, 14(1): 1–13.

Hurst, J. (1950). *The Growth of American Law: The Law Makers.* Boston: Little, Brown.

Hutchins, R. (1928). The law school tomorrow. *The North American Review*, 225(840): 129–140.

Hutchins, R. (1929). Law and medicine and the new institute. *Yale Alumni Weekly*, 38: 697–698.

Hutchins, R. (1933). The American educational system. *American Journal of Education*, 91(4): 480–486.

Hutchins, R. (1934a). The issue in higher learning. *International Journal of Ethics*, 44(2): 175–184.

Hutchins, R. (1934b). The organization of a university. *The Journal of Higher Education*, 5(7): 349–354.

Hutchins, R. (1936). A reply to Professor Whitehead. *Atlantic Monthly*, 158(5): 582–588.

Hutchins, R. (1937). Legal education. *University of Chicago Law Review*, 4(3): 357–368.

Hutchins, R. (1941). The next fifty years. *Science*, 94 (2441): 333–335.

Hutchins, R. (1943). Liberal education for democratic victory and lasting peace. *American Journal of Economics and Sociology*, 2(3): 289–304.

Hutchins, R. (1949). *The State of the University.* Chicago: University of Chicago Press.

Hutchins, R. M. (1968). *The Learning Society.* New York: Frederick A. Praeger.

Ijiri, Y. (2004). Interdisciplinary reasoning and Herb Simon's influence. In M. Augier and J. G. March, eds., *Models of a Man: Essays in Memory of Herbert A Simon.* Cambridge, MA: MIT Press.

Jackson. H. (1958). Farewell remarks. *Stanford Alumni Bulletin.* 25(2): 6–7.

Jackson, T., and D. Cook. (1998). A brief history of accounting for the translation of foreign currencies. *Journal of Management History*, 4(2): 137–144.

Jeanjean, T., and C. Ramirez. (2009, June). Back to the Origins of Positive Theories: A Contribution to an Analysis of Paradigm Changes in Accounting Research. *Accounting in Europe*, 6,(1): 107–126.

Jeuck, J. E. (1973). Business education: Some popular models. *The Library Quarterly*, 43(4): 283–292.

Jeuck, J. E. (1986). Pride and prejudice. 1986 Towers Lecture, University of Chicago. Chicago/Booth Selected Paper Series; Selected Paper no. 64.

Johns, M., M. Barnes, and P. Florencio. (2003). Restoring balance to industry-academia relationships in an era of institutional financial conflicts of interest. *Journal of the American Medical Association*, 289(6): 741–746.

Jones, E. (1913). Some propositions concerning university instruction in business administration. *Journal of Political Economy*, 21(3): 185–195.

Kaplan, F. (1983). *The Wizards of Armageddon*. New York: Simon and Schuster.

Kast, F. (1965). Management education in Europe. *The Academy of Management Journal*, 8(2): 75–89.

Keener, B. (1894). The inductive method in legal education. *American Bar Association Reports* (17): 473–490.

Khurana, R. (2007). *From Higher Aims to Hired Hands: The Social Transformation of American Business Schools and the Unfulfilled Promise of Management as a Profession*. Princeton, NJ: Princeton University Press.

Kiechel, W. (2010). *The Lords of Strategy: The Secret Intellectual History of the New Corporate World*. Boston, MA: Harvard Business Press.

Kierkegaard, S. (2006 [1843]). *Fear and Trembling (Frygt og bæven)*. Cambridge, UK: Cambridge University Press.

Kiesler, S., and L. S. Sproull, eds. (1987). *Computing and Change on Campus*. Cambridge, UK: Cambridge University Press.

King, L. (1984). The Flexner Report of 1910. *Journal of the American Medical Association*, 251(8): 1070–1086.

Kitch, E. (1983). The fire of truth: A remembrance of law and economics at Chicago, 1932–1970. *Journal of Law and Economics*, 26: 163–234.

Kleinman, A., L. Eisenberg, and B. Good. (1978). Clinical lessons from anthropological and cross cultural research. *Annals of Internal Medicine*, 88: 251–258.

Knights, D. (2008). Myopic rhetorics: Reflecting epistemologically and ethically on the demand for relevance in organizational and management research. *Academy of Management Learning & Education*, 7: 537–552.

Koenig, C., and P. Tapie. (2008). Management education in Asia. In T. Durand and S. Dameron, eds., *The Future of Business Schools: Scenarios and Strategies for 2020*, pp. 327–335. London: Palgrave MacMillan.

Kopelman, L. (1994). Case method and casuistry. The problem of bias. *Theoretical Medicine*, 15(1): 21–37.

Labaree, D. (1992). Power, knowledge, and the rationalization of teaching. *Harvard Educational Review*, 62(2): 123–154.

Labaree, D. (1997). *How to Succeed in School without Really Learning: The Credentials Race in American Education.* New Haven, CT: Yale University Press.

Labaree, D. (2004). *The Trouble with Ed Schools.* New Haven, CT: Yale University Press.

Langdell, C. (1871). *A Selection of Cases on the Law of Contract.* Boston: Little, Brown and Company.

Lavelle, Luis. (2005, August 5). A rank offence to business schools? *Business Week.*

Leavitt, H. (1996). The old days, hot groups, and managers lib. *Administrative Science Quarterly*, 41: 288–300.

Leavitt, J., and R. Numbers (1972). *Sickness and Health in America. Readings in the History of Medicine and Public Health.* Madison: Univerity of Wisconsin Press.

Lee, M. (1960, summer). It's good to be in a business school. *Business Horizons*, 3: 4–19.

LeRossingnol, J. (1931). Dr. Flexner on university training for business. *The Journal of Business*, 4(3): 127–137.

Lippard, W. (1974. *A Half Century of American Medical Education: 1920–1970.* New York: Josiah Macy Jr. Foundation.

Litzenberger, R. H. (1991). William F. Sharpe's contributions to financial economics. *The Scandinavian Journal of Economics*, 93: 37–46.

MacDermot, H. E. (1952). Early medical education in North America. *Canadian Medical Association Journal*, 67(4): 370–375.

March, J. G. (1991). Exploration and exploitation in organizational learning. *Organization Science*, 2: 71–87.

March, J. G. (1996). Learning to be risk averse. *Psychological Review*, 103: 309–319.

March, J. G. (2003). A scholar's quest. *Journal of Management Inquiry*, 12: 205–207.

March, J. G. (2004). Experiential knowledge and academic knowledge in management education. In G. Garel and E. Godelier, eds., *Enseigner le management*, pp. 13–17. Paris: Lavosier.

March, J. G. 2006. Rationality, foolishness and adaptive intelligence. *Strategic Management Journal*, 27: 201–214.

March, J. G. (2007). Scholarship, scholarly institutions, and scholarly communities. *Organization Science*, 18: 537–542.

March, J. G. (2010). *The Ambiguities of Experience.* Ithaca, NY: Cornell University Press.

March, J. G., and J. P. Olsen. (1995). *Democratic Governance.* New York: Free Press.

March, J. G., and J. P. Olsen. (2006). The logic of appropriateness. In M. Moran, M. Rein, and R. E. Goodin, eds., *The Oxford Handbook of Public Policy*, pp. 689–708. Oxford, UK: Oxford University Press.

March, J. G., and H. A. Simon. (1958). *Organizations.* New York: Wiley.

March, J. G., and R. Sutton. (1997). Organizational performance as a dependent variable. *Organization Science*, 8: 697–706.

March, J. G., and T. Weil. (2005). *On Leadership*. Oxford, UK: Blackwell Publishers.

Marengo, L. (1993). Knowledge distribution and coordination in organizations: On some social aspects of the exploitation vs exploration trade-off. *Revue Internationale de Systémique*, 7: 553–571.

Marschak, J. (1963). On adaptive programming. *Management Science*, 9(4): 517–526.

Marshack, J., and R. Radner. (1972). *The Economic Theory of Teams*. New Haven, CT: Yale University Press.

Marshall, L. (1913). The College of Commerce and Administration of the University of Chicago. *Journal of Political Economy*, 21(2): 97–110.

Mayer, J. (1925). Modern business education and research. *The Scientific Monthly*, 20(3): 257–269.

McDonald, D. (1956). *The Ford Foundation: The Men and the Millions*. New York: Reynal and Company.

Meisner, S. (1987). *Sanford Meisner on Acting*. New York: Random House.

Merton, R. (1963). The mosaic of the behavioral sciences. In B. Berelson, ed., *The Behavioral Sciences Today*, pp. 247–272. London: Basic Books.

Merton, R. C. (1994). Influence of mathematical models in finance on practice: Past, present and future. *Philosophical Transactions of the Royal Society of London*, Series A. 347 (June 1994): 451–463. (Reprinted in *Financial Practice and Education*, spring 1995.)

Mill, J. S. (1862 [1950]). *Mill on Bentham and Coleridge*. London: Chatoo and Windus.

Miller, M. (1986). Financial innovation: The last twenty years and the next. *Journal of Financial and Quantitative Analysis*, 21(4): 459–471.

Miner, J. (2006). *Organizational Behavior 3: Historical Origins, Theoretical Foundations, and the Future*. New York: M. E. Sharpe.

Miner, J. B. (1984). The validity and usefulness of theories in an emerging organizational science. *Academy of Management Review*, 9: 296–306.

Mintzberg, H. (2004). *Managers, Not MBA's*. San Francisco, CA: Berrett Koeler's Publisher.

Mirowski, P. (2004). *Machine Dreams*. Chicago: Chicago University Press.

Modigliani, F. (1949). Discussion. *American Economic Review*, 39(3): 201–208.

Modigliani, F. (2001). *Adventures of an Economist*. New York: W. W. Norton & Company.

Modigliani, F. (2004): Herbert Simon: Some Cherished Memories. In M. Augier & J. G. March, eds.: *Models of a Man*, pp. 373–375. Cambridge: MIT Press.

Moslein, K., and A. S. Huff. (2008). Management education and research in Germany. In T. Durand and S. Dameron, eds., *The Future of Business Schools: Scenarios and Strategies for 2020*, pp. 133–161. London, UK: Palgrave MacMillan.

Mowery, D. (2009). Plus ça change: Industrial R&D in the "third industrial revolution." *Industrial and Corporate Change*, 18(1): 1–50.

Mulligan, T. (1987). The two cultures in business education. *Academy of Management Review*, 12(4): 593–599.

Muth, J. (1961). Rational expectations and the theory of price movements. *Econometrica*, 29(3): 315–335.

National Academy of Science. (1986). Behavioral and Social Science: Fifty Years of Discovery. Washington, DC: NRC Committee on Basic Research in the Behavioral Social Sciences.

Nelson, R., and S. Winter. (1982). *An Evolutionary Theory of Economic Change*. Cambridge, MA: Harvard University Press.

New York State Journal of Medicine. (1910). Vol, 10, pp. 483–484.

Nietzsche, F. W. (1909). *On the Future of Our Educational Institutions: Homer and Classical Philology*. Edinburgh, UK: T. N. Foulis.

Olkin, I. (1991). A conversation with Allen Wallis. *Statistical Science*, 6(2): 121–140.

Padgett, J. F., and C. K. Ansell. (1993). Robust action and the rise of the Medici, 1400–1434. *The American Journal of Sociology*, 98(6): 1259–1319.

Parmar, N. (2010). Too close for comfort. *Smart Money*, 19(9): September, 62–67.

Patterson, D. (1995). Langdell's legacy. *Northwestern University Law Review*, 90(1): 196–203.

Pechmann, J. (1978). Robert Aaron Gordon, 1908–1978. *Brookings Papers on Economic Activity, No. 2*, pp. 233–236.

Pelz, V. (Ed.). (1926). *Proceedings of the Stanford Conference on Business Education*. Stanford, CA: Stanford University Press.

Perkin, H. (1984). The historical perspective. In B. Clark, ed., *Perspectives on Higher Education*, pp. 17–55. Berkeley: University of California Press.

Pfeffer, J., and C. Fong. (2002). The end of business schools? Less success than meets the eye. *Academy of Management Learning and Education*, 1(1): 78–95.

Pfeffer, J., and C. Fong. (2004). The business school "business": Some lessons from the US experience. *Journal of Management Studies*, 41(8): 1501–1520.

Pierson, F., ed. (1959). *The Education of American Businessmen*. New York: McGraw-Hill.

Porter, A. (1963). The business school transition: From folklore to science. *The Journal of Higher Education*, 34(3): 137–141.

Porter, L., and L. McKibbin. (1988). *Management Education and Development: Drift or Thrust into the 21st Century*. New York: McGraw-Hill.

Posner, R. (1986). The Chicago school of antitrust analysis. *University of Pennsylvania Law Review*,127(4): 925–948.

Poundstone, W. (1992). *Prisoner's Dilemma*. New York: Anchor.

Rader, L. (1965). Roadblocks to progress in the management sciences and operations research. *Management Science*, 11(4): C1–C5.

Raia, A. P. (1966). A study of the educational value of management games. *Journal of Business*, 39: 339–352.

Reed, A. Z. (1921). *Training for the Public Profession of the Law: Historical Development and Principal Contemporary Problems of Legal Education in the United States, with Some Account of Conditions in England and Canada.* Bulletin Number 15 of the Carnegie Foundation for the Advancement of Teaching. New York: C. Scribner's and The Carnegie Foundation.

Reiss, A. J. Jr. (1961). *Occupations and Social Status*. Glencoe, IL: Free Press.

Relman, A. (1980). The new medical-industrial complex. *New England Journal of Medicine*, 303: 963–970.

Relman, A. (1997). The market for health care: Where is the patient? *Clinical Chemistry*, 43(12): 2225–2229.

Relman, A. (2007). Medical professionalism in a commercialized health care market. *Journal of the American Medical Association*, 298(22): 2668–2670.

Reynolds, T., ed. (1991). *The Engineer in America*. Chicago: University of Chicago Press.

Roethlisberger, F. (1977). *The Elusive Phenomena*. Cambridge, MA: Harvard University Press.

Rothstein, W. (1987). *American Medical Schools and the Practice of Medicine: A History*. New York: Oxford University Press.

Sass, S. (1982). *The Pragmatic Imagination: A History of the Wharton School 1881–1981*. Philadelphia: University of Pennsylvania Press.

Schleef, D. (2000). That's a good question! Exploring motivations for law and business school choice. *Sociology of Education*, 73(2): 155–174.

Schlossman, S., M. Sedlak, and H. Wechsler. (1998). The "new look": The Ford Foundation and the revolution in business education. *Selections*, 14(3): 8–27.

Schmotter, J. (2000). An interview with Professor C. Roland Christensen. *Selections* 16(2): 43–49.

Schudson, M. (1974). The Flexner Report and the Reed Report: Notes on the history of professional education in the United States. *Social Science Quarterly*, 55: 347–-361.

Schurr, S., and J. Marschak. (1950). *Economic Aspects of Atomic Power: An Exploratory Study*. Princeton, NJ: Princeton University Press.

Science Magazine. (1962). Strengthening the Behavioral Sciences, 136(3512), April 20, 233–241.

Scott, A. O. (2005). "Where Have All the Howlers Gone?" *New York Times*, December 18.

Sedlak, M., and H. Williamson. (1983). *The Revolution of Management Education, A History of the J. L. Kellogg Graduate School of Management, 1908–1983.* Urbana and Chicago: University of Illinois Press.

Shannon, C., and W. Weaver. (1949). *Mathematical Theory of Communication.* Urbana: University of Illinois Press.

Shepherd, G. R. (1960). *A History of the Council on Medical Education and Hospitals of the American Medical Association, 1904–1959.* Chicago: AMA.

Shryock, R. (1930). Medical practice in the old South. *South Atlantic Quarterley*, 29: 166–171.

Shubik, M. (1960). Simulation of the industry and the firm. *The American Economic Review*, 50(5): 908–919.

Shubik, M. (1962). Some experimental non–zero sum games with lack of information about the rules. *Management Science*, 8: 215–234.

Shugan, S. (2006). Save research—Abandon the case method of teaching. *Marketing Science*, 25(2): 109–115.

Simon, H. (1987, July–August). Two heads are better than one: The collaboration between AI and OR," *Interfaces*, 17: 8–15.

Simon, H. A. (1955). A behavioral model of rational choice. *Quarterly Journal of Economics*, 69(1): 99–118

Simon, H. A. (1967). The business school: A problem in organizational design. *Journal of Management Studies*, 4(1): 1–17.

Simon, H. A. (1991). *Models of My Life.* Cambridge, MA: MIT Press.

Simon, H .A., and C. Holt. (1954). The control of inventories and production rates—a survey. *Journal of the Operations Research Society of America*, 2, 289–301.

Simon, H. A., G. Kotmetzky, H. Guetzkow, and G. Tydall. (1954). *Centralization and Decentralization in Organizing the Controllers Department.* New York: The Controllership Foundation.

Simon, Herbert. (1961). "The corporation: Will it be managed by machines?" In M. Anshen and G. L. Bach, eds., *Management and Corporations 1985*, pp. 17–61. New York: McGraw-Hill.

Smith, A. A. (1962). *Fifty Years of Education for Business at the University of Texas.* Austin, TX: College of Business Administration Foundation.

Smith, B. (1966). *The RAND Corporation: Case Study of a Nonprofit Advisory Corporation.* Cambridge, MA: Harvard University Press.

Sox, H. C. (2007). The ethical foundations of professionalism: A sociological history. *CHEST (Journal of the American College of Chest Physicians)*, 131: 1532–1540.

Spector, B. (2008). Business responsibilities in a divided world: The Cold War roots of the corporate responsibility movement. *Enterprise and Society*, 9:314–336.

Spence, M. 1973. *Market Signaling: Information Transfer in Hiring and Related Processes*. Cambridge, MA: Harvard University Press.

Starbuck, W. (1993). Keeping a butterfly and an elephant in a house of cards. *Journal of Management Studies*, 30: 885–921.

Starkey, K., and N. Tiratsoo. (2007). *The Business School and the Bottom Line*. Cambridge, UK: Cambridge University Press.

Starr, P. (1984). *The Social Transformation of American Medicine*. New York: Basic Books.

Stevens, R. B. (1983 [2001]). *Law School: Legal Education in America from the 1850s to the 1980s*. Union, NJ: Lawbook Exchange.

Swanson, A. E. (1914). The Harvard Bureau of Business Research. *Journal of Political Economy*, 22(9): 896–900.

Taylor, F. (1923). *The Principles of Scientific Management*. New York: Harper Brothers.

Tetlock, P. E., and A. Belkin, eds. (1996). *Counterfactual Thought Experiments in World Politics*. Princeton, NJ: Princeton University Press.

Thomas, H. (2008). U.K. business schools. In T. Durand and S. Dameron, eds., *The Future of Business Schools: Scenarios and Strategies for 2020*, pp. 117–133. London: Palgrave MacMillan.

Thompson, D. (1993). Understanding financial conflicts of interest. *New England Journal of Medicine*, 329: 573–576.

Tinker, T. (2004). The end of business schools? More than meets the eye. *Social Text*, 22(2): 67–80.

Tocqueville, A. (1831/1862). *Democracy in America (De la démocratie en Amérique)*. Cambridge, MA: Sever and Francis.

Trank, C. Q., and S. L. Rynes. (2003). Who moved our cheese? Reclaiming professionalism in business education. *Academy of Management Learning & Education*, 2: 189–205.

Trueblood, R. (1963). Education for a changing profession. *Journal of Accounting Research*, 1(1): 86–94.

Van Overtveldt, J. (2007). *The Chicago School: How the University of Chicago Assembled the Thinkers Who Revolutionized Economics and Business*. Chicago: Agate.

Vermeulen, F. (2005). On rigor and relevance: Fostering dialectic progress in management research. *Academy of Management Journal*, 48: 978–982.

Von Neumann, J., and O. Morgenstern. (1944). *Theory of Games and Economic Behavior*. New York: Wiley.

Walker, E. A. (1971). The major problems facing engineering education. *Proceedings of the IEEE*, 59(6): 823–828.

Wallis, A. (1964). Centripetal and centrifugal forces in university organization. *Daedalus*, 93(4): 1071–1082.

Wanker, C., and R. DeFillippi. (2006). *New Visions of Graduate Management Education*. IAP–Information Age Publishing.

Whitehead, A. N. (1929). *The Aims of Education*. New York: Free Press.

Whitehead, A. N. (1933). *Adventures of Ideas*. New York: Free Press.

Whitehead, A. N. (1936). Harvard: The future. *Atlantic Monthly*, 158(3): 260–270.

Whitehead, A. N. (1938). *Modes of Thought*. New York: MacMillan.

Whitehouse, P. (2008). Why I no longer consult for drug companies. *Culture, Medicine and Psychiatry*, 32(1): 4–10.

Wilbur, R. (1960). *The Memoirs of Ray L. Wilbur*. Stanford, CA: Stanford University Press.

Williams, J. (1962). An overview of RAND. RAND Working Paper D-10053.

Williamson, O. E. (1996). Transaction cost economics and the Carnegie connection. *Journal of Economic Behavior and Organization*, 31: 149–155.

Williamson, O. E. (2002). Herbert Simon and organization theory: Lessons for the theory of the firm. In M. Augier and J. G. March, eds., *Models of a Man: Essays in Honor of Herbert Simon*, pp. 279–296. Cambridge, MA: MIT Press.

Williston, S. (1910). James B. Ames: His service to legal education. *Harvard Law Review*, 23(5): 330–335.

Woodhouse, H. (2000). The seduction of the market: Whitehead, Hutchins, and the Harvard Business School. *Interchange*, 31(2–3): 135–157.

Wren, D. A. (1994). *The Evolution of Management Thought*. New York: Wiley.

Young, O. (1927, July). Dedication address. *Harvard Business Review*, 4: 385–394.

Zalanznick, S. (1986, May). The MBA: The man, the myth, and the method. *Forbes Magazine*: 168–171).

Zald, M. N., and P. Denton. (1963). From evangelism to general service: The transformation of the YMCA. *Administrative Science Quarterly*, 8: 214–234.

Zeff, S. A. (1999). The evolution of the conceptual framework for business enterprises in the United States. *Accounting Historians Journal*, 26: 89–131.

Zimmerman, J. (2001). Can American business schools survive? University of Rochester: Simon School of Business Working Paper No. FR 01-16.

Index

Note: Figures and tables are indicated by *f* or *t*, respectively, following page numbers.

Aristocracy, 242
Arrow, Kenneth, 69, 75, 84, 86, 87, 89, 104, 167
Asia, 187–88, 314
Aspen Institute, 266
Association of American Medical Colleges (AAMC), 36–38
Aumann, Robert, 89

Baccalaureate degrees awarded, 19*f*
Bach, George Leland (Lee), 71, 101, 106, 108, 110, 116, 121, 123, 125–28, 130–34, 136, 137, 143, 168, 176, 197, 221, 227, 244–45, 286, 329*n*30
Bales, Robert Freed, 90
Bane Report, 49
Banta, H. David, 47
Bauer, Raymond, 155
Becker, Gary, 66, 84, 89, 307
Behavioral sciences. *See* Social and behavioral sciences
Bellman, Richard, 80, 89
Bennis, Warren, 222
Bentham, Jeremy, 233
Berelson, Bernard, 70, 75, 82, 102, 103, 133, 168, 176, 329*n*31
Billings, Frank, 38
Bok, Derek, 156
Bonini, Charles, 176
Boulding, Kenneth, 104, 106
Bounded rationality, 140
Bowker, Albert, 167
Brodie, Bernard, 82
Brown, Dyke, 102
Buchanan, James, 89
Bulletin of the World Health Organization, 32–33
Bush, Vannevar, 76, 83, 174
Business: business schools in relation to, 26, 222, 238, 268–71, 304–6, 320–21; the market as chief value of, 63, 93, 180, 224, 261, 263–67, 274–76; post-reform developments in, 305; postwar developments in, 22
Business education: academic respectability of, 264, 305–6, 319–22 (*see also* reputation of); alternatives to utilitarian basis of, 233–38; behavioral sciences and, 109; and continuing education, 317–18; criticisms of, 116; engineering education and, 280–83; Ford Foundation and, 10–11, 57, 75, 94–98, 105–22, 147–48; future of, 311–22; goals of, 3; graduate, 4, 6, 182; information technology and, 283–84; interdisciplinarity in, 92–93; knowledge base for, 261–62; law education as model for, 152, 154; mathematics and, 109–10; medical education as model for, 9, 30–31, 34, 56–59, 109; RAND and, 10, 75, 91–93; reality in relation to, 12–13, 152, 190–214; reform of, 1–6; reputation of, 6, 23 (*see also* academic respectability of; Business schools: reputation of); scholarship on, 6–7; and social trustworthiness, 262–68; statistics and, 110; undergraduate, 6, 18, 157, 160, 182; University of Chicago's influence on, 10, 61–63, 72–73; utilitarian basis of, 223–33. *See also* Business schools
Business Management Games, 206
Business schools, 304–7; business community in relation to, 26, 222, 238, 268–71, 304–6, 320–21; conflicts of interest in, 269–71; criticisms of, 27–29, 114; economics as basis of, 275–76, 307; financial constraints and incentives of, 306, 312; future of, 311–22; institutional context of, 17–18, 23–25, 72, 296–99, 316–17;

Rockefeller Foundation, 60
Roosevelt, Franklin D., 83
Rosenblat, David, 139

Samuelson, Paul, 89
Sass, Steven A., 162
Savage, James, 167
Savage, Leonard, 86
Sawn, Thomas, 256
Schelling, Thomas, 87, 89
Schlesinger, James, 88
Scholarly Contributions to Management
    Award, 142
Schultz, Theodore, 89, 125
Science: Cowles Commission and, 84;
    Ford Foundation and, 101; GSIA and,
    126; higher education and, 20; impact
    of, 10, 30; medical education and,
    44, 48–52; promotion of, 20; Second
    World War and, 29–30, 75–76
Science (journal), 92
Scientific management, 157–58
Scott, A. O., 295
Second World War, 29–30, 75–76, 288–89
Self: counterculture and, 302;
    libertarianism and, 304; social
    responsibility downplayed in favor
    of, 309
Self-interest, 93, 226, 229, 261, 263–65,
    267, 274–76, 309
Selznick, Philip, 75
Shapley, Lloyd, 86, 89
Shareholder interest, 261, 265, 267, 274
Sharpe, William, 89, 146
Shaw, Edward, 82, 106
Shiller, Robert, 266
Shubik, Martin, 69, 89
Shultz, George, 71, 116, 286
Siefkin, Gordon, 106
Simmel, Georg, 40
Simmons, George H., 42

Simon, Herbert, 28–29, 71, 75, 84, 87, 89,
    101, 104, 126, 130–34, 136, 138–40,
    142–44, 216, 227, 250, 283–84, 286;
    "The Control of Inventory and
    Production Rates," 129; "On the
    Relation Between a Heuristic and an
    Exact Production Decision Rule," 129
Simulation games, 193, 204–11; advocacy
    of, 206–8; criticisms of, 208–10;
    development of, 204–5; educational
    use of, 206; research and, 210–11
Sloan, A. P. (Alfred), 126, 280, 286
Sloan Foundation, 78, 97, 126
Sloan School of Management, MIT. *See*
    Massachusetts Institute of Technology
    (MIT): Sloan School of Management
Smart Money (magazine), 270
Smith, E. Dunlap, 125, 128
Smith, Vernon, 75, 89
Social and behavioral sciences: behavioral
    science as a concept, 103; business
    education and, 109, 231–32; criticisms
    of, 103, 105; economics and, 104; Ford
    Foundation and, 99–104; growth
    and importance of, 91–92; post-
    reform changes in, 302; postwar
    developments in, 96–97; promotion
    of, 117, 120; at RAND, 81–82; at
    Wharton, 158
Social intelligence, 16
Socialism, 264–65, 309
Socialization, in business schools, 273
Social responsibility. *See* Social
    trustworthiness
Social Science Research Council, 92, 96,
    101, 145
Social status: higher education and,
    251–53; of management, 259;
    professional education and, 251–53,
    257; the professions and, 241,
    242–43